Get the eBook FREE!
(PDF, ePub, Kindle, and liveBook all included)

We believe that once you buy a book from us, you should be
able to read it in any format we have available. To get electronic
versions of this book at no additional cost to you, purchase and
then register this book at the Manning website.

Go to https://www.manning.com/freebook and follow the
instructions to complete your pBook registration.

That's it!
Thanks from Manning!

T0076334

Python Concurrency
with asyncio

MATTHEW FOWLER

MANNING

SHELTER ISLAND

Manning Publications Co.
20 Baldwin Road
PO Box 761
Shelter Island, NY 11964

Development editor:	Doug Rudder
Technical development editor:	Robert Wenner
Review editor:	Mihaela Batinić
Production editor:	Andy Marinkovich
Copy editor:	Christian Berk
Proofreader:	Keri Hales
Technical proofreader:	Mayur Patil
Typesetter:	Dennis Dalinnik
Cover designer:	Marija Tudor

ISBN: 9781617298660
Printed in the United States of America

To my beautiful wife Kathy,
thank you for always being there.

contents

preface

Nearly 20 years ago, I got my start in professional software engineering writing a mashup of Matlab, C++, and VB.net code to control and analyze data from mass spectrometers and other laboratory devices. The thrill of seeing a line of code trigger a machine to move how I wanted always stuck with me, and ever since then, I knew software engineering was the career for me. Over the years, I gradually moved toward API development and distributed systems, mainly focusing on Java and Scala, learning a lot of Python along the way.

I got my start in Python around 2015, primarily by working on a machine learning pipeline that took sensor data and used it to make predictions—such as sleep tracking, step count, sit-to-stand transitions, and similar activities—about the sensor's wearer. At the time, this machine learning pipeline was slow to the point that it was becoming a customer issue. One of the ways I worked on alleviating the issue was utilizing concurrency. As I dug into the knowledge available for learning concurrent programming in Python, I found things hard to navigate and learn compared to what I was used to in the Java world. Why doesn't multithreading work the same way that it would in Java? Does it make more sense to use multiprocessing? What about the newly introduced asyncio? What is the global interpreter lock, and why does it exist? There weren't a lot of books on the topic of concurrency in Python, and most knowledge was scattered throughout documentation and a smattering of blogs with varying consistency of quality. Fast-forward to today, and things haven't changed much. While there are more resources, the landscape is still sparse, disjointed, and not as friendly for newcomers to concurrency as it should be.

Of course, a lot has changed in the past several years. Back then, asyncio was in its infancy and has since become an important module in Python. Now, single-threaded concurrency models and coroutines are a core component of concurrency in Python, in addition to multithreading and multiprocessing. This means the concurrency landscape in Python has gotten larger and more complex, while still not having comprehensive resources for those wanting to learn it.

My motivation for writing this book was to fill this gap that exists in the Python landscape on the topic of concurrency, specifically with asyncio and single-threaded concurrency. I wanted to make the complex and under-documented topic of single-threaded concurrency more accessible to developers of all skill levels. I also wanted to write a book that would enhance generic understanding of concurrency topics outside of Python. Frameworks such as Node.js and languages such as Kotlin have single-threaded concurrency models and coroutines, so knowledge gained here is helpful in those domains as well. My hope is that all who read it find this book useful in their day-to-day lives as developers—not only within the Python landscape but also within the domain of concurrent programming.

acknowledgments

First, I want to thank my wife, Kathy, who was always there for me to proofread when I wasn't sure if something made sense, and who was extremely supportive through the entire process. A close second goes to my dog, Dug, who was always around to drop his ball near me to remind me to take a break from writing to play.

Next, I'd like to thank my editor, Doug Rudder, and my technical reviewer, Robert Wenner. Your feedback was invaluable in helping keep this book on schedule and high quality, ensuring that my code and explanations made sense and were easy to understand.

To all the reviewers: Alexey Vyskubov, Andy Miles, Charles M. Shelton, Chris Viner, Christopher Kottmyer, Clifford Thurber, Dan Sheikh, David Cabrero, Didier Garcia, Dimitrios Kouzis-Loukas, Eli Mayost, Gary Bake, Gonzalo Gabriel Jiménez Fuentes, Gregory A. Lussier, James Liu, Jeremy Chen, Kent R. Spillner, Lakshmi Narayanan Narasimhan, Leonardo Taccari, Matthias Busch, Pavel Filatov, Phillip Sorensen, Richard Vaughan, Sanjeev Kilarapu, Simeon Leyzerzon, Simon Tschöke, Simone Sguazza, Sumit K. Singh, Viron Dadala, William Jamir Silva, and Zoheb Ainapore, your suggestions helped make this a better book.

Finally, I want to thank the countless number of teachers, coworkers, and mentors I've had over the past years. I've learned and grown so much from all of you. The sum of the experiences we've had together has given me the tools needed to produce this work as well as succeed in my career. Without all of you, I wouldn't be where I am today. Thank you!

about this book

Python Concurrency with asyncio was written to teach you how to utilize concurrency in Python to improve application performance, throughput, and responsiveness. We start by focusing on core concurrency topics, explaining how asyncio's model of single-threaded concurrency works as well as how coroutines and async/await syntax works. We then transition into practical applications of concurrency, such as making multiple web requests or database queries concurrently, managing threads and processes, building web applications, and handling synchronization issues.

Who should read this book?

This book is for intermediate to advanced developers who are looking to better understand and utilize concurrency in their existing or new Python applications. One of the goals of this book is to explain complex concurrency topics in plain, easy-to-understand language. To that end, no prior experience with concurrency is needed, though of course, it is helpful. In this book we'll cover a wide range of uses, from web-based APIs to command-line applications, so this book should be applicable to many problems you'll need to solve as a developer.

How this book is organized: A road map

This book is organized into 14 chapters, covering gradually more advanced topics that build on what you've learned in previous chapters.

- **Chapter 1** focuses on basic concurrency knowledge in Python. We learn what CPU-bound and I/O-bound work is and introduce how asyncio's single-threaded concurrency model works.
- **Chapter 2** focuses on the basics of asyncio coroutines and how to use async/await syntax to build applications utilizing concurrency.
- **Chapter 3** focuses on how non-blocking sockets and selectors work and how to build an echo server using asyncio.
- **Chapter 4** focuses on how to make multiple web requests concurrently. Doing this, we'll learn more about the core asyncio APIs for running coroutines concurrently.
- **Chapter 5** focuses on how to make multiple database queries concurrently using connection pools. We'll also learn about asynchronous context managers and asynchronous generators in the context of databases
- **Chapter 6** focuses on multiprocessing, specifically how to utilize it with asyncio to handle CPU-intensive work. We'll build a map/reduce application to demonstrate this.
- **Chapter 7** focuses on multithreading, specifically how to utilize it with asyncio to handle blocking I/O. This is useful for libraries that don't have native asyncio support but can still benefit from concurrency.
- **Chapter 8** focuses on network streams and protocols. We'll use this to create a chat server and client capable of handling multiple users concurrently.
- **Chapter 9** focuses on asyncio-powered web applications and the ASGI (asynchronous server gateway interface). We'll explore a few ASGI frameworks and discuss how to build web APIs with them. We'll also explore WebSockets.
- **Chapter 10** describes how to use asyncio-based web APIs to build a hypothetical microservice architecture.
- **Chapter 11** focuses on single-threaded concurrency synchronization issues and how to resolve them. We dive into locks, semaphores, events, and conditions.
- **Chapter 12** focuses on asynchronous queues. We'll use these to build a web application that responds to client requests instantly, despite doing time-consuming work in the background.
- **Chapter 13** focuses on creating and managing subprocesses, showing you how to read from and write data to them.
- **Chapter 14** focuses on advanced topics, such as forcing event loop iterations, context variables, and creating your own event loop. This information will be most useful to asyncio API designers and those interested in how the innards of the asyncio event loop function.

At minimum, you should read the first four chapters to get a full understanding of how asyncio works, how to build your first real application, and how to use the core asyncio APIs to run coroutines concurrently (covered in chapter 4). After this you should feel free to move around the book based on your interests.

About the code

This book contains many code examples, both in numbered listings and in-line. Some code listings are reused as imports in later listings in the same chapter, and some are reused across multiple chapters. Code reused across multiple chapters will assume you've created a module named `util`; you'll create this in chapter 2. For each individual code listing, we will assume you have created a module for that chapter named `chapter_{chapter_number}` and then put the code in a file of the format `listing_{chapter_number}_{listing_number}.py` within that module. For example, the code for listing 2.2 in chapter 2 will be in a module called `chapter_2` in a file named `listing_2_2.py`.

Several places in the book go through performance numbers, such as time for a program to complete or web requests completed per second. Code samples in this book were run and benchmarked on a 2019 MacBook Pro with a 2.4 GHz 8-Core Intel Core i9 processor and 32 GB 2667 MHz DDR4 RAM, using a gigabit wireless internet connection. Depending on the machine you run on, these numbers will be different, and factors of speedup or improvement will be different.

Executable snippets of code can be found in the liveBook (online) version of this book at https://livebook.manning.com/book/python-concurrency-with-asyncio. The complete source code can be downloaded free of charge from the Manning website at https://www.manning.com/books/python-concurrency-with-asyncio, and is also available on Github at https://github.com/concurrency-in-python-with-asyncio.

liveBook discussion forum

Purchase of *Python Concurrency with asyncio* includes free access to liveBook, Manning's online reading platform. Using liveBook's exclusive discussion features, you can attach comments to the book globally or to specific sections or paragraphs. It's a snap to make notes for yourself, ask and answer technical questions, and receive help from the author and other users. To access the forum, go to https://livebook.manning.com/#!/book/python-concurrency-with-asyncio/discussion. You can also learn more about Manning's forums and the rules of conduct at https://livebook.manning.com/#!/discussion.

Manning's commitment to our readers is to provide a venue where a meaningful dialogue between individual readers and between readers and the author can take place. It is not a commitment to any specific amount of participation on the part of the author, whose contribution to the forum remains voluntary (and unpaid). We suggest you try asking the author some challenging questions lest his interest stray! The forum and the archives of previous discussions will be accessible from the publisher's website for as long as the book is in print.

about the author

MATTHEW FOWLER has nearly 20 years of software engineering experience in roles from software architect to engineering director. He started out writing software for scientific applications and moved into full-stack web development and distributed systems, eventually leading multiple teams of developers and managers to do the same for an e-commerce site with tens of millions of users. He lives in Lexington, Massachusetts with his wife, Kathy.

about the cover illustration

The figure on the cover of *Python Concurrency with asyncio* is "Paysanne du Marquisat de Bade," or Peasant woman of the Marquisate of Baden, taken from a book by Jacques Grasset de Saint-Sauveur published in 1797. Each illustration is finely drawn and colored by hand.

In those days, it was easy to identify where people lived and what their trade or station in life was just by their dress. Manning celebrates the inventiveness and initiative of the computer business with book covers based on the rich diversity of regional culture centuries ago, brought back to life by pictures from collections such as this one.

Getting to know asyncio

This chapter covers

- What asyncio is and the benefits it provides
- Concurrency, parallelism, threads, and processes
- The global interpreter lock and the challenges it poses to concurrency
- How non-blocking sockets can achieve concurrency with only one thread
- The basics of how event-loop-based concurrency works

Many applications, especially in today's world of web applications, rely heavily on I/O (input/output) operations. These types of operations include downloading the contents of a web page from the internet, communicating over a network with a group of microservices, or running several queries together against a database such as MySQL or Postgres. A web request or communication with a microservice may take hundreds of milliseconds, or even seconds if the network is slow. A database query could be time intensive, especially if that database is under high load or the query is complex. A web server may need to handle hundreds or thousands of requests at the same time.

1

Making many of these I/O requests at once can lead to substantial performance issues. If we run these requests one after another as we would in a sequentially run application, we'll see a compounding performance impact. As an example, if we're writing an application that needs to download 100 web pages or run 100 queries, each of which takes 1 second to execute, our application will take at least 100 seconds to run. However, if we were to exploit concurrency and start the downloads and wait simultaneously, in theory, we could complete these operations in as little as 1 second.

asyncio was first introduced in Python 3.4 as an additional way to handle these highly concurrent workloads outside of multithreading and multiprocessing. Properly utilizing this library can lead to drastic performance and resource utilization improvements for applications that use I/O operations, as it allows us to start many of these long-running tasks together.

In this chapter, we'll introduce the basics of concurrency to better understand how we can achieve it with Python and the asyncio library. We'll explore the differences between CPU-bound work and I/O-bound work to know which concurrency model best suits our specific needs. We'll also learn about the basics of processes and threads and the unique challenges to concurrency in Python caused by its global interpreter lock (GIL). Finally, we'll get an understanding of how we can utilize a concept called *non-blocking I/O* with an event loop to achieve concurrency using only one Python process and thread. This is the primary concurrency model of asyncio.

1.1   *What is asyncio?*

In a synchronous application, code runs sequentially. The next line of code runs as soon as the previous one has finished, and only one thing is happening at once. This model works fine for many, if not most, applications. However, what if one line of code is especially slow? In that case, all other code after our slow line will be stuck waiting for that line to complete. These potentially slow lines can block the application from running any other code. Many of us have seen this before in buggy user interfaces, where we happily click around until the application freezes, leaving us with a spinner or an unresponsive user interface. This is an example of an application being blocked leading to a poor user experience.

While any operation can block an application if it takes long enough, many applications will block waiting on I/O. I/O refers to a computer's input and output devices such as a keyboard, hard drive, and, most commonly, a network card. These operations wait for user input or retrieve the contents from a web-based API. In a synchronous application, we'll be stuck waiting for those operations to complete before we can run anything else. This can cause performance and responsiveness issues, as we can only have one long operation running at any given time, and that operation will stop our application from doing anything else.

One solution to this issue is to introduce concurrency. In the simplest terms, *concurrency* means allowing more than one task being handled at the same time. In the case of concurrent I/O, examples include allowing multiple web requests to be made at the same time or allowing simultaneous connections to a web server.

There are several ways to achieve this concurrency in Python. One of the most recent additions to the Python ecosystem is the asyncio library. *asyncio* is short for *asynchronous I/O*. It is a Python library that allows us to run code using an asynchronous programming model. This lets us handle multiple I/O operations at once, while still allowing our application to remain responsive.

So what is asynchronous programming? It means that a particular long-running task can be run in the background separate from the main application. Instead of blocking all other application code waiting for that long-running task to be completed, the system is free to do other work that is not dependent on that task. Then, once the long-running task is completed, we'll be notified that it is done so we can process the result.

In Python version 3.4, asyncio was first introduced with decorators alongside generator `yield from` syntax to define coroutines. A coroutine is a method that can be paused when we have a potentially long-running task and then resumed when that task is finished. In Python version 3.5, the language implemented first-class support for coroutines and asynchronous programming when the keywords `async` and `await` were explicitly added to the language. This syntax, common in other programming languages such as C# and JavaScript, allows us to make asynchronous code look like it is run synchronously. This makes asynchronous code easy to read and understand, as it looks like the sequential flow most software engineers are familiar with. asyncio is a library to execute these coroutines in an asynchronous fashion using a concurrency model known as a *single-threaded event loop*.

While the name of asyncio may make us think that this library is only good for I/O operations, it has functionality to handle other types of operations as well by interoperating with multithreading and multiprocessing. With this interoperability, we can use `async` and `await` syntax with threads and processes making these workflows easier to understand. This means this library not only is good for I/O based concurrency but can also be used with code that is CPU intensive. To better understand what type of workloads asyncio can help us with and which concurrency model is best for each type of concurrency, let's explore the differences between I/O and CPU-bound operations.

1.2 What is I/O-bound and what is CPU-bound?

When we refer to an operation as I/O-bound or CPU-bound we are referring to the limiting factor that prevents that operation from running faster. This means that if we increased the performance of what the operation was bound on, that operation would complete in less time.

In the case of a CPU-bound operation, it would complete faster if our CPU was more powerful, for instance by increasing its clock speed from 2 GHz to 3 GHz. In the case of an I/O-bound operation, it would get faster if our I/O devices could handle more data in less time. This could be achieved by increasing our network bandwidth through our ISP or upgrading to a faster network card.

CPU-bound operations are typically computations and processing code in the Python world. An example of this is computing the digits of pi or looping over the contents of a dictionary, applying business logic. In an I/O-bound operation we spend most of our time waiting on a network or other I/O device. An example of an I/O-bound operation would be making a request to a web server or reading a file from our machine's hard drive.

Listing 1.1 I/O-bound and CPU-bound operations

```
import requests

response = requests.get('https://www.example.com')      ← I/O-bound
                                                          web request

items = response.headers.items()                          ← CPU-bound
                                                            response
headers = [f'{key}: {header}' for key, header in items]     processing

formatted_headers = '\n'.join(headers)       ← CPU-bound string
                                               concatenation
with open('headers.txt', 'w') as file:
    file.write(formatted_headers)            ← I/O-bound write to disk
```

I/O-bound and CPU-bound operations usually live side by side one another. We first make an I/O-bound request to download the contents of https://www.example.com. Once we have the response, we perform a CPU-bound loop to format the headers of the response and turn them into a string separated by newlines. We then open a file and write the string to that file, both I/O-bound operations.

Asynchronous I/O allows us to pause execution of a particular method when we have an I/O operation; we can run other code while waiting for our initial I/O to complete in the background. This allows us to execute many I/O operations concurrently, potentially speeding up our application.

1.3 Understanding concurrency, parallelism, and multitasking

To better understand how concurrency can help our applications perform better, it is first important to learn and fully understand the terminology of concurrent programming. We'll learn more about what concurrency means and how asyncio uses a concept called multitasking to achieve it. Concurrency and parallelism are two concepts that help us understand how programming schedules and carries out various tasks, methods, and routines that drive action.

1.3.1 Concurrency

When we say two tasks are happening *concurrently*, we mean those tasks are happening at the same time. Take, for instance, a baker baking two different cakes. To bake these cakes, we need to preheat our oven. Preheating can take tens of minutes depending on the oven and the baking temperature, but we don't need to wait for our oven to preheat before starting other tasks, such as mixing the flour and sugar together with eggs. We can do other work until the oven beeps, letting us know it is preheated.

We also don't need to limit ourselves from starting work on the second cake before finishing the first. We can start one cake batter, put it in a stand mixer, and start preparing the second batter while the first batter finishes mixing. In this model, we're switching between different tasks concurrently. This switching between tasks (doing something else while the oven heats, switching between two different cakes) is *concurrent* behavior.

1.3.2 Parallelism

While concurrency implies that multiple tasks are in process simultaneously, it does not imply that they are running together in parallel. When we say something is running *in parallel*, we mean not only are there two or more tasks happening concurrently, but they are also executing at the same time. Going back to our cake baking example, imagine we have the help of a second baker. In this scenario, we can work on the first cake while the second baker works on the second. Two people making batter at once is parallel because we have two distinct tasks running concurrently (figure 1.1).

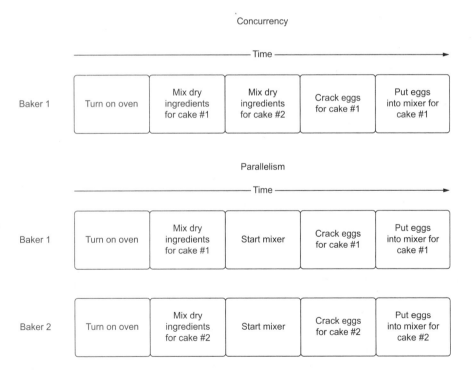

Figure 1.1 With *concurrency*, we have multiple tasks happening at the same time, but only one we're actively doing at a given point in time. With *parallelism*, we have multiple tasks happening and are actively doing more than one simultaneously.

Putting this into terms of applications run by our operating system, let's imagine it has two applications running. In a system that is only concurrent, we can switch between running these applications, running one application for a short while before letting the other one run. If we do this fast enough, it gives the appearance of two things happening at once. In a system that is parallel, two applications are running simultaneously, and we're actively running two things concurrently.

The concepts of concurrency and parallelism are similar (figure 1.2) and slightly confusing to differentiate, but it is important to understand what makes them distinct from one another.

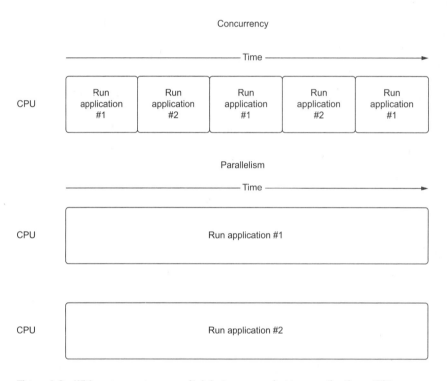

Figure 1.2   With concurrency, we switch between running two applications. With parallelism, we actively run two applications simultaneously.

1.3.3   *The difference between concurrency and parallelism*

Concurrency is about multiple tasks that can happen independently from one another. We can have concurrency on a CPU with only one core, as the operation will employ *preemptive multitasking* (defined in the next section) to switch between tasks. Parallelism, however, means that we must be executing two or more tasks at the same time. On a machine with one core, this is not possible. To make this possible, we need a CPU with multiple cores that can run two tasks together.

While parallelism implies concurrency, concurrency does not always imply parallelism. A multithreaded application running on a multiple-core machine is both concurrent and parallel. In this setup, we have multiple tasks running at the same time, and there are two cores independently executing the code associated with those tasks. However, with multitasking we can have multiple tasks happening concurrently, yet only one of them is executing at a given time.

1.3.4 What is multitasking?

Multitasking is everywhere in today's world. We multitask while making breakfast by taking a call or answering a text while we wait for water to boil to make tea. We even multitask while commuting to work, by reading a book while the train takes us to our stop. Two main kinds of multitasking are discussed in this section: *preemptive multitasking* and *cooperative multitasking*.

PREEMPTIVE MULTITASKING

In this model, we let the operating system decide how to switch between which work is currently being executed via a process called *time slicing*. When the operating system switches between work, we call it *preempting*.

How this mechanism works under the hood is up to the operating system itself. It is primarily achieved through using either multiple threads or multiple processes.

COOPERATIVE MULTITASKING

In this model, instead of relying on the operating system to decide when to switch between which work is currently being executed, we explicitly code points in our application where we can let other tasks run. The tasks in our application operate in a model where they *cooperate*, explicitly saying, "I'm pausing my task for a while; go ahead and run other tasks."

1.3.5 The benefits of cooperative multitasking

asyncio uses cooperative multitasking to achieve concurrency. When our application reaches a point where it could wait a while for a result to come back, we explicitly mark this in code. This allows other code to run while we wait for the result to come back in the background. Once the task we marked has completed, we in effect "wake up" and resume executing the task. This gives us a form of concurrency because we can have multiple tasks started at the same time but, importantly, not in parallel because they aren't executing code simultaneously.

Cooperative multitasking has benefits over preemptive multitasking. First, cooperative multitasking is less resource intensive. When an operating system needs to switch between running a thread or process, it involves a *context switch*. Context switches are intensive operations because the operating system must save information about the running process or thread to be able to reload it.

A second benefit is *granularity*. An operating system knows that a thread or task should be paused based on whichever scheduling algorithm it uses, but that might not be the best time to pause. With cooperative multitasking, we explicitly mark the areas that are the best for pausing our tasks. This gives us some efficiency gains in that we are only switching tasks when we explicitly know it is the right time to do so. Now that we understand concurrency, parallelism, and multitasking, we'll use these concepts to understand how to implement them in Python with threads and processes.

1.4 Understanding processes, threads, multithreading, and multiprocessing

To better set us up to understand how concurrency works in the Python world, we'll first need to understand the basics about how threads and processes work. We'll then examine how to use them for multithreading and multiprocessing to do work concurrently. Let's start with some definitions around processes and threads.

1.4.1 Process

A *process* is an application run that has a memory space that other applications cannot access. An example of creating a Python process would be running a simple "hello world" application or typing `python` at the command line to start up the REPL (read eval print loop).

Multiple processes can run on a single machine. If we are on a machine that has a CPU with multiple cores, we can execute multiple processes at the same time. If we are on a CPU with only one core, we can still have multiple applications running simultaneously, through time slicing. When an operating system uses time slicing, it will switch between which process is running automatically after some amount of time. The algorithms that determine when this switching occurs are different, depending on the operating system.

1.4.2 Thread

Threads can be thought of as lighter-weight processes. In addition, they are the smallest construct that can be managed by an operating system. They do not have their own memory as does a process; instead, they share the memory of the process that created them. Threads are associated with the process that created them. A process will always have at least one thread associated with it, usually known as the *main thread*. A process can also create other threads, which are more commonly known as *worker* or *background* threads. These threads can perform other work concurrently alongside the main thread. Threads, much like processes, can run alongside one another on a multi-core CPU, and the operating system can also switch between them via time slicing. When we run a normal Python application, we create a process as well as a main thread that will be responsible for running our Python application.

Listing 1.2   Processes and threads in a simple Python application

```
import os
import threading

print(f'Python process running with process id: {os.getpid()}')
```

```
total_threads = threading.active_count()
thread_name = threading.current_thread().name

print(f'Python is currently running {total_threads} thread(s)')
print(f'The current thread is {thread_name}')
```

Parent process

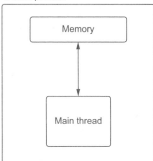

Figure 1.3 A process with one main thread reading from memory

In figure 1.3, we sketch out the process for listing 1.2. We create a simple application to show us the basics of the main thread. We first grab the process ID (a unique identifier for a process) and print it to prove that we indeed have a dedicated process running. We then get the active count of threads running as well as the current thread's name to show that we are running one thread—the main thread. While the process ID will be different each time this code is run, running listing 1.2 will give output similar to the following:

```
Python process running with process id: 98230
Python currently running 1 thread(s)
The current thread is MainThread
```

Processes can also create other threads that share the memory of the main process. These threads can do other work concurrently for us via what is known as *multithreading*.

Listing 1.3 Creating a multithreaded Python application

```
import threading


def hello_from_thread():
    print(f'Hello from thread {threading.current_thread()}!')


hello_thread = threading.Thread(target=hello_from_thread)
hello_thread.start()

total_threads = threading.active_count()
thread_name = threading.current_thread().name

print(f'Python is currently running {total_threads} thread(s)')
print(f'The current thread is {thread_name}')

hello_thread.join()
```

Process

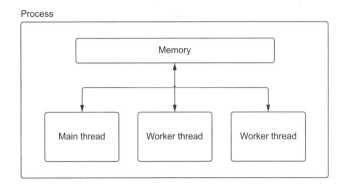

Figure 1.4 **A multithreaded program with two worker threads and one main thread, each sharing the process's memory**

In figure 1.4, we sketch out the process and threads for listing 1.3. We create a method to print out the name of the current thread and then create a thread to run that method. We then call the `start` method of the thread to start running it. Finally, we call the `join` method. `join` will cause the program to pause until the thread we started completed. If we run the previous code, we'll see output similar to the following:

```
Hello from thread <Thread(Thread-1, started 123145541312512)>!
Python is currently running 2 thread(s)
The current thread is MainThread
```

Note that when running this you may see the *hello from thread* and *python is currently running 2 thread(s)* messages print on the same line. This is a *race condition*; we'll explore a bit about this in the next section and in chapters 6 and 7.

Multithreaded applications are a common way to achieve concurrency in many programming languages. There are a few challenges in utilizing concurrency with threads in Python, however. Multithreading is only useful for I/O-bound work because we are limited by the global interpreter lock, which is discussed in section 1.5.

Multithreading is not the only way we can achieve concurrency; we can also create multiple processes to do work concurrently for us. This is known as *multiprocessing*. In multiprocessing, a parent process creates one or more child processes that it manages. It can then distribute work to the child processes.

Python gives us the multiprocessing module to handle this. The API is similar to that of the threading module. We first create a process with a `target` function. Then, we call its `start` method to execute it and finally its `join` method to wait for it to complete running.

Listing 1.4 Creating multiple processes

```
import multiprocessing
import os


def hello_from_process():
    print(f'Hello from child process {os.getpid()}!')
```

```
if __name__ == '__main__':
    hello_process = multiprocessing.Process(target=hello_from_process)
    hello_process.start()

    print(f'Hello from parent process {os.getpid()}')

    hello_process.join()
```

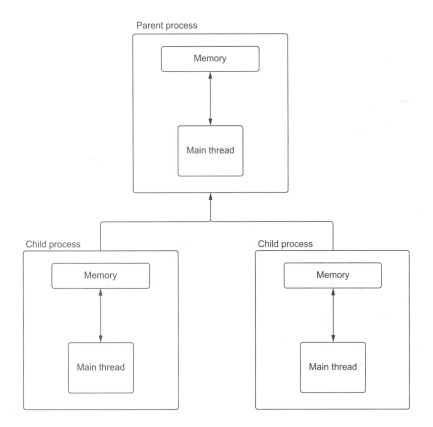

Figure 1.5   An application utilizing multiprocessing with one parent process and two child processes

In figure 1.5, we sketch out the process and threads for listing 1.4. We create one child process that prints its process ID, and we also print out the parent process ID to prove that we are running different processes. Multiprocessing is typically best when we have CPU-intensive work.

Multithreading and multiprocessing may seem like magic bullets to enable concurrency with Python. However, the power of these concurrency models is hindered by an implementation detail of Python—the global interpreter lock.

1.5 Understanding the global interpreter lock

The *global interpreter lock*, abbreviated GIL and pronounced *gill*, is a controversial topic in the Python community. Briefly, the GIL prevents one Python process from executing more than one Python bytecode instruction at any given time. This means that even if we have multiple threads on a machine with multiple cores, a Python process can have only one thread running Python code at a time. In a world where we have CPUs with multiple cores, this can pose a significant challenge for Python developers looking to take advantage of multithreading to improve the performance of their application.

> **NOTE** Multiprocessing can run multiple bytecode instructions concurrently because each Python process has its own GIL.

So why does the GIL exist? The answer lies in how memory is managed in CPython. In CPython, memory is managed primarily by a process known as *reference counting*. Reference counting works by keeping track of who currently needs access to a particular Python object, such as an integer, dictionary, or list. A reference count is an integer keeping track of how many places reference that particular object. When someone no longer needs that referenced object, the reference count is decremented, and when someone else needs it, it is incremented. When the reference count reaches zero, no one is referencing the object, and it can be deleted from memory.

What is CPython?

CPython is the reference implementation of Python. By *reference implementation* we mean it is the standard implementation of the language and is used as the *reference* for proper behavior of the language. There are other implementations of Python such as Jython, which is designed to run on the Java Virtual Machine, and IronPython, which is designed for the .NET framework.

The conflict with threads arises in that the implementation in CPython is not thread safe. When we say CPython is not *thread safe*, we mean that if two or more threads modify a shared variable, that variable may end in an unexpected state. This unexpected state depends on the order in which the threads access the variable, commonly known as a *race condition*. Race conditions can arise when two threads need to reference a Python object at the same time.

As shown in figure 1.6, if two threads increment the reference count at one time, we could face a situation where one thread causes the reference count to be zero when the object is still in use by the other thread. The likely result of this would be an application crash when we try to read the potentially deleted memory.

To demonstrate the effect of the GIL on multithreaded programming, let's examine the CPU-intensive task of computing the nth number in the Fibonacci sequence. We'll use a fairly slow implementation of the algorithm to demonstrate a time-intensive

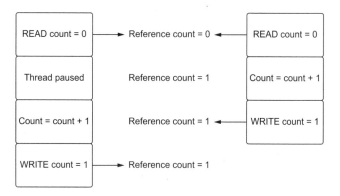

Figure 1.6 A race condition where two threads try to increment a reference count simultaneously. Instead of an expected count of two, we get one.

operation. A proper solution would utilize memoization or mathematical techniques to improve performance.

Listing 1.5 Generating and timing the Fibonacci sequence

```python
import time

def print_fib(number: int) -> None:
    def fib(n: int) -> int:
        if n == 1:
            return 0
        elif n == 2:
            return 1
        else:
            return fib(n - 1) + fib(n - 2)

    print(f'fib({number}) is {fib(number)}')


def fibs_no_threading():
    print_fib(40)
    print_fib(41)


start = time.time()

fibs_no_threading()

end = time.time()

print(f'Completed in {end - start:.4f} seconds.')
```

This implementation uses recursion and is overall a relatively slow algorithm, requiring exponential $O(2^N)$ time to complete. If we are in a situation where we need to print two Fibonacci numbers, it is easy enough to synchronously call them and time the result, as we have done in the preceding listing.

Depending on the speed of the CPU we run on, we will see different timings, but running the code in listing 1.5 will yield output similar to the following:

```
fib(40) is 63245986
fib(41) is 102334155
Completed in 65.1516 seconds.
```

This is a fairly long computation, but our function calls to print_fibs are independent from one another. This means that they can be put in multiple threads that our CPU can, in theory, run concurrently on multiple cores, thus, speeding up our application.

Listing 1.6   Multithreading the Fibonacci sequence

```python
import threading
import time

def print_fib(number: int) -> None:
    def fib(n: int) -> int:
        if n == 1:
            return 0
        elif n == 2:
            return 1
        else:
            return fib(n - 1) + fib(n - 2)

def fibs_with_threads():
    fortieth_thread = threading.Thread(target=print_fib, args=(40,))
    forty_first_thread = threading.Thread(target=print_fib, args=(41,))

    fortieth_thread.start()
    forty_first_thread.start()

    fortieth_thread.join()
    forty_first_thread.join()


start_threads = time.time()

fibs_with_threads()

end_threads = time.time()

print(f'Threads took {end_threads - start_threads:.4f} seconds.')
```

In the preceding listing, we create two threads, one to compute fib(40) and one to compute fib(41) and start them concurrently by calling start() on each thread. Then we make a call to join(), which will cause our main program to wait until the threads finish. Given that we start our computation of fib(40) and fib(41) simultaneously and run them concurrently, you would think we could see a reasonable speedup; however, we will see an output like the following even on a multi-core machine.

```
fib(40) is 63245986
fib(41) is 102334155
Threads took 66.1059 seconds.
```

Our threaded version took almost the same amount of time. In fact, it was even a little slower! This is almost entirely due to the GIL and the overhead of creating and managing threads. While it is true the threads run concurrently, only one of them is allowed to run Python code at a time due to the lock. This leaves the other thread in a waiting state until the first one completes, which completely negates the value of multiple threads.

1.5.1 Is the GIL ever released?

Based on the previous example, you may be wondering if concurrency in Python can ever happen with threads, given that the GIL prevents running two lines of Python concurrently. The GIL, however, is not held forever such that we can't use multiple threads to our advantage.

The global interpreter lock is released when I/O operations happen. This lets us employ threads to do concurrent work when it comes to I/O, but not for CPU-bound Python code itself (there are some notable exceptions that release the GIL for CPU-bound work in certain circumstances, and we'll look at these in a later chapter). To illustrate this, let's use an example of reading the status code of a web page.

Listing 1.7 Synchronously reading status codes

```
import time
import requests


def read_example() -> None:
    response = requests.get('https://www.example.com')
    print(response.status_code)


sync_start = time.time()

read_example()
read_example()

sync_end = time.time()

print(f'Running synchronously took {sync_end - sync_start:.4f} seconds.')
```

In the preceding listing, we retrieve the contents of example.com and print the status code twice. Depending on our network connection speed and our location, we'll see output similar to the following when running this code:

```
200
200
Running synchronously took 0.2306 seconds.
```

Now that we have a baseline for what a synchronous version looks like, we can write a multithreaded version to compare to. In our multithreaded version, in an attempt to run them concurrently, we'll create one thread for each request to example.com.

Listing 1.8   Multithreaded status code reading

```
import time
import threading
import requests


def read_example() -> None:
    response = requests.get('https://www.example.com')
    print(response.status_code)


thread_1 = threading.Thread(target=read_example)
thread_2 = threading.Thread(target=read_example)

thread_start = time.time()

thread_1.start()
thread_2.start()

print('All threads running!')

thread_1.join()
thread_2.join()

thread_end = time.time()

print(f'Running with threads took {thread_end - thread_start:.4f} seconds.')
```

When we execute the preceding listing, we will see output like the following, depending again on our network connection and location:

```
All threads running!
200
200
Running with threads took 0.0977 seconds.
```

This is roughly two times faster than our original version that did not use threads, since we've run the two requests at roughly the same time! Of course, depending on your internet connection and machine specs, you will see different results, but the numbers should be directionally similar.

So how is it that we can release the GIL for I/O but not for CPU-bound operations? The answer lies in the system calls that are made in the background. In the case of I/O, the low-level system calls are outside of the Python runtime. This allows the GIL to be released because it is not interacting with Python objects directly. In this case, the GIL is only reacquired when the data received is translated back into a Python object. Then, at the operating-system level, the I/O operations execute concurrently. This model gives us concurrency but not parallelism. In other languages, such as Java or C++, we would get true parallelism on multi-core machines because we don't have the GIL and can execute simultaneously. However, in Python, because of the GIL, the best we can do is concurrency of our I/O operations, and only one piece of Python code is executing at a given time.

1.5.2   *asyncio and the GIL*

asyncio exploits the fact that I/O operations release the GIL to give us concurrency, even with only one thread. When we utilize asyncio we create objects called *coroutines*. A coroutine can be thought of as executing a lightweight thread. Much like we can have multiple threads running at the same time, each with their own concurrent I/O operation, we can have many coroutines running alongside one another. While we are waiting for our I/O-bound coroutines to finish, we can still execute other Python code, thus, giving us concurrency. It is important to note that asyncio does not circumvent the GIL, and we are still subject to it. If we have a CPU-bound task, we still need to use multiple processes to execute it concurrently (which can be done with asyncio itself); otherwise, we will cause performance issues in our application. Now that we know it is possible to achieve concurrency for I/O with only a single thread, let's dive into the specifics of how this works with non-blocking sockets.

1.6   *How single-threaded concurrency works*

In the previous section, we introduced multiple threads as a mechanism for achieving concurrency for I/O operations. However, we don't need multiple threads to achieve this kind of concurrency. We can do it all within the confines of one process and one thread. We do this by exploiting the fact that, at the system level, I/O operations can be completed concurrently. To better understand this, we'll need to dive into how sockets work and, in particular, how non-blocking sockets work.

1.6.1   *What is a socket?*

A *socket* is a low-level abstraction for sending and receiving data over a network. It is the basis for how data is transferred to and from servers. Sockets support two main operations: sending bytes and receiving bytes. We write bytes to a socket, which will then get sent to a remote address, typically some type of server. Once we've sent those bytes, we wait for the server to write its response back to our socket. Once these bytes have been sent back to our socket, we can then read the result.

Sockets are a low-level concept and are fairly easy to understand if you think of them as mailboxes. You can put a letter in your mailbox that your letter carrier then picks up and delivers to the recipient's mailbox. The recipient opens their mailbox and your letter. Depending on the contents, the recipient may send you a letter back. In this analogy, you may think of the letter as the data or bytes we want to send. Consider that the act of putting a letter into the mailbox is writing the bytes to a socket, and opening the mailbox to read the letter is reading bytes from a socket. The letter carrier can be thought of as the transfer mechanism over the internet, routing the data to the correct address.

In the case of getting the contents from example.com as we saw earlier, we open a socket that connects to example.com's server. We then write a request to get the contents to that socket and wait for the server to reply with the result: in this case, the HTML of the web page. We can visualize the flow of bytes to and from the server in figure 1.7.

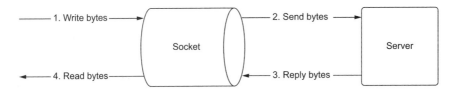

Figure 1.7   Writing bytes to a socket and reading bytes from a socket

Sockets are *blocking* by default. Simply put, this means that when we are waiting for a server to reply with data, we halt our application or *block* it until we get data to read. Thus, our application stops running any other tasks until we get data from the server, an error happens, or there is a timeout.

At the operating system level, we don't need to do this blocking. Sockets can operate in *non-blocking* mode. In non-blocking mode, when we write bytes to a socket, we can just fire and forget the write or read, and our application can go on to perform other tasks. Later, we can have the operating system tell us that we received bytes and deal with it at that time. This lets the application do any number of things while we wait for bytes to come back to us. Instead of blocking and waiting for data to come to us, we become more reactive, letting the operating system inform us when there is data for us to act on.

In the background, this is performed by a few different event notification systems, depending on which operating system we're running. asyncio is abstracted enough that it switches between the different notification systems, depending on which one our operating system supports. The following are the event notification systems used by specific operating systems:

- *kqueue*—FreeBSD and MacOS
- *epoll*—Linux
- *IOCP (I/O completion port)*—Windows

These systems keep track of our non-blocking sockets and notify us when they are ready for us to do something with them. This notification system is the basis of how asyncio can achieve concurrency. In asyncio's model of concurrency, we have only one thread executing Python at any given time. When we hit an I/O operation, we hand it over to our operating system's event notification system to keep track of it for us. Once we have done this handoff, our Python thread is free to keep running other Python code or add more non-blocking sockets for the OS to keep track of for us. When our I/O operation finishes, we "wake up" the task that was waiting for the result and then proceed to run any other Python code that came after that I/O operation. We can visualize this flow in figure 1.8 with a few separate operations that each rely on a socket.

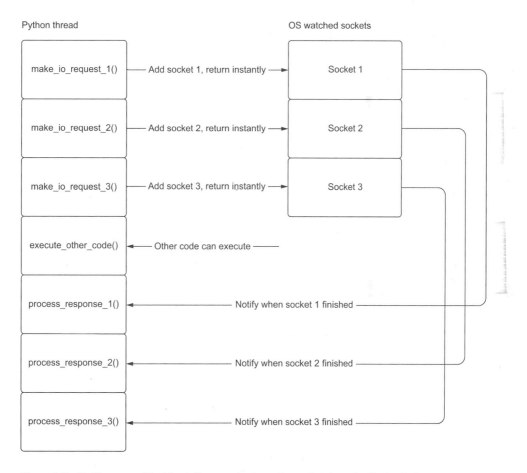

Figure 1.8 Making a non-blocking I/O request returns immediately and tells the O/S to watch sockets for data. This allows `execute_other_code()` **to run right away instead of waiting for the I/O requests to finish. Later, we can be alerted when I/O is complete and process the response.**

But how do we keep track of which tasks are waiting for I/O as opposed to ones that can just run because they are regular Python code? The answer lies in a construct called an event loop.

1.7   How an event loop works

An event loop is at the heart of every asyncio application. *Event loops* are a fairly common design pattern in many systems and have existed for quite some time. If you've ever used JavaScript in a browser to make an asynchronous web request, you've created a task on an event loop. Windows GUI applications use what are called message loops behind the scenes as a primary mechanism for handling events such as keyboard input, while still allowing the UI to draw.

The most basic event loop is extremely simple. We create a queue that holds a list of events or messages. We then loop forever, processing messages one at a time as they come into the queue. In Python, a basic event loop might look something like this:

```
from collections import deque

messages = deque()

while True:
    if messages:
        message = messages.pop()
        process_message(message)
```

In asyncio, the event loop keeps a queue of tasks instead of messages. Tasks are wrappers around a coroutine. A coroutine can pause execution when it hits an I/O-bound operation and will let the event loop run other tasks that are not waiting for I/O operations to complete.

When we create an event loop, we create an empty queue of tasks. We can then add tasks into the queue to be run. Each iteration of the event loop checks for tasks that need to be run and will run them one at a time until a task hits an I/O operation. At that time the task will be "paused," and we instruct our operating system to watch any sockets for I/O to complete. We then look for the next task to be run. On every iteration of the event loop, we'll check to see if any of our I/O has completed; if it has, we'll "wake up" any tasks that were paused and let them finish running. We can visualize this as follows in figure 1.9: the main thread submits tasks to the event loop, which can then run them.

To illustrate this, let's imagine we have three tasks that each make an asynchronous web request. Imagine these tasks have a bit of code to do setup, which is CPU-bound, then they make a web request, and they follow with some CPU-bound postprocessing code. Now, let's submit these tasks to the event loop simultaneously. In pseudocode, we would write something like this:

```
def make_request():
    cpu_bound_setup()
    io_bound_web_request()
    cpu_bound_postprocess()

task_one = make_request()
task_two = make_request()
task_three = make_request()
```

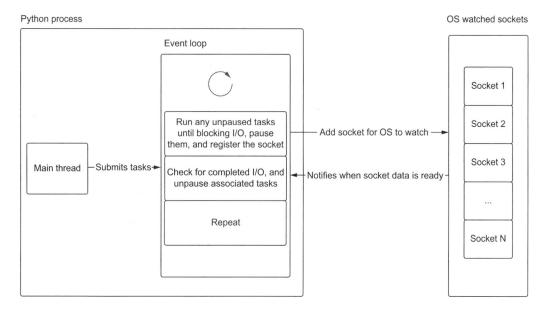

Figure 1.9 An example of a thread submitting tasks to the event loop

All three tasks start with CPU-bound work and we are single-threaded, so only the first task starts executing code, and the other two are left waiting to run. Once the CPU-bound setup work is finished in Task 1, it hits an I/O-bound operation and will pause itself to say, "I'm waiting for I/O; any other tasks waiting to run can run."

Once this happens, Task 2 can begin executing. Task 2 starts its CPU-bound code and then pauses, waiting for I/O. At this time both Task 1 and Task 2 are waiting concurrently for their network request to complete. Since Tasks 1 and 2 are both paused waiting for I/O, we start running Task 3.

Now imagine once Task 3 pauses to wait for its I/O to complete, the web request for Task 1 has finished. We're now alerted by our operating system's event notification system that this I/O has finished. We can now resume executing Task 1 while both Task 2 and Task 3 are waiting for their I/O to finish.

In figure 1.10, we show the execution flow of the pseudocode we just described. If we look at any vertical slice of this diagram, we can see that only one CPU-bound piece of work is running at any given time; however, we have up to two I/O-bound operations happening concurrently. This overlapping of waiting for I/O per each task is where the real time savings of asyncio comes in.

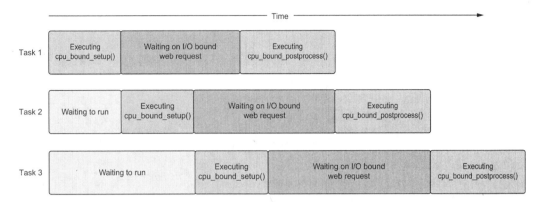

Figure 1.10 **Executing multiple tasks concurrently with I/O operations**

Summary

- CPU-bound work is work that primarily utilizes our computer's processor whereas I/O-bound work primarily utilizes our network or other input/output devices. asyncio primarily helps us make I/O-bound work concurrent, but it exposes APIs for making CPU-bound work concurrent as well.

- Processes and threads are the basic most units of concurrency at the operating system level. Processes can be used for I/O and CPU-bound workloads and threads can (usually) only be used to manage I/O-bound work effectively in Python due to the GIL preventing code from executing in parallel.

- We've seen how, with non-blocking sockets, instead of stopping our application while we wait for data to come in, we can instruct the operating system to tell us when data has come in. Exploiting this is part of what allows asyncio to achieve concurrency with only a single thread.

- We've introduced the event loop, which is the core of asyncio applications. The event loop loops forever, looking for tasks with CPU-bound work to run while also pausing tasks that are waiting for I/O.

asyncio basics

This chapter covers

- The basics of `async await` syntax and coroutines
- Running coroutines concurrently with tasks
- Canceling tasks
- Manually creating the event loop
- Measuring a coroutine's execution time
- Keeping eyes open for problems when running coroutines

Chapter 1 dived into concurrency, looking at how we can achieve it with both processes and threads. We also explored how we could utilize non-blocking I/O and an event loop to achieve concurrency with only one thread. In this chapter, we'll cover the basics of how to write programs using this single-threaded concurrency model with asyncio. Using the techniques in this chapter, you'll be able to take long-running operations, such as web requests, database queries, and network connections and execute them in tandem.

We'll learn more about the *coroutine* construct and how to use `async await` syntax to define and run coroutines. We'll also examine how to run coroutines concurrently by using tasks and examine the time savings we get from running concurrently by

23

creating a reusable timer. Finally, we'll look at common errors software engineers may make when using asyncio and how to use debug mode to spot these problems.

2.1 Introducing coroutines

Think of a coroutine like a regular Python function but with the superpower that it can pause its execution when it encounters an operation that could take a while to complete. When that long-running operation is complete, we can "wake up" our paused coroutine and finish executing any other code in that coroutine. While a paused coroutine is waiting for the operation it paused for to finish, we can run other code. This running of other code while waiting is what gives our application concurrency. We can also run several time-consuming operations concurrently, which can give our applications big performance improvements.

To both create and pause a coroutine, we'll need to learn to use Python's `async` and `await` keywords. The `async` keyword will let us define a coroutine; the `await` keyword will let us pause our coroutine when we have a long-running operation.

> ### Which Python version should I use?
> The code in this book assumes you are using the latest version of Python at the time of writing, which is Python 3.10. Running code with versions earlier than this may have certain API methods missing, may function differently, or may have bugs.

2.1.1 Creating coroutines with the async keyword

Creating a coroutine is straightforward and not much different from creating a normal Python function. The only difference is that, instead of using the `def` keyword, we use `async def`. The `async` keyword marks a function as a coroutine instead of a normal Python function.

Listing 2.1 Using the `async` keyword

```
async def my_coroutine() -> None
    print('Hello world!')
```

The coroutine in the preceding listing does nothing yet other than print "Hello world!" It's also worth noting that this coroutine does not perform any long-running operations; it just prints our message and returns. This means that, when we put the coroutine on the event loop, it will execute immediately because we don't have any blocking I/O, and nothing is pausing execution yet.

This syntax is simple, but we're creating something very different from a plain Python function. To illustrate this, let's create a function that adds one to an integer as well as a coroutine that does the same and compare the results of calling each. We'll also use the `type` convenience function to look at the type returned by calling a coroutine as compared to calling our normal function.

Listing 2.2 Comparing coroutines to normal functions

```
async def coroutine_add_one(number: int) -> int:
    return number + 1


def add_one(number: int) -> int:
    return number + 1


function_result = add_one(1)
coroutine_result = coroutine_add_one(1)

print(f'Function result is {function_result} and the type is
    {type(function_result)}')
print(f'Coroutine result is {coroutine_result} and the type is
    {type(coroutine_result)}')
```

When we run this code, we'll see output like the following:

```
Method result is 2 and the type is <class 'int'>
Coroutine result is <coroutine object coroutine_add_one at 0x1071d6040> and
the type is <class 'coroutine'>
```

Notice how when we call our normal add_one function it executes immediately and returns what we would expect, another integer. However, when we call coroutine_ add_one we don't get our code in the coroutine executed at all. We get a *coroutine object* instead.

This is an important point, as coroutines aren't executed when we call them directly. Instead, we create a coroutine object that can be run later. To run a coroutine, we need to explicitly run it on an event loop. So how can we create an event loop and run our coroutine?

In versions of Python older than 3.7, we had to create an event loop if one did not already exist. However, the asyncio library has added several functions that abstract the event loop management. There is a convenience function, asyncio.run, we can use to run our coroutine. This is illustrated in the following listing.

Listing 2.3 Running a coroutine

```
import asyncio


async def coroutine_add_one(number: int) -> int:
    return number + 1


result = asyncio.run(coroutine_add_one(1))

print(result)
```

Running listing 2.3 will print "2," as we would expect for returning the next integer. We've properly put our coroutine on the event loop, and we have executed it!

asyncio.run is doing a few important things in this scenario. First, it creates a brand-new event. Once it successfully does so, it takes whichever coroutine we pass into it and runs it until it completes, returning the result. This function will also do some cleanup of anything that might be left running after the main coroutine finishes. Once everything has finished, it shuts down and closes the event loop.

Possibly the most important thing about asyncio.run is that it is intended to be the main entry point into the asyncio application we have created. It only executes one coroutine, and that coroutine should launch all other aspects of our application. As we progress further, we will use this function as the entry point into nearly all our applications. The coroutine that asyncio.run executes will create and run other coroutines that will allow us to utilize the concurrent nature of asyncio.

2.1.2   *Pausing execution with the await keyword*

The example we saw in listing 2.3 did not need to be a coroutine, as it executed only non-blocking Python code. The real benefit of asyncio is being able to pause execution to let the event loop run other tasks during a long-running operation. To pause execution, we use the await keyword. The await keyword is usually followed by a call to a coroutine (more specifically, an object known as an *awaitable*, which is not always a coroutine; we'll learn more about awaitables later in the chapter).

Using the await keyword will cause the coroutine following it to be run, unlike calling a coroutine directly, which produces a coroutine object. The await expression will also pause the coroutine where it is contained in until the coroutine we awaited finishes and returns a result. When the coroutine we awaited finishes, we'll have access to the result it returned, and the containing coroutine will "wake up" to handle the result.

We can use the await keyword by putting it in front of a coroutine call. Expanding on our earlier program, we can write a program where we call the add_one function inside of a "main" async function and get the result.

Listing 2.4   Using await to wait for the result of coroutine

```python
import asyncio

async def add_one(number: int) -> int:
    return number + 1


async def main() -> None:
    one_plus_one = await add_one(1)      ◁─── Pause, and wait for the result of add_one(1).
    two_plus_one = await add_one(2)      ◁─── Pause, and wait for the result of add_one(2).
    print(one_plus_one)
    print(two_plus_one)

asyncio.run(main())
```

In listing 2.4, we pause execution twice. We first `await` the call to `add_one(1)`. Once we have the result, the main function will be "unpaused," and we will assign the return value from `add_one(1)` to the variable `one_plus_one`, which in this case will be two. We then do the same for `add_one(2)` and then print the results. We can visualize the execution flow of our application, as shown in figure 2.1. Each block of the figure represents what is happening at any given moment for one or more lines of code.

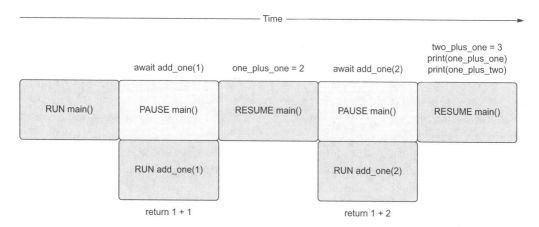

Figure 2.1   **When we hit an `await` expression, we pause our parent coroutine and run the coroutine in the await expression. Once it is finished, we resume the parent coroutine and assign the return value.**

As it stands now, this code does not operate differently from normal, sequential code. We are, in effect, mimicking a normal call stack. Next, let's look at a simple example of how to run other code by introducing a dummy sleep operation while we're waiting.

2.2   *Introducing long-running coroutines with sleep*

Our previous examples did not use any slow operations and were used to help us learn the basic syntax of coroutines. To fully see the benefits and show how we can run multiple events simultaneously, we'll need to introduce some long-running operations. Instead of making web API or database queries right away, which are nondeterministic as to how much time they will take, we'll simulate long-running operations by specifying how long we want to wait. We'll do this with the `asyncio.sleep` function.

We can use `asyncio.sleep` to make a coroutine "sleep" for a given number of seconds. This will pause our coroutine for the time we give it, simulating what would happen if we had a long-running call to a database or web API.

`asyncio.sleep` is itself a coroutine, so we must use it with the `await` keyword. If we call it just by itself, we'll get a coroutine object. Since `asyncio.sleep` is a coroutine, this means that when a coroutine awaits it, other code will be able to run.

Let's examine a simple example, shown in the following listing, that sleeps for 1 second and then prints a `'Hello World!'` message.

Listing 2.5   A first application with `sleep`

```
import asyncio

async def hello_world_message() -> str:
    await asyncio.sleep(1)            ◁——┐  Pause hello_world_message
    return 'Hello World!'                 │  for 1 second.

async def main() -> None:
    message = await hello_world_message()   ◁——┐  Pause main until
    print(message)                               │  hello_world_message
                                                  │  finishes.
asyncio.run(main())
```

When we run this application, our program will wait 1 second before printing our `'Hello World!'` message. Since `hello_world_message` is a coroutine and we pause it for 1 second with `asyncio.sleep`, we now have 1 second where we could be running other code concurrently.

We'll be using `sleep` a lot in the next few examples, so let's invest the time to create a reusable coroutine that sleeps for us and prints out some useful information. We'll call this coroutine `delay`. This is shown in the following listing.

Listing 2.6   A reusable `delay` function

```
import asyncio

async def delay(delay_seconds: int) -> int:
    print(f'sleeping for {delay_seconds} second(s)')
    await asyncio.sleep(delay_seconds)
    print(f'finished sleeping for {delay_seconds} second(s)')
    return delay_seconds
```

`delay` will take in an integer of the duration in seconds that we'd like the function to sleep and will return that integer to the caller once it has finished sleeping. We'll also print when sleep begins and ends. This will help us see what other code, if any, is running concurrently while our coroutines are paused.

To make referencing this utility function easier in future code listings, we'll create a module that we'll import in the remainder of this book when needed. We'll also add to this module as we create additional reusable functions. We'll call this module `util`, and we'll put our delay function in a file called `delay_functions.py`. We'll also add an `__init__.py` file with the following line, so we can nicely import the timer:

```
from util.delay_functions import delay
```

From now on in this book, we'll use `from util import delay` whenever we need to use the `delay` function. Now that we have a reusable delay coroutine, let's combine it with the earlier coroutine `add_one` to see if we can get our simple addition to run concurrently while `hello_world_message` is paused.

Listing 2.7 Running two coroutines

```
import asyncio
from util import delay

async def add_one(number: int) -> int:
    return number + 1

async def hello_world_message() -> str:
    await delay(1)
    return 'Hello World!'

async def main() -> None:
    message = await hello_world_message()
    one_plus_one = await add_one(1)
    print(one_plus_one)
    print(message)

asyncio.run(main())
```

Pause main until
hello_world_message
returns.

Pause main until
add_one returns.

When we run this, 1 second passes before the results of both function calls are printed. What we really want is the value of add_one(1) to be printed immediately while hello_world_message() runs concurrently. So why isn't this happening with this code? The answer is that await pauses our current coroutine and won't execute any other code inside that coroutine until the await expression gives us a value. Since it will take 1 second for our hello_world_message function to give us a value, the main coroutine will be paused for 1 second. Our code behaves as if it were sequential in this case. This behavior is illustrated in figure 2.2.

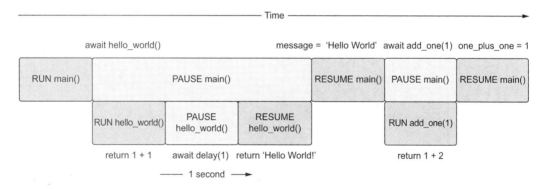

Figure 2.2 Execution flow of listing 2.7

Both main and hello_world paused while we wait for delay(1) to finish. After it has finished, main resumes and can execute add_one.

We'd like to move away from this sequential model and run add_one concurrently with hello_world. To achieve this, we'll need to introduce a concept called *tasks*.

2.3   *Running concurrently with tasks*

Earlier we saw that, when we call a coroutine directly, we don't put it on the event loop to run. Instead, we get a coroutine object that we then need to either use the await keyword on it or pass it in to asyncio.run to run and get a value. With only these tools we can write async code, but we can't run anything concurrently. To run coroutines concurrently, we'll need to introduce *tasks*.

Tasks are wrappers around a coroutine that schedule a coroutine to run on the event loop as soon as possible. This scheduling and execution happen in a non-blocking fashion, meaning that, once we create a task, we can execute other code instantly while the task is running. This contrasts with using the await keyword that acts in a blocking manner, meaning that we pause the entire coroutine until the result of the await expression comes back.

The fact that we can create tasks and schedule them to run instantly on the event loop means that we can execute multiple tasks at roughly the same time. When these tasks wrap a long-running operation, any waiting they do will happen concurrently. To illustrate this, let's create two tasks and try to run them at the same time.

2.3.1   *The basics of creating tasks*

Creating a task is achieved by using the asyncio.create_task function. When we call this function, we give it a coroutine to run, and it returns a task object instantly. Once we have a task object, we can put it in an await expression that will extract the return value once it is complete.

Listing 2.8   Creating a task

```
import asyncio
from util import delay


async def main():
    sleep_for_three = asyncio.create_task(delay(3))
    print(type(sleep_for_three))
    result = await sleep_for_three
    print(result)

asyncio.run(main())
```

In the preceding listing, we create a task that requires 3 seconds to complete. We also print out the type of the task, in this case, <class '_asyncio.Task'>, to show that it is different from a coroutine.

One other thing to note here is that our print statement is executed immediately after we run the task. If we had simply used await on the delay coroutine we would have waited 3 seconds before outputting the message.

Once we've printed our message, we apply an await expression to the task sleep_for_three. This will suspend our main coroutine until we have a result from our task.

It is important to know that we should usually use an `await` keyword on our tasks at some point in our application. In listing 2.8, if we did not use `await`, our task would be scheduled to run, but it would almost immediately be stopped and "cleaned up" when `asyncio.run` shut down the event loop. Using `await` on our tasks in our application also has implications for how exceptions are handled, which we'll look at in chapter 3. Now that we've seen how to create a task and allow other code to run concurrently, we can learn how to run multiple long-running operations at the same time.

2.3.2 *Running multiple tasks concurrently*

Given that tasks are created instantly and are scheduled to run as soon as possible, this allows us to run many long-running tasks concurrently. We can do this by sequentially starting multiple tasks with our long-running coroutine.

Listing 2.9 Running multiple tasks concurrently

```
import asyncio
from util import delay

async def main():
    sleep_for_three = asyncio.create_task(delay(3))
    sleep_again = asyncio.create_task(delay(3))
    sleep_once_more = asyncio.create_task(delay(3))

    await sleep_for_three
    await sleep_again
    await sleep_once_more


asyncio.run(main())
```

In the preceding listing we start three tasks, each taking 3 seconds to complete. Each call to `create_task` returns instantly, so we reach the `await sleep_for_three` statement right away. Previously, we mentioned that tasks are scheduled to run "as soon as possible." Generally, this means the first time we hit an `await` statement after creating a task, any tasks that are pending will run as `await` triggers an iteration of the event loop.

Since we've hit `await sleep_for_three`, all three tasks start running and will carry out any sleep operations concurrently. This means that the program in listing 2.9 will complete in about 3 seconds. We can visualize the concurrency as shown in figure 2.3, noting that all three tasks are running their sleep coroutines at the same time.

Note that in figure 2.3 the code in the tasks labeled RUN delay(3) (in this case, some print statements) does not run concurrently with other tasks; only the sleep coroutines run concurrently. If we were to run these delay operations sequentially, we'd have an application runtime of just over 9 seconds. By doing this concurrently, we've decreased the total runtime of this application three-fold!

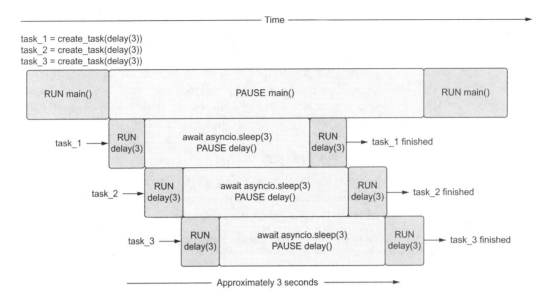

Figure 2.3   Execution flow of listing 2.9

NOTE   This benefit compounds as we add more tasks; if we had launched 10 of these tasks, we would still take roughly 3 seconds, giving us a 10-fold speedup.

Executing these long-running operations concurrently is where asyncio really shines and delivers drastic improvements in our application's performance, but the benefits don't stop there. In listing 2.9, our application was actively doing nothing, while it was waiting for 3 seconds for our delay coroutines to complete. While our code is waiting, we can execute other code. As an example, let's say we wanted to print out a status message every second while we were running some long tasks.

Listing 2.10   Running code while other operations complete

```python
import asyncio
from util import delay


async def hello_every_second():
    for i in range(2):
        await asyncio.sleep(1)
        print("I'm running other code while I'm waiting!")


async def main():
    first_delay = asyncio.create_task(delay(3))
    second_delay = asyncio.create_task(delay(3))
    await hello_every_second()
    await first_delay
    await second_delay
```

In the preceding listing, we create two tasks, each of which take 3 seconds to complete. While these tasks are waiting, our application is idle, which gives us the opportunity to run other code. In this instance, we run a coroutine `hello_every_second`, which prints a message every second 2 times. While our two tasks are running, we'll see messages being output, giving us the following:

```
sleeping for 3 second(s)
sleeping for 3 second(s)
I'm running other code while I'm waiting!
I'm running other code while I'm waiting!
finished sleeping for 3 second(s)
finished sleeping for 3 second(s)
```

We can imagine the execution flow as shown in figure 2.4.

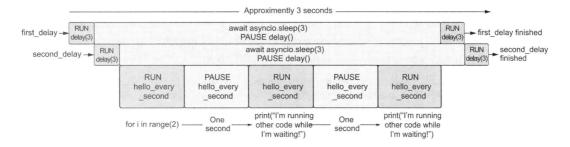

Figure 2.4   Execution flow of listing 2.10

First, we start two tasks that sleep for 3 seconds; then, while our two tasks are idle, we start to see I'm running other code while I'm waiting! being printed every second. This means that even when we're running time-intensive operations, our application can still be performing other tasks.

One potential issue with tasks is that they can take an indefinite amount of time to complete. We could find ourselves wanting to stop a task if it takes too long to finish. Tasks support this use case by allowing cancellation.

2.4   *Canceling tasks and setting timeouts*

Network connections can be unreliable. A user's connection may drop because of a network slowdown, or a web server may crash and leave existing requests in limbo. When making one of these requests, we need to be especially careful that we don't wait indefinitely. Doing so could lead to our application hanging, waiting forever for a result that may never come. It could also lead to a poor user experience; if we allow a user to make a request that takes too long, they are unlikely to wait forever for a response. Additionally, we may want to allow our users a choice if a task continues to run. A user may proactively decide things are taking too long, or they may want to stop a task they made in error.

In our previous examples, if our tasks took forever, we would be stuck waiting for the await statement to finish with no feedback. We also had no way to stop things if we wanted to. asyncio supports both these situations by allowing tasks to be canceled as well as allowing them to specify a timeout.

2.4.1 *Canceling tasks*

Canceling a task is straightforward. Each task object has a method named cancel, which we can call whenever we'd like to stop a task. Canceling a task will cause that task to raise a CancelledError when we await it, which we can then handle as needed.

To illustrate this, let's say we launch a long-running task that we don't want to run for longer than 5 seconds. If the task is not completed within 5 seconds, we'd like to stop that task, reporting back to the user that it took too long and we're stopping it. We also want a status update printed every second, to provide up-to-date information to our user, so they aren't left without information for several seconds.

Listing 2.11 Canceling a task

```
import asyncio
from asyncio import CancelledError
from util import delay


async def main():
    long_task = asyncio.create_task(delay(10))

    seconds_elapsed = 0

    while not long_task.done():
        print('Task not finished, checking again in a second.')
        await asyncio.sleep(1)
        seconds_elapsed = seconds_elapsed + 1
        if seconds_elapsed == 5:
            long_task.cancel()

    try:
        await long_task
    except CancelledError:
        print('Our task was cancelled')

asyncio.run(main())
```

In the preceding listing, we create a task that will take 10 seconds to run. We then create a while loop to check if that task is done. The done method on the task returns True if a task is finished and False otherwise. Every second, we check to see if the task has finished, keeping track of how many seconds we've checked so far. If our task has taken

5 seconds, we cancel the task. Then, we will go on to await `long_task`, and we'll see Our task was cancelled printed out, indicating we've caught a `CancelledError`.

Something important to note about cancellation is that a `CancelledError` can only be thrown from an await statement. This means that if we call cancel on a task when it is executing plain Python code, that code will run until completion until we hit the next await statement (if one exists) and a `CancelledError` can be raised. Calling cancel won't magically stop the task in its tracks; it will only stop the task if you're currently at an await point or its next await point.

2.4.2 Setting a timeout and canceling with wait_for

Checking every second or at some other time interval, and then canceling a task, as we did in the previous example, isn't the easiest way to handle a timeout. Ideally, we'd have a helper function that would allow us to specify this timeout and handle cancellation for us.

asyncio provides this functionality through a function called `asyncio.wait_for`. This function takes in a coroutine or task object, and a timeout specified in seconds. It then returns a coroutine that we can await. If the task takes more time to complete than the timeout we gave it, a `TimeoutException` will be raised. Once we have reached the timeout threshold, the task will automatically be canceled.

To illustrate how `wait_for` works, we'll look at a case where we have a task that will take 2 seconds to complete, but we'll only allow it 1 second to finish. When we get a `TimeoutError` raised, we'll catch the exception and check to see if the task was canceled.

Listing 2.12 Creating a timeout for a task with `wait_for`

```
import asyncio
from util import delay

async def main():
    delay_task = asyncio.create_task(delay(2))
    try:
        result = await asyncio.wait_for(delay_task, timeout=1)
        print(result)
    except asyncio.exceptions.TimeoutError:
        print('Got a timeout!')
        print(f'Was the task cancelled? {delay_task.cancelled()}')

asyncio.run(main())
```

When we run the preceding listing, our application will take roughly 1 second to complete. After 1 second our `wait_for` statement will raise a `TimeoutError`, which we then handle. We'll then see that our original `delay` task was canceled, giving the following output:

```
sleeping for 2 second(s)
Got a timeout!
Was the task cancelled? True
```

Canceling tasks automatically if they take longer than expected is normally a good idea. Otherwise, we may have a coroutine waiting indefinitely, taking up resources that may never be released. However, in certain circumstances we may want to keep our coroutine running. For example, we may want to inform a user that something is taking longer than expected after a certain amount of time but not cancel the task when the timeout is exceeded.

To do this we can wrap our task with the asyncio.shield function. This function will prevent cancellation of the coroutine we pass in, giving it a "shield," which cancellation requests then ignore.

Listing 2.13   Shielding a task from cancellation

```
import asyncio
from util import delay


async def main():
    task = asyncio.create_task(delay(10))

    try:
        result = await asyncio.wait_for(asyncio.shield(task), 5)
        print(result)
    except TimeoutError:
        print("Task took longer than five seconds, it will finish soon!")
        result = await task
        print(result)


asyncio.run(main())
```

In the preceding listing, we first create a task to wrap our coroutine. This differs from our first cancellation example because we'll need to access the task in the except block. If we had passed in a coroutine, wait_for would have wrapped it in a task, but we wouldn't be able to reference it, as it is internal to the function.

Then, inside of a try block, we call wait_for and wrap the task in shield, which will prevent the task from being canceled. Inside our exception block, we print a useful message to the user, letting them know that the task is still running and then we await the task we initially created. This will let it finish in its entirety, and the program's output will be as follows:

```
sleeping for 10 second(s)
Task took longer than five seconds!
finished sleeping for 10 second(s)
finished <function delay at 0x10e8cf820> in 10 second(s)
```

Cancellation and shielding are somewhat tricky subjects with several cases that are noteworthy. We introduce the basics below, but as we get into more complicated cases, we'll explore how cancellation works in greater depth.

We've now introduced the basics of tasks and coroutines. These concepts are intertwined with one another. In the following section, we'll look at how tasks and coroutines are related to one another and understand a bit more about how asyncio is structured.

2.5 *Tasks, coroutines, futures, and awaitables*

Coroutines and tasks can both be used in await expressions. So what is the common thread between them? To understand, we'll need to know about both a future as well as an awaitable. You normally won't need to use futures, but understanding them is a key to understanding the inner workings of asyncio. As some APIs return futures, we will reference them in the rest of the book.

2.5.1 *Introducing futures*

A future is a Python object that contains a single value that you expect to get at some point in the future but may not yet have. Usually, when you create a future, it does not have any value it wraps around because it doesn't yet exist. In this state, it is considered incomplete, unresolved, or simply not done. Then, once you get a result, you can set the value of the future. This will complete the future; at that time, we can consider it finished and extract the result from the future. To understand the basics of futures, let's try creating one, setting its value and extracting that value back out.

Listing 2.14 The basics of futures

```python
from asyncio import Future

my_future = Future()

print(f'Is my_future done? {my_future.done()}')

my_future.set_result(42)

print(f'Is my_future done? {my_future.done()}')
print(f'What is the result of my_future? {my_future.result()}')
```

We can create a future by calling its constructor. At this time, the future will have no result set on it, so calling its done method will return False. We then set the value of the future with its set_result method, which will mark the future as done. Alternatively, if we had an exception we wanted to set on the future, we could call set_exception.

> **NOTE** We don't call the result method before the result is set because the result method will throw an invalid state exception if we do so.

Futures can also be used in await expressions. If we await a future, we're saying "pause until the future has a value set that I can work with, and once I have a value, wake up and let me process it."

To understand this, let's consider an example of making a web request that returns a future. Making a request that returns a future should complete instantly, but as the request will take some time, the future will not yet be defined. Then, later, once the request has finished, the result will be set, then we can access it. If you have used JavaScript in the past, this concept is analogous to *promises*. In the Java world, these are known as *completable futures*.

Listing 2.15   Awaiting a future

```
from asyncio import Future
import asyncio


def make_request() -> Future:
    future = Future()
    asyncio.create_task(set_future_value(future))
    return future


async def set_future_value(future) -> None:
    await asyncio.sleep(1)
    future.set_result(42)

async def main():
    future = make_request()
    print(f'Is the future done? {future.done()}')
    value = await future
    print(f'Is the future done? {future.done()}')
    print(value)


asyncio.run(main())
```

Create a task to asynchronously set the value of the future.

Wait 1 second before setting the value of the future.

Pause main until the future's value is set.

In the preceding listing, we define a function make_request. In that function we create a future and create a task that will asynchronously set the result of the future after 1 second. Then, in the main function, we call make_request. When we call this, we'll instantly get a future with no result; it is, therefore, undone. Then, we await the future. Awaiting this future will pause main for 1 second while we wait for the value of the future to be set. Once this completes, value will be 42 and the future is done.

In the world of asyncio, you should rarely need to deal with futures. That said, you will run into some asyncio APIs which return futures, and you may need to work with callback-based code, which can require futures. You may also need to read or debug some asyncio API code yourself. The implementation of these asyncio APIs heavily rely on futures, so it is ideal to have a basic understanding of how they work.

2.5.2   *The relationship between futures, tasks, and coroutines*

There is a strong relationship between tasks and futures. In fact, task directly inherits from future. A future can be thought as representing a value that we won't have for a while. A task can be thought as a combination of both a coroutine and a future. When we create a task, we are creating an empty future and running the coroutine. Then, when the coroutine has completed with either an exception or a result, we set the result or exception of the future.

Given the relationship between futures and tasks, is there a similar relationship between tasks and coroutines? After all, all these types can be used in await expressions.

The common thread between these is the Awaitable abstract base class. This class defines one abstract double underscore method __await__. We won't go into the specifics about how to create our own awaitables, but anything that implements the __await__ method can be used in an await expression. Coroutines inherit directly from Awaitable, as do futures. Tasks then extend futures, which gives us the inheritance diagram shown in figure 2.5.

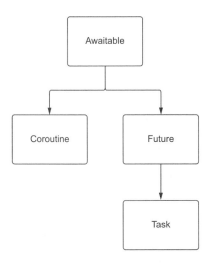

Figure 2.5   The class inheritance hierarchy of Awaitable

Going forward, we'll start to refer to objects that can be used in await expressions as *awaitables.* You'll frequently see the term *awaitable* referenced in the asyncio documentation, as many API methods don't care if you pass in coroutines, tasks, or futures.

Now that we understand the basics of coroutines, tasks, and futures, how do we assess their performance? So far, we've only theorized about how long they take. To make things more rigorous, let's add some functionality to measure execution time.

2.6 *Measuring coroutine execution time with decorators*

So far, we've talked about roughly how long our applications take to run without timing them. To really understand and profile things we'll need to introduce some code to keep track of this for us.

As a first try we could wrap every `await` statement and keep track of the start and end time of the coroutine:

```
import asyncio
import time

async def main():
    start = time.time()
    await asyncio.sleep(1)
    end = time.time()
    print(f'Sleeping took {end - start} seconds')

asyncio.run(main())
```

However, this will get messy quickly when we have multiple `await` statements and tasks to keep track of. A better approach is to come up with a reusable way to keep track of how long any coroutine takes to finish. We can do this by creating a decorator that will run an `await` statement for us (listing 2.16). We'll call this decorator `async_timed`.

> ### What is a decorator?
> A *decorator* is a pattern in Python that allows us to add functionality to existing functions without changing that function's code. We can "intercept" a function as it is being called and apply any decorator code we'd like before or after that call. Decorators are one way to tackle cross-cutting concerns. The following listing illustrates a sample decorator.

Listing 2.16 A decorator for timing coroutines

```
import functools
import time
from typing import Callable, Any


def async_timed():
    def wrapper(func: Callable) -> Callable:
        @functools.wraps(func)
        async def wrapped(*args, **kwargs) -> Any:
            print(f'starting {func} with args {args} {kwargs}')
            start = time.time()
            try:
                return await func(*args, **kwargs)
            finally:
                end = time.time()
```

```
        total = end - start
        print(f'finished {func} in {total:.4f} second(s)')

    return wrapped

return wrapper
```

In this decorator, we create a new coroutine called *wrapped*. This is a wrapper around our original coroutine that takes its arguments, *args and **kwargs, calls an await statement, and then returns the result. We surround that await statement with one message when we start running the function and another message when we end running the function, keeping track of the start and end time in much the same way that we did in our earlier start-time and end-time example. Now, as shown in listing 2.17, we can put this annotation on any coroutine, and any time we run it, we'll see how long it took to run.

Listing 2.17 Timing two concurrent tasks with a decorator

```
import asyncio

@async_timed()
async def delay(delay_seconds: int) -> int:
    print(f'sleeping for {delay_seconds} second(s)')
    await asyncio.sleep(delay_seconds)
    print(f'finished sleeping for {delay_seconds} second(s)')
    return delay_seconds


@async_timed()
async def main():
    task_one = asyncio.create_task(delay(2))
    task_two = asyncio.create_task(delay(3))

    await task_one
    await task_two


asyncio.run(main())
```

When we run the preceding listing, we'll see console output similar to the following:

```
starting <function main at 0x109111ee0> with args () {}
starting <function delay at 0x1090dc700> with args (2,) {}
starting <function delay at 0x1090dc700> with args (3,) {}
finished <function delay at 0x1090dc700> in 2.0032 second(s)
finished <function delay at 0x1090dc700> in 3.0003 second(s)
finished <function main at 0x109111ee0> in 3.0004 second(s)
```

We can see that our two delay calls were both started and finished in roughly 2 and 3 seconds, respectively, for a total of 5 seconds. Notice, however, that our main coroutine only took 3 seconds to complete because we were waiting concurrently.

We'll use this decorator and the resulting output throughout the next several chapters to illustrate how long our coroutines are taking to execute as well as when they start and complete. This will give us a clear picture of where we see performance gains by executing our operations concurrently.

To make referencing this utility decorator easier in future code listings, let's add this to our `util` module. We'll put our timer in a file called `async_timer.py`. We'll also add a line to the module's `__init__.py` file with the following line so we can nicely import the timer:

```
from util.async_timer import async_timed
```

In the rest of this book, we'll use `from util import async_timed` whenever we need to use the timer.

Now that we can use our decorator to understand the performance gains that asyncio can provide when running tasks concurrently, we may be tempted to try and use asyncio all over our existing applications. This can work, but we need to be careful that we aren't running into any of the common pitfalls with asyncio that can degrade our application's performance.

2.7   *The pitfalls of coroutines and tasks*

When seeing the performance improvements we can obtain from running some of our longer tasks concurrently, we can be tempted to start to use coroutines and tasks everywhere in our applications. While it depends on the application you're writing, simply marking functions `async` and wrapping them in tasks may not help application performance. In certain cases, this may degrade performance of your applications.

Two main errors occur when trying to turn your applications asynchronous. The first is attempting to run CPU-bound code in tasks or coroutines without using multiprocessing; the second is using blocking I/O-bound APIs without using multithreading.

2.7.1   *Running CPU-bound code*

We may have functions that perform computationally expensive calculations, such as looping over a large dictionary or doing a mathematical computation. Where we have several of these functions with the potential to run concurrently, we may get the idea to run them in separate tasks. In concept, this is a good idea, but remember that asyncio has a single-threaded concurrency model. This means we are still subject to the limitations of a single thread and the global interpreter lock.

To prove this to ourselves, let's try to run some CPU-bound functions concurrently.

Listing 2.18   Attempting to run CPU-bound code concurrently

```
import asyncio
from util import delay


@async_timed()
async def cpu_bound_work() -> int:
```

```
    counter = 0
    for i in range(100000000):
        counter = counter + 1
    return counter


@async_timed()
async def main():
    task_one = asyncio.create_task(cpu_bound_work())
    task_two = asyncio.create_task(cpu_bound_work())
    await task_one
    await task_two


asyncio.run(main())
```

When we run the preceding listing, we'll see that, despite creating two tasks, our code still executes sequentially. First, we run Task 1, then we run Task 2, meaning our total runtime will be the sum of the two calls to cpu_bound_work:

```
starting <function main at 0x10a8f6c10> with args () {}
starting <function cpu_bound_work at 0x10a8c0430> with args () {}
finished <function cpu_bound_work at 0x10a8c0430> in 4.6750 second(s)
starting <function cpu_bound_work at 0x10a8c0430> with args () {}
finished <function cpu_bound_work at 0x10a8c0430> in 4.6680 second(s)
finished <function main at 0x10a8f6c10> in 9.3434 second(s)
```

Looking at the output above, we may be tempted to think that there are no drawbacks to making all our code use async and await. After all, it ends up taking the same amount of time as if we had run things sequentially. However, by doing this we can run into situations where our application's performance can degrade. This is especially true when we have other coroutines or tasks that have await expressions. Consider creating two CPU-bound tasks alongside a long-running task, such as our delay coroutine.

Listing 2.19   CPU-bound code with a task

```
import asyncio
from util import async_timed, delay


@async_timed()
async def cpu_bound_work() -> int:
    counter = 0
    for i in range(100000000):
        counter = counter + 1
    return counter


@async_timed()
async def main():
    task_one = asyncio.create_task(cpu_bound_work())
    task_two = asyncio.create_task(cpu_bound_work())
```

```
        delay_task = asyncio.create_task(delay(4))
        await task_one
        await task_two
        await delay_task


asyncio.run(main())
```

Running the preceding listing, we might expect to take the same amount of time as in listing 2.18. After all, won't `delay_task` run concurrently alongside the CPU-bound work? In this instance it won't because we create the two CPU-bound tasks first, which, in effect, blocks the event loop from running anything else. This means the runtime of our application will be the sum of time it took for our two `cpu_bound_work` tasks to finish plus the 4 seconds that our `delay` task took.

If we need to perform CPU-bound work and still want to use `async / await` syntax, we can do so. To do this we'll still need to use multiprocessing, and we need to tell asyncio to run our tasks in a *process pool*. We'll learn how to do this in chapter 6.

2.7.2 *Running blocking APIs*

We may also be tempted to use our existing libraries for I/O-bound operations by wrapping them in coroutines. However, this will generate the same issues that we saw with CPU-bound operations. These APIs block the `main` thread. Therefore, when we run a blocking API call inside a coroutine, we're blocking the event loop thread itself, meaning that we stop any other coroutines or tasks from executing. Examples of blocking API calls include libraries such as `requests`, or `time.sleep`. Generally, any function that performs I/O that is not a coroutine or performs time-consuming CPU operations can be considered blocking.

As an example, let's try getting the status code of www.example.com three times concurrently, using the `requests` library. When we run this, since we're running concurrently we'll be expecting this application to finish in about the length of time necessary to get the status code once.

Listing 2.20   Incorrectly using a blocking API in a coroutine

```
import asyncio
import requests
from util import async_timed


@async_timed()
async def get_example_status() -> int:
    return requests.get('http://www.example.com').status_code


@async_timed()
async def main():
    task_1 = asyncio.create_task(get_example_status())
    task_2 = asyncio.create_task(get_example_status())
```

```
    task_3 = asyncio.create_task(get_example_status())
    await task_1
    await task_2
    await task_3

asyncio.run(main())
```

When running the preceding listing, we'll see output similar to the following. Note how the total runtime of the main coroutine is roughly the sum of time for all the tasks to get the status we ran, meaning that we did not have any concurrency advantage:

```
starting <function main at 0x1102e6820> with args () {}
starting <function get_example_status at 0x1102e6700> with args () {}
finished <function get_example_status at 0x1102e6700> in 0.0839 second(s)
starting <function get_example_status at 0x1102e6700> with args () {}
finished <function get_example_status at 0x1102e6700> in 0.0441 second(s)
starting <function get_example_status at 0x1102e6700> with args () {}
finished <function get_example_status at 0x1102e6700> in 0.0419 second(s)
finished <function main at 0x1102e6820> in 0.1702 second(s)
```

This is again because the `requests` library is blocking, meaning it will block whichever thread it is run on. Since asyncio only has one thread, the `requests` library blocks the event loop from doing anything concurrently.

As a rule, most APIs you employ now are blocking and won't work out of the box with asyncio. You need to use a library that supports coroutines and utilizes non-blocking sockets. This means that if the library you are using does not return coroutines and you aren't using `await` in your own coroutines, you're likely making a blocking call.

In the above example we can use a library such as aiohttp, which uses non-blocking sockets and returns coroutines to get proper concurrency. We'll introduce this library later in chapter 4.

If you need to use the `requests` library, you can still use `async` syntax, but you'll need to explicitly tell asyncio to use multithreading with a *thread pool executor*. We'll see how to do this in chapter 7.

We've now seen a few things to look for when using asyncio and have built a few simple applications. So far, we have not created or configured the event loop ourselves but relied on convenience methods to do it for us. Next, we'll learn to create the event loop, which will allow us to access lower-level asyncio functionality and event loop configuration properties.

2.8 *Accessing and manually managing the event loop*

Until now, we have used the convenient `asyncio.run` to run our application and create the event loop for us behind the scenes. Given the ease of use, this is the preferred method to create the event loop. However, there may be cases in which we don't want the functionality that `asyncio.run` provides. As an example, we may want to execute custom logic to stop tasks that differ from what `asyncio.run` does, such as letting any remaining tasks finish instead of stopping them.

In addition, we may want to access methods available on the event loop itself. These methods are typically lower level and, as such, should be used sparingly. However, if you want to perform tasks, such as working directly with sockets or scheduling a task to run at a specific time in the future, you'll need to access the event loop. While we won't, and shouldn't, be managing the event loop extensively, this will be necessary from time to time.

2.8.1 Creating an event loop manually

We can create an event loop by using the `asyncio.new_event_loop` method. This will return an event loop instance. With this, we have access to all the low-level methods that the event loop has to offer. With the event loop we have access to a method named `run_until_complete`, which takes a coroutine and runs it until it finishes. Once we are done with our event loop, we need to close it to free any resources it was using. This should normally be in a `finally` block so that any exceptions thrown don't stop us from closing the loop. Using these concepts, we can create a loop and run an asyncio application.

Listing 2.21   Manually creating the event loop

```
import asyncio

async def main():
    await asyncio.sleep(1)

loop = asyncio.new_event_loop()

try:
    loop.run_until_complete(main())
finally:
    loop.close()
```

The code in this listing is similar to what happens when we call `asyncio.run` with the difference being that this does not perform canceling any remaining tasks. If we want any special cleanup logic, we would do so in our `finally` clause.

2.8.2 Accessing the event loop

From time to time, we may need to access the currently running event loop. asyncio exposes the `asyncio.get_running_loop` function that allows us to get the current event loop. As an example, let's look at `call_soon`, which will schedule a function to run on the next iteration of the event loop.

Listing 2.22   Accessing the event loop

```
import asyncio

def call_later():
    print("I'm being called in the future!")
```

```
async def main():
    loop = asyncio.get_running_loop()
    loop.call_soon(call_later)
    await delay(1)

asyncio.run(main())
```

In the preceding listing, our main coroutine gets the event loop with `asyncio.get_running_loop` and tells it to run `call_later`, which takes a function and will run it on the next iteration of the event loop. In addition, there is an `asyncio.get_event_loop` function that lets you access the event loop.

This function can potentially create a new event loop if it is called when one is not already running, leading to strange behavior. It is recommended to use `get_running_loop`, as this will throw an exception if an event loop isn't running, avoiding any surprises.

While we shouldn't use the event loop frequently in our applications, there are times when we will need to configure settings on the event loop or use low-level functions. We'll see an example of configuring the event loop in the next section on *debug mode*.

2.9 Using debug mode

In previous sections, we mentioned how coroutines should always be awaited at some point in the application. We also saw the drawbacks of running CPU-bound and other blocking code inside coroutines and tasks. It can, however, be hard to tell if a coroutine is taking too much time on CPU, or if we accidently forgot an `await` somewhere in our application. Luckily, asyncio gives us a debug mode to help us diagnose these situations.

When we run in `debug` mode, we'll see a few helpful log messages when a coroutine or task takes more than 100 milliseconds to run. In addition, if we don't `await` a coroutine, an exception is thrown, so we can see where to properly add an `await`. There are a few different ways to run in debug mode.

2.9.1 Using asyncio.run

The `asyncio.run` function we have been using to run coroutines exposes a `debug` parameter. By default, this is set to `False`, but we can set this to `True` to enable debug mode:

```
asyncio.run(coroutine(), debug=True)
```

2.9.2 Using command-line arguments

Debug mode can be enabled by passing a command-line argument when we start our Python application. To do this we apply -X dev:

```
python3 -X dev program.py
```

2.9.3   *Using environment variables*

We can also use environment variables to enable debug mode by setting the
PYTHONASYNCIODEBUG variable to 1:

```
PYTHONASYINCIODEBUG=1 python3 program.py
```

> **NOTE** In versions of Python older than 3.9, there is a bug within debug
> mode. When using asyncio.run, only the boolean debug parameter will
> work. Command-line arguments and environment variables will only work
> when manually managing the event loop.

In debug mode, we'll see informative messages logged when a coroutine takes too
long. Let's test this out by trying to run CPU-bound code in a task to see if we get a
warning, as shown in the following listing.

Listing 2.23   Running CPU-bound code in debug mode

```python
import asyncio
from util import async_timed


@async_timed()
async def cpu_bound_work() -> int:
    counter = 0
    for i in range(100000000):
        counter = counter + 1
    return counter


async def main() -> None:
    task_one = asyncio.create_task(cpu_bound_work())
    await task_one

asyncio.run(main(), debug=True)
```

When running this, we'll see a helpful message that task_one was taking too long,
therefore blocking the event loop from running any other tasks:

```
Executing <Task finished name='Task-2' coro=<cpu_bound_work() done, defined
at listing_2_9.py:5> result=100000000 created at tasks.py:382> took 4.829
seconds
```

This can be helpful for debugging issues where we may inadvertently be making a call
that is blocking. The default settings will log a warning if a coroutine takes longer than
100 milliseconds, but this may be longer or shorter than we'd like. To change this
value, we can set the slow callback duration by accessing the event loop as we do in listing 2.24 and setting slow_callback_duration. This is a floating-point value representing the seconds we want the slow callback duration to be.

Listing 2.24   Changing the slow callback duration

```
import asyncio

async def main():
    loop = asyncio.get_event_loop()
    loop.slow_callback_duration = .250


asyncio.run(main(), debug=True)
```

The preceding listing will set the slow callback duration to 250 milliseconds, meaning we'll get a message printed out if any coroutine takes longer than 250 milliseconds of CPU time to run.

Summary

- We've learned how to create coroutines with the `async` keyword. Coroutines can suspend their execution on a blocking operation. This allows for other coroutines to run. Once the operation where the coroutine suspended completes, our coroutine will wake up and resume where it left off.
- We learned to use `await` in front of a call to a coroutine to run it and wait for it to return a value. To do so, the coroutine with the `await` inside it will suspend its execution, while waiting for a result. This allows other coroutines to run while the first coroutine is awaiting its result.
- We've learned how to use `asyncio.run` to execute a single coroutine. We can use this function to run the coroutine that is the main entry point into our application.
- We've learned how to use tasks to run multiple long-running operations concurrently. Tasks are wrappers around coroutines that will then be run on the event loop. When we create a task, it is scheduled to run on the event loop as soon as possible.
- We've learned how to cancel tasks if we want to stop them and how to add a timeout to a task to prevent them from taking forever. Canceling a task will make it raise a `CancelledError` while we await it. If we have time limits on how long a task should take, we can set timeouts on it by using `asycio.wait_for`.
- We've learned to avoid common issues that newcomers make when using asyncio. The first is running CPU-bound code in coroutines. CPU-bound code will block the event loop from running other coroutines since we're still single-threaded. The second is blocking I/O, since we can't use normal libraries with asyncio, and you must use asyncio-specific ones that return coroutines. If your coroutine does not have an `await` in it, you should consider it suspicious. There are still ways to use CPU-bound and blocking I/O with asyncio, which we will address in chapters 6 and 7.
- We've learned how to use debug mode. Debug mode can help us diagnose common issues in asyncio code, such as running CPU-intensive code in a coroutine.

A first asyncio application

This chapter covers
- Using sockets to transfer data over a network
- Using telnet to communicate with a socket-based application
- Using selectors to build a simple event loop for non-blocking sockets
- Creating a non-blocking echo server that allows for multiple connections
- Handling exceptions in tasks
- Adding custom shutdown logic to an asyncio application

In chapters 1 and 2, we introduced coroutines, tasks, and the event loop. We also examined how to run long operations concurrently and explored some of asyncio's APIs that facilitate this. Up to this point however, we've only simulated long operations with the sleep function.

Since we'd like to build more than just demo applications, we'll use some real-world blocking operations to demonstrate how to create a server that can handle multiple users concurrently. We'll do this with only one thread, leading to a more resource-efficient and simpler application than other solutions that would involve threads or multiple processes. We'll take what we've learned about coroutines, tasks, and asyncio's API methods to build a working command-line echo server application using sockets to demonstrate this. By the end of this chapter, you'll be able to build socket-based network applications with asyncio that can handle multiple users simultaneously with one thread.

First, we'll learn the basics of how to send and receive data with blocking sockets. We'll then use these sockets to attempt building a multi-client echo server. In doing so, we'll demonstrate that we can't build an echo server that works properly for more than one client at a time with only a single thread. We'll then learn how to resolve these issues by making our sockets non-blocking and using the operating system's event notification system. This will help us understand how the underlying machinery of the asyncio event loop works. Then we'll use asyncio's non-blocking socket coroutines to allow multiple clients to connect properly. This application will let multiple users connect simultaneously, letting them send and receive messages concurrently. Finally, we'll add custom shutdown logic to our application, so when our server shuts down, we'll give in-flight messages some time to complete.

3.1 Working with blocking sockets

In chapter 1, we introduced the concept of sockets. Recall that a socket is a way to read and write data over a network. We can think of a socket as a mailbox: we put a letter in, and it is delivered to the recipient's address. The recipient can then read that message, and possibly send us another back.

To get started, we'll create the main mailbox socket, which we'll call our server socket. This socket will first accept connection messages from clients that want to communicate with us. Once that connection is acknowledged by our server socket, we'll create a socket that we can use to communicate with the client. This means our server starts to look more like a post office with multiple PO boxes rather than just one mailbox. The client side can still be thought of as having a single mailbox as they will have one socket to communicate with us. When a client connects to our server, we provide them a PO box. We then use that PO box to send and receive messages to and from that client (see figure 3.1).

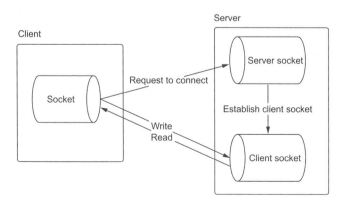

Figure 3.1   A client connects to our server socket. The server then creates a new socket to communicate with the client.

We can create this server socket with Python's built-in socket module. This module provides functionality for reading, writing, and manipulating sockets. To get started creating sockets, we'll create a simple server which listens for a connection from a client and prints a message on a successful connection. This socket will be bound to both a hostname and a port and will be the main "server socket" that any clients will communicate with.

It takes a few steps to create a socket. We first use the socket function to create a socket:

```
import socket

server_socket = socket.socket(socket.AF_INET, socket.SOCK_STREAM)
server_socket.setsockopt(socket.SOL_SOCKET, socket.SO_REUSEADDR, 1)
```

Here, we specify two parameters to the socket function. The first is socket.AF_INET—this tells us what type of address our socket will be able to interact with; in this case a hostname and a port number. The second is socket.SOCK_STREAM; this means that we use the TCP protocol for our communication.

> ### What is the TCP protocol?
> TCP, or transmission control protocol, is a protocol designed to transfer data between applications over a network. This protocol is designed with reliability in mind. It performs error checking, delivers data in order, and can retransmit data when needed. This reliability comes at the cost of some overhead. The vast majority of the web is built on TCP. TCP is in contrast to UDP, or user datagram protocol, which is less reliable but has much less overhead than TCP and tends to be more performant. We will exclusively focus on TCP sockets in this book.

We also call setsockopt to set the SO_REUSEADDR flag to 1. This will allow us to reuse the port number after we stop and restart the application, avoiding any *address already in use* errors. If we didn't do this, it might take some time for the operating system to unbind this port and have our application start without error.

Calling socket.socket lets us create a socket, but we can't start communicating with it yet because we haven't bound it to an address that clients can talk to (our post office needs an address!). For this example, we'll bind the socket to an address on our own computer at 127.0.0.1, and we'll pick an arbitrary port number of 8000:

```
address = (127.0.0.1, 8000)
server_socket.bind(server_address)
```

Now we've set our socket up at the address 127.0.0.1:8000. This means that clients will be able to use this address to send data to our server, and if we write data to a client, they will see this as the address that it's coming from.

Next, we need to actively listen for connections from clients who want to connect to our server. To do this, we can call the listen method on our socket. This tells the socket to listen for incoming connections, which will allow clients to connect to our server socket. Then, we wait for a connection by calling the accept method on our socket. This method will block until we get a connection and when we do, it will return a connection and the address of the client that connected. The connection is just another socket we can use to read data from and write data to our client:

```
server_socket.listen()
connection, client_address = server_socket.accept()
```

With these pieces, we have all the building blocks we need to create a socket-based server application that will wait for a connection and print a message once we have one.

Listing 3.1 Starting a server and listening for a connection

```
import socket                                              Create a TCP server socket.

server_socket = socket.socket(socket.AF_INET, socket.SOCK_STREAM)
server_socket.setsockopt(socket.SOL_SOCKET, socket.SO_REUSEADDR, 1)

server_address = ('127.0.0.1', 8000)                       Set the address of the
server_socket.bind(server_address)                         socket to 127.0.0.1:8000.
server_socket.listen()                                     Listen for connections or
                                                           "open the post office."
connection, client_address = server_socket.accept()        Wait for a connection and
print(f'I got a connection from {client_address}!')        assign the client a PO box.
```

In the preceding listing, when a client connects, we get their connection socket as well as their address and print that we got a connection.

So now that we've built this application, how do we connect to it to test it out? While there are quite a few tools for this, in this chapter we'll use the telnet command-line application.

3.2 Connecting to a server with Telnet

Our simple example of accepting connections left us with no way to connect. There are many command-line applications to read and write data to and from a server, but a popular application that has been around for quite some time is Telnet.

Telnet was first developed in 1969 and is short for "teletype network." Telnet establishes a TCP connection to a server and a host we specify. Once we do so, a terminal is established and we're free to send and receive bytes, all of which will be displayed in the terminal.

On Mac OS you can install telnet with Homebrew with the command `brew install telnet` (see https://brew.sh/ to install Homebrew). On Linux distributions you will need to use the system package manager to install (`apt-get install telnet` or similar). On Windows, PuTTy is the best option, and you can download this from https://putty.org.

> **NOTE**   With PuTTY you'll need to turn on local line editing for code samples in this book to work. To do this go to *Terminal* on the left-hand side of the PuTTy configuration window and set *Local line editing* to *Force on*.

To connect to the server we built in listing 3.1, we can use the Telnet command on a command line and specify that we'd like to connect to localhost on port 8000:

```
telnet localhost 8000
```

Once we do this, we'll see some output on our terminal telling us that we've successfully connected. Telnet then will display a cursor, which allows us to type and select [Enter] to send data to the server.

```
telnet localhost 8000
Trying 127.0.0.1...
Connected to localhost.
Escape character is '^]'.
```

In the console output of our server application, we should now see output like the following, showing that we've established a connection with our Telnet client:

```
I got a connection from ('127.0.0.1', 56526)!
```

You'll also see a Connection closed by foreign host message as the server code exits, indicating the server has shut down the connection to our client. We now have a way to connect to a server and write and read bytes to and from it, but our server can't read or send any data itself. We can do this with our client socket's sendall and recv methods.

3.2.1   *Reading and writing data to and from a socket*

Now that we've created a server capable of accepting connections, let's examine how to read data from our connections. The socket class has a method named recv that we can use to get data from a particular socket. This method takes an integer representing the number of bytes we wish to read at a given time. This is important because we can't read all data from a socket at once; we need to buffer until we reach the end of the input.

In this case, we'll treat the end of input as a carriage return plus a line feed or '\r\n'. This is what gets appended to the input when a user presses [Enter] in telnet. To demonstrate how buffering works with small messages, we'll set a buffer size intentionally low. In a real-world application, we would use a larger buffer size, such as 1024 bytes. We would typically want a larger buffer size, as this will take advantage of the buffering that occurs at the operating system-level, which is more efficient than doing it in your application.

Listing 3.2 Reading data from a socket

```
import socket

server_socket = socket.socket(socket.AF_INET, socket.SOCK_STREAM)
server_socket.setsockopt(socket.SOL_SOCKET, socket.SO_REUSEADDR, 1)

server_address = ('127.0.0.1', 8000)
server_socket.bind(server_address)
server_socket.listen()

try:
    connection, client_address = server_socket.accept()
    print(f'I got a connection from {client_address}!')

    buffer = b''

    while buffer[-2:] != b'\r\n':
        data = connection.recv(2)
        if not data:
            break
        else:
            print(f'I got data: {data}!')
            buffer = buffer + data

    print(f"All the data is: {buffer}")
finally:
    server_socket.close()
```

In the preceding listing, we wait for a connection with server_socket.accept, as before. Once we get a connection, we try to receive two bytes and store it in our buffer. Then, we go into a loop, checking each iteration to see if our buffer ends in a carriage return and a line feed. If it does not, we get two more bytes and print out which bytes we received and append that to the buffer. If we get '\r\n', then we end the loop and we print out the full message we got from the client. We also close the server socket in a finally block. This ensures that we close the connection even if an exception occurs while reading data. If we connect to this application with telnet and send a message 'testing123', we'll see this output:

```
I got a connection from ('127.0.0.1', 49721)!
I got data: b'te'!
I got data: b'st'!
I got data: b'in'!
I got data: b'g1'!
I got data: b'23'!
I got data: b'\r\n'!
All the data is: b'testing123\r\n'
```

Now, we're able to read data from a socket, but how do we write data back to a client? Sockets have a method named sendall that will take a message and write it back to the client for us. We can adapt our code in listing 3.2 to echo the message the client sent to us by calling `connection.sendall` with the buffer once it is filled:

```
while buffer[-2:] != b'\r\n':
    data = connection.recv(2)
    if not data:
        break
    else:
        print(f'I got data: {data}!')
        buffer = buffer + data
print(f"All the data is: {buffer}")
connection.sendall(buffer)
```

Now when we connect to this application and send it a message from Telnet, we should see that message printed back on our telnet terminal. We've created a very basic echo server with sockets!

This application handles one client at a time right now, but multiple clients can connect to a single server socket. Let's adapt this example to allow multiple clients to connect at the same time. In doing this we'll demonstrate how we can't properly support multiple clients with blocking sockets.

3.2.2   *Allowing multiple connections and the dangers of blocking*

A socket in listen mode allows multiple client connections simultaneously. This means that we can call `socket.accept` repeatedly, and each time a client connects we will get a new connection socket to read and write data to and from that client. With that knowledge, we can straightforwardly adapt our previous example to handle multiple clients. We loop forever, calling `socket.accept` to listen for new connections. Each time we get one, we append it to a list of connections we've got so far. Then, we loop over each connection, receiving data as it comes in and writing that data back out to the client connection.

Listing 3.3   Allowing multiple clients to connect

```
import socket

server_socket = socket.socket(socket.AF_INET, socket.SOCK_STREAM)
server_socket.setsockopt(socket.SOL_SOCKET, socket.SO_REUSEADDR, 1)

server_address = ('127.0.0.1', 8000)
server_socket.bind(server_address)
server_socket.listen()

connections = []

try:
    while True:
        connection, client_address = server_socket.accept()
        print(f'I got a connection from {client_address}!')
        connections.append(connection)
```

```
        for connection in connections:
            buffer = b''

            while buffer[-2:] != b'\r\n':
                data = connection.recv(2)
                if not data:
                    break
                else:
                    print(f'I got data: {data}!')
                    buffer = buffer + data

            print(f"All the data is: {buffer}")

            connection.send(buffer)
finally:
    server_socket.close()
```

We can try this by making one connection with telnet and typing a message. Then, once we have done that, we can connect with a second telnet client and send another message. However, if we do this, we will notice a problem right away. Our first client will work fine and will echo messages back as we'd expect, but our second client won't get anything echoed back to it. This is due to the default blocking behavior of sockets. The methods accept and recv block until they receive data. This means that once the first client connects, we will block waiting for it to send its first echo message to us. This causes other clients to be stuck waiting for the next iteration of the loop, which won't happen until the first client sends us data (figure 3.2).

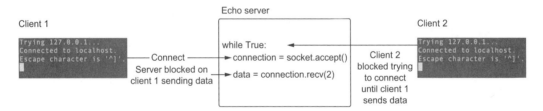

Figure 3.2   With blocking sockets, Client 1 connects, but Client 2 is blocked until client one sends data.

This obviously isn't a satisfactory user experience; we've created something that won't properly scale when we have more than one user. We can solve this issue by putting our sockets in non-blocking mode. When we mark a socket as non-blocking, its methods will not block waiting to receive data before moving on to execute the next line of code.

3.3   *Working with non-blocking sockets*

Our previous echo server allowed multiple clients to connect; however, when more than one connected, we ran into issues where one client could cause others to wait for it to send data. We can address this issue by putting sockets into non-blocking mode.

When we do this, any time we call a method that would block, such as `recv`, it is guaranteed to return instantly. If the socket has data ready for processing, then we will get data returned as we would with a blocking socket. If not, the socket will instantly let us know it does not have any data ready, and we are free to move on to execute other code.

Listing 3.4   Creating a non-blocking socket

```
import socket

server_socket = socket.socket(socket.AF_INET, socket.SOCK_STREAM)
server_socket.setsockopt(socket.SOL_SOCKET, socket.SO_REUSEADDR, 1)
server_socket.bind(('127.0.0.1', 8000))
server_socket.listen()
server_socket.setblocking(False)
```

Fundamentally, creating a non-blocking socket is no different from creating a blocking one, except that we must call `setblocking` with `False`. By default, a socket will have this value set to `True`, indicating it is blocking. Now let's see what happens when we do this in our original application. Does this fix the issue?

Listing 3.5   A first attempt at a non-blocking server

```
import socket

server_socket = socket.socket(socket.AF_INET, socket.SOCK_STREAM)
server_socket.setsockopt(socket.SOL_SOCKET, socket.SO_REUSEADDR, 1)

server_address = ('127.0.0.1', 8000)
server_socket.bind(server_address)          ┐  Mark the server socket
server_socket.listen()                      │  as non-blocking.
server_socket.setblocking(False)    ◁───────┘

connections = []

try:
    while True:
        connection, client_address = server_socket.accept()
        connection.setblocking(False)    ◁───┐  Mark the client
        print(f'I got a connection from {client_address}!')  │  socket as non-
        connections.append(connection)   │  blocking.

        for connection in connections:
            buffer = b''

            while buffer[-2:] != b'\r\n':
                data = connection.recv(2)
                if not data:
                    break
                else:
                    print(f'I got data: {data}!')
                    buffer = buffer + data

            print(f"All the data is: {buffer}")
```

```
            connection.send(buffer)
finally:
    server_socket.close()
```

When we run listing 3.5, we'll notice something different right away. Our application crashes almost instantly! We'll get thrown a `BlockingIOError` because our server socket has no connection yet and therefore no data to process:

```
Traceback (most recent call last):
  File "echo_server.py", line 14, in <module>
    connection, client_address = server_socket.accept()
  File " python3.8/socket.py", line 292, in accept
    fd, addr = self._accept()
BlockingIOError: [Errno 35] Resource temporarily unavailable
```

This is the socket's somewhat unintuitive way of telling us, "I don't have any data, try calling me again later." There is no easy way for us to tell if a socket has data right now, so one solution is to just catch the exception, ignore it, and keep looping until we have data. With this tactic, we'll constantly be checking for new connections and data as fast as we can. This should solve the issue that our blocking socket echo server had.

Listing 3.6 Catching and ignoring blocking IO errors

```
import socket

server_socket = socket.socket(socket.AF_INET, socket.SOCK_STREAM)
server_socket.setsockopt(socket.SOL_SOCKET, socket.SO_REUSEADDR, 1)

server_address = ('127.0.0.1', 8000)
server_socket.bind(server_address)
server_socket.listen()
server_socket.setblocking(False)

connections = []

try:
    while True:
        try:
            connection, client_address = server_socket.accept()
            connection.setblocking(False)
            print(f'I got a connection from {client_address}!')
            connections.append(connection)
        except BlockingIOError:
            pass

        for connection in connections:
            try:
                buffer = b''

                while buffer[-2:] != b'\r\n':
                    data = connection.recv(2)
                    if not data:
                        break
```

```
        else:
            print(f'I got data: {data}!')
            buffer = buffer + data

        print(f"All the data is: {buffer}")
        connection.send(buffer)
    except BlockingIOError:
        pass

finally:
    server_socket.close()
```

Each time we go through an iteration of our infinite loop, none of our calls to accept or recv every block, and we either instantly throw an exception that we ignore, or we have data ready to process and we process it. Each iteration of this loop happens quickly, and we're never dependent on anyone sending us data to proceed to the next line of code. This addresses the issue of our blocking server and allows multiple clients to connect and send data concurrently.

This approach works, but it comes at a cost. The first is code quality. Catching exceptions any time we might not yet have data will quickly get verbose and is potentially error-prone. The second is a resource issue. If you run this on a laptop, you may notice your fan starts to sound louder after a few seconds. This application will always be using nearly 100% of our CPU's processing power (figure 3.3). This is because we are constantly looping and getting exceptions as fast as we can inside our application, leading to a workload that is CPU heavy.

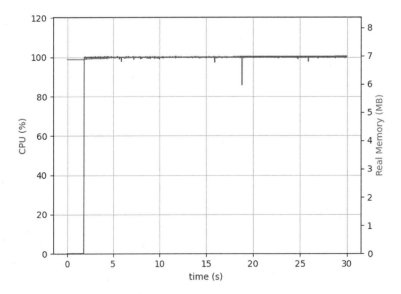

Figure 3.3 When looping and catching exceptions, CPU usage spikes to 100% and stays there.

Earlier, we mentioned operating system-specific event notification systems that can notify us when sockets have data that we can act on. These systems rely on hardware-level notifications and don't involve polling with a `while` loop, as we just did. Python has a library for using this event notification system built in. Next, we'll use this to resolve our CPU utilization issues and build a mini event loop for socket events.

3.4 Using the selectors module to build a socket event loop

Operating systems have efficient APIs that let us watch sockets for incoming data and other events built in. While the actual API is dependent on the operating system (kqueue, epoll, and IOCP are a few common ones), all of these I/O notification systems operate on a similar concept. We give them a list of sockets we want to monitor for events, and instead of constantly checking each socket to see if it has data, the operating system tells us explicitly when sockets have data.

Because this is implemented at the hardware level, very little CPU utilization is used during this monitoring, allowing for efficient resource usage. These notification systems are the core of how asyncio achieves concurrency. Understanding how this works gives us a view of how the underlying machinery of asyncio works.

The event notification systems are different depending on the operating system. Luckily, Python's `selectors` module is abstracted such that we can get the proper event for wherever we run our code. This makes our code portable across different operating systems.

This library exposes an abstract base class called `BaseSelector`, which has multiple implementations for each event notification system. It also contains a `Default-Selector` class, which automatically chooses which implementation is most efficient for our system.

The `BaseSelector` class has important concepts. The first is *registration*. When we have a socket that we're interested in getting notifications about, we register it with the selector and tell it which events we're interested in. These are events such as read and write. Inversely, we can also deregister a socket we're no longer interested in.

The second major concept is *select*. `select` will block until an event has happened, and once it does, the call will return with a list of sockets that are ready for processing along with the event that triggered it. It also supports a timeout, which will return an empty set of events after a specified amount of time.

Given these building blocks, we can create a non-blocking echo server that does not stress our CPU. Once we create our server socket, we'll register it with the default selector, which will listen for any connections from clients. Then, any time someone connects to our server socket, we'll register the client's connection socket with the selector to watch for any data sent. If we get any data from a socket that isn't our server socket, we know it is from a client that has sent data. We then receive that data and write it back to the client. We will also add a timeout to demonstrate that we can have other code execute while we're waiting for things to happen.

Listing 3.7   Using selectors to build a non-blocking server

```python
import selectors
import socket
from selectors import SelectorKey
from typing import List, Tuple

selector = selectors.DefaultSelector()

server_socket = socket.socket()
server_socket.setsockopt(socket.SOL_SOCKET, socket.SO_REUSEADDR, 1)

server_address = ('127.0.0.1', 8000)
server_socket.setblocking(False)
server_socket.bind(server_address)
server_socket.listen()

selector.register(server_socket, selectors.EVENT_READ)

while True:
    events: List[Tuple[SelectorKey, int]] = selector.select(timeout=1)

    if len(events) == 0:
        print('No events, waiting a bit more!')

    for event, _ in events:
        event_socket = event.fileobj

        if event_socket == server_socket:
            connection, address = server_socket.accept()
            connection.setblocking(False)
            print(f"I got a connection from {address}")
            selector.register(connection, selectors.EVENT_READ)
        else:
            data = event_socket.recv(1024)
            print(f"I got some data: {data}")
            event_socket.send(data)
```

Create a selector that will timeout after 1 second.

If there are no events, print it out. This happens when a timeout occurs.

Get the socket for the event, which is stored in the fileobj field.

If the event socket is the same as the server socket, we know this is a connection attempt.

Register the client that connected with our selector.

If the event socket is not the server socket, receive data from the client, and echo it back.

When we run listing 3.7, we'll see "No events, waiting a bit more!" printed roughly every second unless we get a connection event. Once we get a connection, we register that connection to listen for read events. Then, if a client sends us data, our selector will return an event that we have data ready and we can read it with `socket.recv`.

This is fully functioning echo server that supports multiple clients. This server has no issues with blocking, as we only read or write data when we have data to act on. It also has very little CPU utilization as we're using the operating system's efficient event notification system (figure 3.4).

What we've built is akin to a big part of what asyncio's event loop does under the hood. In this case, the events that matter are sockets receiving data. Each iteration of our event loop and the asyncio event loop is triggered by either a socket event happening, or a timeout triggering an iteration of the loop. In the asyncio event loop, when any of these two things happen, coroutines that are waiting to run will do so

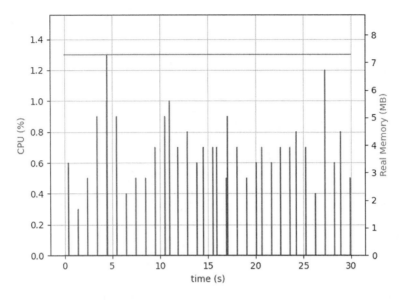

**Figure 3.4   CPU graph of the echo server with selectors. Utilization hovers around
0 and 1 percent with this method.**

until they either complete or they hit the next `await` statement. When we hit an `await`
in a coroutine that utilizes a non-blocking socket, it will register that socket with the
system's selector and keep track that the coroutine is paused waiting for a result. We
can translate this into pseudocode that demonstrates the concept:

```
paused = []
ready = []

while True:
    paused, new_sockets = run_ready_tasks(ready)
selector.register(new_sockets)
    timeout = calculate_timeout()
    events = selector.select(timeout)
    ready = process_events(events)
```

We run any coroutines that are ready to run until they are paused on an `await` statement and store those in the paused array. We also keep track of any new sockets we need
to watch from running those coroutines and register them with the selector. We then
calculate the desired timeout for when we call `select`. While this timeout calculation is
somewhat complicated, it is typically looking at things we have scheduled to run at a specific time or for a specific duration. An example of this is `asyncio.sleep`. We then call
select and wait for any socket events or a timeout. Once either of those happen, we process those events and turn that into a list of coroutines that are ready to run.

While the event loop we've built is only for socket events, it demonstrates the main
concept of using selectors to register sockets we care about, only being woken up

when something we want to process happens. We'll get more in-depth with how to construct a custom event loop at the end of this book.

Now, we understand a large part of the machinery that makes asyncio tick. However, if we just use selectors to build our applications, we would resort to implementing our own event loop to achieve the same functionality, as provided by asyncio. To see how to implement this with asyncio, let's take what we have learned and translate it into async / await code and use an event loop already implemented for us.

3.5   *An echo server on the asyncio event loop*

Working with select is a bit too low-level for most applications. We may want to have code run in the background while we're waiting for socket data to come in, or we may want to have background tasks run on a schedule. If we were to do this with only selectors, we'd likely build our own event loop, while asyncio has a nicely implemented one ready to use. In addition, coroutines and tasks provide abstractions on top of selectors, which make our code easier to implement and maintain, as we don't need to think about selectors at all.

Now that we have a deeper understanding on how the asyncio event loop works, let's take the echo server that we built in the last section and build it again using coroutines and tasks. We'll still use lower-level sockets to accomplish this, but we'll use asyncio-based APIs that return coroutines to manage them. We'll also add some more functionality to our echo server to demonstrate a few key concepts to illustrate how asyncio works.

3.5.1   *Event loop coroutines for sockets*

Given that sockets are a relatively low-level concept, the methods for dealing with them are on asyncio's event loop itself. There are three main coroutines we'll want to work with: sock_accept, sock_recv and sock_sendall. These are analogous to the socket methods that we used earlier, except that they take in a socket as an argument and return coroutines that we can await until we have data to act on.

Let's start with sock_accept. This coroutine is analogous to the socket.accept method that we saw in our first implementation. This method will return a tuple (a data structure that stores an ordered sequence of values) of a socket connection and a client address. We pass it in the socket we're interested in, and we can then await the coroutine it returns. Once that coroutine completes, we'll have our connection and address. This socket must be non-blocking and should already be bound to a port:

```
connection, address = await loop.sock_accept(socket)
```

sock_recv and sock_sendall are called similarly to sock_accept. They take in a socket, and we can then await for a result. sock_recv will await until a socket has bytes we can process. sock_sendall takes in both a socket and data we want to send and will wait until all data we want to send to a socket has been sent and will return None on success:

```
data = await loop.sock_recv(socket)
success = await loop.sock_sendall(socket, data)
```

With these building blocks, we'll be able to translate our previous approaches into one using coroutines and tasks.

3.5.2 *Designing an asyncio echo server*

In chapter 2, we introduced coroutines and tasks. So when should we use just a coroutine, and when should we wrap a coroutine in a task for our echo server? Let's examine how we want our application to behave to make this determination.

We'll start with how we want to listen for connections in our application. When we are listening for connections, we will only be able to process one connection at a time as socket.accept will only give us one client connection. Behind the scenes, incoming connections will be stored in a queue known as the *backlog* if we get multiple connections at the same time, but here, we won't get into how this works.

Since we don't need to process multiple connections concurrently, a single coroutine that loops forever makes sense. This will allow other code to run concurrently while we're paused waiting for a connection. We'll define a coroutine called listen_for_connections that will loop forever and listen for any incoming connections:

```
async def listen_for_connections(server_socket: socket,
                                 loop: AbstractEventLoop):
    while True:
        connection, address = await loop.sock_accept(server_socket)
        connection.setblocking(False)
        print(f"Got a connection from {address}")
```

Now that we have a coroutine for listening to connections, how about reading and writing data to the clients who have connected? Should that be a coroutine, or a coroutine we wrap in a task? In this case, we will have multiple connections, each of which could send data to us at any time. We don't want to wait for data from one connection to block another, so we need to read and write data from multiple clients concurrently. Because we need to handle multiple connections at the same time, creating a task for each connection to read and write data makes sense. On every connection we get, we'll create a task to both read data from and write data to that connection.

We'll create a coroutine named echo that is responsible for handling data from a connection. This coroutine will loop forever listening for data from our client. Once it receives data it will then send it back to the client.

Then, in listen_for_connections we'll create a new task that wraps our echo coroutine for each connection that we get. With these two coroutines defined, we now have all we need to build an asyncio echo server.

Listing 3.8 Building an asyncio echo server

```
import asyncio
import socket
from asyncio import AbstractEventLoop
```

```
async def echo(connection: socket,
               loop: AbstractEventLoop) -> None:
    while data := await loop.sock_recv(connection, 1024):
        await loop.sock_sendall(connection, data)


async def listen_for_connection(server_socket: socket,
                                loop: AbstractEventLoop):
    while True:
        connection, address = await loop.sock_accept(server_socket)
        connection.setblocking(False)
        print(f"Got a connection from {address}")
        asyncio.create_task(echo(connection, loop))


async def main():
    server_socket = socket.socket(socket.AF_INET, socket.SOCK_STREAM)
    server_socket.setsockopt(socket.SOL_SOCKET, socket.SO_REUSEADDR, 1)

    server_address = ('127.0.0.1', 8000)
    server_socket.setblocking(False)
    server_socket.bind(server_address)
    server_socket.listen()

    await listen_for_connection(server_socket, asyncio.get_event_loop())

asyncio.run(main())
```

Loop forever waiting for data from a client connection

Once we have data, send it back to that client.

Whenever we get a connection, create an echo task to listen for client data.

Start the coroutine to listen for connections.

The architecture for the preceding listing looks like figure 3.5. We have one coroutine, `listen_for_connection`, listening for connections. Once a client connects, our
coroutine spawns an `echo` task for each client which then listens for data and writes it
back out to the client.

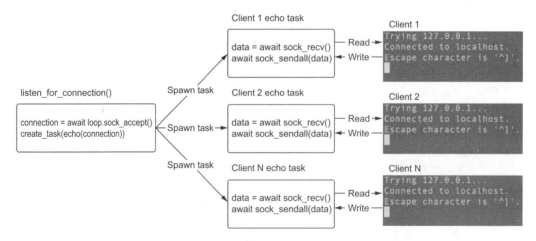

Figure 3.5   The coroutine listening for connections spawns one task per each connection it gets.

When we run this application, we'll be able to connect multiple clients concurrently and send data to them concurrently. Under the hood, this is all using selectors as we saw before, so our CPU utilization remains low.

We've now built a fully functioning echo server entirely using asyncio! So is our implementation error free? It turns out that the way we have designed this echo server does have an issue when our echo task fails that we'll need to handle.

3.5.3 Handling errors in tasks

Network connections are often unreliable, and we may get exceptions we don't expect in our application code. How would our application behave if reading or writing to a client failed and threw an exception? To test this out, let's change our implementation of echo to throw an exception when a client passes us a specific keyword:

```
async def echo(connection: socket,
               loop: AbstractEventLoop) -> None:
    while data := await loop.sock_recv(connection, 1024):
        if data == b'boom\r\n':
            raise Exception("Unexpected network error")
        await loop.sock_sendall(connection, data)
```

Now, whenever a client sends "boom" to us, we will raise an exception and our task will crash. So, what happens when we connect a client to our server and send this message? We will see a traceback with a warning like the following:

```
Task exception was never retrieved
future: <Task finished name='Task-2' coro=<echo() done, defined at
    asyncio_echo.py:5> exception=Exception('Unexpected network error')>
Traceback (most recent call last):
  File "asyncio_echo.py", line 9, in echo
    raise Exception("Unexpected network error")
Exception: Unexpected network error
```

The important part here is `Task exception was never retrieved`. What does this mean? When an exception is thrown inside a task, the task is considered done with its result as an exception. This means that no exception is thrown up the call stack. Furthermore, we have no cleanup here. If this exception is thrown, we can't react to the task failing because we never retrieved the exception.

To have the exception reach us, we must use the task in an `await` expression. When we await a task that failed, the exception will get thrown where we perform the await, and the traceback will reflect that. If we don't `await` a task at some point in our application, we run the risk of never seeing an exception that a task raised. While we did see the exception output in the example, which may lead us to think it isn't that big an issue, there are subtle ways we could change our application so that we would never see this message.

As a demonstration of this, let's say that, instead of ignoring the echo tasks we create in `listen_for_connections`, we kept track of them in a list like so:

```
tasks = []

async def listen_for_connection(server_socket: socket,
                                loop: AbstractEventLoop):
    while True:
        connection, address = await loop.sock_accept(server_socket)
        connection.setblocking(False)
        print(f"Got a connection from {address}")
        tasks.append(asyncio.create_task(echo(connection, loop)))
```

One would expect this to behave in the same way as before. If we send the "boom" message, we'll see the exception printed along with the warning that we never retrieved the task exception. However, this isn't the case, since we'll actually see nothing printed until we forcefully terminate our application!

This is because we've kept a reference around to the task. asyncio can only print this message and the traceback for a failed task when that task is garbage collected. This is because it has no way to tell if that task will be awaited at some other point in the application and would therefore raise an exception then. Due to these complexities, we'll either need to await our tasks or handle all exceptions that our tasks could throw. So how do we do this in our echo server?

The first thing we can do to fix this is wrap the code in our echo coroutine in a try/catch statement, log the exception, and close the connection:

```
import logging

async def echo(connection: socket,
               loop: AbstractEventLoop) -> None:
    try:
        while data := await loop.sock_recv(connection, 1024):
            print('got data!')
            if data == b'boom\r\n':
                raise Exception("Unexpected network error")
            await loop.sock_sendall(connection, data)
    except Exception as ex:
        logging.exception(ex)
    finally:
        connection.close()
```

This will resolve the immediate issue of an exception causing our server to complain that a task exception was never retrieved because we handle it in the coroutine itself. It will also properly shut down the socket within the finally block, so we won't be left with a dangling unclosed exception in the event of a failure.

It's important to note that this implementation will properly close any connections to clients we have open on application shutdown. Why is this? In chapter 2, we noted that asyncio.run will cancel any tasks we have remaining when our application shuts down. We also learned when we cancel a task, a CancelledError is raised whenever we try to await it.

The important thing here is noting where that exception is raised. If our task is waiting on a statement such as `await loop.sock_recv`, and we cancel that task, a `Cancelled-Error` is thrown from the `await loop.sock_recv` line. This means that in the above case our `finally` block will be executed, since we threw an exception on an `await` expression when we canceled the task. If we change the exception block to catch and log these exceptions, you will see one `CancelledError` per each task that was created.

We've now handled the immediate issue of handling errors when our echo tasks fail. What if we want to provide some cleanup of any errors or leftover tasks when our application shuts down? We can do this with asyncio's signal handlers.

3.6 *Shutting down gracefully*

Now, we've created an echo server that handles multiple concurrent connections and also properly logs errors and cleans up when we get an exception. What happens if we need to shut down our application? Wouldn't it be nice if we could allow any in-flight messages to complete before we shut down? We can do this by adding custom shutdown logic to our application that allows any in-progress tasks a few seconds to finish sending any messages they might want to send. While this won't be a production-worthy implementation, we'll learn the concepts around shutting down as well as canceling all running tasks in our asyncio applications.

> ### Signals on Windows
> Windows does not support signals. Therefore, this section only applies to Unix-based systems. Windows uses a different system to handle this, that, at the time of writing this book, does not perform with Python. To learn more about how to make this code work in a cross-platform way, see the following answer on Stack Overflow: https://stackoverflow.com/questions/35772001.

3.6.1 *Listening for signals*

Signals are a concept in Unix-based operating systems for asynchronously notifying a process of an event that occurred at the operating system level. While this sounds very low-level, you're probably familiar with some signals. For instance, a common signal is SIGINT, short for *signal interrupt*. This is triggered when you press CTRL-C to kill a command-line application. In Python, we can often handle this by catching the `KeyboardInterrupt` exception. Another common signal is SIGTERM, short for *signal terminate*. This is triggered when we run the `kill` command on a particular process to stop its execution.

To implement custom shutdown logic, we'll implement listeners in our application for both the SIGINT and SIGTERM signals. Then, in these listeners we'll implement logic to allow any echo tasks we have a few seconds to finish.

How do we listen for signals in our application? The asyncio event loop lets us directly listen for any event we specify with the `add_signal_handler` method. This

differs from the signal handlers that you can set in the signal module with the `signal`
`.signal` function in that `add_signal_handler` can safely interact with the event loop.
This function takes in a signal we want to listen for and a function that we'll call when
our application receives that signal. To demonstrate this, let's look at adding a signal
handler that cancels all currently running tasks. asyncio has a convenience function
that returns a set of all running tasks named `asyncio.all_tasks`.

Listing 3.9   Adding a signal handler to cancel all tasks

```
import asyncio, signal
from asyncio import AbstractEventLoop
from typing import Set

from util.delay_functions import delay


def cancel_tasks():
    print('Got a SIGINT!')
    tasks: Set[asyncio.Task] = asyncio.all_tasks()
    print(f'Cancelling {len(tasks)} task(s).')
    [task.cancel() for task in tasks]


async def main():
    loop: AbstractEventLoop = asyncio.get_running_loop()

    loop.add_signal_handler(signal.SIGINT, cancel_tasks)

    await delay(10)


asyncio.run(main())
```

When we run this application, we'll see that our delay coroutine starts right away
and waits for 10 seconds. If we press CTRL-C within these 10 seconds we should see
`got a SIGINT!` printed out, followed by a message that we're canceling our tasks. We
should also see a `CancelledError` thrown from `asyncio.run(main())`, since we've
canceled that task.

3.6.2   *Waiting for pending tasks to finish*

In the original problem statement, we wanted to give our echo server's echo tasks a
few seconds to keep running before shutting down. One way for us to do this is to
wrap all our echo tasks in a `wait_for` and then `await` those wrapped tasks. Those tasks
will then throw a `TimeoutError` once the timeout has passed and we can terminate
our application.

   One thing you'll notice about our shutdown handler is that this is a normal
Python function, so we can't run any `await` statements inside of it. This poses a
problem for us, since our proposed solution involves `await`. One possible solution is

to just create a coroutine that does our shutdown logic, and in our shutdown handler, wrap it in a task:

```
async def await_all_tasks():
    tasks = asyncio.all_tasks()
    [await task for task in tasks]


async def main():
    loop = asyncio.get_event_loop()
    loop.add_signal_handler(signal.SIGINT,
                            lambda: asyncio.create_task(await_all_tasks()))
```

An approach like this will work, but the drawback is that if something in `await_all_tasks` throws an exception, we'll be left with an orphaned task that failed and a "exception was never retrieved" warning. So, is there a better way to do this?

We can deal with this by raising a custom exception to stop our main coroutine from running. Then, we can catch this exception when we run the main coroutine and run any shutdown logic. To do this, we'll need to create an event loop ourselves instead of using `asyncio.run`. This is because on an exception `asyncio.run` will cancel all running tasks, which means we aren't able to wrap our echo tasks in a `wait_for`:

```
class GracefulExit(SystemExit):
    pass


def shutdown():
    raise GracefulExit()


loop = asyncio.get_event_loop()

loop.add_signal_handler(signal.SIGINT, shutdown)

try:
    loop.run_until_complete(main())
except GracefulExit:
    loop.run_until_complete(close_echo_tasks(echo_tasks))
finally:
    loop.close()
```

With this approach in mind, let's write our shutdown logic:

```
async def close_echo_tasks(echo_tasks: List[asyncio.Task]):
    waiters = [asyncio.wait_for(task, 2) for task in echo_tasks]
    for task in waiters:
        try:
            await task
        except asyncio.exceptions.TimeoutError:
            # We expect a timeout error here
            pass
```

In `close_echo_tasks`, we take a list of echo tasks and wrap them all in a `wait_for` task with a 2-second timeout. This means that any echo tasks will have 2 seconds to finish before we cancel them. Once we've done this, we loop over all these wrapped tasks and await them. We catch any TimeoutErrors, as we expect this to be thrown from our tasks after 2 seconds. Taking all these parts together, our echo server with shutdown logic looks like the following listing.

Listing 3.10   A graceful shutdown

```python
import asyncio
from asyncio import AbstractEventLoop
import socket
import logging
import signal
from typing import List


async def echo(connection: socket,
               loop: AbstractEventLoop) -> None:
    try:
        while data := await loop.sock_recv(connection, 1024):
            print('got data!')
            if data == b'boom\r\n':
                raise Exception("Unexpected network error")
            await loop.sock_sendall(connection, data)
    except Exception as ex:
        logging.exception(ex)
    finally:
        connection.close()


echo_tasks = []


async def connection_listener(server_socket, loop):
    while True:
        connection, address = await loop.sock_accept(server_socket)
        connection.setblocking(False)
        print(f"Got a connection from {address}")
        echo_task = asyncio.create_task(echo(connection, loop))
        echo_tasks.append(echo_task)


class GracefulExit(SystemExit):
    pass


def shutdown():
    raise GracefulExit()


async def close_echo_tasks(echo_tasks: List[asyncio.Task]):
    waiters = [asyncio.wait_for(task, 2) for task in echo_tasks]
    for task in waiters:
        try:
            await task
```

```python
        except asyncio.exceptions.TimeoutError:
            # We expect a timeout error here
            pass


async def main():
    server_socket = socket.socket()
    server_socket.setsockopt(socket.SOL_SOCKET, socket.SO_REUSEADDR, 1)

    server_address = ('127.0.0.1', 8000)
    server_socket.setblocking(False)
    server_socket.bind(server_address)
    server_socket.listen()

    for signame in {'SIGINT', 'SIGTERM'}:
        loop.add_signal_handler(getattr(signal, signame), shutdown)
    await connection_listener(server_socket, loop)


loop = asyncio.new_event_loop()

try:
    loop.run_until_complete(main())
except GracefulExit:
    loop.run_until_complete(close_echo_tasks(echo_tasks))
finally:
    loop.close()
```

Assuming we have at least one client connected, if we stop this application with either CTRL-C, or we issue a kill command to our process, our shutdown logic will execute. We will see the application wait for 2 seconds, while it allows our echo tasks some time to finish before it stops running.

There are a couple reasons why this is not a production-worthy shutdown. The first is we don't shut down our connection listener while we're waiting for our echo tasks to complete. This means that, as we're shutting down, a new connection could come in and then we won't be able to add a 2-second shutdown. The other problem is that in our shutdown logic we await every echo task we're shutting down and only catch TimeoutExceptions. This means that if one of our tasks threw something other than that, we would capture that exception and any other subsequent tasks that may have had an exception will be ignored. In chapter 4, we'll see some asyncio methods for more gracefully handling failures from a group of awaitables.

While our application isn't perfect and is a toy example, we've built a fully functioning server using asyncio. This server can handle many users concurrently—all within one single thread. With a blocking approach we saw earlier, we would need to turn to threading to be able to handle multiple clients, adding complexity and increased resource utilization to our application.

Summary

In this chapter, we've learned about blocking and non-blocking sockets and have explored more in depth how the asyncio event loop functions. We've also made our first application with asyncio, a highly concurrent echo server. We have examined how to handle errors in tasks and add custom shutdown logic in our application.

- We've learned how to create simple applications with blocking sockets. Blocking sockets will stop the entire thread when they are waiting for data. This prevents us from achieving concurrency because we can get data from only one client at a time.

- We've learned how to build applications with non-blocking sockets. These sockets will always return right away, either with data because we have it ready, or with an exception stating we have no data. These sockets let us achieve concurrency because their methods never block and return instantly.

- We've learned how to use the selectors module to listen for events on sockets in an efficient manner. This library lets us register sockets we want to track and will tell us when a non-blocking socket is ready with data.

- If we put select in an infinite loop, we've replicated the core of what the asyncio event loop does. We register sockets we are interested in, and we loop forever, running any code we want once a socket has data available to act on.

- We learned how to use asyncio's event loop methods to build applications with non-blocking sockets. These methods take in a socket and return a coroutine which we can then use this in an `await` expression. This will suspend our parent coroutine until the socket has data. Under the hood, this is using the selectors library.

- We've seen how to use tasks to achieve concurrency for an asyncio-based echo server with multiple clients sending and receiving data at the same time. We've also examined how to handle errors within those tasks.

- We've learned how to add custom shutdown logic to an asyncio application. In our case, we decided that when our server shuts down, we'd give it a few seconds for any remaining clients to finish sending data. Using this knowledge, we can add any logic our application needs when it is shutting down.

Concurrent web requests

This chapter covers

- Asynchronous context managers
- Making asyncio-friendly web requests with aiohttp
- Running web requests concurrently with `gather`
- Processing results as they come in with `as completed`
- Keeping track of in-flight requests with `wait`
- Setting and handling timeouts for groups of requests and canceling requests

In chapter 3, we learned more about the inner workings of sockets and built a basic echo server. Now that we've seen how to design a basic application, we'll take this knowledge and apply it to making concurrent, non-blocking web requests. Utilizing asyncio for web requests allows us to make hundreds of them at the same time, cutting down on our application's runtime compared to a synchronous approach. This is useful for when we must make multiple requests to a set of REST APIs, as can happen in a microservice architecture or when we have a web crawling task. This approach also allows for other code to run as we're waiting for potentially long web requests to finish, allowing us to build more responsive applications.

In this chapter, we'll learn about an asynchronous library called *aiohttp* that enables this. This library uses non-blocking sockets to make web requests and returns coroutines for those requests, which we can then `await` for a result. Specifically, we'll learn how to take a list of hundreds of URLs we'd like to get the contents for, and run all those requests concurrently. In doing so, we'll examine the various API methods that asyncio provides to run coroutines at one time, allowing us to choose between waiting for everything to complete before moving on, or processing results as fast as they come in. In addition, we'll look at how to set timeouts for these requests, both at the individual request level as well as for a group of requests. We'll also see how to cancel a set of in-process requests, based on how other requests have performed. These API methods are useful not only for making web requests but also for whenever we need to run a group of coroutines or tasks concurrently. In fact, we'll use the functions we use here throughout the rest of this book, and you will use them extensively as an asyncio developer.

4.1 *Introducing aiohttp*

In chapter 2, we mentioned that one of the problems that newcomers face when first starting with asyncio is trying to take their existing code and pepper it with `async` and `await` in hopes of a performance gain. In most cases, this won't work, and this is especially true when working with web requests, as most existing libraries are blocking.

One popular library for making web requests is the `requests` library. This library does not perform well with asyncio because it uses blocking sockets. This means that if we make a request, it will block the thread that it runs in, and since asyncio is single-threaded, our entire event loop will halt until that request finishes.

To address this issue and get concurrency, we need to use a library that is non-blocking all the way down to the socket layer. *aiohttp* (Asynchronous HTTP Client/ Server for asyncio and Python) is one library that solves this problem with non-blocking sockets.

aiohttp is an open source library that is part of the *aio-libs* project, which is the self-described "set of asyncio-based libraries built with high quality" (see https://github .com/aio-libs). This library is a fully functioning web client as well as a web server, meaning it can make web requests, and developers can create async web servers using it. (Documentation for the library is available at https://docs.aiohttp.org/.) In this chapter, we'll focus on the client side of aiohttp, but we will also see how to build web servers with it later in the book.

So how do we get started with aiohttp? The first thing to learn is to make a HTTP request. We'll first need to learn a bit of new syntax for asynchronous context managers. Using this syntax will allow us to acquire and close HTTP sessions cleanly. As an asyncio developer, you will use this syntax frequently for asynchronously acquiring resources, such as database connections.

4.2 *Asynchronous context managers*

In any programming language, dealing with resources that must be opened and then closed, such as files, is common. When dealing with these resources, we need to be careful about any exceptions that may be thrown. This is because if we open a resource and an exception is thrown, we may never execute any code to clean up, leaving us in a status with leaking resources. Dealing with this in Python is straightforward using a `finally` block. Though this example is not exactly Pythonic, we can always close a file even if an exception was thrown:

```
file = open('example.txt')

try:
    lines = file.readlines()
finally:
    file.close()
```

This solves the issue of a file handle being left open if there was an exception during `file.readlines`. The drawback is that we must remember to wrap everything in a `try finally`, and we also need to remember the methods to call to properly close our resource. This isn't too hard to do for files, as we just need to remember to close them, but we'd still like something more reusable, especially since our cleanup may be more complicated than just calling one method. Python has a language feature to deal with this known as a *context manager*. Using this, we can abstract the shutdown logic along with the `try/finally` block:

```
with open('example.txt') as file:
    lines = file.readlines()
```

This Pythonic way to manage files is a lot cleaner. If an exception is thrown in the `with` block, our file will automatically be closed. This works for synchronous resources, but what if we want to asynchronously use a resource with this syntax? In this case, the context manager syntax won't work, as it is designed to work only with synchronous Python code and not coroutines and tasks. Python introduced a new language feature to support this use case, called *asynchronous context managers*. The syntax is almost the same as for synchronous context managers with the difference being that we say `async with` instead of just `with`.

Asynchronous context managers are classes that implement two special coroutine methods, `__aenter__`, which asynchronously acquires a resource and `__aexit__`, which closes that resource. The `__aexit__` coroutine takes several arguments that deal with any exceptions that occur, which we won't review in this chapter.

To fully understand async context managers, let's implement a simple one using the sockets we introduced in chapter 3. We can consider a client socket connection a resource we'd like to manage. When a client connects, we acquire a client connection. Once we are done with it, we clean up and close the connection. In chapter 3, we wrapped everything in a try/finally block, but we could have implemented an asynchronous context manager to do so instead.

Listing 4.1   An asynchronous context manager to wait for a client connection

```
import asyncio
import socket
from types import TracebackType
from typing import Optional, Type


class ConnectedSocket:

    def __init__(self, server_socket):
        self._connection = None
        self._server_socket = server_socket

    async def __aenter__(self):
        print('Entering context manager, waiting for connection')
        loop = asyncio.get_event_loop()
        connection, address = await loop.sock_accept(self._server_socket)
        self._connection = connection
        print('Accepted a connection')
        return self._connection

    async def __aexit__(self,
                        exc_type: Optional[Type[BaseException]],
                        exc_val: Optional[BaseException],
                        exc_tb: Optional[TracebackType]):
        print('Exiting context manager')
        self._connection.close()
        print('Closed connection')

async def main():
    loop = asyncio.get_event_loop()

    server_socket = socket.socket()
    server_socket.setsockopt(socket.SOL_SOCKET, socket.SO_REUSEADDR, 1)
    server_address = ('127.0.0.1', 8000)
    server_socket.setblocking(False)
    server_socket.bind(server_address)
    server_socket.listen()

    async with ConnectedSocket(server_socket) as connection:
        data = await loop.sock_recv(connection, 1024)
        print(data)

asyncio.run(main())
```

This coroutine is called when we enter the with block. It waits until a client connects and returns the connection.

This coroutine is called when we exit the with block. In it, we clean up any resources we use. In this case, we close the connection.

This calls __aenter__ and waits for a client connection.

After this statement, __aenter__ will execute, and we'll close our connection.

In the preceding listing, we created a ConnectedSocket async context manager. This class takes in a server socket, and in our __aenter__ coroutine we wait for a client to connect. Once a client connects, we return that client's connection. This lets us access that connection in the as portion of our async with statement. Then, inside our async with block, we use that connection to wait for the client to send us data. Once this block finishes execution, the __aexit__ coroutine runs and closes the connection. Assuming a client connects with Telnet and sends some test data, we should see output like the following when running this program:

```
Entering context manager, waiting for connection
Accepted a connection
b'test\r\n'
Exiting context manager
Closed connection
```

aiohttp uses async context managers extensively for acquiring HTTP sessions and connections, and we'll use this later in chapter 5 when dealing with async database connections and transactions. Normally, you won't need to write your own async context managers, but it's helpful to have an understanding of how they work and are different from normal context managers. Now that we've introduced context managers and their workings, let's use them with aiohttp to see how to make an asynchronous web request.

4.2.1 *Making a web request with aiohttp*

We'll first need to install the aiohttp library. We can do this using pip by running the following:

```
pip install -Iv aiohttp==3.8.1
```

This will install the latest version of aiohttp (3.8.1 at the time of this writing). Once this is complete, you're ready to start making requests.

aiohttp, and web requests in general, employ the concept of a *session*. Think of a session as opening a new browser window. Within a new browser window, you'll make connections to any number of web pages, which may send you cookies that your browser saves for you. With a session, you'll keep many connections open, which can then be recycled. This is known as connection pooling. *Connection pooling* is an important concept that aids the performance of our aiohttp-based applications. Since creating connections is resource intensive, creating a reusable pool of them cuts down on resource allocation costs. A session will also internally save any cookies that we receive, although this functionality can be turned off if desired.

Typically, we want to take advantage of connection pooling, so most aiohttp-based applications run one session for the entire application. This session object is then passed to methods where needed. A session object has methods on it for making any number of web requests, such as GET, PUT, and POST. We can create a session by using async with syntax and the aiohttp.ClientSession asynchronous context manager.

Listing 4.2   Making an aiohttp web request

```
import asyncio
import aiohttp
from aiohttp import ClientSession
from util import async_timed


@async_timed()
async def fetch_status(session: ClientSession, url: str) -> int:
    async with session.get(url) as result:
        return result.status


@async_timed()
async def main():
    async with aiohttp.ClientSession() as session:
        url = 'https://www.example.com'
        status = await fetch_status(session, url)
        print(f'Status for {url} was {status}')


asyncio.run(main())
```

When we run this, we should see that the output Status for http://www.example.com was 200. In the preceding listing, we first created a client session in an async with block with aiohttp.ClientSession(). Once we have a client session, we're free to make any web request desired. In this case, we define a convenience method fetch_status_code that will take in a session and a URL and return the status code for the given URL. In this function, we have another async with block and use the session to run a GET HTTP request against the URL. This will give us a result, which we can then process within the with block. In this case, we just grab the status code and return.

Note that a ClientSession will create a default maximum of 100 connections by default, providing an implicit upper limit to the number of concurrent requests we can make. To change this limit, we can create an instance of an aiohttp TCPConnector specifying the maximum number of connections and passing that to the Client-Session. To learn more about this, review the aiohttp documentation at https://docs.aiohttp.org/en/stable/client_advanced.html#connectors.

We'll reuse fetch_status throughout the chapter, so let's make this function reusable. We'll create a Python module named chapter_04 with its __init__.py containing this function. We'll then import this in future examples in this chapter as from chapter_04 import fetch_status.

A note for Windows users

At the present time, an issue exists with aiohttp on Windows, where you may see errors like RuntimeError: Event loop is closed even though your application works fine. Read more about this issue at https://github.com/aio-libs/aiohttp/issues/4324

and https://bugs.python.org/issue39232. To work around this issue, you can either manually manage the event loop as shown in chapter 2 with `asyncio.get_event_loop().run_until_complete(main())`, or you can change the event loop policy to the Windows selector event loop policy by calling `asyncio.set_event_loop_policy(asyncio.WindowsSelectorEventLoopPolicy())` before `asyncio.run(main())`.

4.2.2 Setting timeouts with aiohttp

Earlier we saw how we could specify a timeout for an awaitable by using `asyncio.wait_for`. This will also work for setting timeouts for an aiohttp request, but a cleaner way to set timeouts is to use the functionality that aiohttp provides out of the box.

By default, aiohttp has a timeout of five minutes, which means that no single operation should take longer than that. This is a long timeout, and many application developers may wish to set this lower. We can specify a timeout at either the session level, which will apply that timeout for every operation, or at the request level, which provides more granular control.

We can specify timeouts using the aiohttp-specific `ClientTimeout` data structure. This structure not only allows us to specify a total timeout in seconds for an entire request but also allows us to set timeouts on establishing a connection or reading data. Let's examine how to use this by specifying a timeout for our session and one for an individual request.

Listing 4.3   Setting timeouts with aiohttp

```
import asyncio
import aiohttp
from aiohttp import ClientSession

async def fetch_status(session: ClientSession,
                       url: str) -> int:
    ten_millis = aiohttp.ClientTimeout(total=.01)
    async with session.get(url, timeout=ten_millis) as result:
        return result.status


async def main():
    session_timeout = aiohttp.ClientTimeout(total=1, connect=.1)
    async with aiohttp.ClientSession(timeout=session_timeout) as session:
        await fetch_status(session, 'https://example.com')

asyncio.run(main())
```

In the preceding listing, we set two timeouts. The first timeout is at the client-session level. Here we set a total timeout of 1 second and explicitly set a connection timeout of 100 milliseconds. Then, in `fetch_status` we override this for our `get` request to set a total timeout of 10 miliseconds. In this instance, if our request to example.com takes more than 10 milliseconds, an `asyncio.TimeoutError` will be raised when we `await` `fetch_status`. In this example, 10 milliseconds should be enough time for the request to example.com to complete, so we're not likely to see an exception. If you'd like to check out this exception, change the URL to a page that takes a bit longer than 10 milliseconds to download.

These examples show us the basics of aiohttp. However, our application's performance won't benefit from running only a single request with asyncio. We'll start to see the real benefits when we run several web requests concurrently.

4.3   *Running tasks concurrently, revisited*

In the first few chapters of this book, we learned how to create multiple tasks to run coroutines concurrently. To do this, we used `asyncio.create_task` and then awaited the task as below:

```
import asyncio

async def main() -> None:
    task_one = asyncio.create_task(delay(1))
    task_two = asyncio.create_task(delay(2))

    await task_one
    await task_two
```

This works for simple cases like the previous one in which we have one or two coroutines we want to launch concurrently. However, in a world where we may make hundreds, thousands, or even more web requests concurrently, this style would become verbose and messy.

We may be tempted to utilize a `for` loop or a list comprehension to make this a little smoother, as demonstrated in the following listing. However, this approach can cause issues if not written correctly.

Listing 4.4   Using tasks with a list comprehension incorrectly

```
import asyncio
from util import async_timed, delay


@async_timed()
async def main() -> None:
    delay_times = [3, 3, 3]
    [await asyncio.create_task(delay(seconds)) for seconds in delay_times]

asyncio.run(main())
```

Given that we ideally want the `delay` tasks to run concurrently, we'd expect the main method to complete in about 3 seconds. However, in this case 9 seconds elapse to run, since everything is done sequentially:

```
starting <function main at 0x10f14a550> with args () {}
starting <function delay at 0x10f7684c0> with args (3,) {}
sleeping for 3 second(s)
finished sleeping for 3 second(s)
finished <function delay at 0x10f7684c0> in 3.0008 second(s)
starting <function delay at 0x10f7684c0> with args (3,) {}
sleeping for 3 second(s)
finished sleeping for 3 second(s)
finished <function delay at 0x10f7684c0> in 3.0009 second(s)
starting <function delay at 0x10f7684c0> with args (3,) {}
sleeping for 3 second(s)
finished sleeping for 3 second(s)
finished <function delay at 0x10f7684c0> in 3.0020 second(s)
finished <function main at 0x10f14a550> in 9.0044 second(s)
```

The problem here is subtle. It occurs because we use await as soon as we create the task. This means that we pause the list comprehension and the main coroutine for every delay task we create until that delay task completes. In this case, we will have only one task running at any given time, instead of running multiple tasks concurrently. The fix is easy, although a bit verbose. We can create the tasks in one list comprehension and await in a second. This lets everything to run concurrently.

Listing 4.5 Using tasks concurrently with a list comprehension

```python
import asyncio
from util import async_timed, delay

@async_timed()
async def main() -> None:
    delay_times = [3, 3, 3]
    tasks = [asyncio.create_task(delay(seconds)) for seconds in delay_times]
    [await task for task in tasks]

asyncio.run(main())
```

This code creates a number of tasks all at once in the tasks list. Once we have created all the tasks, we await their completion in a separate list comprehension. This works because create_task returns instantly, and we don't do any awaiting until all the tasks have been created. This ensures that it only requires at most the maximum pause in delay_times, giving a runtime of about 3 seconds:

```
starting <function main at 0x10d4e1550> with args () {}
starting <function delay at 0x10daff4c0> with args (3,) {}
sleeping for 3 second(s)
starting <function delay at 0x10daff4c0> with args (3,) {}
sleeping for 3 second(s)
starting <function delay at 0x10daff4c0> with args (3,) {}
sleeping for 3 second(s)
finished sleeping for 3 second(s)
finished <function delay at 0x10daff4c0> in 3.0029 second(s)
finished sleeping for 3 second(s)
```

```
finished <function delay at 0x10daff4c0> in 3.0029 second(s)
finished sleeping for 3 second(s)
finished <function delay at 0x10daff4c0> in 3.0029 second(s)
finished <function main at 0x10d4e1550> in 3.0031 second(s)
```

While this does what we want, drawbacks remain. The first is that this consists of multiple lines of code, where we must explicitly remember to separate out our task creation from our awaits. The second is that it is inflexible, and if one of our coroutines finishes long before the others, we'll be trapped in the second list comprehension waiting for all other coroutines to finish. While this may be acceptable in certain circumstances, we may want to be more responsive, processing our results as soon as they arrive. The third, and potentially biggest issue, is exception handling. If one of our coroutines has an exception, it will be thrown when we await the failed task. This means that we won't be able to process any tasks that completed successfully because that one exception will halt our execution.

asyncio has convenience functions to deal with all these situations and more. These functions are recommended when running multiple tasks concurrently. In the following sections, we'll look at some of them, and examine how to use them in the context of making multiple web requests concurrently.

4.4   *Running requests concurrently with gather*

A widely used asyncio API functions for running awaitables concurrently is `asyncio.gather`. This function takes in a sequence of awaitables and lets us run them concurrently, all in one line of code. If any of the awaitables we pass in is a coroutine, gather will automatically wrap it in a task to ensure that it runs concurrently. This means that we don't have to wrap everything with `asyncio.create_task` separately as we used above.

`asyncio.gather` returns an awaitable. When we use it in an await expression, it will pause until all awaitables that we passed into it are complete. Once everything we passed in finishes, `asyncio.gather` will return a list of the completed results.

We can use this function to run as many web requests as we'd like concurrently. To illustrate this, let's see an example where we make 1,000 requests at the same time and grab the status code of each response. We'll decorate our main coroutine with `@async_timed` so we know how long things are taking.

> **Listing 4.6   Running requests concurrently with `gather`**

```python
import asyncio
import aiohttp
from aiohttp import ClientSession
from chapter_04 import fetch_status
from util import async_timed


@async_timed()
async def main():
```

```
async with aiohttp.ClientSession() as session:
    urls = ['https://example.com' for _ in range(1000)]
    requests = [fetch_status(session, url) for url in urls]
    status_codes = await asyncio.gather(*requests)
    print(status_codes)
```

Wait for all requests to complete.

```
asyncio.run(main())
```

Generate a list of coroutines for each request we want to make.

In the preceding listing, we first generate a list of URLs we'd like to retrieve the status code from; for simplicity, we'll request example.com repeatedly. We then take that list of URLs and call fetch_status_code to generate a list of coroutines that we then pass into gather. This will wrap each coroutine in a task and start running them concurrently. When we execute this code, we'll see 1,000 messages printed to standard out, saying that the fetch_status_code coroutines started sequentially, indicating that 1,000 requests started concurrently. As results come in, we'll see messages like finished <function fetch_status_code at 0x10f3fe3a0> in 0.5453 second(s) arrive. Once we retrieve the contents of all the URLs we've requested, we'll see the status codes start to print out. This process is quick, depending on the internet connection and speed of the machine, and this script can finish in as little as 500–600 milliseconds.

So how does this compare with doing things synchronously? It's easy to adapt the main function so that it blocks on each request by using an await when we call fetch_status_code. This will pause the main coroutine for each URL, effectively making things synchronous:

```
@async_timed()
async def main():
    async with aiohttp.ClientSession() as session:
        urls = ['https://example.com' for _ in range(1000)]
        status_codes = [await fetch_status_code(session, url) for url in
    urls]
        print(status_codes)
```

If we run this, notice that things will take much longer. We'll also notice that, instead of getting 1,000 starting function fetch_status_code messages followed by 1,000 finished function fetch_status_code messages, something like the following displays for each request:

```
starting <function fetch_status_code at 0x10d95b310>
finished <function fetch_status_code at 0x10d95b310> in 0.01884 second(s)
```

This indicates that requests occur one after another, waiting for each call to fetch_status_code to finish before moving on to the next request. So how much slower is this than using our async version? While this depends on your internet connection and the machine you run this on, running sequentially can take around 18 seconds to complete. Comparing this with our asynchronous version, which took around 600 milliseconds, the latter runs an impressive 33 times faster.

It is worth noting that the results for each awaitable we pass in may not complete in a deterministic order. For example, if we pass coroutines a and b to gather in that order, b may complete before a. A nice feature of gather is that, regardless of when our awaitables complete, we are guaranteed the results will be returned in the order we passed them in. Let's demonstrate this by looking at the scenario we just described with our delay function.

Listing 4.7   Awaitables finishing out of order

```
import asyncio
from util import delay


async def main():
    results = await asyncio.gather(delay(3), delay(1))
    print(results)

asyncio.run(main())
```

In the preceding listing, we pass two coroutines to gather. The first takes 3 seconds to complete and the second takes 1 second. We may expect the result of this to be [1, 3], since our 1-second coroutine finishes before our 3-second coroutine, but the result is actually [3, 1]—the order we passed things in. The gather function keeps result ordering deterministic despite the inherent nondeterminism behind the scenes. In the background, gather uses a special kind of future implementation to do this. For the curious reader, reviewing the source code of gather can be an instructive way to understand how many asyncio APIs are built using futures.

In the examples above, it's assumed none of the requests will fail or throw an exception. This works well for the "happy path," but what happens when a request fails?

4.4.1 *Handling exceptions with gather*

Of course, when we make a web request, we might not always get a value back; we might get an exception. Since networks can be unreliable, different failure cases are possible. For example, we could pass in an address that is invalid or has become invalid because the site has been taken down. The server we connect to could also close or refuse our connection.

asyncio.gather gives us an optional parameter, return_exceptions, which allows us to specify how we want to deal with exceptions from our awaitables. return_exceptions is a Boolean value; therefore, it has two behaviors that we can choose from:

- return_exceptions=False—This is the default value for gather. In this case, if any of our coroutines throws an exception, our gather call will also throw that exception when we await it. However, even though one of our coroutines failed, our other coroutines are not canceled and will continue to run as long as we handle the exception, or the exception does not result in the event loop stopping and canceling the tasks.

- return_exceptions=True—In this case, gather will return any exceptions as part of the result list it returns when we await it. The call to gather will not throw any exceptions itself, and we'll be able handle all exceptions as we wish.

To illustrate how these options work, let's change our URL list to contain an invalid web address. This will cause aiohttp to raise an exception when we attempt to make the request. We'll then pass that into gather and see how each of these return_exceptions behaves:

```
@async_timed()
async def main():
    async with aiohttp.ClientSession() as session:
        urls = ['https://example.com', 'python://example.com']
        tasks = [fetch_status_code(session, url) for url in urls]
        status_codes = await asyncio.gather(*tasks)
        print(status_codes)
```

If we change our URL list to the above, the request for 'python://example.com' will fail because that URL is not valid. Our fetch_status_code coroutine will throw an AssertionError because of this, meaning that python:// does not translate into a port. This exception will get thrown when we await our gather coroutine. If we run this and look at the output, we'll see that our exception was thrown, but we'll also see that our other request continued to run (we've removed the verbose traceback for brevity):

```
starting <function main at 0x107f4a4c0> with args () {}
starting <function fetch_status_code at 0x107f4a3a0>
starting <function fetch_status_code at 0x107f4a3a0>
finished <function fetch_status_code at 0x107f4a3a0> in 0.0004 second(s)
finished <function main at 0x107f4a4c0> in 0.0203 second(s)
finished <function fetch_status_code at 0x107f4a3a0> in 0.0198 second(s)
Traceback (most recent call last):
  File "gather_exception.py", line 22, in <module>
    asyncio.run(main())
AssertionError

Process finished with exit code 1
```

asyncio.gather won't cancel any other tasks that are running if there is a failure. That may be acceptable for many use cases but is one of the drawbacks of gather. We'll see how to cancel tasks we run concurrently later in this chapter.

Another potential issue with the above code is that if more than one exception happens, we'll only see the first one that occurred when we await the gather. We can fix this by using return_exceptions=True, which will return all exceptions we encounter when running our coroutines. We can then filter out any exceptions and handle them as needed. Let's examine our previous example with invalid URLs to understand how this works:

```
@async_timed()
async def main():
    async with aiohttp.ClientSession() as session:
        urls = ['https://example.com', 'python://example.com']
        tasks = [fetch_status_code(session, url) for url in urls]
        results = await asyncio.gather(*tasks, return_exceptions=True)

        exceptions = [res for res in results if isinstance(res, Exception)]
        successful_results = [res for res in results if not isinstance(res,
    Exception)]

        print(f'All results: {results}')
        print(f'Finished successfully: {successful_results}')
        print(f'Threw exceptions: {exceptions}')
```

When running this, notice that no exceptions are thrown, and we get all the exceptions alongside our successful results in the list that gather returns. We then filter out anything that is an instance of an exception to retrieve the list of successful responses, resulting in the following output:

```
All results: [200, AssertionError()]
Finished successfully: [200]
Threw exceptions: [AssertionError()]
```

This solves the issue of not being able to see all the exceptions that our coroutines throw. It is also nice that now we don't need to explicitly handle any exceptions with a try catch block, since we no longer throw an exception when we await. It is still a little clunky that we must filter out exceptions from successful results, but the API is not perfect.

gather has a few drawbacks. The first, which was already mentioned, is that it isn't easy to cancel our tasks if one throws an exception. Imagine a case in which we're making requests to the same server, and if one request fails, all others will as well, such as reaching a rate limit. In this case, we may want to cancel requests to free up resources, which isn't very easy to do because our coroutines are wrapped in tasks in the background.

The second is that we must wait for all our coroutines to finish before we can process our results. If we want to deal with results as soon as they complete, this poses a problem. For example, if we have one request needing 100 milliseconds, but another that lasts 20 seconds, we'll be stuck waiting for 20 seconds before we can process the request that completed in only 100 milliseconds.

asyncio provides APIs that allow us to solve for both issues. Let's start by looking at the problem of handling results as soon as they come in.

4.5   *Processing requests as they complete*

While asyncio.gather will work for many cases, it has the drawback that it waits for all awaitables to finish before allowing access to any results. This is a problem if we'd like to process results as soon as they come in. It can also be a problem if we have a few awaitables that could complete quickly and a few which could take some time, since gather waits for everything to finish. This can cause our application to become unresponsive; imagine a user makes 100 requests and two of them are slow, but the rest complete quickly. It would be great if once requests start to finish, we could output some information to our users.

To handle this case, asyncio exposes an API function named as_completed. This method takes a list of awaitables and returns an iterator of futures. We can then iterate over these futures, awaiting each one. When the await expression completes, we will retrieve the result of the coroutine that finished first out of all our awaitables. This means that we'll be able to process results as soon as they are available, but there is now no deterministic ordering of results, since we have no guarantees as to which requests will complete first.

To show how this works, let's simulate a case where one request completes quickly, and another needs more time. We'll add a delay parameter to our fetch_status function and call asyncio.sleep to simulate a long request, as follows:

```
async def fetch_status(session: ClientSession,
                       url: str,
                       delay: int = 0) -> int:
    await asyncio.sleep(delay)
    async with session.get(url) as result:
        return result.status
```

We'll then use a for loop to iterate over the iterator returned from as_completed.

Listing 4.8 Using as_completed

```
import asyncio
import aiohttp
from aiohttp import ClientSession
from util import async_timed
from chapter_04 import fetch_status


@async_timed()
async def main():
    async with aiohttp.ClientSession() as session:
        fetchers = [fetch_status(session, 'https://www.example.com', 1),
                    fetch_status(session, 'https://www.example.com', 1),
                    fetch_status(session, 'https://www.example.com', 10)]

        for finished_task in asyncio.as_completed(fetchers):
            print(await finished_task)


asyncio.run(main())
```

In the preceding listing, we create three coroutines—two that require about 1 second to complete and one that will take 10 seconds. We then pass these into as_completed.

Under the hood, each coroutine is wrapped in a task and starts running concurrently. The routine instantly returned an iterator that starts to loop over. When we enter the for loop, we hit await finished_task. Here we pause execution and wait for our first result to come in. In this case, our first result comes in after 1 second, and we print the status code. Then we reach the await result again, and since our requests ran concurrently, we should see the second result almost instantly. Finally, our 10-second request will complete, and our loop will finish. Executing this will give us output as follows:

```
starting <function fetch_status at 0x10dbed4c0>
starting <function fetch_status at 0x10dbed4c0>
starting <function fetch_status at 0x10dbed4c0>
finished <function fetch_status at 0x10dbed4c0> in 1.1269 second(s)
200
finished <function fetch_status at 0x10dbed4c0> in 1.1294 second(s)
200
finished <function fetch_status at 0x10dbed4c0> in 10.0345 second(s)
200
finished <function main at 0x10dbed5e0> in 10.0353 second(s)
```

In total, iterating over result_iterator still takes about 10 seconds, as it would have if we used asynio.gather; however, we're able to execute code to print the result of our first request as soon as it finishes. This gives us extra time to process the result of our first successfully finished coroutine while others are still waiting to finish, making our application more responsive when our tasks complete.

This function also offers better control over exception handling. When a task throws an exception, we'll be able to process it when it happens, as the exception is thrown when we await the future.

4.5.1   *Timeouts with as_completed*

Any web-based request runs the risk of taking a long time. A server could be under a heavy resource load, or we could have a poor network connection. Earlier, we saw how to add timeouts for a particular request, but what if we wanted to have a timeout for a group of requests? The as_completed function supports this use case by supplying an optional timeout parameter, which lets us specify a timeout in seconds. This will keep track of how long the as_completed call has taken; if it takes longer than the timeout, each awaitable in the iterator will throw a TimeoutException when we await it.

To illustrate this, let's take our previous example and create two requests that take 10 seconds to complete and one request that takes 1 second. Then, we'll set a timeout of 2 seconds on as_completed. Once we're done with the loop, we'll print out all the tasks we have that are currently running.

Listing 4.9   Setting a timeout on as_completed

```
import asyncio
import aiohttp
from aiohttp import ClientSession
```

```
from util import async_timed
from chapter_04 import fetch_status


@async_timed()
async def main():
    async with aiohttp.ClientSession() as session:
        fetchers = [fetch_status(session, 'https://example.com', 1),
                    fetch_status(session, 'https://example.com', 10),
                    fetch_status(session, 'https://example.com', 10)]

        for done_task in asyncio.as_completed(fetchers, timeout=2):
            try:
                result = await done_task
                print(result)
            except asyncio.TimeoutError:
                print('We got a timeout error!')

        for task in asyncio.tasks.all_tasks():
            print(task)


asyncio.run(main())
```

When we run this, we'll notice the result from our first fetch, and after 2 seconds, we'll see two timeout errors. We'll also see that two fetches are still running, giving output similar to the following:

```
starting <function main at 0x109c7c430> with args () {}
200
We got a timeout error!
We got a timeout error!
finished <function main at 0x109c7c430> in 2.0055 second(s)
<Task pending name='Task-2' coro=<fetch_status_code()>>
<Task pending name='Task-1' coro=<main>>
<Task pending name='Task-4' coro=<fetch_status_code()>>
```

as_completed works well for getting results as fast as possible but has drawbacks. The first is that while we get results as they come in, there isn't any way to easily see which coroutine or task we're awaiting as the order is completely nondeterministic. If we don't care about order, this may be fine, but if we need to associate the results to the requests somehow, we're left with a challenge.

The second is that with timeouts, while we will correctly throw an exception and move on, any tasks created will still be running in the background. Since it's hard to figure out which tasks are still running if we want to cancel them, we have another challenge. If these are problems we need to deal with, then we'll need some finer-grained knowledge of which awaitables are finished, and which are not. To handle this situation, asyncio provides another API function called wait.

4.6   *Finer-grained control with wait*

One of the drawbacks of both `gather` and `as_completed` is that there is no easy way to cancel tasks that were already running when we saw an exception. This might be okay in many situations, but imagine a use case in which we make several coroutine calls and if the first one fails, the rest will as well. An example of this would be passing in an invalid parameter to a web request or reaching an API rate limit. This has the potential to cause performance issues because we'll consume more resources by having more tasks than we need. Another drawback we noted with `as_completed` is that, as the iteration order is nondeterministic, it is challenging to keep track of exactly which task had completed.

`wait` in asyncio is similar to `gather` wait that offers more specific control to handle these situations. This method has several options to choose from depending on when we want our results. In addition, this method returns two sets: a set of tasks that are finished with either a result or an exception, and a set of tasks that are still running. This function also allows us to specify a timeout that behaves differently from how other API methods operate; it does not throw exceptions. When needed, this function can solve some of the issues we noted with the other asyncio API functions we've used so far.

The basic signature of `wait` is a list of awaitable objects, followed by an optional timeout and an optional `return_when` string. This string has a few predefined values that we'll examine: `ALL_COMPLETED`, `FIRST_EXCEPTION` and `FIRST_COMPLETED`. It defaults to `ALL_COMPLETED`. While as of this writing, `wait` takes a list of awaitables, it will change in future versions of Python to only accept `task` objects. We'll see why at the end of this section, but for these code samples, as this is best practice, we'll wrap all coroutines in tasks.

4.6.1   *Waiting for all tasks to complete*

This option is the default behavior if `return_when` is not specified, and it is the closest in behavior to `asyncio.gather`, though it has a few differences. As implied, using this option will wait for all tasks to finish before returning. Let's adapt this to our example of making multiple web requests concurrently to learn how this function works.

Listing 4.10   **Examining the default behavior of `wait`**

```
import asyncio
import aiohttp
from aiohttp import ClientSession
from util import async_timed
from chapter_04 import fetch_status


@async_timed()
async def main():
    async with aiohttp.ClientSession() as session:
```

```
    fetchers = \
        [asyncio.create_task(fetch_status(session, 'https://example.com')),
         asyncio.create_task(fetch_status(session, 'https://example.com'))]
    done, pending = await asyncio.wait(fetchers)

    print(f'Done task count: {len(done)}')
    print(f'Pending task count: {len(pending)}')

    for done_task in done:
        result = await done_task
        print(result)


asyncio.run(main())
```

In the preceding listing, we run two web requests concurrently by passing a list of coroutines to wait. When we await wait it will return two sets once all requests finish: one set of all tasks that are complete and one set of the tasks that are still running. The done set contains all tasks that finished either successfully or with exceptions. The pending set contains all tasks that have not finished yet. In this instance, since we are using the ALL_COMPLETED option the pending set will always be zero, since asyncio.wait won't return until everything is completed. This will give us the following output:

```
starting <function main at 0x10124b160> with args () {}
Done task count: 2
Pending task count: 0
200
200
finished <function main at 0x10124b160> in 0.4642 second(s)
```

If one of our requests throws an exception, it won't be thrown at the asyncio.wait call in the same way that asyncio.gather did. In this instance, we'll get both the done and pending sets as before, but we won't see an exception until we await the task in done that failed.

With this paradigm, we have a few options on how to handle exceptions. We can use await and let the exception throw, we can use await and wrap it in a try except block to handle the exception, or we can use the task.result() and task.exception() methods. We can safely call these methods since our tasks in the done set are guaranteed to be completed tasks; if they were not calling these methods, it would then produce an exception.

Let's say that we don't want to throw an exception and have our application crash. Instead, we'd like to print the task's result if we have it and log an error if there was an exception. In this case, using the methods on the Task object is an appropriate solution. Let's see how to use these two Task methods to handle exceptions.

Listing 4.11   Exceptions with `wait`

```
import asyncio
import logging

@async_timed()
async def main():
    async with aiohttp.ClientSession() as session:
        good_request = fetch_status(session, 'https://www.example.com')
        bad_request = fetch_status(session, 'python://bad')

        fetchers = [asyncio.create_task(good_request),
                    asyncio.create_task(bad_request)]

        done, pending = await asyncio.wait(fetchers)

        print(f'Done task count: {len(done)}')
        print(f'Pending task count: {len(pending)}')

        for done_task in done:
            # result = await done_task will throw an exception
            if done_task.exception() is None:
                print(done_task.result())
            else:
                logging.error("Request got an exception",
                              exc_info=done_task.exception())

asyncio.run(main())
```

Using `done_task.exception()` will check to see if we have an exception. If we don't, then we can proceed to get the result from `done_task` with the `result` method. It would also be safe to do `result = await done_task` here, although it might throw an exception, which may not be what we want. If the exception is not `None`, then we know that the awaitable had an exception, and we can handle that as desired. Here we just print out the exception's stack trace. Running this will yield output similar to the following (we've removed the verbose traceback for brevity):

```
starting <function main at 0x10401f1f0> with args () {}
Done task count: 2
Pending task count: 0
200
finished <function main at 0x10401f1f0> in 0.12386679649353027 second(s)
ERROR:root:Request got an exception
Traceback (most recent call last):
AssertionError
```

4.6.2   *Watching for exceptions*

The drawbacks of `ALL_COMPLETED` are like the drawbacks we saw with `gather`. We could have any number of exceptions while we wait for other coroutines to complete, which we won't see until all tasks complete. This could be an issue if, because of one exception, we'd like to cancel other running requests. We may also want to immediately handle any errors to ensure responsiveness and continue waiting for other coroutines to complete.

To support these use cases, `wait` supports the `FIRST_EXCEPTION` option. When we use this option, we'll get two different behaviors, depending on whether any of our tasks throw exceptions.

No exceptions from any awaitables

If we have no exceptions from any of our tasks, then this option is equivalent to `ALL_COMPLETED`. We'll wait for all tasks to finish and then the `done` set will contain all finished tasks and the `pending` set will be empty.

One or more exception from a task

If any task throws an exception, `wait` will immediately return once that exception is thrown. The `done` set will have any coroutines that finished successfully alongside any coroutines with exceptions. The `done` set is, at minimum, guaranteed to have one failed task in this case but may have successfully completed tasks. The `pending` set may be empty, but it may also have tasks that are still running. We can then use this `pending` set to manage the currently running tasks as we desire.

To illustrate how `wait` behaves in these scenarios, look at what happens when we have a couple of long-running web requests we'd like to cancel when one coroutine fails immediately with an exception.

Listing 4.12 Canceling running requests on an exception

```
import aiohttp
import asyncio
import logging
from chapter_04 import  fetch_status
from util import async_timed


@async_timed()
async def main():
    async with aiohttp.ClientSession() as session:
        fetchers = \
            [asyncio.create_task(fetch_status(session, 'python://bad.com')),
             asyncio.create_task(fetch_status(session, 'https://www.example
                                        .com', delay=3)),
             asyncio.create_task(fetch_status(session, 'https://www.example
                                        .com', delay=3))]

        done, pending = await asyncio.wait(fetchers,
        return_when=asyncio.FIRST_EXCEPTION)

        print(f'Done task count: {len(done)}')
        print(f'Pending task count: {len(pending)}')
```

```
        for done_task in done:
            if done_task.exception() is None:
                print(done_task.result())
            else:
                logging.error("Request got an exception",
                            exc_info=done_task.exception())

        for pending_task in pending:
            pending_task.cancel()


asyncio.run(main())
```

In the preceding listing, we make one bad request and two good ones; each lasts 3 seconds. When we await our `wait` statement, we return almost immediately since our bad request errors out right away. Then we loop through the done tasks. In this instance, we'll have only one in the done set since our first request ended immediately with an exception. For this, we'll execute the branch that prints the exception.

The pending set will have two elements, as we have two requests that take roughly 3 seconds each to run and our first request failed almost instantly. Since we want to stop these from running, we can call the cancel method on them. This will give us the following output:

```
starting <function main at 0x105cfd280> with args () {}
Done task count: 1
Pending task count: 2
finished <function main at 0x105cfd280> in 0.0044 second(s)
ERROR:root:Request got an exception
```

> **NOTE** Our application took almost no time to run, as we quickly reacted to the fact that one of our requests threw an exception; the power of using this option is we achieve fail fast behavior, quickly reacting to any issues that arise.

4.6.3 *Processing results as they complete*

Both `ALL_COMPLETED` and `FIRST_EXCEPTION` have the drawback that, in the case where coroutines are successful and don't throw an exception, we must wait for all coroutines to complete. Depending on the use case, this may be acceptable, but if we're in a situation where we want to respond to a coroutine as soon as it completes successfully, we are out of luck.

In the instance in which we want to react to a result as soon as it completes, we could use as_completed; however, the issue with as_completed is there is no easy way to see which tasks are remaining and which tasks have completed. We get them only one at a time through an iterator.

The good news is that the return_when parameter accepts a `FIRST_COMPLETED` option. This option will make the `wait` coroutine return as soon as it has at least one result. This can either be a coroutine that failed or one that ran successfully. We can then either cancel the other running coroutines or adjust which ones to keep running, depending on our use case. Let's use this option to make a few web requests and process whichever one finishes first.

```
import asyncio
import aiohttp
from util import async_timed
from chapter_04 import fetch_status


@async_timed()
async def main():
    async with aiohttp.ClientSession() as session:
        url = 'https://www.example.com'
        fetchers = [asyncio.create_task(fetch_status(session, url)),
                    asyncio.create_task(fetch_status(session, url)),
                    asyncio.create_task(fetch_status(session, url))]

        done, pending = await asyncio.wait(fetchers,
     return_when=asyncio.FIRST_COMPLETED)

        print(f'Done task count: {len(done)}')
        print(f'Pending task count: {len(pending)}')

        for done_task in done:
            print(await done_task)


asyncio.run(main())
```

In the preceding listing, we start three requests concurrently. Our wait coroutine will return as soon as any of these requests completes. This means that done will have one complete request, and pending will contain anything still running, giving us the following output:

```
starting <function main at 0x10222f1f0> with args () {}
Done task count: 1
Pending task count: 2
200
finished <function main at 0x10222f1f0> in 0.1138 second(s)
```

These requests can complete at nearly the same time, so we could also see output that says two or three tasks are done. Try running this listing a few times to see how the result varies.

This approach lets us respond right away when our first task completes. What if we want to process the rest of the results as they come in like as_completed? The above example can be adopted easily to loop on the pending tasks until they are empty. This will give us behavior similar to as_completed, with the benefit that at each step we know exactly which tasks have finished and which are still running.

Listing 4.14   Processing all results as they come in

```
import asyncio
import aiohttp
from chapter_04 import fetch_status
from util import async_timed


@async_timed()
async def main():
    async with aiohttp.ClientSession() as session:
        url = 'https://www.example.com'
        pending = [asyncio.create_task(fetch_status(session, url)),
                   asyncio.create_task(fetch_status(session, url)),
                   asyncio.create_task(fetch_status(session, url))]

        while pending:
            done, pending = await asyncio.wait(pending,
        return_when=asyncio.FIRST_COMPLETED)

            print(f'Done task count: {len(done)}')
            print(f'Pending task count: {len(pending)}')

            for done_task in done:
                print(await done_task)

asyncio.run(main())
```

In the preceding listing, we create a set named `pending` that we initialize to the coroutines we want to run. We loop while we have items in the `pending` set and call `wait` with that set on each iteration. Once we have a result from `wait`, we update the `done` and `pending` sets and then print out any `done` tasks. This will give us behavior similar to `as_completed` with the difference being we have better insight into which tasks are done and which tasks are still running. Running this, we'll see the following output:

```
starting <function main at 0x10d1671f0> with args () {}
Done task count: 1
Pending task count: 2
200
Done task count: 1
Pending task count: 1
200
Done task count: 1
Pending task count: 0
200
finished <function main at 0x10d1671f0> in 0.1153 second(s)
```

Since the request function may complete quickly, such that all requests complete at the same time, it's not impossible that we see output similar to this as well:

```
starting <function main at 0x1100f11f0> with args () {}
Done task count: 3
Pending task count: 0
200
200
200
finished <function main at 0x1100f11f0> in 0.1304 second(s)
```

4.6.4 Handling timeouts

In addition to allowing us finer-grained control on how we wait for coroutines to complete, wait also allows us to set timeouts to specify how long we want for all awaitables to complete. To enable this, we can set the timeout parameter with the maximum number of seconds desired. If we've exceeded this timeout, wait will return both the done and pending task set. There are a couple of differences in how timeouts behave in wait as compared to what we have seen thus far with wait_for and as_completed.

> **Coroutines are not canceled**
>
> When we used wait_for, if our coroutine timed out it would automatically request cancellation for us. This is not the case with wait; it behaves closer to what we saw with gather and as_completed. In the case we want to cancel coroutines due to a timeout, we must explicitly loop over the tasks and cancel them.

> **Timeout errors are not raised**
>
> wait does not rely on exceptions in the event of timeouts as do wait_for and as_completed. Instead, if the timeout occurs the wait returns all tasks done and all tasks that are still pending up to that point when the timeout occurred.

For example, let's examine a case where two requests complete quickly and one takes a few seconds. We'll use a timeout of 1 second with wait to understand what happens when we have tasks that take longer than the timeout. For the return_when parameter, we'll use the default value of ALL_COMPLETED.

Listing 4.15 Using timeouts with wait

```
@async_timed()
async def main():
    async with aiohttp.ClientSession() as session:
        url = 'https://example.com'
        fetchers = [asyncio.create_task(fetch_status(session, url)),
                    asyncio.create_task(fetch_status(session, url)),
                    asyncio.create_task(fetch_status(session, url, delay=3))]

        done, pending = await asyncio.wait(fetchers, timeout=1)

        print(f'Done task count: {len(done)}')
        print(f'Pending task count: {len(pending)}')
```

```
        for done_task in done:
            result = await done_task
            print(result)


asyncio.run(main())
```

Running the preceding listing, our `wait` call will return our `done` and `pending` sets after 1 second. In the `done` set we'll see our two fast requests, as they finished within 1 second. Our slow request is still running and is, therefore, in the `pending` set. We then `await` the `done` tasks to extract out their return values. We also could have canceled the pending task if we so desired. Running this code, we will see the following output:

```
starting <function main at 0x11c68dd30> with args () {}
Done task count: 2
Pending task count: 1
200
200
finished <function main at 0x11c68dd30> in 1.0022 second(s)
```

Note that, as before, our tasks in the `pending` set are not canceled and will continue to run despite the timeout. If we have a use case where we want to terminate the `pending` tasks, we'll need to explicitly loop through the `pending` set and call `cancel` on each task.

4.6.5   *Why wrap everything in a task?*

At the start of this section, we mentioned that it is best practice to wrap the coroutines we pass into `wait` in tasks. Why is this? Let's go back to our previous timeout example and change it a little bit. Let's say that we have requests to two different web APIs that we'll call API A and API B. Both can be slow, but our application can run without the result from API B, so it is just a "nice to have." Since we'd like a responsive application, we set a timeout of 1 second for the requests to complete. If the request to API B is still pending after that timeout, we cancel it and move on. Let's see what happens if we implement this without wrapping the requests in tasks.

Listing 4.16   Canceling a slow request

```
import asyncio
import aiohttp
from chapter_04 import fetch_status


async def main():
    async with aiohttp.ClientSession() as session:
        api_a = fetch_status(session, 'https://www.example.com')
        api_b = fetch_status(session, 'https://www.example.com', delay=2)

        done, pending = await asyncio.wait([api_a, api_b], timeout=1)

        for task in pending:
            if task is api_b:
```

```
        print('API B too slow, cancelling')
        task.cancel()

asyncio.run(main())
```

We'd expect for this code to print out API B is too slow and cancelling, but what happens if we don't see this message at all? This can happen because when we call wait with just coroutines they are automatically wrapped in tasks, and the done and pending sets returned are those tasks that wait created for us. This means that we can't do any comparisons to see which specific task is in the pending set such as if task is api_b, since we'll be comparing a task object, we have no access to with a coroutine. However, if we wrap fetch_status in a task, wait won't create any new objects, and the comparison if task is api_b will work as we expect. In this case, we're correctly comparing two task objects.

Summary

- We've learned how to use and create our own asynchronous context managers. These are special classes that allow us to asynchronously acquire resources and then release them, even if an exception occurred. These let us clean up any resources we may have acquired in a non-verbose manner and are useful when working with HTTP sessions as well as database connections. We can use them with the special async with syntax.
- We can use the aiohttp library to make asynchronous web requests. aiohttp is a web client and server that uses non-blocking sockets. With the web client, we can execute multiple web requests concurrently in a way that does not block the event loop.
- The asyncio.gather function lets us run multiple coroutines concurrently and wait for them to complete. This function will return once all awaitables we pass into it have completed. If we want to keep track of any errors that happen, we can set return_exeptions to True. This will return the results of awaitables that completed successfully alongside any exceptions we received.
- We can use the as_completed function to process results of a list of awaitables as soon as they complete. This will give us an iterator of futures that we can loop over. As soon as a coroutine or task has finished, we'll be able to access the result and process it.
- If we want to run multiple tasks concurrently but want to be able to understand which tasks are done and which are still running, we can use wait. This function also allows us greater control on when it returns results. When it returns, we get a set of tasks that have finished and set of tasks that are still running. We can then cancel any tasks we wish or do any other awaiting we need.

Non-blocking
database drivers

This chapter covers

- Running asyncio friendly database queries
  with asyncpg
- Creating database connection pools running
  multiple SQL queries concurrently
- Managing asynchronous database transactions
- Using asynchronous generators to stream query
  results

Chapter 4 explored making non-blocking web requests with the aiohttp library, and
it also addressed using several different asyncio API methods for running these
requests concurrently. With the combination of the asyncio APIs and the aiohttp
library, we can run multiple long-running web requests concurrently, leading to an
improvement in our application's runtime. The concepts we learned in chapter 4
do not apply only to web requests; they also apply to running SQL queries and can
improve the performance of database-intensive applications.

Much like web requests, we'll need to use an asyncio-friendly library since typical SQL libraries block the main thread, and therefore the event loop, until a result
is retrieved. In this chapter, we'll learn more about asynchronous database access

with the asyncpg library. We'll first create a simple schema to keep track of products for an e-commerce storefront that we'll then use to run queries against asynchronously. We'll then look at how to manage transactions and rollbacks within our database, as well as setting up connection pooling.

5.1   *Introducing asyncpg*

As we've mentioned earlier, our existing blocking libraries won't work seamlessly with coroutines. To run queries concurrently against a database, we'll need to use an asyncio-friendly library that uses non-blocking sockets. To do this, we'll use a library called *asyncpg*, which will let us asynchronously connect to Postgres databases and run queries against them.

In this chapter we'll focus on Postgres databases, but what we learn here will also be applicable to MySQL and other databases as well. The creators of aiohttp have also created the *aiomysql* library, which can connect and run queries against a MySQL database. While there are some differences, the APIs are similar, and the knowledge is transferable. It is worth noting that the asyncpg library did not implement the Python database API specification defined in PEP-249 (available at https://www.python.org/ dev/peps/pep-0249). This was a conscious choice on the part of the library implementors, since a concurrent implementation is inherently different from a synchronous one. The creators of aiomysql, however, took a different route and do implement PEP-249, so this library's API will feel familiar to those who have used synchronous database drivers in Python.

The current documentation for asynpg is available at https://magicstack.github .io/asyncpg/current/. Now that we've learned a little about the driver we'll be using, let's connect to our first database.

5.2   *Connecting to a Postgres database*

To get started with asyncpg, we'll use a real-world scenario of creating a product database for an e-commerce storefront. We'll use this example database throughout the chapter to demonstrate database problems in this domain that we might need to solve.

The first thing for getting started creating our product database and running queries is establishing a database connection. For this section and the rest of the chapter, we'll assume that you have a Postgres database running on your local machine on the default port of 5432, and we'll assume the default user `postgres` has a password of `'password'`.

> **WARNING** We'll be hardcoding the password in these code examples for transparency and learning purposes; but note you should *never* hardcode a password in your code as this violates security principles. Always store passwords in environment variables or some other configuration mechanism.

You can download and install a copy of Postgres from https://www.postgresql.org/ download/; just choose the appropriate operating system you're working on. You may also consider using the Docker Postgres image; more information can be found at https://hub.docker.com/_/postgres/.

Once we have our database set up, we'll install the asyncpg library. We'll use pip3 to do this, and we'll install the latest version at the time of writing, 0.0.23:

```
pip3 install -Iv asyncpg==0.23.0
```

Once installed, we can now import the library and establish a connection to our database. asyncpg provides this with the asyncpg.connect function. Let's use this to connect and print out the database version number.

Listing 5.1 Connecting to a Postgres database as the default user

```
import asyncpg
import asyncio


async def main():
    connection = await asyncpg.connect(host='127.0.0.1',
                                       port=5432,
                                       user='postgres',
                                       database='postgres',
                                       password='password')
    version = connection.get_server_version()
    print(f'Connected! Postgres version is {version}')
    await connection.close()


asyncio.run(main())
```

In the preceding listing, we create a connection to our Postres instance as the default postgres user and the default postgres database. Assuming our Postgres instance is up and running, we should see something like "Connected! Postgres version is ServerVersion(major=12, minor=0, micro=3, releaselevel='final' serial=0)" displayed on our console, indicating we've successfully connected to our database. Finally, we close the connection to the database with await connection.close().

Now we've connected, but nothing is currently stored in our database. The next step is to create a product schema that we can interact with. In creating this schema, we'll learn how to execute basic queries with asyncpg.

5.3   *Defining a database schema*

To begin running queries against our database, we'll need to create a database schema. We're going to select a simple schema that we'll call products, modeling real-world products that an online storefront might have in stock. Let's define a few different entities that we can then turn into tables in our database.

Brand

A *brand* is a manufacturer of many distinct products. For instance, Ford is a brand that produces many different models of cars (e.g., Ford F150, Ford Fiesta, etc.).

Product

A *product* is associated with one brand and there is a one-to-many relationship between brands and products. For simplicity, in our product database, a product will just have a product name. In the Ford example, a product is a compact car called the *Fiesta*; the brand is *Ford*. In addition, each product in our database will come in multiple sizes and colors. We'll define the available sizes and colors as SKUs.

SKU

SKU stands for *stock keeping unit*. A SKU represents a distinct item that a storefront has for sale. For instance, *jeans* may be a product for sale and a SKU might be *Jeans, size: medium, color: blue;* or *jeans, size: small, color: black.* There is a one-to-many relationship between a product and a SKU.

Product size

A product can come in multiple sizes. For this example, we'll consider that there are only three sizes available: small, medium, and large. Each SKU has one product size associated with it, so there is a one-to-many relationship between product sizes and SKUs.

Product color

A product can come in multiple colors. For this example, we'll say our inventory consists of only two colors: black and blue. There is a one-to-many relationship between product color and SKUs.

Putting this all together, we'll be modeling a database schema, as shown in figure 5.1.

Now, let's define some variables with the SQL we'll need to create this schema. Using asyncpg, we'll execute these statements to create our product database. Since our sizes and colors are known ahead of time, we'll also insert a few records into the product_size and product_color tables. We'll reference these variables in the upcoming code listings, so we don't need to repeat lengthy SQL create statements.

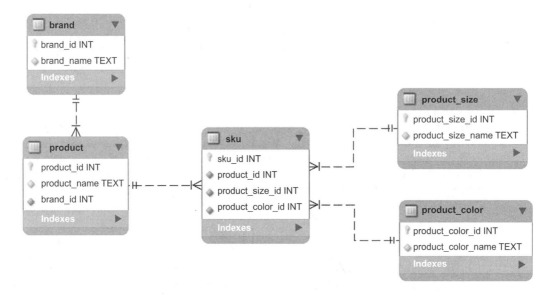

Figure 5.1   The entity diagram for the products database

Listing 5.2   Product schema table create statements

```
CREATE_BRAND_TABLE = \
    """
    CREATE TABLE IF NOT EXISTS brand(
        brand_id SERIAL PRIMARY KEY,
        brand_name TEXT NOT NULL
    );"""

CREATE_PRODUCT_TABLE = \
    """
    CREATE TABLE IF NOT EXISTS product(
        product_id SERIAL PRIMARY KEY,
        product_name TEXT NOT NULL,
        brand_id INT NOT NULL,
        FOREIGN KEY (brand_id) REFERENCES brand(brand_id)
    );"""

CREATE_PRODUCT_COLOR_TABLE = \
    """
    CREATE TABLE IF NOT EXISTS product_color(
        product_color_id SERIAL PRIMARY KEY,
        product_color_name TEXT NOT NULL
    );"""

CREATE_PRODUCT_SIZE_TABLE = \
    """
    CREATE TABLE IF NOT EXISTS product_size(
        product_size_id SERIAL PRIMARY KEY,
```

```
        product_size_name TEXT NOT NULL
    );"""

CREATE_SKU_TABLE = \
    """
    CREATE TABLE IF NOT EXISTS sku(
        sku_id SERIAL PRIMARY KEY,
        product_id INT NOT NULL,
        product_size_id INT NOT NULL,
        product_color_id INT NOT NULL,
        FOREIGN KEY (product_id)
        REFERENCES product(product_id),
        FOREIGN KEY (product_size_id)
        REFERENCES product_size(product_size_id),
        FOREIGN KEY (product_color_id)
        REFERENCES product_color(product_color_id)
    );"""

COLOR_INSERT = \
    """
    INSERT INTO product_color VALUES(1, 'Blue');
    INSERT INTO product_color VALUES(2, 'Black');
    """

SIZE_INSERT = \
    """
    INSERT INTO product_size VALUES(1, 'Small');
    INSERT INTO product_size VALUES(2, 'Medium');
    INSERT INTO product_size VALUES(3, 'Large');
    """
```

Now that we have the statements to create our tables and insert our sizes and colors, we need a way to run queries against them.

5.4 *Executing queries with asyncpg*

To run queries against our database, we'll first need to connect to our Postgres instance and create the database directly outside of Python. We can create the database by executing the following statement once connected to the database as the default Postgres user:

```
CREATE DATABASE products;
```

You can execute this via the command line by running `sudo -u postgres psql -c "CREATE TABLE products;"`. In the next examples, we'll assume you have executed this statement, as we'll connect to the products database directly.

Now that we've created our products database, we'll connect to it and execute our create statements. The connection class has a coroutine called `execute` that we can use to run our create statements one by one. This coroutine returns a string representing the status of the query that Postgres returned. Let's take the statements we created in the last section and execute them.

Listing 5.3   Using an execute coroutine to run `create` statements

```
import asyncpg
import asyncio


async def main():
    connection = await asyncpg.connect(host='127.0.0.1',
                                       port=5432,
                                       user='postgres',
                                       database='products',
                                       password='password')
    statements = [CREATE_BRAND_TABLE,
                  CREATE_PRODUCT_TABLE,
                  CREATE_PRODUCT_COLOR_TABLE,
                  CREATE_PRODUCT_SIZE_TABLE,
                  CREATE_SKU_TABLE,
                  SIZE_INSERT,
                  COLOR_INSERT]

    print('Creating the product database...')
    for statement in statements:
        status = await connection.execute(statement)
        print(status)
    print('Finished creating the product database!')
    await connection.close()


asyncio.run(main())
```

We first create a connection to our products database similarly to what we did in our first example, the difference being that here we connect to the products database. Once we have this connection, we then start to execute our CREATE TABLE statements one at a time with `connection.execute()`. Note that `execute()` is a coroutine, so to run our SQL we need to `await` the call. Assuming everything worked properly, the status of each execute statement should be CREATE TABLE, and each insert statement should be INSERT 0 1. Finally, we close the connection to the product database. Note that in this example we await each SQL statement in a `for` loop, which ensures that we run the INSERT statements synchronously. Since some tables depend on others, we can't run them concurrently.

These statements don't have any results associated with them, so let's insert a few pieces of data and run some simple select queries. We'll first insert a few brands and then query them to ensure we've inserted them properly. We can insert data with the execute coroutine, as before, and we can run a query with the `fetch` coroutine.

Listing 5.4   Inserting and selecting brands

```
import asyncpg
import asyncio
from asyncpg import Record
from typing import List
```

```
async def main():
    connection = await asyncpg.connect(host='127.0.0.1',
                                        port=5432,
                                        user='postgres',
                                        database='products',
                                        password='password')
    await connection.execute("INSERT INTO brand VALUES(DEFAULT, 'Levis')")
    await connection.execute("INSERT INTO brand VALUES(DEFAULT, 'Seven')")

    brand_query = 'SELECT brand_id, brand_name FROM brand'
    results: List[Record] = await connection.fetch(brand_query)

    for brand in results:
        print(f'id: {brand["brand_id"]}, name: {brand["brand_name"]}')

    await connection.close()


asyncio.run(main())
```

We first insert two brands into the brand table. Once we've done this, we use `connection`
`.fetch` to get all brands from our brand table. Once this query has finished, we will
have all results in memory in the `results` variable. Each result will be an `asyncpg`
`Record` object. These objects act similarly to dictionaries; they allow us to access data
by passing in a column name with subscript syntax. Executing this will give us the following output:

```
id: 1, name: Levis
id: 2, name: Seven
```

In this example, we fetch all data for our query into a list. If we wanted to fetch a single result, we could call `connection.fetchrow()`, which will return a single record
from the query. The default asyncpg connection will pull all results from our query
into memory, so for the time being there is no performance difference between
`fetchrow` and `fetch`. Later in this chapter, we'll see how to use streaming result sets
with cursors. These will only pull a few results into memory at a time, which is a useful
technique for times when queries may return large amounts of data.

These examples run queries one after another, and we could have had similar performance by using a non-asyncio database driver. However, since we're now returning
coroutines, we can use the asyncio API methods we learned in chapter 4 to execute
queries concurrently.

5.5 Executing queries concurrently with connection pools

The true benefit of asyncio for I/O-bound operations is the ability to run multiple
tasks concurrently. Queries independent from one another that we need to make repeatedly are good examples of where we can apply concurrency to make our application perform better. To demonstrate this, let's pretend that we're a successful e-commerce
storefront. Our company carries 100,000 SKUs for 1,000 distinct brands.

We'll also pretend that we sell our items through partners. These partners make requests for thousands of products at a given time through a batch process we have built. Running all these queries sequentially could be slow, so we'd like to create an application that executes these queries concurrently to ensure a speedy experience.

Since this is an example, and we don't have 100,000 SKUs on hand, we'll start by creating a fake product and SKU records in our database. We'll randomly generate 100,000 SKUs for random brands and products, and we'll use this data set as a basis for running our queries.

5.5.1   *Inserting random SKUs into the product database*

Since we don't want to list brands, products, and SKUs ourselves, we'll randomly generate them. We'll pick random names from a list of the 1,000 most frequently occurring English words. For the sake of this example, we'll assume we have a text file that contains these words, called common_words.txt. You can download a copy of this file from the book's GitHub data repository at https://github.com/concurrency-in-python-with-asyncio/data.

The first thing we'll want to do is insert our brands, since our product table depends on brand_id as a foreign key. We'll use the connection.executemany coroutine to write parameterized SQL to insert these brands. This will allow us to write one SQL query and pass in a list of parameters we want to insert instead of having to create one INSERT statement for each brand.

The executemany coroutine takes in one SQL statement and a list of tuples with values we'd like to insert. We can parameterize the SQL statement by using $1, $2 ... $N syntax. Each number after the dollar sign represents the index of the tuple we'd like to use in the SQL statement. For instance, if we have a query we write as "INSERT INTO table VALUES($1, $2)" and a list of tuples [('a', 'b'), ('c', 'd')] this would execute two inserts for us:

```
INSERT INTO table ('a', 'b')
INSERT INTO table ('c', 'd')
```

We'll first generate a list of 100 random brand names from our list of common words. We'll return this as a list of tuples each with one value inside of it, so we can use this in the executemany coroutine. Once we've created this list, it's a matter of passing a parameterized INSERT statement alongside this list of tuples.

Listing 5.5   Inserting random brands

```
import asyncpg
import asyncio
from typing import List, Tuple, Union
from random import sample


def load_common_words() -> List[str]:
    with open('common_words.txt') as common_words:
        return common_words.readlines()
```

```
def generate_brand_names(words: List[str]) -> List[Tuple[Union[str, ]]]:
    return [(words[index],) for index in sample(range(100), 100)]


async def insert_brands(common_words, connection) -> int:
    brands = generate_brand_names(common_words)
    insert_brands = "INSERT INTO brand VALUES(DEFAULT, $1)"
    return await connection.executemany(insert_brands, brands)


async def main():
    common_words = load_common_words()
    connection = await asyncpg.connect(host='127.0.0.1',
                                       port=5432,
                                       user='postgres',
                                       database='products',
                                       password='password')
    await insert_brands(common_words, connection)


asyncio.run(main())
```

Internally, executemany will loop through our brands list and generate one INSERT statement per each brand. Then it will execute all those insert statements at once. This method of parameterization will also prevent us from SQL injection attacks, as the input data is sanitized. Once we run this, we should have 100 brands in our system with random names.

Now that we've seen how to insert random brands, let's use the same technique to insert products and SKUs. For products, we'll create a description of 10 random words and a random brand ID. For SKUs, we'll pick a random size, color, and product. We'll assume that our brand ID starts at 1 and ends at 100.

Listing 5.6   Inserting random products and SKUs

```
import asyncio
import asyncpg
from random import randint, sample
from typing import List, Tuple
from chapter_05.listing_5_5 import load_common_words


def gen_products(common_words: List[str],
                 brand_id_start: int,
                 brand_id_end: int,
                 products_to_create: int) -> List[Tuple[str, int]]:
    products = []
    for _ in range(products_to_create):
        description = [common_words[index] for index in sample(range(1000), 10)]
        brand_id = randint(brand_id_start, brand_id_end)
        products.append((" ".join(description), brand_id))
    return products
```

```python
def gen_skus(product_id_start: int,
             product_id_end: int,
             skus_to_create: int) -> List[Tuple[int, int, int]]:
    skus = []
    for _ in range(skus_to_create):
        product_id = randint(product_id_start, product_id_end)
        size_id = randint(1, 3)
        color_id = randint(1, 2)
        skus.append((product_id, size_id, color_id))
    return skus


async def main():
    common_words = load_common_words()
    connection = await asyncpg.connect(host='127.0.0.1',
                                       port=5432,
                                       user='postgres',
                                       database='products',
                                       password='password')

    product_tuples = gen_products(common_words,
                                  brand_id_start=1,
                                  brand_id_end=100,
                                  products_to_create=1000)
    await connection.executemany("INSERT INTO product VALUES(DEFAULT, $1, $2)",
                                 product_tuples)

    sku_tuples = gen_skus(product_id_start=1,
                          product_id_end=1000,
                          skus_to_create=100000)
    await connection.executemany("INSERT INTO sku VALUES(DEFAULT, $1, $2, $3)",
                                 sku_tuples)

    await connection.close()


asyncio.run(main())
```

When we run this listing, we should have a database with 1,000 products and 100,000 SKUs. Depending on your machine, this may take several seconds to run. With a few joins, we can now query all available SKUs for a particular product. Let's see what this query would look like for product id 100:

```sql
product_query = \
"""
SELECT
p.product_id,
p.product_name,
p.brand_id,
s.sku_id,
pc.product_color_name,
ps.product_size_name
FROM product as p
JOIN sku as s on s.product_id = p.product_id
```

```
JOIN product_color as pc on pc.product_color_id = s.product_color_id
JOIN product_size as ps on ps.product_size_id = s.product_size_id
WHERE p.product_id = 100"""
```

When we execute this query, we'll get one row for each SKU for a product, and we'll also get the proper English name for size and color instead of an ID. Assuming we have a lot of product IDs we'd like to query at a given time, this provides us a good opportunity to apply concurrency. We may naively try to apply `asyncio.gather` with our existing connection like so:

```
async def main():
    connection = await asyncpg.connect(host='127.0.0.1',
                                       port=5432,
                                       user='postgres',
                                       database='products',
                                       password='password')
    print('Creating the product database...')
    queries = [connection.execute(product_query),
               connection.execute(product_query)]
    results = await asyncio.gather(*queries)
```

However, if we run this we'll be greeted with an error:

```
RuntimeError: readexactly() called while another coroutine is already waiting
    for incoming data
```

Why is this? In the SQL world, one connection means one socket connection to our database. Since we have only one connection and we're trying to read the results of multiple queries concurrently, we experience an error. We can resolve this by creating multiple connections to our database and executing one query per connection. Since creating connections is resource expensive, caching them so we can access them when needed makes sense. This is commonly known as a *connection pool.*

5.5.2 Creating a connection pool to run queries concurrently

Since we can only run one query per connection at a time, we need a mechanism for creating and managing multiple connections. A connection pool does just that. You can think of a connection pool as a cache of existing connections to a database instance. They contain a finite number of connections that we can access when we need to run a query.

Using connection pools, we *acquire* connections when we need to run a query. Acquiring a connection means we ask the pool, "Does the pool currently have any connections available? If so, give me one so I can run my queries." Connection pools facilitate the reuse of these connections to execute queries. In other words, once a connection is acquired from the pool to run a query and that query finishes, we return or "release" it to the pool for others to use. This is important because establishing a connection with a database is time-expensive. If we had to create a new connection for every query we wanted to run, our application's performance would quickly degrade.

Since the connection pool has a finite number of connections, we could be waiting for some time for one to become available, as other connections may be in use. This means connection acquisition is an operation that may take time to complete. If we only have 10 connections in the pool, each of which is in use, and we ask for another, we'll need to wait until 1 of the 10 connections becomes available for our query to execute.

To illustrate how this works in terms of asyncio, let's imagine we have a connection pool with two connections. Let's also imagine we have three coroutines and each runs a query. We'll run these three coroutines concurrently as tasks. With a connection pool set up this way, the first two coroutines that attempt to run their queries will acquire the two available connections and start running their queries. While this is happening, the third coroutine will be waiting for a connection to become available. When either one of the first two coroutines finishes running its query, it will release its connection and return it to the pool. This lets the third coroutine acquire it and start using it to run its query (figure 5.2).

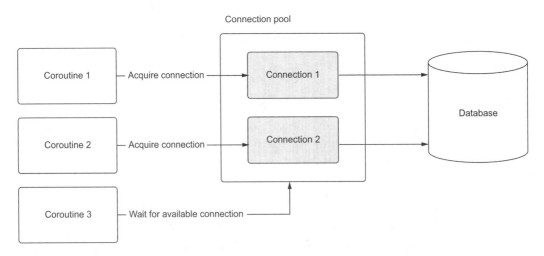

Figure 5.2   Coroutines 1 and 2 acquire connections to run their queries while Coroutine 3 waits for a connection. Once either Coroutine 1 or 2 finishes, Coroutine 3 will be able to use the newly released connection and will be able to execute its query.

In this model, we can have at most two queries running concurrently. Normally, the connection pool will be a bit bigger to enable more concurrency. For our examples, we'll use a connection pool of six, but the actual number you want to use is dependent on the hardware your database and your application run on. In this case, you'll need to benchmark which connection pool size works best. Keep in mind, bigger is not always better, but that's a much larger topic.

Now that we understand how connection pools work, how do we create one with asyncpg? asyncpg exposes a coroutine named `create_pool` to accomplish this. We use this instead of the `connect` function we used earlier to establish a connection to our database. When we call `create_pool`, we'll specify the number of connections we wish to create in the pool. We'll do this with the `min_size` and `max_size` parameters. The `min_size` parameter specifies the minimum number of connections in our connection pool. This means that once we set up our pool, we are guaranteed to have this number of connections inside of it already established. The `max_size` parameter specifies the maximum number of connections we want in our pool, determining the maximum number of connections we can have. If we don't have enough connections available, the pool will create a new one for us if the new connection won't cause the pool size to be above the value set in `max_size`. For our first example, we'll set both these values to six. This guarantees we always have six connections available.

asyncpg pools are *asynchronous context managers*, meaning that we must use `async with` syntax to create a pool. Once we've established a pool, we can acquire connections using the `acquire` coroutine. This coroutine will suspend execution until we have a connection available. Once we do, we can then use that connection to execute whatever SQL query we'd like. Acquiring a connection is also an async context manager that returns the connection to the pool when we are done with it, so we'll need to use `async with` syntax just like we did when we created the pool. Using this, we can rewrite our code to run several queries concurrently.

Listing 5.7 Establishing a connection pool and running queries concurrently

```
import asyncio
import asyncpg

product_query = \
    """
SELECT
p.product_id,
p.product_name,
p.brand_id,
s.sku_id,
pc.product_color_name,
ps.product_size_name
FROM product as p
JOIN sku as s on s.product_id = p.product_id
JOIN product_color as pc on pc.product_color_id = s.product_color_id
JOIN product_size as ps on ps.product_size_id = s.product_size_id
WHERE p.product_id = 100"""


async def query_product(pool):
    async with pool.acquire() as connection:
        return await connection.fetchrow(product_query)


async def main():
    async with asyncpg.create_pool(host='127.0.0.1',
                                   port=5432,
                                   user='postgres',
```

```
                                password='password',
                                database='products',        ┌ Create a
                                min_size=6,                 │ connection
                                max_size=6) as pool:   ◁────┤ pool with six
        await asyncio.gather(query_product(pool),          └ connections.
                             query_product(pool))  ◁──┐ Execute two
                                                      │ product queries
    asyncio.run(main())                               └ concurrently.
```

In the preceding listing, we first create a connection pool with six connections. We then create two query coroutine objects and schedule them to run concurrently with `asyncio.gather`. In our `query_product` coroutine, we first acquire a connection from the pool with `pool.acquire()`. This coroutine will then suspend running until a connection is available from the connection pool. We do this in an `async with` block; this will ensure that once we leave the block, the connection will be returned to the pool. This is important because if we don't do this we can run out of connections, and we'll end up with an application that hangs forever, waiting for a connection that will never become available. Once we've acquired a connection, we can then run our query as we did in previous examples.

We can expand this example to run 10,000 queries by creating 10,000 different query coroutine objects. To make this interesting, we'll write a version that runs the queries synchronously and compare how long things take.

Listing 5.8 Synchronous queries vs. concurrent

```
import asyncio
import asyncpg
from util import async_timed

product_query = \
    """
SELECT
p.product_id,
p.product_name,
p.brand_id,
s.sku_id,
pc.product_color_name,
ps.product_size_name
FROM product as p
JOIN sku as s on s.product_id = p.product_id
JOIN product_color as pc on pc.product_color_id = s.product_color_id
JOIN product_size as ps on ps.product_size_id = s.product_size_id
WHERE p.product_id = 100"""


async def query_product(pool):
    async with pool.acquire() as connection:
        return await connection.fetchrow(product_query)
```

```
@async_timed()
async def query_products_synchronously(pool, queries):
    return [await query_product(pool) for _ in range(queries)]


@async_timed()
async def query_products_concurrently(pool, queries):
    queries = [query_product(pool) for _ in range(queries)]
    return await asyncio.gather(*queries)


async def main():
    async with asyncpg.create_pool(host='127.0.0.1',
                                   port=5432,
                                   user='postgres',
                                   password='password',
                                   database='products',
                                   min_size=6,
                                   max_size=6) as pool:
        await query_products_synchronously(pool, 10000)
        await query_products_concurrently(pool, 10000)


asyncio.run(main())
```

In query_products_synchronously, we put an await in a list comprehension, which will force each call to query_product to run sequentially. Then, in query_products_concurrently we create a list of coroutines we want to run and then run them concurrently with gather. In the main coroutine, we then run our synchronous and concurrent version with 10,000 queries each. While the exact results can vary substantially based on your hardware, the concurrent version is nearly five times as fast as the serial version:

```
starting <function query_products_synchronously at 0x1219ea1f0> with args
    (<asyncpg.pool.Pool object at 0x12164a400>, 10000) {}
finished <function query_products_synchronously at 0x1219ea1f0> in 21.8274
    second(s)
starting <function query_products_concurrently at 0x1219ea310> with args
    (<asyncpg.pool.Pool object at 0x12164a400>, 10000) {}
finished <function query_products_concurrently at 0x1219ea310> in 4.8464
    second(s)
```

An improvement like this is significant, but there are still more improvements we can make if we need more throughput. Since our query is relatively fast, this code is a mixture of CPU-bound in addition to I/O-bound. In chapter 6, we'll see how to squeeze even more performance out of this setup.

So far, we've seen how to insert data into our database assuming we don't have any failures. But what happens if we are in the middle of inserting products, and we get a failure? We don't want an inconsistent state in our database, so this is where database transactions come into play. Next, we'll see how to use asynchronous context managers to acquire and manage transactions.

5.6   *Managing transactions with asyncpg*

Transactions are a core concept in many databases that satisfy the ACID (atomic, consistent, isolated, durable) properties. A *transaction* consists of one or more SQL statements that are executed as one atomic unit. If no errors occur when we execute the statements within a transaction, we *commit* the statements to the database, making any changes a permanent part of the database. If there are any errors, we *roll back* the statements, and it is as if none of them ever happened. In the context of our product database, we may need to roll back a set of updates if we attempt to insert a duplicate brand, or if we have violated a database constraint we've set.

In asyncpg, the easiest way to deal with transactions is to use the `connection` `.transaction` asynchronous context manager to start them. Then, if there is an exception in the `async with` block, the transaction will automatically be rolled back. If everything executes successfully, it will be automatically committed. Let's look at how to create a transaction and execute two simple `insert` statements to add a couple of brands.

Listing 5.9   Creating a transaction

```
import asyncio
import asyncpg


async def main():
    connection = await asyncpg.connect(host='127.0.0.1',
                                       port=5432,
                                       user='postgres',
                                       database='products',
                                       password='password')
    async with connection.transaction():
        await connection.execute("INSERT INTO brand "
                                 "VALUES(DEFAULT, 'brand_1')")
        await connection.execute("INSERT INTO brand "
                                 "VALUES(DEFAULT, 'brand_2')")

    query = """SELECT brand_name FROM brand
                  WHERE brand_name LIKE 'brand%'"""
    brands = await connection.fetch(query)
    print(brands)

    await connection.close()


asyncio.run(main())
```

Start a database transaction. → `async with connection.transaction():`

`brands = await connection.fetch(query)` ← **Select brands to ensure that our transaction was committed.**

Assuming our transaction committed successfully, we should see [<Record brand_name='brand_1'>, <Record brand_name='brand_2'>] printed out to the console. This example assumes zero errors running the two `insert` statements, and everything was committed successfully. To demonstrate what happens when a rollback occurs, let's force a SQL error. To test this out, we'll try and insert two brands with the same primary key `id`. Our first insert will work successfully, but our second insert will raise a duplicate key error.

Listing 5.10 Handling an error in a transaction

```
import asyncio
import logging
import asyncpg

async def main():
    connection = await asyncpg.connect(host='127.0.0.1',
                                       port=5432,
                                       user='postgres',
                                       database='products',
                                       password='password')
    try:
        async with connection.transaction():
            insert_brand = "INSERT INTO brand VALUES(9999, 'big_brand')"
            await connection.execute(insert_brand)
            await connection.execute(insert_brand)
    except Exception:
        logging.exception('Error while running transaction')
    finally:
        query = """SELECT brand_name FROM brand
                   WHERE brand_name LIKE 'big_%'"""
        brands = await connection.fetch(query)
        print(f'Query result was: {brands}')

        await connection.close()

asyncio.run(main())
```

If we had an exception, log the error.

This insert statement will error because of a duplicate primary key.

Select the brands to ensure we didn't insert anything.

In the following code, our second insert statement throws an error. This leads to the following output:

```
ERROR:root:Error while running transaction
Traceback (most recent call last):
  File "listing_5_10.py", line 16, in main
    await connection.execute("INSERT INTO brand "
  File "asyncpg/connection.py", line 272, in execute
    return await self._protocol.query(query, timeout)
  File "asyncpg/protocol/protocol.pyx", line 316, in query
asyncpg.exceptions.UniqueViolationError: duplicate key value violates unique
    constraint "brand_pkey"
DETAIL:  Key (brand_id)=(9999) already exists.
Query result was: []
```

We first retrieved an exception because we attempted to insert a duplicate key and then see that the result of our select statement was empty, indicating that we successfully rolled back the transaction.

5.6.1 *Nested transactions*

asyncpg also supports the concept of a *nested transaction* through a Postgres feature called *savepoints*. Savepoints are defined in Postgres with the SAVEPOINT command. When we define a savepoint, we can roll back to that savepoint and any queries executed after the savepoint will roll back, but any queries successfully executed before it will not roll back.

In asyncpg, we can create a savepoint by calling the `connection.transaction` context manager within an existing transaction. Then, if there is any error within this inner transaction it is rolled back, but the outer transaction is not affected. Let's try this out by inserting a brand in a transaction and then within a nested transaction attempting to insert a color that already exists in our database.

Listing 5.11   A nested transaction

```
import asyncio
import asyncpg
import logging


async def main():
    connection = await asyncpg.connect(host='127.0.0.1',
                                       port=5432,
                                       user='postgres',
                                       database='products',
                                       password='password')
    async with connection.transaction():
        await connection.execute("INSERT INTO brand VALUES(DEFAULT,
    'my_new_brand')")

        try:
            async with connection.transaction():
                await connection.execute("INSERT INTO product_color VALUES(1,
    'black')")
        except Exception as ex:
            logging.warning('Ignoring error inserting product color',
    exc_info=ex)

    await connection.close()


asyncio.run(main())
```

When we run this code, our first `INSERT` statement runs successfully, since we don't have this brand in our database yet. Our second `INSERT` statement fails with a duplicate key error. Since this second insert statement is within a transaction and we catch and log the exception, despite the error our outer transaction is not rolled back, and the brand is properly inserted. If we did not have the nested transaction, the second insert statement would have also rolled back our brand insert.

5.6.2   *Manually managing transactions*

So far, we have used asynchronous context managers to handle committing and rolling back our transactions. Since this is less verbose than managing things ourselves, it is usually the best approach. That said, we may find ourselves in situations where we need to manually manage a transaction. For example, we may want to have custom code execute on rollback, or we may want to roll back on a condition other than an exception.

To manually manage a transaction, we can use the transaction manager returned by `connection.transaction` outside of a context manager. When we do this, we'll manually need to call its `start` method to start a transaction and then `commit` on success and `rollback` on failure. Let's look at how to do this by rewriting our first example.

Listing 5.12 Manually managing a transaction

```
import asyncio
import asyncpg
from asyncpg.transaction import Transaction


async def main():
    connection = await asyncpg.connect(host='127.0.0.1',
                                        port=5432,
                                        user='postgres',
                                        database='products',
                                        password='password')      ⟵┐ Create a
                                                                     transaction
    transaction: Transaction = connection.transaction()  ⟵────────┘ instance.
    await transaction.start()
    try:
        await connection.execute("INSERT INTO brand "
                                 "VALUES(DEFAULT, 'brand_1')")
        await connection.execute("INSERT INTO brand "
                                 "VALUES(DEFAULT, 'brand_2')")
    except asyncpg.PostgresError:
        print('Errors, rolling back transaction!')
        await transaction.rollback()          ⟵──────── If there was an
    else:                                               exception, roll back.
        print('No errors, committing transaction!')
        await transaction.commit()            ⟵──────── If there was no
                                                         exception, commit.
    query = """SELECT brand_name FROM brand
                WHERE brand_name LIKE 'brand%'"""
    brands = await connection.fetch(query)
    print(brands)

    await connection.close()

asyncio.run(main())
```

Start the transaction. points to `await transaction.start()`

We first start by creating a transaction with the same method call we used with async context manager syntax, but instead, we store the `Transaction` instance that this call returns. Think of this class as a manager for our transaction, since with this we'll be able to perform any commits and rollbacks we need. Once we have a transaction instance, we can then call the `start` coroutine. This will execute a query to start the transaction in

Postgres. Then, within a `try` block we can execute any queries we'd like. In this case we insert two brands. If there were errors with any of those INSERT statements, we'll experience the `except` block and roll back the transaction by calling the `rollback` coroutine. If there were no errors, we call the `commit` coroutine, which will end the transaction and make any changes in our transaction permanent in the database.

Up until now we have been running our queries in a way that pulls all query results into memory at once. This makes sense for many applications, since many queries will return small result sets. However, we may have a situation where we are dealing with a large result set that may not fit in memory all at once. In these cases, we may want to stream results to avoid taxing our system's random access memory (RAM). Next, we'll explore how to do this with asyncpg and, along the way, introduce asynchronous generators.

5.7 Asynchronous generators and streaming result sets

One drawback of the default `fetch` implementation asynpg provides is that it pulls all data from any query we execute into memory. This means that if we have a query that returns millions of rows, we'd attempt to transfer that entire set from the database to the requesting machine. Going back to our product database example, imagine we're even more successful and have billions of products available. It is highly likely that we'll have some queries that will return very large result sets, potentially hurting performance.

Of course, we could apply LIMIT statements to our query and paginate things, and this makes sense for many, if not most, applications. That said, there is overhead with this approach in that we are sending the same query multiple times, potentially creating extra stress on the database. If we find ourselves hampered by these issues, it can make sense to stream results for a particular query only as we need them. This will save on memory consumption at our application layer as well as save load on the database. However, it does come at the expense of making more round trips over the network to the database.

Postgres supports streaming query results through the concept of *cursors*. Consider a cursor as a pointer to where we currently are in iterating through a result set. When we get a single result from a streamed query, we advance the cursor to the next element, and so on, until we have no more results.

Using asyncpg, we can get a cursor directly from a connection which we can then use to execute a streaming query. Cursors in asyncpg use an asyncio feature we have not used yet called *asynchronous generators*. Asynchronous generators generate results asynchronously one by one, similarly to regular Python generators. They also allow us to use a special `for` loop style syntax to iterate over any results we get. To fully understand how this works, we'll first introduce asynchronous generators as well as `async for` syntax to loop these generators.

5.7.1 Introducing asynchronous generators

Many developers will be familiar with generators from the synchronous Python world. Generators are an implementation of the iterator design pattern made famous in the book *Design Patterns: Elements of Reusable Object-Oriented Software* by the "gang of four" (Addison-Wesley Professional, 1994). This pattern allows us to define sequences of data "lazily" and iterate through them one element at a time. This is useful for potentially large sequences of data, where we don't need to store everything in memory all at once.

A simple synchronous generator is a normal Python function which contains a `yield` statement instead of a `return` statement. For example, let's see how creating and using a generator returns positive integers, starting from zero until a specified end.

Listing 5.13 A synchronous generator

```
def positive_integers(until: int):
    for integer in range(until):
        yield integer


positive_iterator = positive_integers(2)

print(next(positive_iterator))
print(next(positive_iterator))
```

In the preceding listing, we create a function which takes an integer that we want to count to. We then start a loop until our specified end integer. Then, at each iteration of the loop, we `yield` the next integer in the sequence. When we call `positive_integers(2)`, we don't return an entire list or even run the loop in our method. In fact, if we check the type of `positive_iterator`, we'll get `<class 'generator'>`.

We then use the `next` utility function to iterate over our generator. Each time we call `next`, this will trigger one iteration of the `for` loop in `positive_integers`, giving us the result of the `yield` statement per each iteration. Thus, the code in listing 5.13 will print 0 and 1 to the console. Instead of using `next`, we could have used a `for` loop with our generator to loop through all values in our generator.

This works for synchronous methods, but what if we wanted to use coroutines to generate a sequence of values asynchronously? Using our database example, what if we wanted to generate a sequence of rows that we "lazily" get from our database? We can do this with Python's asynchronous generators and special `async for` syntax. To demonstrate a simple asynchronous generator, let's start with our positive integer example but introduce a call to a coroutine that takes a few seconds to complete. We'll use the `delay` function from chapter 2 for this.

Listing 5.14 A simple asynchronous generator

```
import asyncio
from util import delay, async_timed
```

```
async def positive_integers_async(until: int):
    for integer in range(1, until):
        await delay(integer)
        yield integer


@async_timed()
async def main():
    async_generator = positive_integers_async(3)
    print(type(async_generator))
    async for number in async_generator:
        print(f'Got number {number}')


asyncio.run(main())
```

Running the preceding listing, we'll see the type is no longer a plain generator but `<class 'async_generator'>`, an asynchronous generator. An asynchronous generator differs from a regular generator in that, instead of generating plain Python objects as elements, it generates coroutines that we can then await until we get a result. Because of this, our normal for loops and next functions won't work with these types of generators. Instead, we have a special syntax, async for, to deal with these types of generators. In this example, we use this syntax to iterate over `positive_integers_async`.

This code will print the numbers 1 and 2, waiting 1 second before returning the first number and 2 seconds before returning the second. Note that this is not running the coroutines generated concurrently; instead, it is generating and awaiting them one at a time in a series.

5.7.2   *Using asynchronous generators with a streaming cursor*

The concept of asynchronous generators pairs nicely with the concept of a `streaming` database cursor. Using these generators, we'll be able to fetch one row at a time with a simple for loop-like syntax. To perform streaming with asyncpg, we'll first need to start a transaction, as Postgres requires this to use cursors. Once we've started a transaction, we can then call the cursor method on the Connection class to obtain a cursor. When we call the cursor method, we'll pass in the query we'd like to stream. This method will return an asynchronous generator that we can use to stream results one at a time.

To get familiar with how to do this, let's run a query to get all products from our database with a cursor. We'll then use async for syntax to fetch elements one at a time from our result set.

Listing 5.15   Streaming results one by one

```
import asyncpg
import asyncio
import asyncpg


async def main():
    connection = await asyncpg.connect(host='127.0.0.1',
```

```
                                    port=5432,
                                    user='postgres',
                                    database='products',
                                    password='password')

    query = 'SELECT product_id, product_name FROM product'
    async with connection.transaction():
        async for product in connection.cursor(query):
            print(product)

    await connection.close()


asyncio.run(main())
```

The preceding listing will print all our products out one at a time. Despite having put 1,000 products in this table, we'll only pull a few into memory at a time. At the time of writing, to cut down on network traffic the cursor defaults to prefetching 50 records at a time. We can change this behavior by setting the `prefetch` parameter with however many elements we'd like to prefetch.

We can also use these cursors to skip around our result set and fetch an arbitrary number of rows at a time. Let's see how to do this by getting a few records from the middle of the query we just used.

Listing 5.16 Moving the cursor and fetching records

```
import asyncpg
import asyncio


async def main():
    connection = await asyncpg.connect(host='127.0.0.1',
                                    port=5432,
                                    user='postgres',
                                    database='products',
                                    password='password')
    async with connection.transaction():
        query = 'SELECT product_id, product_name from product'
        cursor = await connection.cursor(query)
        await cursor.forward(500)
        products = await cursor.fetch(100)
        for product in products:
            print(product)

    await connection.close()


asyncio.run(main())
```

Create a cursor for the query.

Move the cursor forward 500 records.

Get the next 100 records.

The code in the preceding listing will first create a cursor for our query. Note that we use this in an `await` statement like a coroutine instead of an asynchronous generator; this is because in asyncpg a cursor is both an asynchronous generator *and* an awaitable. For the most part, this is similar to using an async generator, but there is a difference in prefetch behavior when creating a cursor this way. Using this method, we cannot set a prefetch value. Doing so would raise an `InterfaceError`.

Once we have the cursor, we use its `forward` coroutine method to move forward in the result set. This will effectively skip the first 500 records in our product table. Once we've moved our cursor forward, we then fetch the next 100 products and print them each out to the console.

These types of cursors are non-scrollable by default, meaning we can only advance forward in the result set. If you want to use scrollable cursors that can move both forwards and backwards, you'll need to execute the SQL to do so manually using `DECLARE ... SCROLL CURSOR` (you can read more on how to do this in the Postgres documentation at https://www.postgresql.org/docs/current/plpgsql-cursors.html).

Both techniques are useful if we have a really large result set and don't want to have the entire set residing in memory. The `async for` loops we saw in listing 5.16 are useful for looping over the entire set, while creating a cursor and using the `fetch` coroutine method is useful for fetching a chunk of records or skipping a set of records.

However, what if we only want to retrieve a fixed set of elements at a time with prefetching and still use an `async for` loop? We could add a counter in our `async for` loop and break out after we've seen a certain number of elements, but that isn't particularly reusable if we need to do this often in our code. What we can do to make this easier is build our own async generator. We'll call this generator `take`. This generator will take an async generator and the number of elements we wish to extract. Let's investigate creating this and grabbing the first five elements from a result set.

Listing 5.17   Getting a specific number of elements with an asynchronous generator

```
import asyncpg
import asyncio


async def take(generator, to_take: int):
    item_count = 0
    async for item in generator:
        if item_count > to_take - 1:
            return
        item_count = item_count + 1
        yield item


async def main():
    connection = await asyncpg.connect(host='127.0.0.1',
                                       port=5432,
                                       user='postgres',
                                       database='products',
                                       password='password')
    async with connection.transaction():
        query = 'SELECT product_id, product_name from product'
        product_generator = connection.cursor(query)
```

```
        async for product in take(product_generator, 5):
            print(product)

        print('Got the first five products!')

    await connection.close()


asyncio.run(main())
```

Our `take` async generator keeps track of how many items we've seen so far with `item_count`. We then enter an `async_for` loop and `yield` each record that we see. Once we `yield`, we check `item_count` to see if we have yielded the number of items the caller requested. If we have, we `return`, which ends the async generator. In our main coroutine, we can then use `take` within a normal async for loop. In this example, we use it to ask for the first five elements from the cursor, giving us the following output:

```
<Record product_id=1 product_name='among paper foot see shoe ride age'>
<Record product_id=2 product_name='major wait half speech lake won't'>
<Record product_id=3 product_name='war area speak listen horse past edge'>
<Record product_id=4 product_name='smell proper force road house planet'>
<Record product_id=5 product_name='ship many dog fine surface truck'>
Got the first five products!
```

While we've defined this in code ourselves, an open source library, *aiostream*, has this functionality and more for processing asynchronous generators. You can view the documentation for this library at aiostream.readthedocs.io.

Summary

In this chapter, we've learned the basics around creating and selecting records in Postgres using an asynchronous database connection. You should now be able to take this knowledge and create concurrent database clients.

- We've learned how to use asyncpg to connect to a Postgres database.
- We've learned how to use various asyncpg coroutines to create tables, insert records, and execute single queries.
- We've learned how to create a connection pool with asyncpg. This allows us to run multiple queries concurrently with asyncio's API methods such as `gather`. Using this we can potentially speed up our applications by running our queries in tandem.
- We've learned how to manage transactions with asyncpg. Transactions allow us to roll back any changes we make to a database as the result of a failure, keeping our database in a consistent state even when something unexpected happens.
- We've learned how to create asynchronous generators and how to use them for streaming database connections. We can use these two concepts together to work with large data sets that can't fit in memory all at once.

Handling CPU-bound work

This chapter covers

- The multiprocessing library
- Creating process pools to handle CPU-bound work
- Using `async` and `await` to manage CPU-bound work
- Using MapReduce to solve a CPU-intensive problem with asyncio
- Handling shared data between multiple processes with locks
- Improving the performance of work with both CPU- and I/O-bound operations

Until now, we've been focused on performance gains we can get with asyncio when running I/O-bound work concurrently. Running I/O-bound work is asyncio's bread and butter, and with the way we've written code so far, we need to be careful not to run any CPU-bound code in our coroutines. This seems like it severely limits asyncio, but the library is more versatile than just handling I/O-bound work.

asyncio has an API for interoperating with Python's multiprocessing library. This lets us use async await syntax as well as asyncio APIs with multiple processes.

Using this, we can get the benefits of the asyncio library even when using CPU-bound code. This allows us to achieve performance gains for CPU-intensive work, such as mathematical computations or data processing, letting us sidestep the global interpreter lock and take full advantage of a multicore machine.

In this chapter, we'll first learn about the multiprocessing module to become familiar with the concept of executing multiple processes. We'll then learn about *process pool executors* and how we can hook them into asyncio. We'll then take this knowledge and use it to solve a CPU-intensive problem with MapReduce. We'll also learn about managing shared states amongst multiple processes, and we'll introduce the concept of locking to avoid concurrency bugs. Finally, we'll look at how to use multiprocessing to improve the performance of an application that is both I/O- and CPU-bound as we saw in chapter 5.

6.1 Introducing the multiprocessing library

In chapter 1, we introduced the global interpreter lock. The global interpreter lock prevents more than one piece of Python bytecode from running in parallel. This means that for anything other than I/O-bound tasks, excluding some small exceptions, using multithreading won't provide any performance benefits, the way it would in languages such as Java and C++. It seems like we might be stuck with no solution for our parallelizable CPU-bound work in Python, but this is where the multiprocessing library provides a solution.

Instead of our parent process spawning threads to parallelize things, we instead spawn subprocesses to handle our work. Each subprocess will have its own Python interpreter and be subject to the GIL, but instead of one interpreter we'll have several, each with its own GIL. Assuming we run on a machine with multiple CPU cores, this means that we can parallelize any CPU-bound workload effectively. Even if we have more processes than cores, our operating system will use preemptive multitasking to allow our multiple tasks to run concurrently. This setup is both concurrent *and* parallel.

To get started with the multiprocessing library, let's start by running a couple of functions in parallel. We'll use a very simple CPU-bound function that counts from zero to a large number to examine how the API works as well as the performance benefits.

Listing 6.1 Two parallel processes with multiprocessing

```python
import time
from multiprocessing import Process


def count(count_to: int) -> int:
    start = time.time()
    counter = 0
    while counter < count_to:
        counter = counter + 1
    end = time.time()
```

```
        print(f'Finished counting to {count_to} in {end-start}')
        return counter
```

Create a process to run the countdown function.

```
if __name__ == "__main__":
    start_time = time.time()

    to_one_hundred_million = Process(target=count, args=(100000000,))   ◄─
    to_two_hundred_million = Process(target=count, args=(200000000,))
```

```
    to_one_hundred_million.start()     ◄─┐  Start the process. This
    to_two_hundred_million.start()       │  method returns instantly.
```

```
    to_one_hundred_million.join()      ◄─┐  Wait for the process to finish.
    to_two_hundred_million.join()        │  This method blocks until the
                                         │  process is done.
    end_time = time.time()
    print(f'Completed in {end_time-start_time}')
```

In the preceding listing, we create a simple count function which takes an integer and loops one by one until we count to the integer we pass in. We then create two processes, one to count to 100,000,000 and one to count to 200,000,000. The Process class takes in two arguments, a target which is the function name we wish to run in the process and args representing a tuple of arguments we wish to pass to the function. We then call the start method on each process. This method returns instantly and will start running the process. In this example we start both processes one after another. We then call the join method on each process. This will cause our main process to block until each process has finished. Without this, our program would exit almost instantly and terminate the subprocesses, as nothing would be waiting for their completion. Listing 6.1 runs both count functions concurrently; assuming we're running on a machine with at least two CPU cores, we should see a speedup. When this code runs on a 2.5 GHz 8-core machine, we achieve the following results:

```
Finished counting down from 100000000 in 5.3844
Finished counting down from 200000000 in 10.6265
Completed in 10.8586
```

In total, our countdown functions took a bit over 16 seconds, but our application finished in just under 11 seconds. This gives us a time savings over running sequentially of about 5 seconds. Of course, the results you see when you run this will be highly variable depending on your machine, but you should see something directionally equivalent to this.

Notice the addition of if __name__ == "__main__": to our application where we haven't before. This is a quirk of the multiprocessing library; if you don't add this you may receive the following error: An attempt has been made to start a new process before the current process has finished its bootstrapping phase. The reason this happens is to prevent others who may import your code from accidentally launching multiple processes.

This gives us a decent performance gain; however, it is awkward because we must call start and join for each process we start. We also don't know which process will complete first; if we want to do something like asyncio.as_completed and process results as they finish, we're out of luck. The join method also does not return the value our target function returns; in fact, currently there is no way to get the value our function returns without using shared inter-process memory!

This API will work for simple cases, but it clearly won't work if we have functions where we want to get the return value out or want to process results as soon as they come in. Luckily, process pools provide a way for us to deal with this.

6.2 Using process pools

In the previous example, we manually created processes and called their start and join methods to run and wait for them. We identified several issues with this approach, from code quality to not having the ability to access the results our process returned. The multiprocessing module has an API that lets us deal with this issue, called *process pools*.

Process pools are a concept similar to the connection pools that we saw in chapter 5. The difference in this case is that, instead of a collection of connections to a database, we create a collection of Python processes that we can use to run functions in parallel. When we have a CPU-bound function we wish to run in a process, we ask the pool directly to run it for us. Behind the scenes, this will execute this function in an available process, running it and returning the return value of that function. To see how a process pool works, let's create a simple one and run a few "hello world"-style functions with it.

Listing 6.2 Creating a process pool

```
from multiprocessing import Pool


def say_hello(name: str) -> str:
    return f'Hi there, {name}'


if __name__ == "__main__":
    with Pool() as process_pool:                                   ◀── Create a new process pool.
        hi_jeff = process_pool.apply(say_hello, args=('Jeff',))    ◀── Run say_hello with the argument 'Jeff' in a separate process and get the result.
        hi_john = process_pool.apply(say_hello, args=('John',))
        print(hi_jeff)
        print(hi_john)
```

In the preceding listing, we create a process pool using with Pool() as process_pool. This is a context manager because once we are done with the pool, we need to appropriately shut down the Python processes we created. If we don't do this, we run the risk of leaking processes, which can cause resource-utilization issues. When we instantiate this pool, it will automatically create Python processes equal to the number of CPU cores on the machine you're running on. You can determine the number of CPU cores you have in Python by running the `multiprocessing.cpu_count()` function. You can set the `processes` argument to any integer you'd like when you call `Pool()`. The default value is usually a good starting point.

Next, we use the `apply` method of the process pool to run our `say_hello` function in a separate process. This method looks similar to what we did previously with the `Process` class, where we passed in a target function and a tuple of arguments. The difference here is that we don't need to start the process or call `join` on it ourselves. We also get back the return value of our function, which we couldn't do in the previous example. Running this code, you should see the following printed out:

```
Hi there, Jeff
Hi there, John
```

This works, but there is a problem. The `apply` method blocks until our function completes. That means that, if each call to `say_hello` took 10 seconds, our entire program's run time would be about 20 seconds because we've run things sequentially, negating the point of running in parallel. We can solve this problem by using the process pool's `apply_async` method.

6.2.1   *Using asynchronous results*

In the previous example, each call to `apply` blocked until our function completed. This doesn't work if we want to build a truly parallel workflow. To work around this, we can use the `apply_async` method instead. This method returns an `AsyncResult` instantly and will start running the process in the background. Once we have an `AsyncResult`, we can use its `get` method to block and obtain the results of our function call. Let's take our `say_hello` example and adapt it to use asynchronous results.

Listing 6.3   **Using async results with process pools**

```python
from multiprocessing import Pool


def say_hello(name: str) -> str:
    return f'Hi there, {name}'


if __name__ == "__main__":
    with Pool() as process_pool:
        hi_jeff = process_pool.apply_async(say_hello, args=('Jeff',))
        hi_john = process_pool.apply_async(say_hello, args=('John',))
        print(hi_jeff.get())
        print(hi_john.get())
```

When we call `apply_async`, our two calls to `say_hello` start instantly in separate processes. Then, when we call the `get` method, our parent process will block until each process returns a value. This lets things run concurrently, but what if `hi_jeff` took 10 seconds, but `hi_john` only took one? In this case, since we call `get` on `hi_jeff` first, our program would block for 10 seconds before printing our hi_john message even though we were ready after only 1 second. If we want to respond to things as soon as they finish, we're left with an issue. What we really want is something like asyncio's as_completed in this instance. Next, let's see how to use process pool executors with asyncio, so we can address this issue.

6.3 *Using process pool executors with asyncio*

We've seen how to use process pools to run CPU-intensive operations concurrently. These pools are good for simple use cases, but Python offers an abstraction on top of multiprocessing's process pools in the concurrent.futures module. This module contains *executors* for both processes and threads that can be used on their own but also interoperate with asyncio. To get started, we'll learn the basics of ProcessPool-Executor, which is similar to ProcessPool. Then, we'll see how to hook this into asyncio, so we can use the power of its API functions, such as gather.

6.3.1 *Introducing process pool executors*

Python's process pool API is strongly coupled to processes, but multiprocessing is one of two ways to implement preemptive multitasking, the other being multithreading. What if we need to easily change the way in which we handle concurrency, seamlessly switching between processes and threads? If we want a design like this, we need to build an abstraction that encompasses the core of distributing work to a pool of resources that does not care if those resources are processes, threads, or some other construct.

The concurrent.futures module provides this abstraction for us with the Executor abstract class. This class defines two methods for running work asynchronously. The first is submit, which will take a callable and return a Future (note that this is not the same as asyncio futures but is part of the concurrent.futures module)—this is equivalent to the Pool.apply_async method we saw in the last section. The second is map. This method will take a callable and a list of function arguments and then execute each argument in the list asynchronously. It returns an iterator of the results of our calls similarly to asyncio.as_completed in that results are available once they complete. Executor has two concrete implementations: ProcessPool-Executor and ThreadPoolExecutor. Since we're using multiple processes to handle CPU-bound work, we'll focus on ProcessPoolExecutor. In chapter 7, we'll examine threads with ThreadPoolExecutor. To learn how a ProcessPoolExecutor works, we'll reuse our count example with a few small numbers and a few large numbers to show how results come in.

Listing 6.4 Process pool executors

```
import time
from concurrent.futures import ProcessPoolExecutor
```

```
def count(count_to: int) -> int:
    start = time.time()
    counter = 0
    while counter < count_to:
        counter = counter + 1
    end = time.time()
    print(f'Finished counting to {count_to} in {end - start}')
    return counter


if __name__ == "__main__":
    with ProcessPoolExecutor() as process_pool:
        numbers = [1, 3, 5, 22, 100000000]
        for result in process_pool.map(count, numbers):
            print(result)
```

Much like before, we create a `ProcessPoolExecutor` in context manager. The number of resources also defaults to the number of CPU cores our machine has, as process pools did. We then use `process_pool.map` with our `count` function and a list of numbers that we want to count to.

When we run this, we'll see that our calls to countdown with a low number will finish quickly and be printed out nearly instantly. Our call with `100000000` will, however, take much longer and will be printed out after the few small numbers, giving us the following output:

```
Finished counting down from 1 in 9.5367e-07
Finished counting down from 3 in 9.5367e-07
Finished counting down from 5 in 9.5367e-07
Finished counting down from 22 in 3.0994e-06
1
3
5
22
Finished counting down from 100000000 in 5.2097
100000000
```

While it seems that this works the same as `asyncio.as_completed`, the order of iteration is deterministic based on the order we passed in the `numbers` list. This means that if `100000000` was our first number, we'd be stuck waiting for that call to finish before we could print out the other results that completed earlier. This means we aren't quite as responsive as `asyncio.as_completed`.

6.3.2 *Process pool executors with the asyncio event loop*

Now that we've know the basics of how process pool executors work, let's see how to hook them into the asyncio event loop. This will let us use the API functions such as `gather` and `as_completed` that we learned of in chapter 4 to manage multiple processes.

Creating a process pool executor to use with asyncio is no different from what we just learned; that is, we create one in within a context manager. Once we have a pool, we can use a special method on the asyncio event loop called run_in_executor. This method will take in a callable alongside an executor (which can be either a thread pool or process pool) and will run that callable inside the pool. It then returns an awaitable, which we can use in an await statement or pass into an API function such as gather.

Let's implement our previous count example with a process pool executor. We'll submit multiple count tasks to the executor and wait for them all to finish with gather. run_in_executor only takes a callable and does not allow us to supply function arguments; so, to get around this, we'll use partial function application to build countdown calls with 0 arguments.

What is partial function application?

Partial function application is implemented in the functools module. Partial application takes a function that accepts some arguments and turns it into a function that accepts fewer arguments. It does this by "freezing" some arguments that we supply. As an example, our count function takes one argument. We can turn it into a function with 0 arguments by using functools.partial with the parameter we want to call it with. If we want to have a call to count(42) but pass in no arguments we can say call_with_42 = functools.partial(count, 42) that we can then call as call_with_42().

Listing 6.5   Process pool executors with asyncio

```
import asyncio
from asyncio.events import AbstractEventLoop
from concurrent.futures import ProcessPoolExecutor
from functools import partial
from typing import List


def count(count_to: int) -> int:
    counter = 0
    while counter < count_to:
        counter = counter + 1
    return counter


async def main():
    with ProcessPoolExecutor() as process_pool:
        loop: AbstractEventLoop = asyncio.get_running_loop()       ⟵─── Create a partially applied function for countdown with its argument.
        nums = [1, 3, 5, 22, 100000000]
        calls: List[partial[int]] = [partial(count, num) for num in nums]   ⟵─── Submit each call to the process pool and append it to a list.
        call_coros = []

        for call in calls:
            call_coros.append(loop.run_in_executor(process_pool, call))

        results = await asyncio.gather(*call_coros)       ⟵─── Wait for all results to finish.
```

```
        for result in results:
            print(result)


if __name__ == "__main__":
    asyncio.run(main())
```

We first create a process pool executor, as we did before. Once we have this, we get the asyncio event loop, since run_in_executor is a method on the `AbstractEventLoop`. We then partially apply each number in nums to the count function, since we can't call count directly. Once we have count function calls, then we can submit them to the executor. We loop over these calls, calling `loop.run_in_executor` for each partially applied count function and keep track of the awaitable it returns in call_coros. We then take this list and wait for everything to finish with `asyncio.gather`.

If we had wanted, we could also use `asyncio.as_completed` to get the results from the subprocesses as they completed. This would solve the problem we saw earlier with process pool's map method, where if we had a task it took a long time.

We've now seen all we need to start using process pools with asyncio. Next, let's look at how to improve the performance of a real-world problem with multiprocessing and asyncio.

6.4   *Solving a problem with MapReduce using asyncio*

To understand the type of problem we can solve with MapReduce, we'll introduce a hypothetical real-world problem. We'll then take that understanding and use it to solve a similar problem with a large, freely available data set.

Going back to our example of an e-commerce storefront from chapter 5, we'll pretend our site receives a lot of text data through our customer support portal's *questions and concerns* field. Since our site is successful, this data set of customer feedback is multiple terabytes in size and growing every day.

To better understand the common issues our users are facing, we've been tasked to find the most frequently used words in this data set. A simple solution would be to use a single process to loop through each comment and keep track of how many times each word occurs. This will work, but since our data is large, going through this in serial could take a long time. Is there a faster way we could approach this type of problem?

This is the exact kind of problem that MapReduce can solve. The MapReduce programming model solves a problem by first partitioning up a large data set into smaller chunks. We can then solve our problem for that smaller subset of data instead of entire set—this is known as *mapping*, as we "map" our data to a partial result.

Once the problem for each subset is solved, we can then combine the results into a final answer. This step is known as *reducing*, as we "reduce" multiple answers into one. Counting the frequency of words in a large text data set is a canonical MapReduce problem. If we have a large enough dataset, splitting it into smaller chunks can yield performance benefits as each map operation can run in parallel, as shown in figure 6.1.

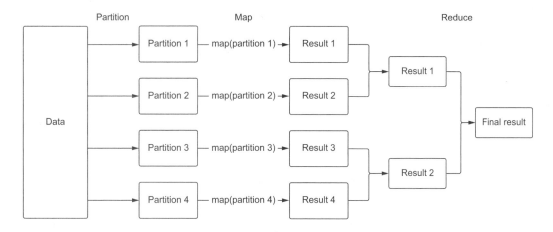

Figure 6.1 A large set of data is split into partitions, then a map function produces intermediate results. These intermediate results are combined into a result.

Systems such as Hadoop and Spark exist to perform MapReduce operations in a cluster of computers for truly large datasets. However, many smaller workloads can be processed on one computer with multiprocessing. In this section, we'll see how to implement a MapReduce workflow with multiprocessing to find how frequently certain words have appeared in literature since the year 1500.

6.4.1 A simple MapReduce example

To fully understand how MapReduce works, let's walk through a concrete example. Let's say we have text data on each line of a file. For this example, we'll pretend we have four lines to handle:

```
I know what I know.
I know that I know.
I don't know that much.
They don't know much.
```

We'd like to count how many times each distinct word occurs in this data set. This example is small enough that we could solve it with a simple `for` loop, but let's approach it using a MapReduce model.

First, we need to partition this data set into smaller chunks. For simplicity, we'll define a smaller chunk as one line of text. Next, we need to define the mapping operation. Since we want to count word frequencies, we'll split the line of text on a space. This will get us an array of each individual word in the string. We can then loop over this, keeping track of each distinct word in the line of text in a dictionary.

Finally, we need to define a *reduce* operation. This will take one or more results from our map operation and combine them into an answer. In this example, we need to take two dictionaries from our map operation and combine them into one. If a word exists in both dictionaries, we add their word counts together; if not, we copy over the word count to the result dictionary. Once we've defined these operations, we can then run our map operation on each individual line of text and our reduce operation on each pair of results from our map. Let's see how to do this example in code with the four lines of text we introduced earlier.

Listing 6.6   Single-threaded MapReduce

```
import functools
from typing import Dict


def map_frequency(text: str) -> Dict[str, int]:
    words = text.split(' ')
    frequencies = {}
    for word in words:
        if word in frequencies:
            frequencies[word] = frequencies[word] + 1
        else:
            frequencies[word] = 1
    return frequencies

def merge_dictionaries(first: Dict[str, int],
                       second: Dict[str, int]) -> Dict[str, int]:
    merged = first
    for key in second:
        if key in merged:
            merged[key] = merged[key] + second[key]
        else:
            merged[key] = second[key]
    return merged

lines = ["I know what I know",
         "I know that I know",
         "I don't know much",
         "They don't know much"]

mapped_results = [map_frequency(line) for line in lines]

for result in mapped_results:
    print(result)

print(functools.reduce(merge_dictionaries, mapped_results))
```

- **If we have the word in our frequency dictionary, add one to the count.**
- **If we do not have the word in our frequency dictionary, set its count to one.**
- **If the word is in both dictionaries, combine frequency counts.**
- **If the word is not in both dictionaries, copy over the frequency count.**
- **For each line of text, perform our map operation.**
- **Reduce all our intermediate frequency counts into one result.**

For each line of text, we apply our map operation, giving us the frequency count for each line of text. Once we have these mapped partial results, we can begin to combine them. We use our merge function merge_dictionaries along with the functools .reduce function. This will take our intermediate results and add them together into one result, giving us the following output:

```
Mapped results:
{'I': 2, 'know': 2, 'what': 1}
{'I': 2, 'know': 2, 'that': 1}
{'I': 1, "don't": 1, 'know': 1, 'much': 1}
{'They': 1, "don't": 1, 'know': 1, 'much': 1}

Final Result:
{'I': 5, 'know': 6, 'what': 1, 'that': 1, "don't": 2, 'much': 2, 'They': 1}
```

Now that we understand the basics of MapReduce with a sample problem, we'll see how to apply this to a real-world data set where multiprocessing can yield performance improvements.

6.4.2 *The Google Books Ngram dataset*

We'll need a sufficiently large set of data to process to see the benefits of MapReduce with multiprocessing. If our dataset is too small, we'll see no benefit from Map-Reduce and will likely see performance degradation from the overhead of managing processes. A data set of a few uncompressed should be enough for us to show a meaningful performance gain.

The Google Books Ngram dataset is a sufficiently large data set for this purpose. To understand what this data set is, we'll first define what an n-gram is.

An *n-gram* is a concept from natural language processing and is a phrase of N words from a sample of given text. The phrase "the fast dog" has six n-grams. Three 1-grams or *unigrams,* each of one single word (*the, fast,* and *dog*), two 2-grams or *digrams* (*the fast* and *fast dog*), and one 3-gram or *trigram* (*the fast dog*).

The Google Books Ngram dataset is a scan of n-grams from a set of over 8,000,000 books, going back to the year 1500, comprising more than six percent of all books published. It counts the number of times a distinct n-gram appears in text, grouped by the year it appears. This data set has everything from unigrams to 5-grams in tab-separated format. Each line of this data set has an n-gram, the year when it was seen, the number of times it was seen, and how many books it occurred in. Let's look at the first few entries in the unigram dataset for the word *aardvark*:

```
Aardvark    1822    2     1
Aardvark    1824    3     1
Aardvark    1827    10    7
```

This means that in the year 1822, the word *aardvark* appeared twice in one book. Then, in 1827, the word *aardvark* appeared ten times in seven different books. The dataset has many more entries for *aardvark* (for example, aardvark occurred 1,200 times in 2007), demonstrating the upwards trajectory of aardvarks in literature over the years.

For the sake of this example, we'll count the occurrences of single words (unigrams) for words that start with *a.* This dataset is approximately 1.8 GB in size. We'll aggregate this to the number of times each word has been seen in literature since 1500.

We'll use this to answer the question, "How many times has the word *aardvark* appeared in literature since the year 1500?" The relevant file we want to work with is downloadable at https://storage.googleapis.com/books/ngrams/books/googlebooks-eng-all-1gram-20120701-a.gz or at https://mattfowler.io/data/googlebooks-eng-all-1gram-20120701-a.gz. You can also download any other part of the dataset from http://storage.googleapis.com/books/ngrams/books/datasetsv2.html.

6.4.3   *Mapping and reducing with asyncio*

To have a baseline to compare to, let's first write a synchronous version to count the frequencies of words. We'll then use this frequency dictionary to answer the question, "How many times has the word *aardvark* appeared in literature since 1500?" We'll first load the entire contents of the dataset into memory. Then we can use a dictionary to keep track of a mapping of words to the total time they have occurred. For each line of our file, if the word on that line is in our dictionary, we add to the count in our dictionary with the count for that word. If it is not, we add the word and the count on that line to the dictionary.

Listing 6.7   Counting frequencies of words that start with *a*

```
import time

freqs = {}

with open('googlebooks-eng-all-1gram-20120701-a', encoding='utf-8') as f:
    lines = f.readlines()

    start = time.time()

    for line in lines:
        data = line.split('\t')
        word = data[0]
        count = int(data[2])
        if word in freqs:
            freqs[word] = freqs[word] + count
        else:
            freqs[word] = count

    end = time.time()
    print(f'{end-start:.4f}')
```

To test how long the CPU-bound operation takes, we'll time how long the frequency counting takes and won't include the length of time needed to load the file. For multiprocessing to be a viable solution, we need to run on a machine with sufficient CPU cores to make parallelization worth the effort. To see sufficient gains, we'll likely need a machine with more CPUs than most laptops have. To test on such a machine, we'll use a large Elastic Compute Cloud (EC2) instance on Amazon Web Servers (AWS).

AWS is a cloud computing service run by Amazon. AWS is a collection of cloud services that enable users to handle tasks from file storage to large-scale machine learning jobs—all without managing their own physical servers. One such service offered is EC2. Using this, you can rent a virtual machine in AWS to run any application you want, specifying how many CPU cores and memory you need on your virtual machine. You can learn more about AWS and EC2 at https://aws.amazon.com/ec2.

We'll test on a c5ad.8xlarge instance. At the time of writing, this machine has 32 CPU cores, 64 GB of RAM, and a solid-state drive, or SSD. On this instance, listing 6.7's script requires approximately 76 seconds. Let's see if we can do any better with multiprocessing and asyncio. If you run this on a machine with fewer CPU cores or other resources, your results may vary.

Our first step is to take our data set and partition it into a smaller set of chunks. Let's define a partition generator which can take our large list of data and grab chunks of arbitrary size.

```
def partition(data: List,
              chunk_size: int) -> List:
    for i in range(0, len(data), chunk_size):
        yield data[i:i + chunk_size]
```

We can use this partition generator to create slices of data that are chunk_size long. We'll use this to generate the data to pass into our map functions, which we will then run in parallel. Next, let's define our map function. This is almost the same as our map function from the previous example, adjusted to work with our data set.

```
def map_frequencies(chunk: List[str]) -> Dict[str, int]:
    counter = {}
    for line in chunk:
        word, _, count, _ = line.split('\t')
        if counter.get(word):
            counter[word] = counter[word] + int(count)
        else:
            counter[word] = int(count)
    return counter
```

For now, we'll keep our reduce operation, as in the previous example. We now have all the blocks we need to parallelize our map operations. We'll create a process pool, partition our data into chunks, and for each partition run map_frequencies in a resource ("worker") on the pool. We have almost everything we need, but one question remains: what partition size should I use?

There isn't an easy answer for this. One rule of thumb is the *Goldilocks approach*; that is, the partition should not be too big or too small. The reason the partition size should not be small is that when we create our partitions they are serialized ("pickled") and sent to our worker processes, then the worker process unpickles them. The process of serializing and deserializing this data can take up a significant amount of time, quickly eating into any performance gains if we do it too often. For example, a chunk size of two would be a poor choice as we would have nearly 1,000,000 pickle and unpickle operations.

We also don't want the partition size to be too large; otherwise, we might not fully utilize the power of our machine. For example, if we have 10 CPU cores but only create two partitions, we're missing out on eight cores that could run workloads in parallel.

For this example, we'll chose a partition size of 60,000, as this seems to offer reasonable performance for the AWS machine we're using based on benchmarking. If you're considering this approach for your data processing task, you'll need to test out a few different partition sizes to find the one for your data and the machine you're running on, or develop a heuristic algorithm for determining the right partition size. We can now combine all these parts together with a process pool and the event loop's run_in_executor coroutine to parallelize our map operations.

Listing 6.8   Parallel MapReduce with process pools

```python
import asyncio
import concurrent.futures
import functools
import time
from typing import Dict, List


def partition(data: List,
              chunk_size: int) -> List:
    for i in range(0, len(data), chunk_size):
        yield data[i:i + chunk_size]


def map_frequencies(chunk: List[str]) -> Dict[str, int]:
    counter = {}
    for line in chunk:
        word, _, count, _ = line.split('\t')
        if counter.get(word):
            counter[word] = counter[word] + int(count)
        else:
            counter[word] = int(count)
    return counter


def merge_dictionaries(first: Dict[str, int],
                       second: Dict[str, int]) -> Dict[str, int]:
    merged = first
    for key in second:
        if key in merged:
            merged[key] = merged[key] + second[key]
        else:
            merged[key] = second[key]
    return merged


async def main(partition_size: int):
    with open('googlebooks-eng-all-1gram-20120701-a', encoding='utf-8') as f:
        contents = f.readlines()
```

```
        loop = asyncio.get_running_loop()
        tasks = []
        start = time.time()
        with concurrent.futures.ProcessPoolExecutor() as pool:
            for chunk in partition(contents, partition_size):
                tasks.append(loop.run_in_executor(pool,
    functools.partial(map_frequencies, chunk)))
```

For each partition, run our map operation in a separate process.

```
        intermediate_results = await asyncio.gather(*tasks)
        final_result = functools.reduce(merge_dictionaries,
        intermediate_results)
```

Wait for all map operations to complete.

Reduce all our intermediate map results into a result.

```
        print(f"Aardvark has appeared {final_result['Aardvark']} times.")

        end = time.time()
        print(f'MapReduce took: {(end - start):.4f} seconds')


if __name__ == "__main__":
    asyncio.run(main(partition_size=60000))
```

In the main coroutine we create a process pool and partition the data. For each partition, we launch a map_frequencies function in a separate process. We then use asyncio.gather to wait for all intermediate dictionaries to finish. Once all our map operations are complete, we run our reduce operation to produce our result.

Running this on the instance we described, this code completes in roughly 18 seconds, delivering a significant speedup compared with our serial version. This is quite a nice performance gain for not a whole lot more code! You may also wish to experiment with a machine with more CPU cores to see if you can further improve the performance of this algorithm.

You may notice in this implementation that we still have some CPU-bound work happening in our parent process that is parallelizable. Our reduce operation takes thousands of dictionaries and combines them together. We can apply the partitioning logic we used on the original data set and split these dictionaries into chunks and combine them across multiple processes. Let's write a new reduce function that does that. In this function, we'll partition the list and call reduce on each chunk in a worker process. Once this completes, we'll keep partitioning and reducing until we have one dictionary remaining. (In this listing, we've removed the partition, map, and merge functions for brevity.)

Listing 6.9 Parallelizing the reduce operation

```
import asyncio
import concurrent.futures
import functools
import time
from typing import Dict, List
from chapter_06.listing_6_8 import partition, merge_dictionaries,
    map_frequencies
```

```
async def reduce(loop, pool, counters, chunk_size) -> Dict[str, int]:
    chunks: List[List[Dict]] = list(partition(counters, chunk_size))
    reducers = []
    while len(chunks[0]) > 1:
        for chunk in chunks:
            reducer = functools.partial(functools.reduce,
                merge_dictionaries, chunk)
            reducers.append(loop.run_in_executor(pool, reducer))
        reducer_chunks = await asyncio.gather(*reducers)
        chunks = list(partition(reducer_chunks, chunk_size))
        reducers.clear()
    return chunks[0][0]
```

Partition the dictionaries into parallelizable chunks.

Reduce each partition into a single dictionary.

Wait for all reduce operations to complete.

Partition the results again, and start a new iteration of the loop.

```
async def main(partition_size: int):
    with open('googlebooks-eng-all-1gram-20120701-a', encoding='utf-8') as f:
        contents = f.readlines()
        loop = asyncio.get_running_loop()
        tasks = []
        with concurrent.futures.ProcessPoolExecutor() as pool:
            start = time.time()

            for chunk in partition(contents, partition_size):
                tasks.append(loop.run_in_executor(pool,
        functools.partial(map_frequencies, chunk)))

            intermediate_results = await asyncio.gather(*tasks)
            final_result = await reduce(loop, pool, intermediate_results, 500)

            print(f"Aardvark has appeared {final_result['Aardvark']} times.")

            end = time.time()
            print(f'MapReduce took: {(end - start):.4f} seconds')


if __name__ == "__main__":
    asyncio.run(main(partition_size=60000))
```

If we run this parallelized reduce, we may see some small performance gain or only a small gain, depending on the machine you run on. In this instance, the overhead of pickling the intermediate dictionaries and sending them to the children processes will eat away much of the time savings by running in parallel. This optimization may not do much to make this problem less troublesome; however, if our reduce operation was more CPU-intensive, or we had a much larger data set, this approach can yield benefits.

Our multiprocessing approach has clear performance benefits over a synchronous approach, but right now there isn't an easy way to see how many map operations we've completed at any given time. In the synchronous version, we would only need to add a counter we incremented for every line we processed to see how far along we were. Since multiple processes by default do not share any memory, how can we create a counter to track our job's progress?

6.5   *Shared data and locks*

In chapter 1, we discussed the fact that, in multiprocessing, each process has its own memory, separate from other processes. This presents a challenge when we have shared state to keep track of. So how can we share data between processes if their memory spaces are all distinct?

Multiprocessing supports a concept called *shared memory objects*. A shared memory object is a chunk of memory allocated that a set of separate processes can access. Each process, as shown in figure 6.2, can then read and write into that memory space as needed.

Shared state is complicated and can lead to hard-to-reproduce bugs if not properly implemented. Generally, it is best to avoid shared state if possible. That said, sometimes it is necessary to introduce shared state. One such instance is a shared counter.

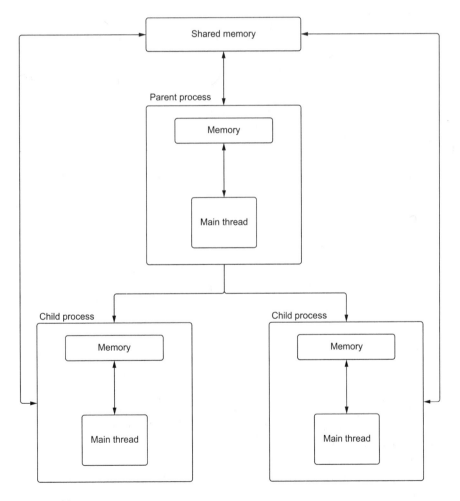

Figure 6.2   A parent process with two children processes, all sharing memory

To learn more about shared data, we'll take our MapReduce example from above and keep a counter of how many map operations we've completed. We'll then periodically output this number to show how far along we are to the user.

6.5.1   *Sharing data and race conditions*

Multiprocessing supports two kinds of shared data: values and array. A *value* is a singular value, such as an integer or floating-point number. An *array* is an array of singular values. The types of data that we can share in memory are limited by the types defined in the Python array module, available at https://docs.python.org/3/library/array .html#module-array.

To create a value or array, we first need to use the typecode from the array module that is just a character. Let's create two shared pieces of data—one integer value and one integer array. We'll then create two processes to increment each of these shared pieces of data in parallel.

Listing 6.10   Shared values and arrays

```python
from multiprocessing import Process, Value, Array


def increment_value(shared_int: Value):
    shared_int.value = shared_int.value + 1


def increment_array(shared_array: Array):
    for index, integer in enumerate(shared_array):
        shared_array[index] = integer + 1


if __name__ == '__main__':
    integer = Value('i', 0)
    integer_array = Array('i', [0, 0])

    procs = [Process(target=increment_value, args=(integer,)),
             Process(target=increment_array, args=(integer_array,))]

    [p.start() for p in procs]
    [p.join() for p in procs]

    print(integer.value)
    print(integer_array[:])
```

In the preceding listing, we create two processes—one to increment our shared integer value and one to increment each element in our shared array. Once our two subprocesses complete, we print out the data.

Since our two pieces of data are never touched by different processes, this code works well. Will this code continue to work if we have multiple processes modifying the same shared data? Let's test this out by creating two processes to increment a shared integer value in parallel. We'll run this code repeatedly in a loop to see if we get consistent results. Since we have two processes, each incrementing a shared counter by one, once the processes finish we expect the shared value to always be two.

Listing 6.11   Incrementing a shared counter in parallel

```
from multiprocessing import Process, Value

def increment_value(shared_int: Value):
    shared_int.value = shared_int.value + 1

if __name__ == '__main__':
    for _ in range(100):
        integer = Value('i', 0)
        procs = [Process(target=increment_value, args=(integer,)),
                 Process(target=increment_value, args=(integer,))]

        [p.start() for p in procs]
        [p.join() for p in procs]
        print(integer.value)
        assert(integer.value == 2)
```

While you will see different output because this problem is nondeterministic, at some point you should see that the result isn't always 2.

```
2
2
2
Traceback (most recent call last):
  File "listing_6_11.py", line 17, in <module>
    assert(integer.value == 2)
AssertionError
1
```

Sometimes our result is 1! Why is this? What we've encountered is called a *race condition*. A race condition occurs when the outcome of a set of operations is dependent on which operation finishes first. You can imagine the operations as racing against one another; if the operations win the race in the right order, everything works fine. If they win the race in the wrong order, bizarre behavior results.

So where is the race occurring in our example? The problem lies in that incrementing a value involves both read and write operations. To increment a value, we first need to read the value, add one to it, then write the result back to memory. The value each process sees in the shared data is entirely dependent on when it reads the shared value.

If the processes run in the following order, everything works fine, as seen in figure 6.3.

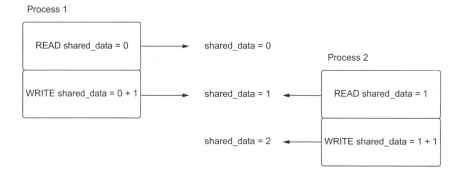

Figure 6.3 Successfully avoiding a race condition

In this example, Process 1 increments the value just before Process 2 reads it and wins the race. Since Process 2 finishes second, this means that it will see the correct value of one and will add to it, producing the correct final value.

What happens if there is a tie in our virtual race? Look at figure 6.4.

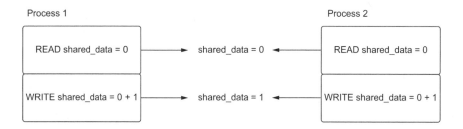

Figure 6.4 A race condition

In this instance, Processes 1 and 2 both read the initial value of zero. They then increment that value to 1 and write it back at the same time, producing the incorrect value.

You may ask, "But our code is only one line. Why are there two operations!?" Under the hood, incrementing is written as two operations, which causes this issue. This makes it *non-atomic* or not *thread-safe*. This isn't easy to figure out. An explanation of which operations are atomic and which operations are non-atomic is available at http://mng.bz/5Kj4.

These types of errors are tricky because they are often difficult to reproduce. They aren't like normal bugs, since they depend on the order in which our operating system runs things, which is out of our control when we use multiprocessing. So how do we fix this nasty bug?

6.5.2 *Synchronizing with locks*

We can avoid race conditions by *synchronizing* access to any shared data we want to modify. What does it mean to synchronize access? Revisiting our race example, it means that we control access to any shared data so that any operations we have finish the race in an order that makes sense. If we're in a situation where a tie between two operations could occur, we explicitly block the second operation from running until the first completes, guaranteeing operations to finish the race in a consistent manner. You can imagine this as a referee at the finish line, seeing that a tie is about to happen and telling the runners, "Hold up a minute. One racer at a time!" and picking one runner to wait while the other crosses the finish line.

One mechanism for synchronizing access to shared data is a *lock*, also known as a *mutex* (short for *mutual exclusion*). These structures allow for a single process to "lock" a section of code, preventing other processes from running that code. The locked section of code is commonly called a *critical section*. This means that if one process is executing the code of a locked section and a second process tries to access that code, the second process will need to wait (blocked by the referee) until the first process is finished with the locked section.

Locks support two primary operations: *acquiring* and *releasing*. When a process acquires a lock, it is guaranteed that it will be the only process running that section of code. Once the section of code that needs synchronized access is finished, we release the lock. This allows other processes to acquire the lock and run any code in the critical section. If a process tries to run code that is locked by another process, acquiring the lock will block until the other process releases that lock.

Revisiting our counter race condition example, and using figure 6.5, let's visualize what happens when two processes try and acquire a lock at roughly the same time. Then, let's see how it prevents the counter from getting the wrong value.

In this diagram, Process 1 first acquires the lock successfully and reads and increments the shared data. The second process tries to acquire the lock but is blocked from advancing further until the first process releases the lock. Once the first process releases the lock, the second process can successfully acquire the lock and increment the shared data. This prevents the race condition because the lock prevents more than one process from reading and writing the shared data at the same time.

So how do we implement this synchronization with our shared data? The multiprocessing API implementors thought of this and nicely included a method to get a lock on both value and array. To acquire a lock, we call `get_lock().acquire()` and to release a lock we call `get_lock().release()`. Using listing 6.12, let's apply this to our previous example to fix our bug.

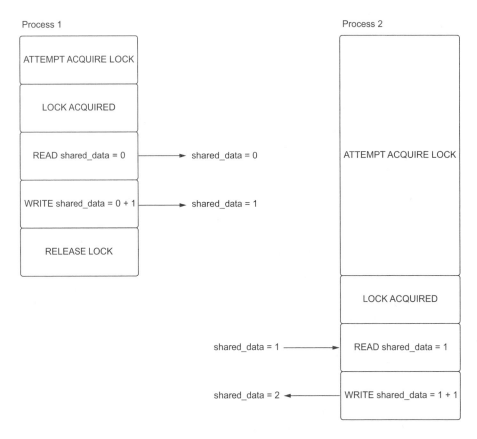

Figure 6.5   Process 2 is blocked from reading shared data until Process 1 releases the lock.

Listing 6.12   Acquiring and releasing a lock

```
from multiprocessing import Process, Value

def increment_value(shared_int: Value):
    shared_int.get_lock().acquire()
    shared_int.value = shared_int.value + 1
    shared_int.get_lock().release()

if __name__ == '__main__':
    for _ in range(100):
        integer = Value('i', 0)
        procs = [Process(target=increment_value, args=(integer,)),
                 Process(target=increment_value, args=(integer,))]

        [p.start() for p in procs]
        [p.join() for p in procs]
        print(integer.value)
        assert (integer.value == 2)
```

When we run this code, every value we get should be 2. We've fixed our race condition! Note that locks are also context managers, and to clean up our code we could have written increment_value using a with block. This will acquire and release the lock for us automatically:

```
def increment_value(shared_int: Value):
    with shared_int.get_lock():
        shared_int.value = shared_int.value + 1
```

Notice that we have taken concurrent code and have just forced it to be sequential, negating the value of running in parallel. This is an important observation and is a caveat of synchronization and shared data in concurrency in general. To avoid race conditions, we must make our parallel code sequential in critical sections. This can hurt the performance of our multiprocessing code. Care must be taken to lock only the sections that absolutely need it so that other parts of the application can execute concurrently. When faced with a race condition bug, it is easy to protect all your code with a lock. This will "fix" the problem but will likely degrade your application's performance.

6.5.3 Sharing data with process pools

We've just seen how to share data within a couple of processes, so how do we apply this knowledge to process pools? Process pools operate a bit differently than creating processes manually, posing a challenge with shared data. Why is this?

When we submit a task to a process pool, it may not run immediately because the processes in the pool may be busy with other tasks. How does the process pool handle this? In the background, process pool executors keep a queue of tasks to manage this. When we submit a task to the process pool, its arguments are pickled (serialized) and put on the task queue. Then, each worker process asks for a task from the queue when it is ready for work. When a worker process pulls a task off the queue, it unpickles (deserializes) the arguments and begins to execute the task.

Shared data is, by definition, shared among worker processes. Therefore, pickling and unpickling it to send it back and forth between processes makes little sense. In fact, neither Value nor Array objects can be pickled, so if we try to pass the shared data in as arguments to our functions as we did before, we'll get an error along the lines of can't pickle Value objects.

To handle this, we'll need to put our shared counter in a global variable and somehow let our worker processes know about it. We can do this with *process pool initializers*. These are special functions that are called when each process in our pool starts up. Using this, we can create a reference to the shared memory that our parent process created. We can pass this function in when we create a process pool. To see how this works, let's create a simple example that increments a counter.

Listing 6.13   Initializing a process pool

```
from concurrent.futures import ProcessPoolExecutor
import asyncio
from multiprocessing import Value

shared_counter: Value

def init(counter: Value):
    global shared_counter
    shared_counter = counter

def increment():
    with shared_counter.get_lock():
        shared_counter.value += 1

async def main():
    counter = Value('d', 0)
    with ProcessPoolExecutor(initializer=init,
                             initargs=(counter,)) as pool:
        await asyncio.get_running_loop().run_in_executor(pool, increment)
        print(counter.value)


if __name__ == "__main__":
    asyncio.run(main())
```

This tells the pool to execute the function init with the argument counter for each process.

We first define a global variable, shared_counter, which will contain the reference to the shared Value object we create. In our init function, we take in a Value and initialize shared_counter to that value. Then, in the main coroutine, we create the counter and initialize it to 0, then pass in our init function and our counter to the initializer and initargs parameter when creating the process pool. The init function will be called for each process that the process pool creates, correctly initializing our shared_counter to the one we created in our main coroutine.

You may ask, "Why do we need to bother with all this? Can't we just initialize the global variable as shared_counter: Value = Value('d', 0) instead of leaving it empty?" The reason we can't do this is that when each process is created, the script we created it from is run again, per each process. This means that each process that starts will execute shared_counter: Value = Value('d', 0), meaning that if we have 100 processes, we'd get 100 shared_counter values, each set to 0, resulting in some strange behavior.

Now that we know how to initialize shared data properly with a process pool, let's see how to apply this to our MapReduce application. We'll create a shared counter that we'll increment each time a map operation completes. We'll also create a progress reporter1 task that will run in the background and output our progress to the console every second. For this example, we'll import some of our code around partitioning and reducing, to avoid repeating ourselves.

Listing 6.14 Keeping track of map operation progress

```python
from concurrent.futures import ProcessPoolExecutor
import functools
import asyncio
from multiprocessing import Value
from typing import List, Dict
from chapter_06.listing_6_8 import partition, merge_dictionaries


map_progress: Value


def init(progress: Value):
    global map_progress
    map_progress = progress


def map_frequencies(chunk: List[str]) -> Dict[str, int]:
    counter = {}
    for line in chunk:
        word, _, count, _ = line.split('\t')
        if counter.get(word):
            counter[word] = counter[word] + int(count)
        else:
            counter[word] = int(count)

    with map_progress.get_lock():
        map_progress.value += 1

    return counter


async def progress_reporter(total_partitions: int):
    while map_progress.value < total_partitions:
        print(f'Finished {map_progress.value}/{total_partitions} map
    operations')
        await asyncio.sleep(1)


async def main(partiton_size: int):
    global map_progress

    with open('googlebooks-eng-all-1gram-20120701-a', encoding='utf-8') as f:
        contents = f.readlines()
        loop = asyncio.get_running_loop()
        tasks = []
        map_progress = Value('i', 0)

        with ProcessPoolExecutor(initializer=init,
                                 initargs=(map_progress,)) as pool:
            total_partitions = len(contents) // partiton_size
            reporter =
    asyncio.create_task(progress_reporter(total_partitions))
```

```
        for chunk in partition(contents, partiton_size):
            tasks.append(loop.run_in_executor(pool,
    functools.partial(map_frequencies, chunk)))

        counters = await asyncio.gather(*tasks)

        await reporter

        final_result = functools.reduce(merge_dictionaries, counters)

        print(f"Aardvark has appeared {final_result['Aardvark']} times.")


if __name__ == "__main__":
    asyncio.run(main(partiton_size=60000))
```

The main change from our original MapReduce implementation, aside from initializing a shared counter, is inside our map_frequencies function. Once we have finished counting all words in that chunk, we acquire the lock for the shared counter and increment it. We also added a progress_reporter coroutine, which will run in the background and report how many jobs we've completed every second. When running this, you should see output similar to the following:

```
Finished 17/1443 map operations
Finished 144/1443 map operations
Finished 281/1443 map operations
Finished 419/1443 map operations
Finished 560/1443 map operations
Finished 701/1443 map operations
Finished 839/1443 map operations
Finished 976/1443 map operations
Finished 1099/1443 map operations
Finished 1230/1443 map operations
Finished 1353/1443 map operations
Aardvark has appeared 15209 times.
```

We now know how to use multiprocessing with asyncio to improve the performance of CPU-intensive work. What happens if we have a workload that has work that has both heavily CPU-bound and I/O-bound operations? We can use multiprocessing, but is there a way for us to combine the ideas of multiprocessing and a single-threaded concurrency model to further improve performance?

6.6   *Multiple processes, multiple event loops*

While multiprocessing is mainly useful for CPU-bound tasks, it can have benefits for workloads that are I/O-bound as well. Let's take our example of running multiple SQL queries concurrently from listing 5.8 in the previous chapter. Can we use multiprocessing to further improve its performance? Let's look at what its CPU usage graph looks like on a single core, as illustrated in figure 6.6.

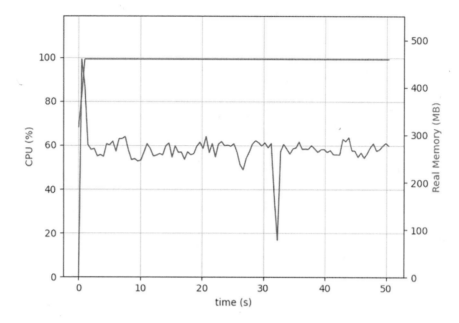

Figure 6.6   The CPU utilization graph for the code in listing 5.8

While this code is mostly making I/O-bound queries to our database, there is still a significant amount of CPU utilization happening. Why is this? In this instance, there is work happening to process the raw results we get from Postgres, leading to higher CPU utilization. Since we're single-threaded, while this CPU-bound work is happening, our event loop isn't processing results from other queries. This poses a potential throughput issue. If we issue 10,000 SQL queries concurrently, but we can only process one result at a time, we may end up with a backlog of query results to process.

Is there a way for us to improve our throughput by using multiprocessing? Using multiprocessing, each process has its own thread and its own Python interpreter. This opens up the opportunity to create one event loop per each process in our pool. With this model, we can distribute our queries over several processes. As seen in figure 6.7, this will spread the CPU load across multiple processes.

While this won't make our I/O throughput increase, it will increase how many query results we can process at a time. This will increase the overall throughout of our application. Let's take our example from listing 5.7 and use it to create this architecture, as shown in listing 6.15.

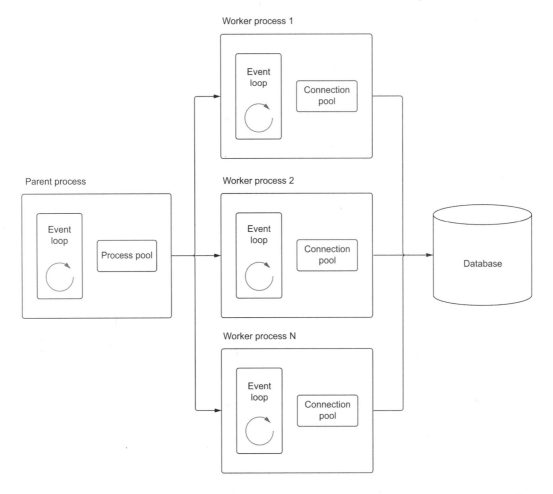

Figure 6.7   A parent process creates a process pool. The parent process then creates workers, each with its own event loop.

Listing 6.15   One event loop per process

```
import asyncio
import asyncpg
from util import async_timed
from typing import List, Dict
from concurrent.futures.process import ProcessPoolExecutor


product_query = \
    """
SELECT
p.product_id,
p.product_name,
```

```
        p.brand_id,
        s.sku_id,
        pc.product_color_name,
        ps.product_size_name
        FROM product as p
        JOIN sku as s on s.product_id = p.product_id
        JOIN product_color as pc on pc.product_color_id = s.product_color_id
        JOIN product_size as ps on ps.product_size_id = s.product_size_id
        WHERE p.product_id = 100"""

async def query_product(pool):
    async with pool.acquire() as connection:
        return await connection.fetchrow(product_query)


@async_timed()
async def query_products_concurrently(pool, queries):
    queries = [query_product(pool) for _ in range(queries)]
    return await asyncio.gather(*queries)


def run_in_new_loop(num_queries: int) -> List[Dict]:
    async def run_queries():
        async with asyncpg.create_pool(host='127.0.0.1',
                                       port=5432,
                                       user='postgres',
                                       password='password',
                                       database='products',
                                       min_size=6,
                                       max_size=6) as pool:
            return await query_products_concurrently(pool, num_queries)

    results = [dict(result) for result in asyncio.run(run_queries())]     ⟵
    return results


@async_timed()
async def main():
    loop = asyncio.get_running_loop()
    pool = ProcessPoolExecutor()
    tasks = [loop.run_in_executor(pool, run_in_new_loop, 10000) for _ in
      range(5)]                                               ⟵
    all_results = await asyncio.gather(*tasks)                ⟵
    total_queries = sum([len(result) for result in all_results])
    print(f'Retrieved {total_queries} products the product database.')


if __name__ == "__main__":
    asyncio.run(main())
```

> **Run queries in a new event loop, and convert them to dictionaries.**

> **Create five processes each with their own event loop to run queries.**

> **Wait for all query results to complete.**

We create a new function: run_in_new_loop. This function has an inner coroutine, run_queries, which creates a connection pool and runs the number of queries we specify concurrently. We then call run_queries with asyncio.run, which creates a new event loop and runs the coroutine.

One thing to note here is that we convert our results into dictionaries because asyncpg record objects cannot be pickled. Converting to a data structure that is serializable ensures that we can send our result back to our parent process.

In our main coroutine, we create a process pool and make five calls to run_in_ new_loop. This will concurrently kick off 50,000 queries—10,000 per each of five processes. When you run this, you should see five processes launched quickly, followed by each of these processes finishing at roughly the same time. The runtime of the entire application should take slightly longer than the slowest process. When running this on an eight-core machine, this script was able to complete in roughly 13 seconds. Going back to our previous example from chapter 5, we made 10,000 queries in about 6 seconds. This output means we were getting a throughput of roughly 1,666 queries per second. With the multiprocessing and multiple event loop approach, we completed 50,000 queries in 13 seconds, or roughly 3,800 queries per second, more than doubling our throughput.

Summary

- We've learned how to run multiple Python functions in parallel with a process pool.
- We've learned how to create a process pool executor and run Python functions in parallel. A process pool executor lets us use asyncio API methods such as gather to run multiple processes concurrently and wait for the results.
- We've learned how to solve a problem with MapReduce using process pools and asyncio. This workflow not only applies to MapReduce but can be used in general with any CPU-bound work that we can split into multiple smaller chunks.
- We've learned how to share state between multiple processes. This lets us keep track of data that is relevant for subprocesses we kick off, such as a status counter.
- We've learned how to avoid race conditions by using locks. Race conditions happen when multiple processes attempt to access data at roughly the same time and can lead to hard-to reproduce bugs.
- We've learned how to use multiprocessing to extend the power of asyncio by creating an event loop per each process. This has the potential to improve performance of workloads that have a mixture of CPU-bound and I/O-bound work.

Handling blocking
work with threads

This chapter covers

- Reviewing the multithreading library
- Creating thread pools to handle blocking I/O
- Using `async` and `await` to manage threads
- Handling blocking I/O libraries with thread pools
- Handling shared data and locking with threads
- Handling CPU-bound work in threads

When developing a new I/O-bound application from scratch, asyncio may be a natural technology choice. From the beginning, you'll be able to use non-blocking libraries that work with asyncio, such as asyncpg and aiohttp, as you begin development. However, greenfields (a project lacking constraints imposed by prior work) development is a luxury that many software developers don't have. A large portion of our work may be managing existing code using blocking I/O libraries, such as requests for HTTP requests, psycopg for Postgres databases, or any number of blocking libraries. We may also be in a situation where an asyncio-friendly library does not yet exist. Is there a way to get the performance gains of concurrency while still using asyncio APIs in these cases?

Multithreading is the solution to this question. Since blocking I/O releases the global interpreter lock, this enables the possibility to run I/O concurrently in separate threads. Much like the multiprocessing library, asyncio exposes a way for us to utilize pools of threads, so we can get the benefits of threading while still using the asyncio APIs, such as `gather` and `wait`.

In this chapter, we'll learn how to use multithreading with asyncio to run blocking APIs, such as requests, in threads. In addition, we'll learn how to synchronize shared data like we did in the last chapter and examine more advanced locking topics such as *reentrant locks* and *deadlocks*. We'll also see how to combine asyncio with synchronous code by building a responsive GUI to run a HTTP stress test. Finally, we'll look at the few exceptions for which threading can be used for CPU-bound work.

7.1 *Introducing the threading module*

Python lets developers create and manage threads via the threading module. This module exposes the `Thread` class, which, when instantiated, accepts a function to run in a separate thread. The Python interpreter runs single-threaded within a process, meaning that only one piece of Python bytecode can be running at one time even if we have code running in multiple threads. The global interpreter lock will only allow one thread to execute code at a time.

This seems like Python limits us from using multithreading to any advantage, but there are a few cases in which the global interpreter lock is released, the primary one being during I/O operations. Python can release the GIL in this case because, under the hood, Python is making low-level operating system calls to perform I/O. These system calls are outside the Python interpreter, meaning that no Python bytecode needs to run while we're waiting for I/O to finish.

To get a better sense of how to create and run threads in the context of blocking I/O, we'll revisit our example of an echo server from chapter 3. Recall that to handle multiple connections, we needed to switch our sockets to non-blocking mode and use the `select` module to watch for events on the sockets. What if we were working with a legacy codebase where non-blocking sockets weren't an option? Could we still build an echo server that can handle more than one client at a time?

Since a socket's `recv` and `sendall` are I/O-bound methods, and therefore release the GIL, we should be able to run them in separate threads concurrently. This means that we can create one thread per each connected client and read and write data in that thread. This model is a common paradigm in web servers such as Apache and is known as a *thread-per-connection* model. Let's give this idea a try by waiting for connections in our main thread and then creating a thread to echo for each client that connects.

Listing 7.1 A multithreaded echo server

```
from threading import Thread
import socket
```

```
def echo(client: socket):
    while True:
        data = client.recv(2048)
        print(f'Received {data}, sending!')
        client.sendall(data)


with socket.socket(socket.AF_INET, socket.SOCK_STREAM) as server:
    server.setsockopt(socket.SOL_SOCKET, socket.SO_REUSEADDR, 1)
    server.bind(('127.0.0.1', 8000))
    server.listen()
    while True:
        connection, _ = server.accept()
        thread = Thread(target=echo, args=(connection,))
        thread.start()
```

Block waiting for a client to connect.

Once a client connects, create a thread to run our echo function.

Start running the thread.

In the preceding listing, we enter an infinite loop listening for connections on our server socket. Once we have a client connected, we create a new thread to run our echo function. We supply the thread with a `target` that is the `echo` function we want to run and `args`, which is a tuple of arguments passed to `echo`. This means that we'll call `echo(connection)` in our thread. Then, we start the thread and loop again, waiting for a second connection. Meanwhile, in the thread we created, we loop forever listening for data from our client, and when we have it, we echo it back.

You should be able to connect an arbitrary amount of telnet clients concurrently and have messages echo properly. Since each `recv` and `sendall` operates in a separate thread per client, these operations never block each other; they only block the thread they are running in.

This solves the problem of multiple clients being unable to connect at the same time with blocking sockets, although the approach has some issues unique to threads. What happens if we try to kill this process with CTRL-C while we have clients connected? Does our application shut down the threads we created cleanly?

It turns out that things don't shut down quite so cleanly. If you kill the application, you should see a `KeyboardInterrupt` exception thrown on `server.accept()`, but your application will hang as the background thread will keep the program alive. Furthermore, any connected clients will still be able to send and receive messages!

Unfortunately, user-created threads in Python do not receive `KeyboardInterrupt` exceptions; only the main thread will receive them. This means that our threads will keep running, happily reading from our clients and preventing our application from exiting.

There are a couple approaches to handle this; specifically, we can use what are called *daemon* threads (pronounced *demon*), or we can come up with our own way of canceling or "interrupting" a running thread. Daemon threads are a special kind of thread for long-running background tasks. These threads won't prevent an application from shutting down. In fact, when only daemon threads are running, the application will shut down automatically. Since Python's main thread is not a daemon thread, this means that, if we make all our connection threads daemonic, our application will terminate on a `KeyboardInterrupt`. Adapting our code from listing 7.1

to use daemonic threads is easy; all we need to do is set `thread.daemon = True` before we run `thread.start()`. Once we make that change, our application will terminate properly on CTRL-C.

The problem with this approach is we have no way to run any cleanup or shutdown logic when our threads stop, since daemon threads terminate abruptly. Let's say that on shutdown we want to write out to each client that the server is shutting down. Is there a way we can have some type of exception interrupt our thread and cleanly shut down the socket? If we call a socket's `shutdown` method, any existing calls to `recv` will return `zero`, and `sendall` will throw an exception. If we call `shutdown` from the main thread, this will have the effect of interrupting our client threads that are blocking a `recv` or `sendall` call. We can then handle the exception in the client thread and perform any cleanup logic we'd like.

To do this, we'll create threads slightly differently than before, by subclassing the `Thread` class itself. This will let us define our own thread with a `cancel` method, inside of which we can shut down the client socket. Then, our calls to `recv` and `sendall` will be interrupted, allowing us to exit our `while` loop and close out the thread.

The `Thread` class has a `run` method that we can override. When we subclass `Thread`, we implement this method with the code that we want the thread to run when we start it. In our case, this is the `recv` and `sendall` echo loop.

> **Listing 7.2   Subclassing the thread class for a clean shutdown**

```python
from threading import Thread
import socket


class ClientEchoThread(Thread):

    def __init__(self, client):
        super().__init__()
        self.client = client

    def run(self):
        try:
            while True:
                data = self.client.recv(2048)
                if not data:
                    raise BrokenPipeError('Connection closed!')
                print(f'Received {data}, sending!')
                self.client.sendall(data)
        except OSError as e:
            print(f'Thread interrupted by {e} exception, shutting down!')

    def close(self):
        if self.is_alive():
            self.client.sendall(bytes('Shutting down!', encoding='utf-8'))
            self.client.shutdown(socket.SHUT_RDWR)
```

If there is no data, raise an exception. This happens when the connection was closed by the client or the connection was shut down.

When we have an exception, exit the run method. This terminates the thread.

Shut down the connection if the thread is alive; the thread may not be alive if the client closed the connection.

Shut down the client connection for reads and writes.

```
with socket.socket(socket.AF_INET, socket.SOCK_STREAM) as server:
    server.setsockopt(socket.SOL_SOCKET, socket.SO_REUSEADDR, 1)
    server.bind(('127.0.0.1', 8000))
    server.listen()
    connection_threads = []
    try:
        while True:
            connection, addr = server.accept()
            thread = ClientEchoThread(connection)
            connection_threads.append(thread)
            thread.start()
    except KeyboardInterrupt:
        print('Shutting down!')
        [thread.close() for thread in connection_threads]
```

> Call the close method on our threads to shut down each client connection on keyboard interrupt.

We first create a new class, ClientEchoThread, that inherits from Thread. This class overrides the run method with the code from our original echo function, but with a few changes. First, we wrap everything in a try catch block and intercept OSError exceptions. This type of exception is thrown from methods such as sendall when we close the client socket. We also check to see if the data from recv is 0. This happens in two cases: if the client closes the connection (someone quits telnet, for example) or when we shut down the client connection ourselves. In this case we throw a Broken-PipeError ourselves (a subclass of OSError), execute the print statement in the except block, and exit the run method, which shuts down the thread.

We also define a close method on our ClientEchoThread class. This method first checks to see if the thread is alive before shutting down the client connection. What does it mean for a thread to be "alive," and why do we need to do this? A thread is alive if its run method is executing; in this case this is true if our run method does not throw any exceptions. We need this check because the client itself may have closed the connection, resulting in a BrokenPipeError exception in the run method before we call close. This means that calling sendall would result in an exception, as the connection is no longer valid.

Finally, in our main loop, which listens for new incoming connections, we intercept KeyboardInterrupt exceptions. Once we have one, we call the close method on each thread we've created. This will send a message to the client, assuming the connection is still active and shut down the connection.

Overall, canceling running threads in Python, and in general, is a tricky problem and depends on the specific shutdown case you're trying to handle. You'll need to take special care that your threads do not block your application from exiting and to figure out where to put in appropriate interrupt points to exit your threads.

We've now seen a couple ways to manage threads manually ourselves, creating a thread object with a target function and subclassing Thread and overriding the run method. Now that we understand threading basics, let's see how to use them with asyncio to work with popular blocking libraries.

7.2   *Using threads with asyncio*

We now know how to create and manage multiple threads to handle blocking work. The drawback of this approach is that we must individually create and keep track of threads. We'd like to be able to use all the asyncio-based APIs we've learned to wait for results from threads without having to manage them ourselves. Like process pools from chapter 6, we can use *thread pools* to manage threads in this manner. In this section, we'll introduce a popular blocking HTTP client library and see how to use threads with asyncio to run web requests concurrently.

7.2.1   *Introducing the requests library*

The *requests library* is a popular HTTP client library for Python, self-described as "HTTP for humans." You can view the latest documentation for the library at https://requests .readthedocs.io/en/master/. Using it, you can make HTTP requests to web servers much like we did with aiohttp. We'll use the latest version (as of this writing, version 2.24.0). You can install this library by running the following pip command:

```
pip install -Iv requests==2.24.0
```

Once we've installed the library, we're ready to make some basic HTTP requests. Let's start out by making a couple of requests to example.com to retrieve the status code, as we did earlier with aiohttp.

Listing 7.3   Basic usage of requests

```
import requests


def get_status_code(url: str) -> int:
    response = requests.get(url)
    return response.status_code


url = 'https://www.example.com'
print(get_status_code(url))
print(get_status_code(url))
```

The preceding listing executes two HTTP GET requests in series. Running this, you should see two 200 outputs. We didn't create a HTTP session here, as we did with aiohttp, but the library does support this as needed to keep cookies persistent across different requests.

The requests library is blocking, meaning that each call to requests.get will stop any thread from executing other Python code until the request finishes. This has implications for how we can use this library in asyncio. If we try to use this library in a coroutine or a task by itself, it will block the entire event loop until the request finishes. If we had a HTTP request that took 2 seconds, our application wouldn't be able to do anything other than wait for those 2 seconds. To properly use this library with asyncio, we must run these blocking operations inside of a thread.

7.2.2 *Introducing thread pool executors*

Much like process pool executors, the `concurrent.futures` library provides an implementation of the `Executor` abstract class to work with threads named `Thread-PoolExecutor`. Instead of maintaining a pool of worker processes like a process pool does, a thread pool executor will create and maintain a pool of threads that we can then submit work to.

While a process pool will by default create one worker process for each CPU core our machine has available, determining how many worker threads to create is a bit more complicated. Internally, the formula for the default number of threads is `min(32, os.cpu_count() + 4)`. This causes the maximum (upper) bound of worker threads to be 32 and the minimum (lower) bound to be 5. The upper bound is set to 32 to avoid creating a surprising number of threads on machines with large amounts of CPU cores (remember, threads are resource-expensive to create and maintain). The lower bound is set to 5 because on smaller 1–2 core machines, spinning up only a couple of threads isn't likely to improve performance much. It often makes sense to create a few more threads than your available CPUs for I/O-bound work. For example, on an 8-core machine the above formula means we'll create 12 threads. While only 8 threads can run concurrently, we can have other threads paused waiting for I/O to finish, letting our operating resume them when I/O is done.

Let's adapt our example from listing 7.3 to run 1,000 HTTP requests concurrently with a thread pool. We'll time the results to get an understanding of what the benefit is.

Listing 7.4 Running requests with a thread pool

```
import time
import requests
from concurrent.futures import ThreadPoolExecutor


def get_status_code(url: str) -> int:
    response = requests.get(url)
    return response.status_code



start = time.time()

with ThreadPoolExecutor() as pool:
    urls = ['https://www.example.com' for _ in range(1000)]
    results = pool.map(get_status_code, urls)
    for result in results:
        print(result)
```

```
end = time.time()

print(f'finished requests in {end - start:.4f} second(s)')
```

On an 8-core machine with a speedy internet connection, this code can execute in as little as 8–9 seconds with the default number of threads. It is easy to write this synchronously to understand the impact that threading has by doing something, as in the following:

```
start = time.time()

urls = ['https://www.example.com' for _ in range(1000)]

for url in urls:
    print(get_status_code(url))

end = time.time()

print(f'finished requests in {end - start:.4f} second(s)')
```

Running this code can take upwards of 100 seconds! This makes our threaded code a bit more than 10 times faster than our synchronous code, giving us a pretty big performance bump.

   While this is clearly an improvement, you may remember from chapter 4, on aiohttp, that we were able to make 1,000 requests concurrently in less than 1 second. Why is this so much slower than our threading version? Remember that our maximum number of worker threads is limited to 32 (that is, the number of CPUs plus 4), meaning that by default we can only run a maximum of 32 requests concurrently. We can try to get around this by passing in max_workers=1000 when we create our thread pool, as in the following:

```
with ThreadPoolExecutor(max_workers=1000) as pool:
    urls = ['https://www.example.com' for _ in range(1000)]
    results = pool.map(get_status_code, urls)
    for result in results:
        print(result)
```

This approach can yield some improvements, as we now have one thread per each request we make. However, this still won't come very close to our coroutine-based code. This is due to the resource overhead associated with threads. Threads are created at the operating-system level and are more expensive to create than coroutines. In addition, threads have a context-switching cost at the OS level. Saving and restoring thread state when a context switch happens eats up some of the performance gains obtained by using threads.

   When you're determining the number of threads to use for a particular problem, it is best to start small (the amount of CPU cores plus a few is a good starting point), test it, and benchmark it, gradually increasing the number of threads. You'll usually find a "sweet spot," after which the run time will plateau and may even degrade, no matter how many more threads you add. This sweet spot is usually a fairly low number relative to the requests you want to make (to make it clear, creating 1,000 threads for 1,000 requests probably isn't the best use of resources).

7.2.3 *Thread pool executors with asyncio*

Using thread pool executors with the asyncio event loop isn't much different than using ProcessPoolExecutors. This is the beauty of having the abstract Executor base class in that we can use the same code to run threads or processes by only having to change one line of code. Let's adapt our example of running 1,000 HTTP requests to use asyncio.gather instead of pool.map.

Listing 7.5 Using a thread pool executor with asyncio

```python
import functools
import requests
import asyncio
from concurrent.futures import ThreadPoolExecutor
from util import async_timed


def get_status_code(url: str) -> int:
    response = requests.get(url)
    return response.status_code


@async_timed()
async def main():
    loop = asyncio.get_running_loop()
    with ThreadPoolExecutor() as pool:
        urls = ['https://www.example.com' for _ in range(1000)]
        tasks = [loop.run_in_executor(pool,
    functools.partial(get_status_code, url)) for url in urls]
        results = await asyncio.gather(*tasks)
        print(results)

asyncio.run(main())
```

We create the thread pool as we did before, but instead of using map we create a list of tasks by calling our get_status_code function with loop.run_in_executor. Once we have a list of tasks, we can wait for them to finish with asyncio.gather or any of the other asyncio APIs we learned earlier.

Internally, loop.run_in_executor calls the thread pool executor's submit method. This will put each function we pass in onto a queue. Worker threads in the pool then pull from the queue, running each work item until it completes. This approach does not yield any performance benefits over using a pool without asyncio, but while we're waiting for await asyncio.gather to finish, other code can run.

7.2.4   *Default executors*

Reading the asyncio documentation, you may notice that the run_in_executor method's executor parameter can be None. In this case, run_in_executor will use the event loop's *default executor.* What is a default executor? Think of it as a reusable singleton executor for your entire application. The default executor will always default to a ThreadPoolExecutor unless we set a custom one with the loop.set_default_executor method. This means that we can simplify the code from listing 7.5, as shown in the following listing.

Listing 7.6   Using the default executor

```
import functools
import requests
import asyncio
from util import async_timed


def get_status_code(url: str) -> int:
    response = requests.get(url)
    return response.status_code


@async_timed()
async def main():
    loop = asyncio.get_running_loop()
    urls = ['https://www.example.com' for _ in range(1000)]
    tasks = [loop.run_in_executor(None, functools.partial(get_status_code,
     url)) for url in urls]
    results = await asyncio.gather(*tasks)
    print(results)


asyncio.run(main())
```

In the preceding listing, we eliminate creating our own ThreadPoolExecutor and using it in a context manager as we did before and, instead, pass in None as the executor. The first time we call run_in_executor, asyncio creates and caches a default thread pool executor for us. Each subsequent call to run_in_executor reuses the previously created default executor, meaning the executor is then global to the event loop. Shutdown of this pool is also different from what we saw before. Previously, the thread pool executor we created was shut down when we exited a context manager's with block. When using the default executor, it won't shut down until the event loop closes, which usually happens when our application finishes. Using the default thread pool executor when we want to use threads simplifies things, but can we make this even easier?

In Python 3.9, the asyncio.to_thread coroutine was introduced to further simplify putting work on the default thread pool executor. It takes in a function to run in a thread and a set of arguments to pass to that function. Previously, we had to use functools.partial to pass in arguments, so this makes our code a little cleaner. It then runs the function with its arguments in the default thread pool executor and the currently running event loop. This lets us simplify our threading code even more. Using the to_thread coroutine eliminates using functools.partial and our call to asyncio.get_running_loop, cutting down our total lines of code.

Listing 7.7 Using the `to_thread` coroutine

```
import requests
import asyncio
from util import async_timed


def get_status_code(url: str) -> int:
    response = requests.get(url)
    return response.status_code


@async_timed()
async def main():
    urls = ['https://www.example.com' for _ in range(1000)]
    tasks = [asyncio.to_thread(get_status_code, url) for url in urls]
    results = await asyncio.gather(*tasks)
    print(results)

asyncio.run(main())
```

So far, we've only seen how to run blocking code inside of threads. The power of combining threads with asyncio is that we can run other code while we're waiting for our threads to finish. To see how to run other code while threads are running, we'll revisit our example from chapter 6 of periodically outputting the status of a long-running task.

7.3 Locks, shared data, and deadlocks

Much like multiprocessing code, multithreaded code is also susceptible to race conditions when we have shared data, as we do not control the order of execution. Any time you have two threads or processes that could modify a shared piece of non-thread-safe data, you'll need to utilize a lock to properly synchronize access. Conceptually, this is no different from the approach we took with multiprocessing; however, the memory model of threads changes the approach slightly.

Recall that with multiprocessing, by default the processes we create do not share memory. This meant we needed to create special shared memory objects and properly initialize them so that each process could read from and write to that object. Since threads *do* have access to the same memory of their parent process, we no longer need to do this, and threads can access shared variables directly.

This simplifies things a bit, but since we won't be working with shared Value objects that have locks built in, we'll need to create them ourselves. To do this, we'll need to use the threading module's Lock implementation, which is different from the one we used with multiprocessing. This is as easy as importing Lock from the threading module and calling its `acquire` and `release` methods around critical sections of code or using it in a context manager.

To see how to use locks with threading, let's revisit our task from chapter 6 of keeping track and displaying the progress of a long task. We'll take our previous example of making thousands of web requests and use a shared counter to keep track of how many requests we've completed so far.

Listing 7.8   Printing status of requests

```python
import functools
import requests
import asyncio
from concurrent.futures import ThreadPoolExecutor
from threading import Lock
from util import async_timed

counter_lock = Lock()
counter: int = 0


def get_status_code(url: str) -> int:
    global counter
    response = requests.get(url)
    with counter_lock:
        counter = counter + 1
    return response.status_code


async def reporter(request_count: int):
    while counter < request_count:
        print(f'Finished {counter}/{request_count} requests')
        await asyncio.sleep(.5)


@async_timed()
async def main():
    loop = asyncio.get_running_loop()
    with ThreadPoolExecutor() as pool:
        request_count = 200
        urls = ['https://www.example.com' for _ in range(request_count)]
        reporter_task = asyncio.create_task(reporter(request_count))
        tasks = [loop.run_in_executor(pool,
       functools.partial(get_status_code, url)) for url in urls]
        results = await asyncio.gather(*tasks)
        await reporter_task
        print(results)


asyncio.run(main())
```

This should look familiar, as it is like the code we wrote to output progress of our `map` operation in chapter 6. We create a global `counter` variable as well as a `counter_lock` to synchronize access to it in critical sections. In our `get_status_code` function we acquire the lock when we increment the counter. Then, in our main coroutine we kick off a reporter background task that outputs how many requests we've finished every 500 milliseconds. Running this, you should see output similar to the following:

```
Finished 0/200 requests
Finished 48/200 requests
Finished 97/200 requests
Finished 163/200 requests
```

We now know the basics around locks with both multithreading and multiprocessing, but there is still quite a bit to learn about locking. Next, we'll look at the concept of *reentrancy*.

7.3.1 Reentrant locks

Simple locks work well for coordinating access to a shared variable across multiple threads, but what happens when a thread tries to acquire a lock it has already acquired? Is this even safe? Since the same thread is acquiring the lock, this should be okay since this is single-threaded by definition and, therefore, thread-safe.

While this access should be okay, it does cause problems with the locks we have been using so far. To illustrate this, let's imagine we have a recursive sum function that takes a list of integers and produces the sum of the list. The list we want to sum can be modified from multiple threads, so we need to use a lock to ensure the list we're summing does not get modified during our sum operation. Let's try implementing this with a normal lock to see what happens. We'll also add some console output to see how our function is executing.

Listing 7.9   Recursion with locks

```python
from threading import Lock, Thread
from typing import List

list_lock = Lock()


def sum_list(int_list: List[int]) -> int:
    print('Waiting to acquire lock...')
    with list_lock:
        print('Acquired lock.')
        if len(int_list) == 0:
            print('Finished summing.')
            return 0
        else:
            head, *tail = int_list
            print('Summing rest of list.')
            return head + sum_list(tail)
```

```
thread = Thread(target=sum_list, args=([1, 2, 3, 4],))
thread.start()
thread.join()
```

If you run this code, you'll see the following few messages and then the application will hang forever:

```
Waiting to acquire lock...
Acquired lock.
Summing rest of list.
Waiting to acquire lock...
```

Why is this happening? If we walk through this, we acquire list_lock the first time perfectly fine. We then unpack the list and recursively call sum_list on the remainder of the list. This then causes us to attempt to acquire list_lock a second time. This is where our code hangs because, since we already acquired the lock, we block forever trying to acquire the lock a second time. This also means we never exit the first with block and can't release the lock; we're waiting for a lock that will never be released!

Since this recursion is coming from the same thread that originated it, acquiring the lock more than once shouldn't be a problem as this won't cause race conditions. To support these use cases, the threading library provides *reentrant* locks. A reentrant lock is a special kind of lock that can be acquired by the same thread more than once, allowing that thread to "reenter" critical sections. The threading module provides reentrant locks in the RLock class. We can take our above code and fix the problem by modifying only two lines of code—the import statement and the creation of the list_lock:

```
from threading import Rlock

list_lock = RLock()
```

If we modify these lines our code will work properly, and a single thread will be able to acquire the lock multiple times. Internally, reentrant locks work by keeping a recursion count. Each time we acquire the lock from the thread that first acquired the lock, the count increases, and each time we release the lock it decreases. When the count is 0, the lock is finally released for other threads to acquire it.

Let's examine a more real-world application to truly understand the concept of recursion with locks. Imagine we're trying to build a thread-safe integer list class with a method to find and replace all elements of a certain value with a different value. This class will contain a normal Python list and a lock we use to prevent race conditions. We'll pretend our existing class already has a method called indices_of(to_find: int) that takes in an integer and returns all the indices in the list that match to_find. Since we want to follow the DRY (don't repeat yourself) rule, we'll reuse this method when we define our find-and-replace method (note this is not the technically the most efficient way to do this, but we'll do it to illustrate the concept). This means our class and method will look something like the following listing.

Listing 7.10 A thread-safe list class

```python
from threading import Lock
from typing import List


class IntListThreadsafe:

    def __init__(self, wrapped_list: List[int]):
        self._lock = Lock()
        self._inner_list = wrapped_list

    def indices_of(self, to_find: int) -> List[int]:
        with self._lock:
            enumerator = enumerate(self._inner_list)
            return [index for index, value in enumerator if value == to_find]

    def find_and_replace(self,
                         to_replace: int,
                         replace_with: int) -> None:
        with self._lock:
            indices = self.indices_of(to_replace)
            for index in indices:
                self._inner_list[index] = replace_with


threadsafe_list = IntListThreadsafe([1, 2, 1, 2, 1])
threadsafe_list.find_and_replace(1, 2)
```

If someone from another thread modifies the list during our `indices_of` call, we could obtain an incorrect return value, so we need to acquire the lock before we search for matching indices. Our `find_and_replace` method must acquire the lock for the same reason. However, with a normal lock we wind up hanging forever when we call `find_and_replace`. The find-and-replace method first acquires the lock and then calls another method, which tries to acquire the same lock. Switching to an `RLock` in this case will fix this problem because one call to `find_and_replace` will always acquire any locks from the same thread. This illustrates a generic formula for when you need to use reentrant locks. If you are developing a thread-safe class with a method A, which acquires a lock, and a method B that also needs to acquire a lock *and* call method A, you likely need to use a reentrant lock.

7.3.2 Deadlocks

You may be familiar with the concept of *deadlock* from political negotiations on the news, where one party makes a demand of the other side, and the other side makes a counterdemand. Both sides disagree on the next step and negotiation reaches a standstill. The concept in computer science is similar in that we reach a state where there is contention over a shared resource with no resolution, and our application hangs forever.

The issue we saw in the previous section, where non-reentrant locks can cause our program to hang forever, is one example of a deadlock. In that case, we reach a state where we're stuck in a standstill negotiation with ourselves, demanding to acquire a lock that is never released. This situation can also arise when we have two threads using more than one lock. Figure 7.1 illustrates this scenario: if thread A asks for a lock that thread B has acquired, and thread B is asking for a lock that A has acquired, we reach a standstill and a deadlock. In that instance, using reentrant locks won't help, as we have multiple threads stuck waiting on a resource the other thread holds.

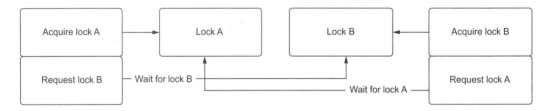

Figure 7.1 Threads 1 and 2 acquire locks A and B at roughly the same time. Then, thread 1 waits for lock B, which thread 2 holds; meanwhile, thread 2 is waiting for A, which thread 1 holds. This circular dependency causes a deadlock and will hang the application.

Let's look at how to create this type of deadlock in code. We'll create two locks, lock A and B, and two methods which need to acquire both locks. One method will acquire A first and then B and another will acquire B first and then A.

Listing 7.11 A deadlock in code

```python
from threading import Lock, Thread
import time

lock_a = Lock()
lock_b = Lock()


def a():                                    Acquire lock A.      Sleep for 1 second; this
    with lock_a:                                                 ensures we create the right
        print('Acquired lock a from method a!')                 conditions for deadlock.
        time.sleep(1)
        with lock_b:          Acquire
            print('Acquired both locks from method a!')  lock B.


def b():
    with lock_b:
        print('Acquired lock b from method b!')
    Acquire   with lock_a:
    lock A.       print('Acquired both locks from method b!')
```

```
thread_1 = Thread(target=a)
thread_2 = Thread(target=b)
thread_1.start()
thread_2.start()
thread_1.join()
thread_2.join()
```

When we run this code, we'll see the following output, and our application will hang forever:

```
Acquired lock a from method a!
Acquired lock b from method b!
```

We first call method A and acquire lock A, then we introduce an artificial delay to give method B a chance to acquire lock B. This leaves us in a state where method A holds lock A and method B holds lock B. Next, method A attempts to acquire lock B, but method B is holding that lock. At the same time, method B tries to acquire lock A, but method A is holding it, stuck waiting for B to release its lock. Both methods are stuck waiting on one another to release a resource, and we reach a standstill.

How do we handle this situation? One solution is the so-called "ostrich algorithm," named for the situation (although ostriches don't *actually* behave this way) where an ostrich sticks its head in the sand whenever it senses danger. With this strategy, we ignore the problem and devise a strategy to restart our application when we encounter the issue. The driving idea behind this approach is if the issue happens rarely enough, investing in a fix isn't worth it. If you remove the sleep from the above code, you'll only rarely see deadlock occur, as it relies on a very specific sequence of operations. This isn't really a fix and isn't ideal but is a strategy used with deadlocks that rarely occur.

However, in our situation there is an easy fix, where we change the locks in both methods to always be acquired in the same order. For instance, both methods A and B can acquire lock A first then lock B. This resolves the issue, as we'll never acquire locks in an order where a deadlock could occur. The other option would be to refactor the locks so we use only one instead of two. It is impossible to have a deadlock with one lock (excluding the reentrant deadlock we saw earlier). Overall, when dealing with multiple locks that you need to acquire, ask yourself, "Am I acquiring these locks in a consistent order? Is there a way I can refactor this to use only one lock?"

We've now seen how to use threads effectively with asyncio and have investigated more complex locking scenarios. Next, let's see how to use threads to integrate asyncio into existing synchronous applications that may not work smoothly with asyncio.

7.4 *Event loops in separate threads*

We have mainly focused on building applications that are completely implemented from the bottom up with coroutines and asyncio. When we've had any work that does not fit within a single-threaded concurrency model, we have run it inside of threads or processes. Not all applications will fit into this paradigm. What if we're working in an existing synchronous application and we want to incorporate asyncio?

One such situation where we can run into this scenario is building desktop user interfaces. The frameworks to build GUIs usually run their own event loop, and the event loop blocks the main thread. This means that any long-running operations can cause the user interface to freeze. In addition, this UI event loop will block us from creating an asyncio event loop. In this section, we'll learn how to use multithreading to run multiple event loops at the same time by building a responsive HTTP stress-testing user interface in Tkinter.

7.4.1   *Introducing Tkinter*

Tkinter is a platform-independent desktop graphical user interface (GUI) toolkit provided in the default Python installation. Short for "Tk interface," it is an interface to the low-level Tk GUI toolkit that is written in the tcl language. With the creation of the Tkinter Python library, Tk has grown into a popular way for Python developers to build desktop user interfaces.

Tkinter has a set of "widgets," such as labels, text boxes, and buttons, that we can place in a desktop window. When we interact with a widget, such as entering text or pressing a button, we can trigger a function to execute code. The code that runs in response to a user action could be as simple as updating another widget or triggering another operation.

Tkinter, and many other GUI libraries, draw their widgets and handle widget interactions through their own event loops. The event loop is constantly redrawing the application, processing events, and checking to see if any code should run in response to a widget event. To get familiar with Tkinter and its event loop, let's create a basic hello world application. We'll create an application with a "say hello" button that will output "Hello there!" to the console when we click on it.

Listing 7.12   "Hello world" with Tkinter

```
import tkinter
from tkinter import ttk

window = tkinter.Tk()
window.title('Hello world app')
window.geometry('200x100')


def say_hello():
    print('Hello there!')


hello_button = ttk.Button(window, text='Say hello', command=say_hello)
hello_button.pack()

window.mainloop()
```

This code first creates a Tkinter window (see figure 7.2) and sets the application title and window size. We then place a button on the window and set its command to the say_hello function. When a user presses this button, the say_hello function executes, printing out our message. We then call window.mainloop() that starts the Tk event loop, running our application.

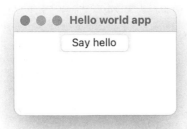

Figure 7.2 The "hello world" application from listing 7.12

One thing to note here is that our application will block on window.mainloop(). Internally, this method runs the Tk event loop. This is an infinite loop that is checking for window events and constantly redrawing the window until we close it. The Tk event loop has interesting parallels to the asyncio event loop. For example, what happens if we try to run blocking work in our button's command? If we add a 10-second delay to the say_hello function with time.sleep(10), we'll start to see a problem: our application will freeze for 10 seconds!

Much like asyncio, Tkinter runs *everything* in its event loop. This means that if we have a long-running operation, such as making a web request or loading a large file, we'll block the tk event loop until that operation finishes. The effect on the user is that the UI hangs and becomes unresponsive. The user can't click on any buttons, we can't update any widgets with status or progress, and the operating system will likely display a spinner (like the example in figure 7.3) to indicate the application is hanging. This is clearly an undesirable, unresponsive user interface.

Figure 7.3 The dreaded "beach ball of doom" occurs as we block the event loop on a Mac.

This is an instance where asynchronous programming can, in theory, help us out. If we can make asynchronous requests that don't block the tk event loop, we can avoid this problem. This is trickier than it may seem as Tkinter is not asyncio-aware, and you can't pass in a coroutine to run on a button click. We could try running two event loops at the same time in the same thread, but this won't work. Both Tkinter and asyncio are single-threaded—this idea is the same as trying to run two infinite loops in the same thread at the same time, which can't be done. If we start the asyncio event loop before the Tkinter event loop, the asyncio event loop will block the Tkinter loop from running, and vice versa. Is there a way for us to run an asyncio application alongside a single-threaded application?

We can in fact combine these two event loops to create a functioning application by running the asyncio event loop in a separate thread. Let's look at how to do this with an application that will responsively update the user on the status of a long-running task with a progress bar.

7.4.2 *Building a responsive UI with asyncio and threads*

First, let's introduce our application and sketch out a basic UI. We'll build a URL stress test application. This application will take a URL and many requests to send as input. When we press a submit button, we'll use aiohttp to send out web requests as fast as we can, delivering a predefined load to the web server we choose. Since this may take a long time, we'll add a progress bar to visualize how far along we are in the test. We'll update the progress bar after every 1% of total requests are finished to show progress. Further, we'll let the user cancel the request if they'd like. Our UI will have a few widgets, including a text input for the URL to test, a text input for the number of requests we wish to issue, a start button, and a progress bar. We'll design a UI that looks like the illustration in figure 7.4.

Figure 7.4   The URL requester GUI

Now that we have our UI sketched out, we need to think through how to have two event loops running alongside one another. The basic idea is that we'll have the Tkinter event loop running in the main thread, and we'll run the asyncio event loop in a separate thread. Then, when the user clicks "Submit," we'll submit a coroutine to the asyncio event loop to run the stress test. As the stress test is running, we'll issue commands from the asyncio event loop back to the Tkinter event loop to update our progress. This gives us an architecture that looks like the drawing in figure 7.5.

This new architecture includes communication across threads. We need to be careful about race conditions in this situation, especially since the asyncio event loop is *not*

GUI process

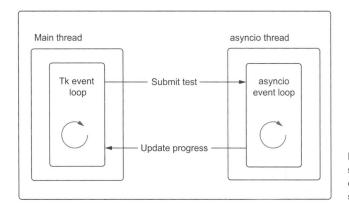

Figure 7.5 The tk event loop submits a task to the asyncio event loop, which runs in a separate thread.

thread-safe! Tkinter is designed with thread safety in mind, so there are fewer concerns with calling it from a separate thread (in Python 3+ at least; we'll look more closely at this soon).

We may be tempted to submit coroutines from Tkinter using `asyncio.run`, but this function blocks until the coroutine we pass in finishes and will cause the Tkinter application to hang. We'll need a function which submits a coroutine to the event loop without any blocking. There are a few new asyncio functions to learn that are both non-blocking and have thread safety built in to submit this kind of work properly. The first is a method on the asyncio event loop named `call_soon_threadsafe`. This function takes in a Python function (not a coroutine) and schedules it to execute it in a thread-safe manner at the next iteration of the asyncio event loop. The second function is `asyncio.run_coroutine_threadsafe`. This function takes in a coroutine and submits it to run in a thread-safe manner, immediately returning a future that we can use to access a result of the coroutine. Importantly, and confusingly, this future is *not* an asyncio future but rather from the `concurrent.futures` module. The logic behind this is that asyncio futures are not thread-safe, but `concurrent.futures` futures are. This `future` class does however have the same functionality as the future from the asyncio module.

Let's start defining and implementing a few classes to build our stress test application based on what we described above. The first thing we'll build is a stress test class. This class will be responsible for starting and stopping one stress test and keeping track of how many requests have completed. Its constructor will take in a URL, an asyncio event loop, the number of desired requests to make, and a progress updater callback. We'll call this callback when we want to trigger a progress bar update. When we get to implementing the UI, this callback will trigger an update to the progress bar. Internally, we'll calculate a refresh rate, which is the rate at which we'll execute the callback. We'll default this rate to every 1% of the total requests we plan to send.

Listing 7.13   The stress test class

```
import asyncio
from concurrent.futures import Future
from asyncio import AbstractEventLoop
from typing import Callable, Optional
from aiohttp import ClientSession


class StressTest:

    def __init__(self,
                 loop: AbstractEventLoop,
                 url: str,
                 total_requests: int,
                 callback: Callable[[int, int], None]):
        self._completed_requests: int = 0
        self._load_test_future: Optional[Future] = None
        self._loop = loop
        self._url = url
        self._total_requests = total_requests
        self._callback = callback
        self._refresh_rate = total_requests // 100

    def start(self):
        future = asyncio.run_coroutine_threadsafe(self._make_requests(),
 self._loop)
        self._load_test_future = future

    def cancel(self):
        if self._load_test_future:
            self._loop.call_soon_threadsafe(self._load_test_future.cancel)

    async def _get_url(self, session: ClientSession, url: str):
        try:
            await session.get(url)
        except Exception as e:
            print(e)
        self._completed_requests = self._completed_requests + 1
        if self._completed_requests % self._refresh_rate == 0 \
                or self._completed_requests == self._total_requests:
            self._callback(self._completed_requests, self._total_requests)

    async def _make_requests(self):
        async with ClientSession() as session:
            reqs = [self._get_url(session, self._url) for _ in
 range(self._total_requests)]
            await asyncio.gather(*reqs)
```

> Start making the requests, and store the future, so we can later cancel if needed.

> If we want to cancel, call the cancel function on the load test future.

> Once we've completed 1% of requests, call the callback with the number of completed requests and the total requests.

In our start method, we call run_coroutine_threadsafe with _make_requests that will start making requests on the asyncio event loop. We also keep track of the future this returns in _load_test_future. Keeping track of this future lets us cancel the load test in our cancel method. In our _make_requests method we create a list coroutines to make all our web requests, passing them into `asyncio.gather` to run them. Our `_get_url` coroutine makes the request, increments the `_completed_requests` counter, and calls the callback with the total number of completed requests if necessary. We can use this class by simply instantiating it and calling the `start` method, optionally canceling by calling the `cancel` method.

One interesting thing to note is that we didn't use any locking around the `_completed_requests` counter despite updates happening to it from multiple coroutines. Remember that asyncio is single-threaded, and the asyncio event loop only runs a piece of Python code at any given time. This has the effect of making incrementing the counter atomic when used with asyncio, despite it being non-atomic when happening between multiple threads. asyncio saves us from many kinds of race conditions that we see with multithreading but not all. We'll examine this more in a later chapter.

Next, let's implement our Tkinter GUI to use this load tester class. For code cleanliness, we'll subclass the `TK` class directly and initialize our widgets in the constructor. When a user clicks the start button, we'll create a new `StressTest` instance and start it. The question now becomes what do we pass in as a callback to our `StressTest` instance? Thread safety becomes an issue here as our callback will be called in the worker thread. If our callback modifies shared data from the worker thread that our main thread can also modify, this could cause race conditions. In our case, since Tkinter has thread safety built in and all we're doing is updating the progress bar, we should be okay. But what if we needed to do something with shared data? Locking is one approach, but if we could run our callback in the main thread, we'd avoid any race conditions. We'll use a generic pattern to demonstrate how to do this, though updating the progress bar directly should be safe.

One common pattern to accomplish this is to use a shared thread-safe queue from the `queue` module. Our asyncio thread can put progress updates into this queue. Then, our Tkinter thread can check this queue for updates in its thread, updating the progress bar in the correct thread. We'll need to tell Tkinter to poll the queue in the main thread to do this.

Tkinter has a method that lets us queue up a function to run after a specified time increment in the main thread called `after`. We'll use this to run a method that asks the queue if it has a new progress update (listing 7.14). If it does, we can update the progress bar safely from the main thread. We'll poll the queue every 25 milliseconds to ensure we get updates with reasonable latency.

Is Tkinter really thread-safe?

If you search for Tkinter and thread safety, you'll find a lot of conflicting information. The threading situation in Tkinter is quite complicated. This is in part because, for several years, Tk and Tkinter lacked proper thread support. Even when threaded mode was added, it had several bugs that have since been fixed. Tk supports both non-threaded and threaded modes. In non-threaded mode, there is no thread safety; and using Tkinter from anything other than the main thread is inviting a crash. In older

(continued)

versions of Python, Tk thread safety was not turned on; however, in versions of Python 3 and later, thread safety is turned on by default and we have thread-safe guarantees. In threaded mode, if an update is issued from a worker thread, Tkinter acquires a mutex and writes the update event to a queue for the main thread to later process. The relevant code where this happens is in CPython in the `Tkapp_Call` function in `Modules/_tkinter.c`.

Listing 7.14   The Tkinter GUI

```python
from queue import Queue
from tkinter import Tk
from tkinter import Label
from tkinter import Entry
from tkinter import ttk
from typing import Optional
from chapter_07.listing_7_13 import StressTest


class LoadTester(Tk):

    def __init__(self, loop, *args, **kwargs):       ◁─── In our constructor, we
        Tk.__init__(self, *args, **kwargs)                 set up the text inputs,
        self._queue = Queue()                              labels, submit button,
        self._refresh_ms = 25                              and progress bar.

        self._loop = loop
        self._load_test: Optional[StressTest] = None
        self.title('URL Requester')

        self._url_label = Label(self, text="URL:")
        self._url_label.grid(column=0, row=0)

        self._url_field = Entry(self, width=10)
        self._url_field.grid(column=1, row=0)

        self._request_label = Label(self, text="Number of requests:")
        self._request_label.grid(column=0, row=1)

        self._request_field = Entry(self, width=10)       When clicked, our
        self._request_field.grid(column=1, row=1)         submit button will call
                                                          the _start method.
        self._submit = ttk.Button(self, text="Submit", command=self._start)  ◁──┘
        self._submit.grid(column=2, row=1)

        self._pb_label = Label(self, text="Progress:")
        self._pb_label.grid(column=0, row=3)

        self._pb = ttk.Progressbar(self, orient="horizontal", length=200,
    mode="determinate")
        self._pb.grid(column=1, row=3, columnspan=2)
```

```
    def _update_bar(self, pct: int):
        if pct == 100:
            self._load_test = None
            self._submit['text'] = 'Submit'
        else:
            self._pb['value'] = pct
            self.after(self._refresh_ms, self._poll_queue)
```

The update bar method will set the progress bar to a percentage complete value from 0 to 100. This method should only be called in the main thread.

```
    def _queue_update(self, completed_requests: int, total_requests: int):
        self._queue.put(int(completed_requests / total_requests * 100))
```

This method is the callback we pass to the stress test; it adds a progress update to the queue.

```
    def _poll_queue(self):
        if not self._queue.empty():
            percent_complete = self._queue.get()
            self._update_bar(percent_complete)
        else:
            if self._load_test:
                self.after(self._refresh_ms, self._poll_queue)
```

Try to get a progress update from the queue; if we have one, update the progress bar.

```
    def _start(self):
        if self._load_test is None:
            self._submit['text'] = 'Cancel'
            test = StressTest(self._loop,
                              self._url_field.get(),
                              int(self._request_field.get()),
                              self._queue_update)
            self.after(self._refresh_ms, self._poll_queue)
            test.start()
            self._load_test = test
        else:
            self._load_test.cancel()
            self._load_test = None
            self._submit['text'] = 'Submit'
```

Start the load test, and start polling every 25 milliseconds for queue updates.

In our application's constructor, we create all the widgets we need for the user interface. Most notably, we create Entry widgets for the URL to test and the number of requests to run, a submit button, and a horizontal progress bar. We also use the grid method to arrange these widgets in the window appropriately.

When we create the submit button widget, we specify the command as the _start method. This method will create a StressTest object and starts running it unless we already have a load test running, in which case we will cancel it. When we create a StressTest object, we pass in the _queue_update method as a callback. The Stress-Test object will call this method whenever it has a progress update to issue. When this method runs, we calculate the appropriate percentage and put this into the queue. We then use Tkinter's after method to schedule the _poll_queue method to run every 25 milliseconds.

Using the queue as a shared communication mechanism instead of directly calling _update_bar will ensure that our _update_bar method runs in the Tkinter event loop thread. If we don't do this, the progress bar update would happen in the asyncio event loop as the callback is run within that thread.

Now that we've implemented the UI application, we can glue these pieces all together to create a fully working application. We'll create a new thread to run the event loop in the background and then start our newly created `LoadTester` application.

> **Listing 7.15 The load tester app**

```
import asyncio
from asyncio import AbstractEventLoop
from threading import Thread
from chapter_07.listing_7_14 import LoadTester        We create a new thread
                                                       class to run the asyncio
                                                       event loop forever.
class ThreadedEventLoop(Thread):          ◄──────────
    def __init__(self, loop: AbstractEventLoop):
        super().__init__()
        self._loop = loop
        self.daemon = True

    def run(self):
        self._loop.run_forever()


loop = asyncio.new_event_loop()                   Start the new thread
                                                  to run the asyncio event
asyncio_thread = ThreadedEventLoop(loop)          loop in the background.
asyncio_thread.start()              ◄─────────

app = LoadTester(loop)      ◄──    Create the load tester Tkinter application,
app.mainloop()                     and start its main event loop.
```

We first define a `ThreadedEventLoopClass` that inherits from `Thread` to run our event loop. In this class's constructor, we take in an event loop and set the thread to be a daemon thread. We set the thread to be daemon because the asyncio event loop will block and run forever in this thread. This type of infinite loop would prevent our GUI application from shutting down if we ran in non-daemon mode. In the thread's `run` method, we call the event loop's `run_forever` method. This method is well named, as it quite literally just starts the event loop running forever, blocking until we stop the event loop.

Once we've created this class, we create a new asyncio event loop with the `new_event_loop` method. We then create a `ThreadedEventLoop` instance, passing in the loop we just created and start it. This creates a new thread with our event loop running inside of it. Finally, we create an instance of our `LoadTester` app and call the `mainloop` method, kicking off the Tkinter event loop.

When we run a stress test with this application, we should see the progress bar update smoothly without freezing the user interface. Our application remains responsive, and we can click cancel to stop the load test whenever we please. This technique of running the asyncio event loop in a separate thread is useful for building responsive GUIs, but also is useful for any synchronous legacy applications where coroutines and asyncio don't fit smoothly.

We've now seen how to utilize threads for various I/O-bound workloads, but what about CPU-bound workloads? Recall that the GIL prevents us from running Python bytecode concurrently in threads, but there are a few notable exceptions to this that let us do some CPU-bound work in threads.

7.5 *Using threads for CPU-bound work*

The global interpreter lock is a tricky subject in Python. The rule of thumb is multithreading only makes sense for blocking I/O work, as I/O will release the GIL. This is true in most cases but not all. To properly release the GIL and avoid any concurrency bugs, the code that is running needs to avoid interacting with Python objects (dictionaries, lists, Python integers, and so on). This can happen when a large portion of our libraries' work is done in low-level C code. There are a few notable libraries, such as hashlib and NumPy, that perform CPU-intensive work in pure C and release the GIL. This enables us to use multithreading to improve the performance of certain CPU-bound workloads. We'll examine two such instances: hashing sensitive text for security and solving a data analysis problem with NumPy.

7.5.1 *Multithreading with hashlib*

In today's world, security has never been more important. Ensuring that data is not read by hackers is key to avoiding leaking sensitive customer data, such as passwords or other information that can be used to identify or harm them.

Hashing algorithms solve this problem by taking a piece of input data and creating a new piece of data that is unreadable and unrecoverable (if the algorithm is secure) to a human. For example, the password "password" may be hashed to a string that looks more like `'a12bc21df'`. While no one can read or recover the input data, we're still able to check if a piece of data matches a hash. This is useful for scenarios such as validating a user's password on login or checking if a piece of data has been tampered with.

There are many different hashing algorithms today, such as SHA512, BLAKE2, and scrypt, though SHA is not the best choice for storing passwords, as it is susceptible to brute-force attacks. Several of these algorithms are implemented in Python's `hashlib` library. Many functions in this library release the GIL when hashing data greater than 2048 bytes, so multithreading is an option to improve this library's performance. In addition, the `scrypt` function, used for hashing passwords, always releases the GIL.

Let's introduce a (hopefully) hypothetical scenario to see when multithreading might be useful with `hashlib`. Imagine you've just started a new job as principal software architect at a successful organization. Your manager assigns you your first bug to get started learning the company's development process—a small issue with the login system. To debug this issue, you start to look at a few database tables, and to your horror you notice that all your customers' passwords are stored in plaintext! This means that if your database is compromised, attackers could get all your customers' passwords and log in as them, potentially exposing sensitive data such as saved credit card numbers. You bring this to your manager's attention, and they ask you to find a solution to the problem as soon as possible.

Using the scrypt algorithm to hash the plaintext passwords is a good solution for this kind of problem. It is secure and the original password is unrecoverable, as it introduces a *salt*. A salt is a random number that ensures that the hash we get for the password is unique. To test out using scrypt, we can quickly write a synchronous script to create random passwords and hash them to get a sense of how long things will take. For this example, we'll test on 10,000 random passwords.

Listing 7.16   Hashing passwords with scrypt

```
import hashlib
import os
import string
import time
import random


def random_password(length: int) -> bytes:
    ascii_lowercase = string.ascii_lowercase.encode()
    return b''.join(bytes(random.choice(ascii_lowercase)) for _ in
      range(length))


passwords = [random_password(10) for _ in range(10000)]


def hash(password: bytes) -> str:
    salt = os.urandom(16)
    return str(hashlib.scrypt(password, salt=salt, n=2048, p=1, r=8))


start = time.time()

for password in passwords:
    hash(password)

end = time.time()
print(end - start)
```

We first write a function to create random lowercase passwords and then use that to create 10,000 random passwords of 10 characters each. We then hash each password with the scrypt function. We'll gloss over the details (n, p, and r parameters of the scrypt function), but these are used to tune how secure we'd like our hash to be and memory/CPU usage.

Running this on the servers you have, which are 2.4 Ghz 8-core machines, this code completes in just over 40 seconds, which is not too bad. The issue is that you have a large user base, and you need to hash 1,000,000,000 passwords. Doing the calculation based on this test, it will take a bit over 40 days to hash the entire database! We could split up our data set and run this procedure on multiple machines, but we'd need a lot of machines to do that, given how slow this is. Can we use threading to improve the speed and therefore cut down on the time and machines we need to use? Let's apply what we know about multithreading to give this a shot. We'll create a thread pool and hash passwords in multiple threads.

Listing 7.17 Hashing with multithreading and asyncio

```
import asyncio
import functools
import hashlib
import os
from concurrent.futures.thread import ThreadPoolExecutor
import random
import string

from util import async_timed


def random_password(length: int) -> bytes:
    ascii_lowercase = string.ascii_lowercase.encode()
    return b''.join(bytes(random.choice(ascii_lowercase)) for _ in
     range(length))


passwords = [random_password(10) for _ in range(10000)]


def hash(password: bytes) -> str:
    salt = os.urandom(16)
    return str(hashlib.scrypt(password, salt=salt, n=2048, p=1, r=8))


@async_timed()
async def main():
    loop = asyncio.get_running_loop()
    tasks = []

    with ThreadPoolExecutor() as pool:
        for password in passwords:
            tasks.append(loop.run_in_executor(pool, functools.partial(hash,
     password)))

    await asyncio.gather(*tasks)


asyncio.run(main())
```

This approach involves us creating a thread pool executor and creating a task for each password we want to hash. Since hashlib releases the GIL we realize some decent performance gains. This code runs in about 5 seconds as opposed to the 40 we got earlier. We've just cut our runtime down from 47 days to a bit over 5! As a next step, we could take this application and run it concurrently on different machines to further cut runtime, or we could get a machine with more CPU cores.

7.5.2   *Multithreading with NumPy*

NumPy is an extremely popular Python library, widely used in data science and machine learning projects. It has a multitude of mathematical functions common to arrays and matrices that tend to outperform plain Python arrays. This increased performance is because much of the underlying library is implemented in C and Fortran that are low-level languages and tend to be more performant than Python.

Because many of this library's operations are in low-level code outside of Python, this opens the opportunity for NumPy to release the GIL and allow us to multithread some of our code. The caveat here is this functionality is not well-documented, but it is generally safe to assume matrix operations can potentially be multithreaded for a performance win. That said, depending on how the numpy function is implemented, the win could be large or small. If the code directly calls C functions and releases the GIL there is a potential bigger win; if there is a lot of supporting Python code around any low-level calls, the win will be smaller. Given that this is not well documented, you may have to try adding multithreading to specific bottlenecks in your application (you can determine where the bottlenecks are with profiling) and benchmarking what gains you get. You'll then need to decide if the extra complexity is worth any potential gains you get.

To see this in practice, we'll create a large matrix of 4,000,000,000 data points in 50 rows. Our task will be to obtain the mean for reach row. NumPy has an efficient function, mean, to compute this. This function has an axis parameter which lets us calculate all the means across an axis without having to write a loop. In our case, an axis of 1 will calculate the mean for every row.

Listing 7.18   Means of a large matrix with NumPy

```
import numpy as np
import time

data_points = 4000000000
rows = 50
columns = int(data_points / rows)

matrix = np.arange(data_points).reshape(rows, columns)

s = time.time()

res = np.mean(matrix, axis=1)

e = time.time()
print(e - s)
```

This script first creates an array with 4,000,000,000 integer data points, ranging from 1,000,000,000–4,000,000,000 (note that this takes quite a bit of memory; if your application crashes with an out-of-memory error, lower this number). We then "reshape" the array into a matrix with 50 rows. Finally, we call NumPy's mean function with an axis of 1, calculating the mean for each individual row. All told, this script runs in about 25–30 seconds on an 8-core 2.4 Ghz CPU. Let's adapt this code slightly to work with threads. We'll run the median for each row in a separate thread and use `asyncio.gather` to wait for all the median of all rows.

Listing 7.19   Threading with NumPy

```
import functools
from concurrent.futures.thread import ThreadPoolExecutor
import numpy as np
import asyncio
from util import async_timed


def mean_for_row(arr, row):
    return np.mean(arr[row])


data_points = 4000000000
rows = 50
columns = int(data_points / rows)

matrix = np.arange(data_points).reshape(rows, columns)

@async_timed()
async def main():
    loop = asyncio.get_running_loop()
    with ThreadPoolExecutor() as pool:
        tasks = []
        for i in range(rows):
            mean = functools.partial(mean_for_row, matrix, i)
            tasks.append(loop.run_in_executor(pool, mean))

        results = asyncio.gather(*tasks)


asyncio.run(main())
```

First, we create a `mean_for_row` function that calculates the mean for one row. Since our plan is to calculate the mean for every row in a separate thread, we can no longer use the `mean` function with an axis as we did before. We then create a main coroutine with a thread pool executor and create a task to calculate the mean for each row, waiting for all the calculations to finish with `gather`.

On the same machine, this code runs in roughly 9–10 seconds, nearly a 3× boost in performance! Multithreading can help us in certain cases with NumPy, although the documentation for what can benefit from threads is lacking at the time of writing. When in doubt, if threading will help a CPU-bound workload, the best way to see if it will help is to test it out and benchmark.

In addition, keep in mind that your NumPy code should be as vectorized as possible before trying threading or multiprocessing to improve performance. This means avoiding things like Python loops or functions like NumPy's `apply_along_axis`, which just hides a loop. With NumPy, you will often see much better performance by pushing as much computation as you can to the library's low-level implementations.

Summary

- We've learned how to run I/O-bound work using the threading module.
- We've learned how to cleanly terminate threads on application shutdown.
- We've learned how to use thread pool executors to distribute work to a pool of threads. This allows us to use asyncio API methods like `gather` to wait for results from threads.
- We've learned how to take existing blocking I/O APIs, such as requests, and run them in threads with thread pools and asyncio for performance wins.
- We've learned how to avoid race conditions with locks from the threading module. We've also learned how to avoid deadlocks with reentrant locks.
- We've learned how to run the asyncio event loop in a separate thread and send coroutines to it in a thread-safe manner. This lets us build responsive user interfaces with frameworks such as Tkinter.
- We've learned how to use multithreading with `hashlib` and `numpy`. Low-level libraries will sometimes release the GIL, which lets us use threading for CPU-bound work.

Streams

8

This chapter covers

- Transports and protocols
- Using streams for network connections
- Processing command-line input asynchronously
- Creating client/server applications with streams

When writing network applications, such as our echo clients in prior chapters, we've employed the socket library to read from and write to our clients. While directly using sockets is useful when building low-level networking libraries, they are ultimately complex creatures with nuances outside the scope of this book. That said, many use cases of sockets rely on a few conceptually simple operations, such as starting a server, waiting for client connections, and sending data to clients. The designers of asyncio realized this and built network stream APIs to abstract away handling the nuances of sockets for us. These higher-level APIs are much easier to work with than sockets, making any client-server applications easier to build and more robust than using sockets ourselves. Using streams is the recommended way to build network-based applications in asyncio.

In this chapter, we'll first learn using the lower-level transport and protocol APIs by building a simple HTTP client. Learning about these APIs will give us the foundation for understanding how the higher-level stream APIs work in the background. We'll then use this knowledge to learn about stream readers and writers and use them to build a non-blocking command-line SQL client. This application will asynchronously process user input, allowing us to run multiple queries concurrently from the command line. Finally, we'll learn how to use asyncio's server API to create client and server applications, building a functional chat server and chat client.

8.1 *Introducing streams*

In asyncio, *streams* are a high-level set of classes and functions that create and manage network connections and generic streams of data. Using them, we can create client connections to read and write to servers, or even create servers and manage them ourselves. These APIs abstract a lot of knowledge around managing sockets, such as dealing with SSL or lost connections, making our lives as developers a little easier.

The stream APIs are built on top of a lower-level set of APIs known as *transports* and *protocols*. These APIs directly wrap the sockets we used in previous chapters (generally, any generic stream of data), providing us with a clean API for reading and writing data to sockets.

These APIs are structured a little differently from others in that they use a callback style design. Instead of actively waiting for data from a socket like we did previously, a method on a class we implement is called for us when data is available. We then process the data we receive in this method as needed. To get started learning how these callback-based APIs work, let's first see how to use the lower-level transport and protocol APIs by building a basic HTTP client.

8.2 *Transports and protocols*

At a high level, a transport is an abstraction for communication with an arbitrary stream of data. When we communicate with a socket or any data stream such as standard input, we work with a familiar set of operations. We read data from or write data to a source, and when we're finished working with it, we close it. A socket cleanly fits how we've defined this transport abstraction; that is, we read and write data to it and once we've finished, we close it. In short, a transport provides definitions for sending and receiving data to and from a source. Transports have several implementations depending on which type of source we're using. We're mainly concerned with `Read-Transport`, `WriteTransport`, and `Transport`, though there are others for dealing with UDP connections and subprocess communication. Figure 8.1 illustrates the class hierarchy of transports.

Transmitting data to and from a socket is only part of the equation. What about the lifecycle of a socket? We establish a connection; we write data and then process any response we get. These are the set of operations a protocol owns. Note that a protocol simply refers to a Python class here and not a protocol like HTTP or FTP. A transport manages data transmission and calls methods on a protocol when events occur, such as a connection being established or data being ready to process, as shown in figure 8.2.

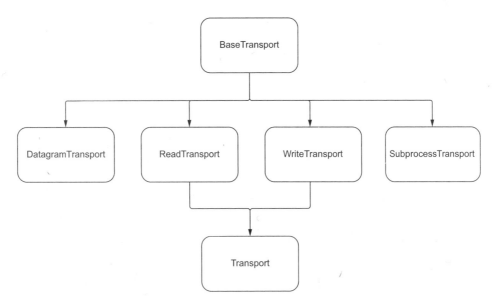

Figure 8.1 The class hierarchy of transports

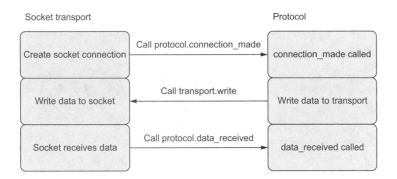

**Figure 8.2 A transport calls methods on a protocol when events happen.
A protocol can write data to a transport.**

To understand how transports and protocols work together, we'll build a basic application to run a single HTTP GET request. The first thing we'll need to do is define a class that extends asyncio.Protocol. We'll implement a few methods from the base class to make the request, receive data from the request, and handle any errors with the connection.

The first protocol method we'll need to implement is connection_made. The transport calls this method when the underlying socket has successfully connected with the HTTP server. This method employs a Transport as an argument that we can use to communicate with the server. In this case, we'll use the transport to send the HTTP request immediately.

The second method we'll need to implement is `data_received`. The transport calls this method whenever it receives data, passing it to us as bytes. This method can be called multiple times, so we'll need to create an internal buffer to store the data.

The question now becomes, how do we tell when our response is finished? To answer this, we'll implement a method called `eof_received`. This method is called when we receive the *end of file*, which, in the case of a socket, happens when the server closes the connection. Once this method is called, we are guaranteed that `data_received` will never be called again. The `eof_received` method returns a `Boolean` value that determines how to shut down the transport (close the client socket in this example). Returning `False` ensures that the transport will shut itself down, whereas `True` means that the protocol implementation we wrote will shut things down. In this case, as we don't need to do any special logic on shutdown, our method should return `False`, so we don't need to handle closing the transport ourselves.

With what we've described, we have only a way to store things in an internal buffer. So, how do consumers of our protocol get the result once the request is finished? To do this, we can create a `Future` internally to hold the result when it is complete. Then, in the `eof_received` method we'll set the result of the `future` to the result of the HTTP response. We'll then define a coroutine we'll name `get_response` that will await the future.

Let's take what we've described above and implement it as our own protocol. We'll call it `HTTPGetClientProtocol`.

Listing 8.1 Running a HTTP request with transports and protocols

```python
import asyncio
from asyncio import Transport, Future, AbstractEventLoop
from typing import Optional


class HTTPGetClientProtocol(asyncio.Protocol):

    def __init__(self, host: str, loop: AbstractEventLoop):
        self._host: str = host
        self._future: Future = loop.create_future()
        self._transport: Optional[Transport] = None
        self._response_buffer: bytes = b''

    async def get_response(self):                    ◁─┐ Await the internal future until we
        return await self._future                      │ get a response from the server.

    def _get_request_bytes(self) -> bytes:           ◁─┐ Create the
        request = f"GET / HTTP/1.1\r\n" \              │ HTTP request.
                  f"Connection: close\r\n" \
                  f"Host: {self._host}\r\n\r\n"
        return request.encode()
```

```
        def connection_made(self, transport: Transport):
            print(f'Connection made to {self._host}')
            self._transport = transport
            self._transport.write(self._get_request_bytes())
```

Once we've established a connection, use the transport to send the request.

Once we have data, save it to our internal buffer.

```
        def data_received(self, data):
            print(f'Data received!')
            self._response_buffer = self._response_buffer + data
```

Once the connection closes, complete the future with the buffer.

```
        def eof_received(self) -> Optional[bool]:
            self._future.set_result(self._response_buffer.decode())
            return False

        def connection_lost(self, exc: Optional[Exception]) -> None:
            if exc is None:
                print('Connection closed without error.')
            else:
                self._future.set_exception(exc)
```

If the connection closes without error, do nothing; otherwise, complete the future with an exception.

Now that we've implemented our protocol, let's use it to make a real request. To do this, we'll need to learn a new coroutine method on the asyncio event loop named `create_connection`. This method will create a socket connection to a given host and wrap it in an appropriate transport. In addition to a host and port, it takes in a *protocol factory*. A protocol factory is a function that creates protocol instances; in our case, an instance of the `HTTPGetClientProtocol` class we just created. When we call this coroutine, we're returned both the transport that the coroutine created along with the protocol instance the factory created.

Listing 8.2 Using the protocol

```
import asyncio
from asyncio import AbstractEventLoop
from chapter_08.listing_8_1 import HTTPGetClientProtocol


async def make_request(host: str, port: int, loop: AbstractEventLoop) -> str:
    def protocol_factory():
        return HTTPGetClientProtocol(host, loop)

    _, protocol = await loop.create_connection(protocol_factory, host=host,
     port=port)

    return await protocol.get_response()


async def main():
    loop = asyncio.get_running_loop()
    result = await make_request('www.example.com', 80, loop)
    print(result)


asyncio.run(main())
```

We first define a `make_request` method that takes in the host and port we'd like to make a request to, and the server's response. Inside this method, we create an inner method for our protocol factory that creates a new `HTTPGetClientProtocol`. We then call `create_connection` with the host and port that returns both a transport and the protocol our factory created. We won't need the transport, and we ignore it, but we will need the protocol because we'll want to use the `get_response` coroutine; therefore, we'll keep track of it in the `protocol` variable. Finally, we await the `get_response` coroutine of our protocol that will wait until the HTTP server has responded with a result. In our main coroutine, we await `make_request` and print the response. Executing this, you should see a HTTP response like the following (we've omitted the HTML body for brevity):

```
Connection made to www.example.com
Data received!
HTTP/1.1 200 OK
Age: 193241
Cache-Control: max-age=604800
Content-Type: text/html; charset=UTF-8
Connection closed without error.
```

We've learned to use transports and protocols. These APIs are lower-level and, as such, aren't the recommended way to work with streams in asyncio. Let's see how to use *streams*, a higher-level abstraction that expands on transports and protocols.

8.3   *Stream readers and stream writers*

Transports and protocols are lower-level APIs that are best suited for when we need direct control over what is happening as we send and receive data. As an example, if we're designing a networking library or web framework, we may consider transports and protocols. For most applications, we don't need this level of control, and using transports and protocols would involve us writing a bunch of repetitive code.

The designers of asyncio realized this and created the higher-level *streams* APIs. This API encapsulates the standard use cases of transports and protocols into two classes that are easy to understand and use: `StreamReader` and `StreamWriter`. As you can guess, they handle reading from and writing to streams, respectively. Using these classes is the recommended way to develop networking applications in asyncio.

To get an understanding of how to use these APIs, let's take our example of making a HTTP GET request and translate it into streams. Instead of directly instantiating `StreamReader` and `StreamWriter` instances, asyncio provides a library coroutine function named `open_connection` that will create them for us. This coroutine takes in a host and port that we'll connect to and returns a `StreamReader` and a `StreamWriter` as a tuple. Our plan will be to use the `StreamWriter` to send out the HTTP request and the `StreamReader` to read the response. `StreamReader` methods are easy to understand, and we have a convenient `readline` coroutine that waits until we have a line of data. Alternatively, we could also use `StreamReader`'s `read` coroutine that waits for a specified number of bytes to arrive.

StreamWriter is a little more complex. It has a write method as we'd expect, but it is a plain method and *not* a coroutine. Internally, stream writers try to write to a socket's output buffer right away, but this buffer can be full. If the socket's write buffer is full, the data is instead stored in an internal queue where it can later go into to the buffer. This poses a potential problem in that calling write does not necessarily send out data immediately. This can cause potential memory issues. Imagine our network connection becomes slow, able to send out 1 KB per second, but our application is writing out 1 MB per second. In this case, our application's write buffer will fill up at a much faster rate than we can send the data out to the socket's buffer, and eventually we'll start to hit memory limits on the machine, inviting a crash.

How can we wait until all our data is properly sent out? To solve this issue, we have a coroutine method called drain. This coroutine will block until all queued data gets sent to the socket, ensuring we've written everything before moving on. The pattern we'll want to use functions after we call write we'll always await a call to drain. Technically, it's not necessary to call drain after every write, but it is a good idea to help prevent bugs.

Listing 8.3 A HTTP request with stream readers and writers

```
import asyncio
from asyncio import StreamReader
from typing import AsyncGenerator


async def read_until_empty(stream_reader: StreamReader) ->
        AsyncGenerator[str, None]:
    while response := await stream_reader.readline():      ⬅──┐  Read a line and
        yield response.decode()                                decode it until
                                                               we don't have
                                                               any left.

async def main():
    host: str = 'www.example.com'
    request: str = f"GET / HTTP/1.1\r\n" \
                    f"Connection: close\r\n" \
                    f"Host: {host}\r\n\r\n"

    stream_reader, stream_writer = await
     asyncio.open_connection('www.example.com', 80)
                                                          Write the http
    try:                                                  request, and drain
        stream_writer.write(request.encode())       ⬅──  the writer.
        await stream_writer.drain()

        responses = [response async for response in
     read_until_empty(stream_reader)]          ⬅──┐  Read each
                                                      line, and store
        print(''.join(responses))                     it in a list.
    finally:
        stream_writer.close()                   ⬅──  Close the writer,
        await stream_writer.wait_closed()            and wait for it to
                                                     finish closing.
asyncio.run(main())
```

In the preceding listing, we first create a convenience async generator to read all lines from a `StreamReader`, decoding them into strings until we don't have any left to process. Then, in our main coroutine we open a connection to example.com, creating a `StreamReader` and `StreamWriter` instance in the process. We then write the request and drain the stream writer, using `write` and `drain`, respectively. Once we've written our request, we use our async generator to get each line from the response back, storing them in the `responses` list. Finally, we close the `StreamWriter` instance by calling `close` and then awaiting the `wait_closed` coroutine. Why do we need to call a method *and* a coroutine here? The reason is that when we call `close` a few things happen, such as deregistering the socket and calling the underlying transport's `connection_lost` method. These all happen asynchronously on a later iteration of the event loop, meaning that immediately after we call `close` our connection isn't closed until sometime later. If you need to wait for the connection to close before proceeding or are concerned about any exceptions that may happen while you're closing, calling `wait_closed` is best practice.

We've now learned the basics around the stream APIs by making web requests. The usefulness of these classes extends beyond web- and network-based applications. Next, we'll see how to utilize stream readers to create non-blocking command-line applications.

8.4   *Non-blocking command-line input*

Traditionally in Python, when we need to get user input, we use the `input` function. This function will stop execution flow until the user has provided input and presses Enter. What if we want to run code in the background while remaining responsive to input? For example, we may want to let the user launch multiple long-running tasks concurrently, such as long-running SQL queries. In the case of a command-line chat application, we likely want the user to be able to type a message while receiving messages from other users.

Since asyncio is single-threaded, using `input` in an asyncio application means we stop the event loop from running until the user provides input, halting our entire application. Even using tasks to kick off an operation in the background won't work. To demonstrate this, let's attempt to create an application where the user enters a time for the application to sleep. We'd like to be able to run multiple of these sleep operations concurrently while still accepting user input, so we'll ask for the number of seconds to sleep and create a `delay` task in a loop.

Listing 8.4   Attempting background tasks

```
import asyncio
from util import delay


async def main():
    while True:
```

```
delay_time = input('Enter a time to sleep:')
asyncio.create_task(delay(int(delay_time)))
```

```
asyncio.run(main())
```

If this code worked the way we intended, after we input a number we'd expect to see `sleeping for n second(s)` printed out followed by `finished sleeping for n second(s)` *n* seconds later. However, this isn't the case, and we see nothing except our prompt to enter a time to sleep. This is because there is no `await` inside our code and, therefore, the task never gets a chance to run on the event loop. We can hack around this by putting `await asyncio.sleep(0)` after the `create_task` line that will schedule the task (this is known as "yielding to the event loop" and will be covered in chapter 14). Even with this trick, as it stops the entire thread the `input` call still blocks any background task we create from running to completion.

What we really want is for the `input` function to be a coroutine instead, so we could write something like `delay_time = await input('Enter a time to sleep:')`. If we could do this, our task would schedule properly and continue to run while we waited for user input. Unfortunately, there is no coroutine variant of `input`, so we'll need to do something else.

This is where protocols and stream readers can help us out. Recall that a stream reader has the `readline` coroutine that is the type of coroutine we're looking for. If we had a way to hook a stream reader to standard input, we could then use this coroutine for user input.

asyncio has a coroutine method on the event loop called `connect_read_pipe` that connects a protocol to a file-like object, which is almost what we want. This coroutine method accepts a *protocol factory* and a *pipe*. A protocol factory is just a function that creates a protocol instance. A pipe is a file-like object, which is defined as an object with methods such as `read` and `write` on it. The `connect_read_pipe` coroutine will then connect the pipe to the protocol the factory creates, taking data from the pipe and sending it to the protocol.

In terms of standard console input, `sys.stdin` fits the bill of a file-like object that we can pass in to `connect_read_pipe`. Once we call this coroutine, we'll get a tuple of the protocol our factory function created and a `ReadTransport`. The question now becomes what protocol should we create in our factory, and how do we connect this with a `StreamReader` that has the `readline` coroutine we'd like to use?

asyncio provides a utility class called `StreamReaderProtocol` for connecting instances of stream readers to protocols. When we instantiate this class, we pass in an instance of a stream reader. The protocol class then delegates to the stream reader we created, allowing us to use the stream reader to read data from standard input. Putting all these pieces together, we can create a command-line application that does not block the event loop when waiting for user input.

> ### For Windows users
>
> Unfortunately, on Windows `connect_read_pipe` will not work with `sys.stdin`. This is due to an unfixed bug caused by the way Windows implements file descriptors. For this to work on Windows, you'll need to call `sys.stdin.readline()` in a separate thread using techniques we explored in chapter 7. You can read more about this issue at https://bugs.python.org/issue26832.

Since we'll be reusing the asynchronous standard in reader throughout the rest of the chapter, let's create it in its own file, `listing_8_5.py`. We'll then import it in the rest of the chapter.

Listing 8.5 An asynchronous standard input reader

```
import asyncio
from asyncio import StreamReader
import sys


async def create_stdin_reader() -> StreamReader:
    stream_reader = asyncio.StreamReader()
    protocol = asyncio.StreamReaderProtocol(stream_reader)
    loop = asyncio.get_running_loop()
    await loop.connect_read_pipe(lambda: protocol, sys.stdin)
    return stream_reader
```

In the preceding listing, we create a reusable coroutine named `create_stdin_reader` that creates a `StreamReader` that we'll use to asynchronously read standard input. We first create a stream reader instance and pass it to a stream reader protocol. We then call `connect_read_pipe`, passing in a protocol factory as a lambda function. This lambda returns the stream reader protocol we created earlier. We also pass `sys.stdin` to connect standard input to our stream reader protocol. Since we won't need them, we ignore the transport and protocol that `connect_read_pipe` returns. We can now use this function to asynchronously read from standard input and build our application.

Listing 8.6 Using stream readers for input

```
import asyncio
from chapter_08.listing_8_5 import create_stdin_reader
from util import delay


async def main():
    stdin_reader = await create_stdin_reader()
    while True:
        delay_time = await stdin_reader.readline()
        asyncio.create_task(delay(int(delay_time)))


asyncio.run(main())
```

In our main coroutine, we call `create_stdin_reader` and loop forever, waiting for input from the user with the `readline` coroutine. Once user presses Enter on the keyboard, this coroutine will deliver the input text entered. Once we have input from the user, we convert it into an integer (note here that for a real application, we should add code to handle bad input, as we'll crash if we pass in a string right now) and create a `delay` task. Running this, you'll be able to run multiple `delay` tasks concurrently while still entering command-line input. For instance, entering delays of 5, 4, and 3 seconds, respectively, you should see the following output:

```
5
sleeping for 5 second(s)
4
sleeping for 4 second(s)
3
sleeping for 3 second(s)
finished sleeping for 5 second(s)
finished sleeping for 4 second(s)
finished sleeping for 3 second(s)
```

This works, but this approach has a critical flaw. What happens if a message appears on the console while we're typing an input delay time? To test this out, we'll enter a delay time of 3 seconds and then start rapidly pressing 1. Doing this, we'll see something like the following:

```
3
sleeping for 3 second(s)
111111finished sleeping for 3 second(s)
11
```

While we were typing, the message from our delay task prints out, disrupting our input line and forcing it to continue on the next line. In addition, the input buffer is now only `11`, meaning if we press Enter, we'll create a `delay` task for that amount of time, losing the first few pieces of input. This is because, by default, the terminal runs in *cooked* mode. In this mode, the terminal echoes user input to standard output, and also processes special keys, such as Enter and CTRL-C. This issue arises because the `delay` coroutine writes to standard out at the same time the terminal is echoing output, causing a race condition.

There is also a single position on the screen where standard out writes to. This is known as a *cursor* and is much like a cursor you'd see in a word processor. As we enter input, the cursor rests on the line where our keyboard input prints out. This means that any output messages from other coroutines will print on the same line as our input, since this is where the cursor is, causing odd behavior.

To solve these issues, we need a combination of two solutions. The first is to bring the echoing of input from the terminal into our Python application. This will ensure that, while echoing input from the user, we don't write any output messages from other coroutines as we're single-threaded. The second is to move the cursor around the screen when we write output messages, ensuring that we don't write output messages on the same line as our input. We can do these by manipulating the settings of our terminal and using escape sequences.

8.4.1   *Terminal raw mode and the read coroutine*

Because our terminal is running in cooked mode, it handles echoing user input on `readline` for us outside of our application. How can we bring this processing into our application, so we can avoid the race conditions we saw previously?

The answer is switching the terminal to *raw* mode. In raw mode, instead of the terminal doing buffering, preprocessing, and echoing for us, every keystroke is sent to the application. It is then up to us to echo and preprocess as we'd like. While this means we must do extra work, it also means we have fine-grained control around writing to standard out, giving us the needed power to avoid race conditions.

Python allows us to change the terminal to raw mode but also allows for `cbreak` mode. This mode behaves like raw mode with the difference being that keystrokes like CTRL-C will still be interpreted for us, saving us some work. We can enter raw mode by using the `tty` module and the `setcbreak` function like so:

```
import tty
import sys
tty.setcbreak(sys.stdin)
```

Once we're in `cbreak` mode, we'll need to rethink how we designed our application. The `readline` coroutine will no longer work, as it won't echo any input for us in raw mode. Instead, we'll want to read one character at a time and store it in our own internal buffer, echoing each character typed in. The standard input stream reader we created has a method called `read` that takes in a number of bytes to read from the stream. Calling `read(1)` will read one character at a time, which we can then store in a buffer and echo to standard out.

We now have two pieces of the puzzle to solve this, entering `cbreak` mode and reading one input character at a time, echoing it to standard out. We need to think through how to display the output of the `delay` coroutines, so it won't interfere with our input.

Let's define a few requirements to make our application more user-friendly and solve the issue with output writing on the same line as input. We'll then let these requirements inform how we implement things:

1. The user input field should always remain at the bottom of the screen.
2. Coroutine output should start from the top of the screen and move down.
3. When there are more messages than available lines on the screen, existing messages should scroll up.

Given these requirements, how can we display the output from the `delay` coroutine? Given that we want to scroll messages up when there are more messages than available lines, writing directly to standard out with print will prove tricky. Instead of doing this, the approach we'll take is keeping a *deque* (double-ended queue) of the messages we want to write to standard out. We'll set the maximum number of elements in the deque to the number of rows on the terminal screen. This will give us the scrolling behavior we want when the deque is full, as items in the back of the deque will be discarded. When a new message is appended to the deque, we'll move to the top of the screen and redraw each message. This will get us the scrolling behavior we desire without having to keep much information about the state of standard out. This makes our application flow look like the illustration in figure 8.3.

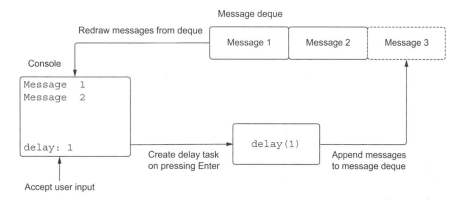

Figure 8.3   The delay console application

Our game plan for the application will then be as follows:

1   Move the cursor to the bottom of the screen, and when a key is pressed, append it to our internal buffer, and echo the keypress to standard out.

2   When the user presses Enter, create a `delay` task. Instead of writing output messages to standard out, we'll append them to a deque with a maximum number of elements equal to the number of rows on the console.

3   Once a message goes into the deque, we'll redraw the output on the screen. We first move the cursor to the top left of the screen. We then print out all messages in the deque. Once we're done, we return the cursor to the input row and column where it was before.

To implement the application in this way, we'll first need to learn how to move the cursor around the screen. We can use ANSI *escape codes* to do this. These are special codes we can write to standard out performing actions like changing the color of text, moving the cursor up or down, and deleting lines. Escape sequences are first introduced with an escape code; in Python, we can do this by printing \033 to the console. Many of the escape sequences we'll need to use are introduced by *control sequence introducers,* which are started by printing \033[. To better understand this, let's see how to move the cursor to five lines below where it currently is.

```
sys.stdout.write('\033[5E')
```

This escape sequence starts with the control sequence introducer followed by 5E. 5 represents the number of rows from the current cursor row we'd like to move down, and E is the code for "move the cursor down this number of lines." Escape sequences are terse and a little hard to follow. In the next listing, we'll create several functions with clear names to explain what each escape code does, and we'll import them in future listings. If you'd like more explanation on ANSI escape sequences and how they work, the Wikipedia article on the subject has great information at https://en .wikipedia.org/wiki/ANSI_escape_code.

Let's think through how we'll need to move the cursor around the screen to figure out which functions we'll need to implement. First, we'll need to move the cursor to the bottom of the screen to accept user input. Then, once the user presses Enter, we'll need to clear any text they have entered. To print coroutine output messages from the top of the screen, we'll need to be able to move to the first line of the screen. We'll also need to save and restore the current position of the cursor, since while we're typing a message from a coroutine it may print a message, meaning we'll need to move it back to the proper spot. We can do these with the following escape code functions:

Listing 8.7   Escape sequence convenience functions

```python
import sys
import shutil

def save_cursor_position():
    sys.stdout.write('\0337')


def restore_cursor_position():
    sys.stdout.write('\0338')


def move_to_top_of_screen():
    sys.stdout.write('\033[H')


def delete_line():
    sys.stdout.write('\033[2K')


def clear_line():
    sys.stdout.write('\033[2K\033[0G')


def move_back_one_char():
    sys.stdout.write('\033[1D')
```

```
def move_to_bottom_of_screen() -> int:
    _, total_rows = shutil.get_terminal_size()
    input_row = total_rows - 1
    sys.stdout.write(f'\033[{input_row}E')
    return total_rows
```

Now that we have a set of reusable functions to move the cursor around the screen, let's implement a reusable coroutine for reading standard input one character at a time. We'll use the read coroutine to do this. Once we have read a character, we'll write it to standard output, storing the character in an internal buffer. Since we also want to handle a user pressing Delete, we'll watch for the Delete key. When a user presses it, we'll delete the character from the buffer and standard output.

Listing 8.8 Reading input one character at a time

```
import sys
from asyncio import StreamReader
from collections import deque
from chapter_08.listing_8_7 import move_back_one_char, clear_line


async def read_line(stdin_reader: StreamReader) -> str:
    def erase_last_char():                          ◁――――  Convenience function to
        move_back_one_char()                               delete the previous character
        sys.stdout.write(' ')                              from standard output
        move_back_one_char()

    delete_char = b'\x7f'
    input_buffer = deque()
    while (input_char := await stdin_reader.read(1)) != b'\n':
        if input_char == delete_char:               ◁―――  If the input character
            if len(input_buffer) > 0:                     is backspace, remove
                input_buffer.pop()                        the last character.
                erase_last_char()
                sys.stdout.flush()
        else:
            input_buffer.append(input_char)         ◁―――  If the input character is
            sys.stdout.write(input_char.decode())         not backspace, append it
            sys.stdout.flush()                            to the buffer and echo.
    clear_line()
    return b''.join(input_buffer).decode()
```

Our coroutine takes in a stream reader that we've attached to standard input. We then define a convenience function to erase the previous character from standard output, as we'll need this when a user presses Delete. We then enter a while loop reading character by character until the user hits Enter. If the user presses Delete, we remove the last character from the buffer and from standard out. Otherwise, we append it to the buffer and echo it. Once the user presses Enter, we clear the input line and return the contents of the buffer.

Next, we'll need to define the queue where we'll store the messages we want to print to standard out. Since we want to redraw output whenever we append a message, we'll define a class that wraps a deque and takes in a callback awaitable. The callback we pass in will be responsible for redrawing output. We'll also add an `append` coroutine method to our class that will append items to the deque and call the callback with the current set of items in the deque.

Listing 8.9   A message store

```
from collections import deque
from typing import Callable, Deque, Awaitable


class MessageStore:
    def __init__(self, callback: Callable[[Deque], Awaitable[None]],
      max_size: int):
        self._deque = deque(maxlen=max_size)
        self._callback = callback

    async def append(self, item):
        self._deque.append(item)
        await self._callback(self._deque)
```

Now, we have all the pieces to create the application. We'll rewrite our `delay` coroutine to add messages to the message store. Then, in our main coroutine, we'll create a helper coroutine to redraw messages in our deque to standard out. This is the callback we'll pass to our `MessageStore`. Then, we'll use the `read_line` coroutine we implemented earlier to accept user input, creating a delay task when the user hits Enter.

Listing 8.10   The asynchronous delay application

```
import asyncio
import os
import tty
from collections import deque
from chapter_08.listing_8_5 import create_stdin_reader
from chapter_08.listing_8_7 import *
from chapter_08.listing_8_8 import read_line
from chapter_08.listing_8_9 import MessageStore


async def sleep(delay: int, message_store: MessageStore):
    await message_store.append(f'Starting delay {delay}')      ◁── Append the output messages to the message store.
    await asyncio.sleep(delay)
    await message_store.append(f'Finished delay {delay}')


async def main():
    tty.setcbreak(sys.stdin)
    os.system('clear')
    rows = move_to_bottom_of_screen()           Callback to move the cursor to the top of the screen; redraw output and move the cursor back.

    async def redraw_output(items: deque):      ◁──
        save_cursor_position()
```

```
        move_to_top_of_screen()
        for item in items:
            delete_line()
            print(item)
        restore_cursor_position()

    messages = MessageStore(redraw_output, rows - 1)

    stdin_reader = await create_stdin_reader()

    while True:
        line = await read_line(stdin_reader)
        delay_time = int(line)
        asyncio.create_task(sleep(delay_time, messages))


asyncio.run(main())
```

Running this, you'll be able to create delays and watch input write to the console even as you type. While it is more complicated than our first attempt, we've built an application that avoids the problems writing to standard out that we faced earlier.

What we've built works for the delay coroutine, but what about something more real-world? The pieces we've just defined are robust enough we can make more useful applications by reusing them. For example, let's think through how to create a command-line SQL client. Certain queries may take a long time to execute, but we may want to run other queries in the meantime or cancel a running query. Using what we've just built, we can create this type of client. Let's build one using our previous e-commerce product database from chapter 5, where we created a schema with a set of clothing brands, products, and SKUs. We'll create a connection pool to connect to our database, and we'll reuse our code from previous examples to accept and run queries. We'll output basic information about the queries to the console—for now, just the number of rows returned.

Listing 8.11 An asynchronous command-line sql client

```
import asyncio
import asyncpg
import os
import tty
from collections import deque
from asyncpg.pool import Pool
from chapter_08.listing_8_5 import create_stdin_reader
from chapter_08.listing_8_7 import *
from chapter_08.listing_8_8 import read_line
from chapter_08.listing_8_9 import MessageStore


async def run_query(query: str, pool: Pool, message_store: MessageStore):
    async with pool.acquire() as connection:
        try:
```

```
            result = await connection.fetchrow(query)
            await message_store.append(f'Fetched {len(result)} rows from:
    {query}')
        except Exception as e:
            await message_store.append(f'Got exception {e} from: {query}')


async def main():
    tty.setcbreak(0)
    os.system('clear')
    rows = move_to_bottom_of_screen()

    async def redraw_output(items: deque):
        save_cursor_position()
        move_to_top_of_screen()
        for item in items:
            delete_line()
            print(item)
        restore_cursor_position()

    messages = MessageStore(redraw_output, rows - 1)

    stdin_reader = await create_stdin_reader()

    async with asyncpg.create_pool(host='127.0.0.1',
                                   port=5432,
                                   user='postgres',
                                   password='password',
                                   database='products',
                                   min_size=6,
                                   max_size=6) as pool:

        while True:
            query = await read_line(stdin_reader)
            asyncio.create_task(run_query(query, pool, messages))


asyncio.run(main())
```

Our code is almost the same as before, with the difference that instead of a delay coroutine, we create a run_query coroutine. Instead of just sleeping for an arbitrary amount of time, this runs a query the user entered that can take an arbitrary amount of time. This lets us issue new queries from the command line while others are still running; it and also lets us see output from completed ones even as we are typing in new queries.

We now know how to create command-line clients that can handle input while other code executes and writes to the console. Next, we'll learn how to create servers using higher-level asyncio APIs.

8.5 Creating servers

When we have built servers, such as our echo server, we've created a server socket, bound it to a port and waited for incoming connections. While this works, asyncio lets us create servers at a higher level of abstraction, meaning we can create them without ever worrying about managing sockets. Creating servers this way simplifies the code we need to write with sockets, and as such, using these higher-level APIs is the recommended way to create and manage servers using asyncio.

We can create a server with the `asyncio.start_server` coroutine. This coroutine takes in several optional parameters to configure things such as SSL, but the main parameters we'll be interested in are the `host`, `port`, and `client_connected_cb`. The host and port are like what we've seen before: the address that the server socket will listen for connections. The more interesting piece is `client_connected_cb`, which is either a callback function or a coroutine that will run whenever a client connects to the server. This callback takes in a `StreamReader` and `StreamWriter` as parameters that will let us read from and write to the client that connected to the server.

When we await `start_server`, it will return an `AbstractServer` object. This class lacks many interesting methods that we'll need to use, other than `serve_forever`, which runs the server forever until we terminate it. This class is also an asynchronous context manager. This means we can use an instance of it with `async with` syntax to have the server properly shut down on exit.

To get a handle on creating servers, let's create an echo server again but make it a little more advanced. Instead of just echoing back output, we'll display information about how many other clients are connected. We'll also display information when a client disconnects from the server. To manage this, we'll create a class we'll call `ServerState` to manage how many users are connected. Once a user connects, we'll add them to the server state and notify other clients that they connected.

Listing 8.12 Creating an echo server with server objects

```python
import asyncio
import logging
from asyncio import StreamReader, StreamWriter


class ServerState:

    def __init__(self):
        self._writers = []

    async def add_client(self, reader: StreamReader, writer: StreamWriter):    # Add a client to the server state, and create an echo task.
        self._writers.append(writer)
        await self._on_connect(writer)
        asyncio.create_task(self._echo(reader, writer))

    async def _on_connect(self, writer: StreamWriter):    # On a new connection, tell the client how many users are online, and notify others of a new user.
        writer.write(f'Welcome! {len(self._writers)} user(s) are
    online!\n'.encode())
```

```
            await writer.drain()
            await self._notify_all('New user connected!\n')

    async def _echo(self, reader: StreamReader, writer: StreamWriter):
        try:
            while (data := await reader.readline()) != b'':
                writer.write(data)
                await writer.drain()
            self._writers.remove(writer)
            await self._notify_all(f'Client disconnected. {len(self._writers)}
    user(s) are online!\n')
        except Exception as e:
            logging.exception('Error reading from client.', exc_info=e)
            self._writers.remove(writer)

    async def _notify_all(self, message: str):
        for writer in self._writers:
            try:
                writer.write(message.encode())
                await writer.drain()
            except ConnectionError as e:
                logging.exception('Could not write to client.', exc_info=e)
                self._writers.remove(writer)


async def main():
    server_state = ServerState()

    async def client_connected(reader: StreamReader, writer:
      StreamWriter) -> None:
        await server_state.add_client(reader, writer)

    server = await asyncio.start_server(client_connected, '127.0.0.1', 8000)

    async with server:
        await server.serve_forever()


asyncio.run(main())
```

Handle echoing user input when a client disconnects, and notify other users of a disconnect.

Helper method to send a message to all other users. If a message fails to send, remove that user.

When a client connects, add that client to the server state.

Start the server, and start serving forever.

When a user connects to our server, our `client_connected` callback responds with a reader and writer for that user, which in turn calls the server state's `add_client` coroutine. In the `add_client` coroutine, we store the `StreamWriter`, so we can send messages to all connected clients and remove it when a client disconnects. We then call `_on_connect`, which sends a message to the client informing them how many other users are connected. In `_on_connect`, we also notify any other connected clients that a new user has connected.

The `_echo` coroutine is similar to what we've done in the past with the twist being that when a user disconnects, we notify any other connected clients that someone disconnected. When running this, you should have a functioning echo server that lets each individual client know when a new user connects and disconnects from the server.

We've now seen how to create an asyncio server that is a little more advanced than what we've done previously. Next, let's build on top of this knowledge and create a chat server and chat client—something even more advanced.

8.6   *Creating a chat server and client*

We now know how to both create servers and handle asynchronous command-line input. We can combine what we know in these two areas to create two applications. The first is a chat server that accepts multiple chat clients at the same time, and the second is a chat client that connects to the server and sends and receives chat messages.

Before we begin designing our application, let's start with some requirements that will help us make the correct design choices. First, for our server:

1 A chat client should be able to connect to the server when they provide a username.
2 Once a user is connected, they should be able to send chat messages to the server, and each message should be sent to every user connected to the server.
3 To prevent idle users taking up resources, if a user is idle for more than one minute, the server should disconnect them.

Second, for our client:

1 When a user starts the application, the client should prompt for a username and attempt to connect to the server.
2 Once connected, the user will see any messages from other clients scroll down from the top of the screen.
3 The user should have an input field at the bottom of the screen. When the user presses Enter, the text in the input should be sent to the server and then to all other connected clients.

Given these requirements, let's first think through what our communication between the client and server should look like. First, we'll need to send a message from the client to the server with our username. We need to disambiguate connecting with a username from a message send, so we'll introduce a simple command protocol to indicate that we're sending a username. To keep things simple, we'll just pass a string with a command name called CONNECT followed by the user-provided username. For example, CONNECT MissIslington will be the message we'll send to the server to connect a user with the username "MissIslington."

Once we've connected, we'll just send messages directly to the server, which will then send the message to all connected clients (including ourselves; as needed, you could optimize this away). For a more robust application, you may want to consider a command that the server sends back to the client to acknowledge that the message was received, but we'll skip this for brevity.

With this in mind, we have enough to start designing our server. We'll create a ChatServerState class similar to what we did in the previous section. Once a client connects, we'll wait for them to provide a username with the CONNECT command.

Assuming they provide it, we'll create a task to listen for messages from the client and write them to all other connected clients. To keep track of connected clients, we'll keep a dictionary of the connected usernames to their StreamWriter instances. If a connected user is idle for more than a minute, we'll disconnect them and remove them from the dictionary, sending a message to other users that they left the chat.

Listing 8.13   A chat server

```python
import asyncio
import logging
from asyncio import StreamReader, StreamWriter


class ChatServer:

    def __init__(self):
        self._username_to_writer = {}

    async def start_chat_server(self, host: str, port: int):
        server = await asyncio.start_server(self.client_connected, host, port)

        async with server:
            await server.serve_forever()

    async def client_connected(self, reader: StreamReader, writer: StreamWriter):    ◁─┐
        command = await reader.readline()
        print(f'CONNECTED {reader} {writer}')
        command, args = command.split(b' ')
        if command == b'CONNECT':
            username = args.replace(b'\n', b'').decode()
            self._add_user(username, reader, writer)
            await self._on_connect(username, writer)
        else:
            logging.error('Got invalid command from client, disconnecting.')
            writer.close()
            await writer.wait_closed()

    def _add_user(self, username: str, reader:
      StreamReader, writer: StreamWriter):
        self._username_to_writer[username] = writer
        asyncio.create_task(self._listen_for_messages(username, reader))

    async def _on_connect(self, username: str, writer: StreamWriter):    ◁─┐
        writer.write(f'Welcome! {len(self._username_to_writer)} user(s) are
      online!\n'.encode())
        await writer.drain()
        await self._notify_all(f'{username} connected!\n')

    async def _remove_user(self, username: str):
        writer = self._username_to_writer[username]
        del self._username_to_writer[username]
        try:
            writer.close()
```

> **Wait for the client to provide a valid username command; otherwise, disconnect them.**

> **Store a user's stream writer instance and create a task to listen for messages.**

> **Once a user connects, notify all others that they have connected.**

```
                    await writer.wait_closed()
            except Exception as e:
                logging.exception('Error closing client writer, ignoring.',
        exc_info=e)

        async def _listen_for_messages(self,
                                    username: str,
                                    reader: StreamReader):
            try:
                while (data := await asyncio.wait_for(reader.readline(), 60)) != b'':
                    await self._notify_all(f'{username}: {data.decode()}')
                await self._notify_all(f'{username} has left the chat\n')
            except Exception as e:
                logging.exception('Error reading from client.', exc_info=e)
                await self._remove_user(username)

        async def _notify_all(self, message: str):
            inactive_users = []
            for username, writer in self._username_to_writer.items():
                try:
                    writer.write(message.encode())
                    await writer.drain()
                except ConnectionError as e:
                    logging.exception('Could not write to client.', exc_info=e)
                    inactive_users.append(username)

            [await self._remove_user(username) for username in inactive_users]


    async def main():
        chat_server = ChatServer()
        await chat_server.start_chat_server('127.0.0.1', 8000)


    asyncio.run(main())
```

Listen for messages from a client and send them to all other clients, waiting a maximum of a minute for a message.

Send a message to all connected clients, removing any disconnected users.

Our `ChatServer` class encapsulates everything about our chat server in one clean interface. The main entry point is the `start_chat_server` coroutine. This coroutine starts a server on the specified host and port, and calls `serve_forever`. For our server's client connected callback, we use our `client_connected` coroutine. This coroutine waits for the first line of data from the client, and if it receives a valid `CONNECT` command, it calls `_add_user` and then `_on_connect`; otherwise, it terminates the connection.

The `_add_user` function stores the username and user's stream writer in an internal dictionary and then creates a task to listen for chat messages from the user. The `_on_connect` coroutine sends a message to the client welcoming them to the chat room and then notifies all other connected clients that the user connected.

When we called `_add_user`, we created a task for the `_listen_for_messages` coroutine. This coroutine is where the meat of our application lies. We loop forever, reading messages from the client until we see an empty line, indicating the client disconnected.

Once we get a message, we call _notify_all to send the chat message to all connected clients. To satisfy the requirement that a client should be disconnected after being idle for a minute, we wrap our readline coroutine in wait_for. This will throw a TimeoutError if the client has idled for longer than a minute. In this case, we have a broad exception clause that catches TimeoutError and any other exceptions thrown. We handle any exception by removing the client from the _username_to_writer dictionary, so we stop sending messages to them.

We now have a complete server, but the server is meaningless without a client to connect to it. We'll implement the client similarly to the command-line SQL client we wrote earlier. We'll create a coroutine to listen for messages from the server and append them to a message store, redrawing the screen when a new message comes in. We'll also put the input at the bottom of the screen, and when the user presses Enter, we'll send the message to the chat server.

Listing 8.14   The chat client

```python
import asyncio
import os
import logging
import tty
from asyncio import StreamReader, StreamWriter
from collections import deque
from chapter_08.listing_8_5 import create_stdin_reader
from chapter_08.listing_8_7 import *
from chapter_08.listing_8_8 import read_line
from chapter_08.listing_8_9 import MessageStore


async def send_message(message: str, writer: StreamWriter):
    writer.write((message + '\n').encode())
    await writer.drain()


async def listen_for_messages(reader: StreamReader,                    # Listen for
                              message_store: MessageStore):            # messages from
    while (message := await reader.readline()) != b'':                 # the server,
        await message_store.append(message.decode())                  # appending
    await message_store.append('Server closed connection.')           # them to the
                                                                       # message store.

async def read_and_send(stdin_reader: StreamReader,                    # Read input from
                        writer: StreamWriter):                         # the user, and
    while True:                                                        # send it to the
        message = await read_line(stdin_reader)                        # server.
        await send_message(message, writer)


async def main():
    async def redraw_output(items: deque):
        save_cursor_position()
        move_to_top_of_screen()
```

```
        for item in items:
            delete_line()
            sys.stdout.write(item)
        restore_cursor_position()

    tty.setcbreak(0)
    os.system('clear')
    rows = move_to_bottom_of_screen()

    messages = MessageStore(redraw_output, rows - 1)

    stdin_reader = await create_stdin_reader()
    sys.stdout.write('Enter username: ')
    username = await read_line(stdin_reader)

    reader, writer = await asyncio.open_connection('127.0.0.1', 8000)

    writer.write(f'CONNECT {username}\n'.encode())
    await writer.drain()

    message_listener = asyncio.create_task(listen_for_messages(reader, messages))
    input_listener = asyncio.create_task(read_and_send(stdin_reader, writer))

    try:
        await asyncio.wait([message_listener, input_listener],
     return_when=asyncio.FIRST_COMPLETED)
    except Exception as e:
        logging.exception(e)
        writer.close()
        await writer.wait_closed()


asyncio.run(main())
```

Open a connection to the server, and send the connect message with the username.

Create a task to listen for messages, and listen for input; wait until one finishes.

We first ask the user for their username, and once we have one, we send our CONNECT message to the server. Then, we create two tasks: one to listen for messages from the server and one to continuously read chat messages and send them to the server. We then take these two tasks and wait for whichever one completes first by wrapping them in asyncio.wait. We do this because the server could disconnect us, or the input listener could throw an exception. If we just awaited each task independently, we may find ourselves stuck. For instance, if the server disconnected us, we'd have no way to stop the input listener if we had awaited that task first. Using the wait coroutine prevents this issue because if either the message listener or input listener finishes, our application will exit. If we wanted to have more robust logic here, we could do this by checking the done and pending sets wait returns. For instance, if the input listener threw an exception, we could cancel the message listener task.

If you first run the server, then run a couple of chat clients, you'll be able to send and receive messages in the client like a normal chat application. For example, two users connecting to the chat may produce output like the following:

```
Welcome! 1 user(s) are online!
MissIslington connected!
SirBedevere connected!
SirBedevere: Is that your nose?
MissIslington: No, it's a false one!
```

We've built a chat server and client that can handle multiple users connected simultaneously with only one thread. This application could stand to be more robust. For example, you may want to consider retrying message sends on failure or a protocol to acknowledge a client received a message. Making this a production-worthy application is rather complex and is outside the scope of this book, though it might be a fun exercise for the reader, as there are many failure points to think through. Using similar concepts to what we've explored in this example, you'll be able to create robust client and server applications to suit your needs.

Summary

- We've learned how to use the lower-level transport and protocol APIs to build a simple HTTP client. These APIs are the bedrock of the higher-level stream asyncio stream APIs and are generally not recommended for general use.
- We've learned how to use the `StreamReader` and `StreamWriter` classes to build network applications. These higher-level APIs are the recommended approach to work with streams in asyncio.
- We've learned how to use streams to create non-blocking command-line applications that can remain responsive to user input while running tasks in the background.
- We've learned how to create servers using the `start_server` coroutine. This approach is the recommended way to create servers in asyncio, as opposed to using sockets directly.
- We've learned how to create responsive client and server applications using streams and servers. Using this knowledge, we can create network-based applications, such as chat servers and clients.

Web applications

9

This chapter covers

- Creating web applications with aiohttp
- The asynchronous server gateway interface (ASGI)
- Creating ASGI web applications with Starlette
- Using Django's asynchronous views

Web applications power most of the sites we use on the internet today. If you've worked as a developer for a company with an internet presence, you've likely worked on a web application at some point in your career. In the world of synchronous Python, this means you've used frameworks such as Flask, Bottle, or the extremely popular Django. With the exception of more recent versions of Django, these web frameworks were not built to work with asyncio out of the box. As such, when our web applications perform work that could be parallelized, such as querying a database or making calls to other APIs, we don't have options outside of multithreading or multiprocessing. This means that we'll need to explore new frameworks that are compatible with asyncio.

In this chapter, we'll learn about a few popular asyncio-ready web frameworks. We'll first see how to use a framework we've already dealt with, aiohttp, to build async

RESTful APIs. We'll then learn about the asynchronous server gateway interface, or ASGI, which is the async replacement for the WSGI (web server gateway interface) and is how many web applications run. Using ASGI with Starlette, we'll build a simple REST API with WebSocket support. We'll also look at using Django's asynchronous views. Performance of web applications is always a consideration when scaling, so we'll also take a look at performance numbers by benchmarking with a load testing tool.

9.1   Creating a REST API with aiohttp

Previously, we used aiohttp as a HTTP client to make thousands of concurrent web requests to web applications. aiohttp has not only support as a HTTP client but also has functionality to create asyncio-ready web application servers as well.

9.1.1   What is REST?

REST is an abbreviation for *representational state transfer*. It is a widely used paradigm in modern web application development, especially in conjunction with single-page applications with frameworks like React and Vue. REST provides us with a stateless, structured way to design our web APIs independently of client-side technology. A REST API should be able to interoperate with any number of clients from a mobile phone to a browser, and all that should need to change is the client-side presentation of the data.

The key concept in REST is a *resource*. A resource is typically anything that can be represented by a noun. For example, a customer, a product, or an account can be RESTful resources. The resources we just listed reference a single customer or product. Resources can also be collections, for example, "customers" or "products" that have singletons we can access by some unique identifier. Singletons may also have sub-resources. A customer could have a list of favorite products as an example. Let's take a look at a couple of REST APIs to get a better understanding:

```
customers
customers/{id}
customers/{id}/favorites
```

We have three REST API endpoints here. Our first endpoint, `customers`, references a collection of customers. As consumers of this API, we would expect this to return a list of customers (this may be paginated as it could potentially be a large set). Our second endpoint references a single customer and takes in an `id` as a parameter. If we uniquely identify customers with an integer ID, calling `customers/1` would give us data for the customer with an `id` of 1. Our final endpoint is an example of a sub-entity. A customer could have a list of favorite products, making the list of favorites a sub-entity of a customer. Calling `customers/1/favorites` would return the list of favorites for the customer with `id` of 1.

We'll design our REST APIs going forward to return JSON as this is typical, though we could choose any format that suits our need. REST APIs can sometimes support multiple data representations through content negotiation via HTTP headers.

While a proper look into all the details of REST is outside the scope of this book, the creator of REST's PhD dissertation is a good place to learn about the concepts. It is available at http://mng.bz/1jAg.

9.1.2 *aiohttp server basics*

Let's get started by creating a simple "hello world"-style API with aiohttp. We'll start by creating a simple GET endpoint that will give us some basic data in JSON format about the time and date. We'll call our endpoint /time and will expect it to return the month, day, and current time.

aiohttp provides web server functionality in the web module. Once we import this, we can define endpoints (called *routes* in aiohttp) with a RouteTableDef. A RouteTableDef provides a decorator that lets us specify a request type (GET, POST, etc.) and a string representing the endpoint name. We can then use the RouteTableDef decorator to decorate coroutines that will execute when we call that endpoint. Inside these decorated coroutines, we can perform whatever application logic we'd like and then return data to the client.

Creating these endpoints by themselves does nothing, however, and we still need to start the web application to serve the routes. We do this by first creating an Application instance, adding the routes from our RouteTableDef and running the application.

Listing 9.1 The current time endpoint

```
from aiohttp import web
from datetime import datetime
from aiohttp.web_request import Request
from aiohttp.web_response import Response

routes = web.RouteTableDef()

@routes.get('/time')                 ◁──┐  Create a time GET endpoint;
async def time(request: Request) -> Response:    when a client calls this endpoint,
    today = datetime.today()                     the time coroutine will run.

    result = {
        'month': today.month,
        'day': today.day,
        'time': str(today.time())
    }                                ┌─ Take the result
                                     │  dictionary, and turn it
    return web.json_response(result) ◁┘  into a JSON response.


app = web.Application()              ◁─┐  Create the web application,
app.add_routes(routes)                 │  register the routes, and
web.run_app(app)                       │  run the application.
```

In the preceding listing, we first create a time endpoint. @routes.get('/time') specifies that the decorated coroutine will execute when a client executes a HTTP GET request against the /time URI. In our `time` coroutine, we get the month, day, and time and store it in a dictionary. We then call `web.json_response`, which takes the dictionary and serializes it into JSON format. It also configures the HTTP response we send back. In particular, it sets the status code to `200` and the content type to `'application/json'`.

We then create the web application and start it. First, we create an `Application` instance and call `add_routes`. This registers all the decorators we created with the web application. We then call `run_app`, which starts the web server. By default, this starts the web server on localhost port 8080.

When we run this, we'll be able to test this out by either going to local-host:8080/time in a web browser or using a command-line utility, such as cURL or Wget. Let's test it out with cURL to take a look at the full response by running `curl -i localhost:8080/time`. You should see something like the following:

```
HTTP/1.1 200 OK
Content-Type: application/json; charset=utf-8
Content-Length: 51
Date: Mon, 23 Nov 2020 16:35:32 GMT
Server: Python/3.9 aiohttp/3.6.2

{"month": 11, "day": 23, "time": "11:35:32.033271"}
```

This shows that we've successfully created our first endpoint with aiohttp! One thing you may have noticed from our code listing is that our `time` coroutine had a single parameter named `request`. While we didn't need to use it in this example, it will soon become important. This data structure has information about the web request the client sent, such as the body, query parameters, and so on. To get a glimpse of the headers in the request, add `print(request.headers)` somewhere inside the `time` coroutine, and you should see something similar to this:

```
<CIMultiDictProxy('Host': 'localhost:8080', 'User-Agent': 'curl/7.64.1',
    'Accept': '*/*')>
```

9.1.3   *Connecting to a database and returning results*

While our time endpoint shows us the basics, most web applications are not this simple. We'll usually need to connect to a database such as Postgres or Redis, and may need to communicate with other REST APIs, for example, if we query or update a vendor API we use.

To see how to do this, we'll build a REST API around our e-commerce storefront database from chapter 5. Specifically, we'll design a REST API to get existing products from our database as well as create new ones.

The first thing we'll need to do is create a connection to our database. Since we expect our application will have many concurrent users, using a connection pool instead of a single connection makes the most sense. The question becomes: where can we create and store the connection pool for easy use by our application's endpoints?

To answer the question of where we can store the connection pool, we'll need to first answer the broader question of where we can store shared application data in aiohttp applications. We'll then use this mechanism to hold a reference to our connection pool.

To store shared data, aiohttp's `Application` class acts as a dictionary. For example, if we had some shared dictionary we wanted all our routes to have access to, we could store it in our application as follows:

```
app = web.Application()
app['shared_dict'] = {'key' : 'value'}
```

We can now access the shared dictionary by executing `app['shared_dict']`. Next, we need to figure out how to access the application from within a route. We could make the app instance global, but aiohttp provides a better way though the `Request` class. Every request that our route gets will have a reference to the application instance through the `app` field, allowing us easy access to any shared data. For example, getting the shared dictionary and returning it as a response might look like the following:

```
@routes.get('/')
async def get_data(request: Request) -> Response:
    shared_data = request.app['shared_dict']
    return web.json_response(shared_data)
```

We'll use this paradigm to store and retrieve our database connection pool once we create it. Now we decide the best place to create our connection pool. We can't easily do it when we create our application instance, as this happens outside of any coroutine meaning, and we can't use the needed `await` expressions.

aiohttp provides a signal handler on the application instance to handle setup tasks like this called `on_startup`. You can think of this as a list of coroutines that will execute when we start the application. We can add coroutines to run on startup by calling `app.on_startup.append(coroutine)`. Each coroutine we append to `on_startup` has a single parameter: the `Application` instance. We can store our database pool in the application instance passed in to this coroutine once we've instantiated it.

We also need to consider what happens when our web application shuts down. We want to actively close and clean up database connections when we shut down; otherwise, we could leave dangling connections, putting unneeded stress on our database. aiohttp also provides a second signal handler: `on_cleanup`. The coroutines in this handler will run when our application closes, giving us an easy place to shut down the connection pool. This behaves like the `on_startup` handler in that we just call `append` with coroutines we'd like to run.

Putting all these pieces together, we can create a web application that creates a connection pool to our product database. To test this out, let's create an endpoint that gets all brand data in our database. This will be a GET endpoint called /brands.

Listing 9.2   Connecting to a product database

```python
import asyncpg
from aiohttp import web
from aiohttp.web_app import Application
from aiohttp.web_request import Request
from aiohttp.web_response import Response
from asyncpg import Record
from asyncpg.pool import Pool
from typing import List, Dict


routes = web.RouteTableDef()
DB_KEY = 'database'


async def create_database_pool(app: Application):          ◄──┐  Create the database
    print('Creating database pool.')                             pool, and store it in
    pool: Pool = await asyncpg.create_pool(host='127.0.0.1',     the application
                                           port=5432,            instance.
                                           user='postgres',
                                           password='password',
                                           database='products',
                                           min_size=6,
                                           max_size=6)

    app[DB_KEY] = pool


async def destroy_database_pool(app: Application):         ◄──   Destroy the pool in the
    print('Destroying database pool.')                           application instance.
    pool: Pool = app[DB_KEY]
    await pool.close()


@routes.get('/brands')                                           Query all brands and
async def brands(request: Request) -> Response:            ◄──   return results to the client.
    connection: Pool = request.app[DB_KEY]
    brand_query = 'SELECT brand_id, brand_name FROM brand'
    results: List[Record] = await connection.fetch(brand_query)
    result_as_dict: List[Dict] = [dict(brand) for brand in results]
    return web.json_response(result_as_dict)


app = web.Application()                                          Add the create
app.on_startup.append(create_database_pool)                ◄──  and destroy pool
app.on_cleanup.append(destroy_database_pool)                    coroutines to startup
                                                                and cleanup.

app.add_routes(routes)
web.run_app(app)
```

We first define two coroutines to create and destroy the connection pool. In create_
database_pool, we create a pool and store it in the application under the DB_KEY.
Then, in destroy_database_pool, we get the pool from the application instance and
wait for it to close. When we start our application, we append these two coroutines to
the on_startup and on_cleanup signal handlers, respectively.

Next, we define our brands route. We first grab the database pool from the request and run a query to get all brands in our database. We then loop over each brand, casting them to dictionaries. This is because aiohttp does not know how to serialize asyncpg `Record` instances. When running this application, you should be able to go to `localhost:8080/brands` in a browser and see all brands in your database displayed as a JSON list, giving you something like the following:

```
[{"brand_id": 1, "brand_name": "his"}, {"brand_id": 2, "brand_name": "he"},
    {"brand_id": 3, "brand_name": "at"}]
```

We've now created our first RESTful collection API endpoint. Next, let's see how to create endpoints to create and update singleton resources. We'll implement two endpoints: one GET endpoint to retrieve a product by a specific ID and one POST endpoint to create a new product.

Let's start with our GET endpoint for a product. This endpoint will take in an integer ID parameter, meaning to get the product with ID 1 we'd call /products/1. How can we create a route that has a parameter in it? aiohttp lets us parameterize our routes by wrapping any parameters in curly brackets, so our product route will be `/products/{id}`. When we parameterize like this, we'll see an entry in our request's `match_info` dictionary. In this case, whatever the user passed into the `id` parameter will be available in `request.match_info['id']` as a string.

Since we could pass in an invalid string for an ID, we'll need to add some error handling. A client could also ask for an ID that does not exist, so we'll need to handle the "not found" case appropriately as well. For these error cases, we'll return a HTTP 400 status code to indicate the client issued a bad request. For the case where the product does not exist, we'll return a HTTP 404 status code. To represent these error cases, aiohttp provides a set of exceptions for each HTTP status code. In the error cases, we can just raise them, and the client will receive the appropriate status code.

Listing 9.3 Getting a specific product

```
import asyncpg
from aiohttp import web
from aiohttp.web_app import Application
from aiohttp.web_request import Request
from aiohttp.web_response import Response
from asyncpg import Record
from asyncpg.pool import Pool

routes = web.RouteTableDef()
DB_KEY = 'database'


@routes.get('/products/{id}')
async def get_product(request: Request) -> Response:
    try:
```

```
        str_id = request.match_info['id']          ◄─┐   Get the product_id
        product_id = int(str_id)                      │   parameter from the URL.

        query = \
            """
            SELECT
            product_id,
            product_name,
            brand_id
            FROM product
            WHERE product_id = $1
            """                                                    Run the query for
                                                                   a single product.
        connection: Pool = request.app[DB_KEY]
        result: Record = await connection.fetchrow(query, product_id)   ◄─┘

        if result is not None:            ◄─────────────┐   If we have a result, convert
            return web.json_response(dict(result))      │   it to JSON and send to the
        else:                                           │   client; otherwise, send a
            raise web.HTTPNotFound()                    │   "404 not found."
    except ValueError:
        raise web.HTTPBadRequest()


async def create_database_pool(app: Application):
    print('Creating database pool.')
    pool: Pool = await asyncpg.create_pool(host='127.0.0.1',
                                           port=5432,
                                           user='postgres',
                                           password='password',
                                           database='products',
                                           min_size=6,
                                           max_size=6)

    app[DB_KEY] = pool


async def destroy_database_pool(app: Application):
    print('Destroying database pool.')
    pool: Pool = app[DB_KEY]
    await pool.close()


app = web.Application()
app.on_startup.append(create_database_pool)
app.on_cleanup.append(destroy_database_pool)

app.add_routes(routes)
web.run_app(app)
```

Next, let's see how to create a POST endpoint to create a new product in the database. We'll send the data we want in the request body as a JSON string, and we'll then translate that into an insert query. We'll need to do some error checking here to see if the JSON is valid, and if it isn't, send the client a bad request error.

Listing 9.4   A create product endpoint

```
import asyncpg
from aiohttp import web
from aiohttp.web_app import Application
from aiohttp.web_request import Request
from aiohttp.web_response import Response
from chapter_09.listing_9_2 import create_database_pool,
    destroy_database_pool


routes = web.RouteTableDef()
DB_KEY = 'database'


@routes.post('/product')
async def create_product(request: Request) -> Response:
    PRODUCT_NAME = 'product_name'
    BRAND_ID = 'brand_id'

    if not request.can_read_body:
        raise web.HTTPBadRequest()

    body = await request.json()

    if PRODUCT_NAME in body and BRAND_ID in body:
        db = request.app[DB_KEY]
        await db.execute('''INSERT INTO product(product_id,
                                                product_name,
                                                brand_id)
                                         VALUES(DEFAULT, $1, $2)''',
                         body[PRODUCT_NAME],
                         int(body[BRAND_ID]))
        return web.Response(status=201)
    else:
        raise web.HTTPBadRequest()


app = web.Application()
app.on_startup.append(create_database_pool)
app.on_cleanup.append(destroy_database_pool)

app.add_routes(routes)
web.run_app(app)
```

We first check to see if we even have a body with request.can_read_body, and if we don't, we quickly return a bad response. We then grab the request body as a dictionary with the json coroutine. Why is this a coroutine and not a plain method? If we have an especially large request body, the result may be buffered and could take some time to read. Instead of blocking our handler waiting for all data to come in, we await until all data is there. We then insert the record into the product table and return a HTTP 201 created status back to the client.

Using cURL, you should be able to execute something like the following to insert a product into your database, getting a HTTP 201 response.

```
curl -i -d '{"product_name":"product_name", "brand_id":1}'
    localhost:8080/product
HTTP/1.1 201 Created
Content-Length: 0
Content-Type: application/octet-stream
Date: Tue, 24 Nov 2020 13:27:44 GMT
Server: Python/3.9 aiohttp/3.6.2
```

While the error handling here should be more robust (what happens if the brand ID is a string and not an integer or the JSON is malformed?), this illustrates how to process `postdata` to insert a record into our database.

9.1.4   *Comparing aiohttp with Flask*

Working with aiohttp and an asyncio-ready web framework gives us the benefit of using libraries such as asyncpg. Outside of the use of asyncio libraries, are there any benefits to using a framework like aiohttp as opposed to a similar synchronous framework such as Flask?

While it highly depends on server configuration, database hardware, and other factors, asyncio-based applications can have better throughput with fewer resources. In a synchronous framework, each request handler runs from start to finish without interruption. In an asynchronous framework, when our `await` expressions suspend execution, they give the framework a chance to handle other work, resulting in greater efficiency.

To test this out, let's build a Flask replacement for our brands endpoint. We'll assume basic familiarity with Flask and synchronous database drivers, although even if you don't know these you should be able to follow the code. To get started, we'll install Flask and psycopg2, a synchronous Postgres driver, with the following commands:

```
pip install -Iv flask==2.0.1
pip install -Iv psycopg2==2.9.1
```

For psycopg, you may run into compile errors on install. If you do, you may need to install Postgres tools, and open SSL or another library. A web search with your error should yield the answer. Now, let's implement our endpoint. We'll first create a connection to the database. Then, in our request handler we'll reuse the brand query from our previous example and return the results as a JSON array.

Listing 9.5   A Flask application to retrieve brands

```
from flask import Flask, jsonify
import psycopg2

app = Flask(__name__)
```

```
conn_info = "dbname=products user=postgres password=password host=127.0.0.1"
db = psycopg2.connect(conn_info)


@app.route('/brands')
def brands():
    cur = db.cursor()
    cur.execute('SELECT brand_id, brand_name FROM brand')
    rows = cur.fetchall()
    cur.close()
    return jsonify([{'brand_id': row[0], 'brand_name': row[1]} for row in rows])
```

Now, we need to run our application. Flask comes with a development server, but it is not production-ready and wouldn't be a fair comparison, especially since it would only run one process, meaning we could only handle one request at a time. We'll need to use a production WSGI server to test this. We'll use Gunicorn for this example, though there are many you could choose. Let's start by installing Gunicorn with the following command:

```
pip install -Iv gunicorn==20.1.0
```

We'll be testing this out on an 8-core machine, so we'll spawn eight workers with Gunicorn. Running `gunicorn -w 8 chapter_09.listing_9_5:app`, and you should see eight workers start up:

```
[2020-11-24 09:53:39 -0500] [16454] [INFO] Starting gunicorn 20.0.4
[2020-11-24 09:53:39 -0500] [16454] [INFO] Listening at:
     http://127.0.0.1:8000 (16454)
[2020-11-24 09:53:39 -0500] [16454] [INFO] Using worker: sync
[2020-11-24 09:53:39 -0500] [16458] [INFO] Booting worker with pid: 16458
[2020-11-24 09:53:39 -0500] [16459] [INFO] Booting worker with pid: 16459
[2020-11-24 09:53:39 -0500] [16460] [INFO] Booting worker with pid: 16460
[2020-11-24 09:53:39 -0500] [16461] [INFO] Booting worker with pid: 16461
[2020-11-24 09:53:40 -0500] [16463] [INFO] Booting worker with pid: 16463
[2020-11-24 09:53:40 -0500] [16464] [INFO] Booting worker with pid: 16464
[2020-11-24 09:53:40 -0500] [16465] [INFO] Booting worker with pid: 16465
[2020-11-24 09:53:40 -0500] [16468] [INFO] Booting worker with pid: 16468
```

This means we have created eight connections to our database and can serve eight requests concurrently. Now, we need a tool to benchmark performance between Flask and aiohttp. A command-line load tester will work for a quick test. While this won't be the most accurate picture, it will give us a directional idea of performance. We'll use a load tester called wrk, though any load tester, such as Apache Bench or Hey, will work. You can view installation instructions on wrk at https://github.com/wg/wrk.

Let's start by running a 30-second load test on our Flask server. We'll use one thread and 200 connections, simulating 200 concurrent users hitting our app as fast as they can. On an 8-core 2.4 Ghz machine you could see results similar to the following:

```
Running 30s test @ http://localhost:8000/brands
  1 threads and 200 connections
  16534 requests in 30.02s, 61.32MB read
  Socket errors: connect 0, read 1533, write 276, timeout 0
Requests/sec:    550.82
Transfer/sec:    2.04MB
```

We served about 550 requests per second—not a bad result. Let's rerun the same with aiohttp and compare the results:

```
Running 30s test @ http://localhost:8080/brands
  1 threads and 200 connections
  46774 requests in 30.01s, 191.45MB read
Requests/sec:    1558.46
Transfer/sec:    6.38MB
```

Using aiohttp, we were able to serve over 1,500 requests per second, which is about three times what we were able to do with Flask. More importantly, we did this with only one process, where Flask needed a total of *eight processes* to handle *one-third* of the requests! You could further improve the performance of aiohttp by putting NGINX in front of it and starting more worker processes.

We now know the basics of how to use aiohttp to build a database-backed web application. In the world of web applications, aiohttp is a little different than most in that it is a web server itself, and it does not conform to WSGI and can stand alone on its own. As we saw with Flask, this is not usually the case. Next, let's understand how ASGI works and see how to use it with an ASGI-compliant framework called Starlette.

9.2   *The asynchronous server gateway interface*

When we used Flask in the previous example, we used the Gunicorn WSGI server to serve our application. WSGI is a standardized way to forward web requests to a web framework, such as Flask or Django. While there are many WSGI servers, they were not designed to support asynchronous workloads, as the WSGI specification long predates asyncio. As asynchronous web applications become more widely used, a way to abstract frameworks from their servers proved necessary. Thus, the *asynchronous server gateway interface*, or ASGI, was created. ASGI is a relative newcomer to the internet space but already has several popular implementations and frameworks that support it, including Django.

9.2.1   *How does ASGI compare to WSGI?*

WSGI was born out of a fractured landscape of web application frameworks. Prior to WSGI, the choice of one framework could limit the kinds of usable interface web servers, as there was no standardized interface between the two. WSGI addressed this by providing a simple API for web servers to talk to Python frameworks. WSGI received formal acceptance into the Python ecosystem in 2004 with the acceptance of PEP-333

(Python enhancement proposal; https://www.python.org/dev/peps/pep-0333/) and is now the de facto standard for web application deployment.

When it comes to asynchronous workloads however, WSGI does not work. The heart of the WSGI specification is a simple Python function. For example, let's see the simplest WSGI application we can build.

Listing 9.6   A WSGI application

```
def application(env, start_response):
    start_response('200 OK', [('Content-Type','text/html')])
    return [b"WSGI hello!"]
```

We can run this application with Gunicorn by running `gunicorn chapter_09.listing_9_6` and test it out with `curl http://127.0.0.1:8000`. As you can see, there isn't any place for us to use an `await`. In addition, WSGI only supports response/request life-cycles, meaning it won't work with long-lived connection protocols, such as WebSockets. ASGI fixes this by redesigning the API to use coroutines. Let's translate our WSGI example to ASGI.

Listing 9.7   A simple ASGI application

```
async def application(scope, receive, send):
    await send({
        'type': 'http.response.start',
        'status': 200,
        'headers': [[b'content-type', b'text/html']]
    })
    await send({'type': 'http.response.body', 'body': b'ASGI hello!'})
```

An ASGI application function has three parameters: a scope dictionary, a receive coroutine, and a send coroutine, which allow us to send and receive data, respectively. In our example, we send the start of the HTTP response, followed by the body.

Now, how do we serve the above application? There are a few implementations of ASGI available, but we'll use a popular one called Uvicorn (https://www.uvicorn .org/). Uvicorn is built on top of uvloop and httptools, which are fast C implementations of the asyncio event loop (we're actually not tied to the event loop that comes with asyncio, as we'll learn more in chapter 14) and HTTP parsing. We can install Uvicorn by running the following:

```
pip install -Iv uvicorn==0.14.0
```

Now, we can run our application with the following command:

```
uvicorn chapter_09.listing_9_7:application
```

And we should see our "hello" message printed if we go to http://localhost:8000. While we used Uvicorn directly here to test things out, it is better practice to use

Uvicorn with Gunicorn, as Gunicorn will have logic to restart workers on crashes for us. We'll see how to do this with Django in section 9.4.

We should keep in mind that, while WSGI is an accepted PEP, ASGI is not yet accepted, and as of this writing it is still relatively new. Expect the details of how ASGI works to evolve and change as the asyncio landscape changes.

Now, we know the basics of ASGI and how it compares to WSGI. What we have learned is very low-level, though; we want a framework to handle ASGI for us! There are a few ASGI-compliant frameworks, let's look at a popular one.

9.3   *ASGI with Starlette*

Starlette is a small ASGI-compliant framework created by Encode, the creators of Uvicorn and other popular libraries such as Django REST framework. It offers fairly impressive performance (at the time of writing), WebSocket support, and more. You can view its documentation at https://www.starlette.io/. Let's see how to implement simple REST and WebSocket endpoints using it. To get started, let's first install it with the following command:

```
pip install -Iv starlette==0.15.0
```

9.3.1   *A REST endpoint with Starlette*

Let's start to learn Starlette by reimplementing our brands endpoint from previous sections. We'll create our application by creating an instance of the `Starlette` class. This class takes a few parameters that we'll be interested in using: a list of `route` objects and a list of coroutines to run on startup and shutdown. `Route` objects are mappings from a string path—brands, in our case—to a coroutine or another callable object. Much like aiohttp, these coroutines have one parameter representing the request, and they return a response, so our route handle will look very similar to our aiohttp version. What is slightly different is how we handle sharing our database pool. We still store it on our Starlette application instance, but it is inside a state object instead.

Listing 9.8   A Starlette brands endpoint

```
import asyncpg
from asyncpg import Record
from asyncpg.pool import Pool
from starlette.applications import Starlette
from starlette.requests import Request
from starlette.responses import JSONResponse, Response
from starlette.routing import Route
from typing import List, Dict


async def create_database_pool():
    pool: Pool = await asyncpg.create_pool(host='127.0.0.1',
                                           port=5432,
                                           user='postgres',
                                           password='password',
```

```
                                                  database='products',
                                                  min_size=6,
                                                  max_size=6)
            app.state.DB = pool


async def destroy_database_pool():
    pool = app.state.DB
    await pool.close()


async def brands(request: Request) -> Response:
    connection: Pool = request.app.state.DB
    brand_query = 'SELECT brand_id, brand_name FROM brand'
    results: List[Record] = await connection.fetch(brand_query)
    result_as_dict: List[Dict] = [dict(brand) for brand in results]
    return JSONResponse(result_as_dict)


app = Starlette(routes=[Route('/brands', brands)],
                on_startup=[create_database_pool],
                on_shutdown=[destroy_database_pool])
```

Now that we have our brands endpoint, let's use Uvicorn to start it up. We'll start up eight workers, as we did before, with the following command:

```
uvicorn --workers 8 --log-level error chapter_09.listing_9_8:app
```

You should be able to hit this endpoint at localhost:8000/brands and see the contents of the brand table, as before. Now that we have our application running, let's run a quick benchmark to see how it compares to aiohttp and Flask. We'll use the same wrk command as before with 200 connections over 30 seconds:

```
Running 30s test @ http://localhost:8000/brands
  1 threads and 200 connections
Requests/sec:   4365.37
Transfer/sec:   16.07MB
```

We've served over 4,000 requests per second, outperforming Flask and even aiohttp by a wide margin! Since we only ran one aiohttp worker process earlier, this isn't exactly a fair comparison (we'd get similar numbers with eight aiohttp workers behind NGINX), but this shows the throughput power that async frameworks offer.

9.3.2 *WebSockets with Starlette*

In a traditional HTTP request, the client sends a request to the server, the server hands a back a response, and that is the end of the transaction. What if we want to build a web page that updates without a user having to refresh? For example, we may have a live counter of how many users are currently on the site. We can do this over HTTP with some JavaScript that polls an endpoint, telling us how many users are on the site. We could hit the endpoint every few seconds, updating the page with the latest result.

While this will work, it has drawbacks. The main drawback is that we're creating an extra load on our web server, each request and response cycle taking time and resources. This is especially egregious because our user count might not change between requests, causing a strain on our system for no new information (we could mitigate this with caching, but the point still stands, and caching introduces other complexity and overhead). HTTP polling is the digital equivalent of a child in the backseat of the car repeatedly asking, "Are we there yet?"

WebSockets provide an alternative to HTTP polling. Instead of a request/response cycle like HTTP, we establish one persistent socket. Then, we just send data freely across that socket. This socket is bidirectional, meaning we can both send data to and receive data from our server without having to go through a HTTP request lifecycle every time. To apply this to the example of displaying an up-to-date user count, once we connect to a WebSocket the server can just *tell* us when there is a new user count. As shown in figure 9.1, we don't need to ask repeatedly, creating extra load and potentially receiving data that isn't new.

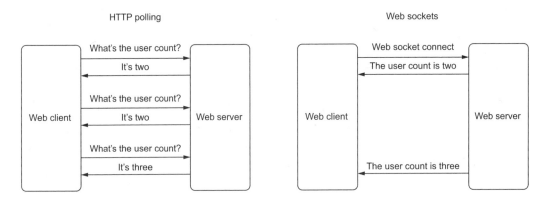

Figure 9.1   HTTP polling to retrieve data compared to WebSockets

Starlette provides out-of-the-box support for WebSockets using an easy-to-understand interface. To see this in action, we'll build a simple WebSocket endpoint that will tell us how many users are connected to a WebSocket endpoint simultaneously. To get started we'll first need to install WebSocket support:

```
pip install -Iv websockets==9.1
```

Next, we'll need to implement our WebSocket endpoint. Our game plan will be to keep an in-memory list of all connected client WebSockets. When a new client connects, we'll add them to the list and send the new count of users to all clients in the list. When a client disconnects, we'll remove them from the list and update other clients about the change in user count as well. We'll also add some basic error handling. If sending one of these messages results in an exception, we'll remove the client from the list.

In Starlette, we can subclass WebSocketEndpoint to create an endpoint to handle a WebSocket connection. This class has a few coroutines we'll need to implement. The first is on_connect, which gets fired when a client connects to our socket. In on_connect, we'll store the client's WebSocket in a list and send the length of the list to all other sockets. The second coroutine is on_receive; this gets fired when the client connection sends a message to the server. In our case, we won't need to implement this, as we don't expect the client to send us any data. The final coroutine is on_disconnect, which runs when a client disconnects. In this case, we'll remove the client from the list of connected Web-Sockets and update other connected clients with the latest user count.

Listing 9.9 A Starlette WebSocket endpoint

```
import asyncio
from starlette.applications import Starlette
from starlette.endpoints import WebSocketEndpoint
from starlette.routing import WebSocketRoute


class UserCounter(WebSocketEndpoint):
    encoding = 'text'
    sockets = []

    async def on_connect(self, websocket):         ◁──┘  When a client connects, add it
        await websocket.accept()                          to the list of sockets and notify
        UserCounter.sockets.append(websocket)             other users of the new count.
        await self._send_count()

    async def on_disconnect(self, websocket, close_code):  ◁──
        UserCounter.sockets.remove(websocket)
        await self._send_count()

    async def on_receive(self, websocket, data):
        pass

    async def _send_count(self):                    ◁────────────
        if len(UserCounter.sockets) > 0:
            count_str = str(len(UserCounter.sockets))
            task_to_socket =
      {asyncio.create_task(websocket.send_text(count_str)): websocket
                      for websocket
                      in UserCounter.sockets}

            done, pending = await asyncio.wait(task_to_socket)

            for task in done:
                if task.exception() is not None:
                    if task_to_socket[task] in UserCounter.sockets:
                        UserCounter.sockets.remove(task_to_socket[task])


app = Starlette(routes=[WebSocketRoute('/counter', UserCounter)])
```

When a client disconnects, remove it from the list of sockets and notify other users of the new count.

Notify other users how many users are connected. If there is an exception while sending, remove them from the list.

Now, we'll need to define a page to interact with our WebSocket. We'll add create a basic script to connect to our WebSocket endpoint. When we receive a message, we'll update a counter on the page with the latest value.

Listing 9.10   Using the WebSocket endpoint

```html
<!DOCTYPE html>
<html lang="">
<head>
    <title>Starlette Web Sockets</title>
    <script>
        document.addEventListener("DOMContentLoaded", () => {
            let socket = new WebSocket("ws://localhost:8000/counter");

            socket.onmessage = (event) => {
                const counter = document.querySelector("#counter");
                counter.textContent = event.data;
            };
        });
    </script>
</head>
<body>
    <span>Users online: </span>
    <span id="counter"></span>
</body>
</html>
```

In the preceding listing, the script is where most of the work happens. We first connect to our endpoint and then define an `onmessage` callback. When the server sends us data, this callback runs. In this callback, we grab a special element from the DOM and set its content to the data we receive. Note that in our script we don't execute this code until after the `DOMContentLoaded` event, without which our counter element may not exist when the script executes.

If you start the server with `uvicorn --workers 1 chapter_09.listing_9_9:app` and open the web page, you should see the `1` displayed on the page. If you open the page multiple times in separate tabs, you should see the count increment on all the tabs. When you close a tab, you should see the count decrement across all other open tabs. Note that we only use one worker here, as we have shared state (the `socket` list) in memory; if we use multiple workers, each worker will have its own `socket` list. To deploy properly, you'll need some persistent store, such as a database.

We can now use both aiohttp and Starlette to create asyncio-based web applications for both REST and WebSocket endpoints. While these frameworks are popular, they are not close in popularity to Django, the 1,000-pound gorilla of Python web frameworks.

9.4 *Django asynchronous views*

Django is one of the most popular and widely used Python frameworks. It has a wealth of functionality out of the box, from an ORM (object relational mapper) to handle databases to a customizable admin console. Until version 3.0, Django applications supported deploying as a WSGI application alone and had little support for asyncio outside of the channels library. Version 3.0 introduced support for ASGI and began the process of making Django fully asynchronous. More recently, version 3.1 gained support for asynchronous views, allowing you to use asyncio libraries directly in your Django views. At the time of writing, async support for Django is new, and the overall feature set is still lacking (for example, the ORM is entirely synchronous, but supporting async is in the future). Expect support for this to grow and evolve as Django becomes more async-aware.

Let's learn how to use async views by building a small application that uses aiohttp in a view. Imagine that we're integrating with an external REST API, and we want to build a utility to run a few requests concurrently to see response times, body length, and how many failures (exceptions) we have. We'll build a view that takes in a URL and request count as query parameters and calls out to this URL and aggregates the results, returning them in a tabular format.

Let's get started by ensuring that we have the appropriate version of Django installed:

```
pip install -Iv django==3.2.8
```

Now, let's use the Django admin tool to create the skeleton for our application. We'll call our project async_views:

```
django-admin startproject async_views
```

Once you run this command, you should see a directory named async_views created with the following structure:

```
async_views/
    manage.py
    async_views/
        __init__.py
        settings.py
        urls.py
        asgi.py
        wsgi.py
```

Note that we have both a wsgi.py and an asgi.py file, showing that we can deploy to both types of gateway interfaces. You should now be able to use Uvicorn to serve the basic Django hello world page. Run the following command from the top-level async_views directory:

```
gunicorn async_views.asgi:application -k uvicorn.workers.UvicornWorker
```

Then, when you go to `localhost:8000`, you should see the Django welcome page (figure 9.2).

Figure 9.2   The Django welcome page

Next, we'll need to create our app, which we'll call `async_api`. Within the `async_views` directory, run `python manage.py startapp async_api`. This will build `model`, `view`, and other files for the `async_api` app.

Now, we have everything we need to create our first asynchronous view. Within the `async_api` directory there should be a `views.py` file. Inside of this, we can specify a view as asynchronous by simply declaring it as a coroutine. In this file, we'll add an async view to make HTTP requests concurrently and display their status codes and other data in an HTML table.

Listing 9.11   A Django asynchronous view

```
import asyncio
from datetime import datetime
from aiohttp import ClientSession
from django.shortcuts import render
import aiohttp
```

```
async def get_url_details(session: ClientSession, url: str):
    start_time = datetime.now()
    response = await session.get(url)
    response_body = await response.text()
    end_time = datetime.now()
    return {'status': response.status,
            'time': (end_time - start_time).microseconds,
            'body_length': len(response_body)}


async def make_requests(url: str, request_num: int):
    async with aiohttp.ClientSession() as session:
        requests = [get_url_details(session, url) for _ in range(request_num)]
        results = await asyncio.gather(*requests, return_exceptions=True)
        failed_results = [str(result) for result in results if
    isinstance(result, Exception)]
        successful_results = [result for result in results if not
    isinstance(result, Exception)]
        return {'failed_results': failed_results, 'successful_results':
    successful_results}


async def requests_view(request):
    url: str = request.GET['url']
    request_num: int = int(request.GET['request_num'])
    context = await make_requests(url, request_num)
    return render(request, 'async_api/requests.html', context)
```

In the preceding listing, we first create a coroutine to make a request and return a dictionary of the response status, the total time of the request, and the length of the response body. Next, we define an async view coroutine named `requests_view`. This view gets the URL and request count from the query parameters and then makes requests via `get_url_details` concurrently with `gather`. Finally, we filter out the successful responses from any failures and put the results in a context dictionary that we then pass to `render` to build the response. Note that we haven't built our template for the response yet and are passing in `async_views/requests.html` only for right now. Next, let's build the template, so we can view the results.

First, we'll need to create a `templates` directory under the `async_api` directory, then within the templates directory we'll need to create an `async_api` folder. Once we have this directory structure in place, we can add a view inside `async_api/templates/async_api`. We'll call this view `requests.html`, and we'll loop over the context dictionary from our view, putting the results in table format.

Listing 9.12 The `requests` view

```
<!DOCTYPE html>
<html lang="en">
<head>
    <meta charset="UTF-8">
    <title>Request Summary</title>
</head>
```

```
<body>
<h1>Summary of requests:</h1>
<h2>Failures:</h2>
<table>
    {% for failure in failed_results %}
    <tr>
        <td>{{failure}}</td>
    </tr>
    {% endfor %}
</table>
<h2>Successful Results:</h2>
<table>
    <tr>
        <td>Status code</td>
        <td>Response time (microseconds)</td>
        <td>Response size</td>
    </tr>
    {% for result in successful_results %}
    <tr>
        <td>{{result.status}}</td>
        <td>{{result.time}}</td>
        <td>{{result.body_length}}</td>
    </tr>
    {% endfor %}
</table>
</body>
</html>
```

In our view, we create two tables: one to display any exceptions we encountered, and a second to display the successful results we were able to get. While this won't be the prettiest web page ever created, it will have all the relevant information we want.

Next, we'll need to hook our template and view up to a URL, so it will run when we hit it in a browser. In the async_api folder, create a url.py file with the following:

Listing 9.13 The async_api/url.py file

```
from django.urls import path
from . import views

app_name = 'async_api'

urlpatterns = [
    path('', views.requests_view, name='requests'),
]
```

Now, we'll need to include the async_api app's URLs within our Django application. Within the async_views/async_views directory, you should already have a urls.py file. Inside this file, you'll need to modify the urlpatterns list to reference async_api, and once done this should look like the following:

```
from django.contrib import admin
from django.urls import path, include
```

```
urlpatterns = [
    path('admin/', admin.site.urls),
    path('requests/', include('async_api.urls'))
]
```

Finally, we'll need to add the async_views application to the installed apps. In async_views/async_views/settings.py, modify the INSTALLED_APPS list to include async_api; once done it should look like this:

```
INSTALLED_APPS = [
    'django.contrib.admin',
    'django.contrib.auth',
    'django.contrib.contenttypes',
    'django.contrib.sessions',
    'django.contrib.messages',
    'django.contrib.staticfiles',
    'async_api'
]
```

Now, we finally have everything we need to run our application. You can start the app with the same gunicorn command we used when we first created the Django app. Now, you can go to our endpoint and make requests. For example, to hit example.com 10 times concurrently and get the results, go to:

```
http://localhost:8000/requests/?url=http://example.com&request_num=10
```

While numbers will differ on your machine, you should see a page like that shown in figure 9.3 displayed.

We've now built a Django view that can make an arbitrary amount of HTTP requests concurrently by hosting it with ASGI, but what if you're in a situation where ASGI isn't an option? Perhaps you're working with an older application that relies on it; can you still host an async view? We can try this out by running our application under Gunicorn with the WSGI application from wsgi.py with the synchronous worker with the following command:

```
gunicorn async_views.wsgi:application
```

You should still be able to hit the requests endpoint, and everything will work fine. So how does this work? When we run as a WSGI application, a fresh event loop is created each time we hit an asynchronous view. We can prove this to ourselves by adding a couple of lines of code somewhere in our view:

```
loop = asyncio.get_running_loop()
print(id(loop))
```

The id function will return an integer that is guaranteed to be unique over the lifetime of an object. When running as a WSGI application, each time you hit the requests endpoint, this will print a distinct integer, indicating that we create a fresh event loop

Summary of requests:

Failures:

Successful Results:

Status code	Response time (microseconds)	Response size
200	51604	1256
200	46196	1256
200	63883	1256
200	61545	1256
200	62322	1256
200	61387	1256
200	63271	1256
200	61143	1256
200	62448	1256
200	62659	1256

Figure 9.3 The `requests` asynchronous view

on a per-request basis. Keep the same code when running as an ASGI application, and you'll see the same integer printed every time, since ASGI will only have one event loop for the entire application.

This means we can get the benefits of async views and running things concurrently even when running as a WSGI application. However, anything that needs an event loop to live across multiple requests won't work unless you deploy as an ASGI application.

9.4.1 *Running blocking work in an asynchronous view*

What about blocking work in an async view? We're still in a world where many libraries are synchronous, but this is incompatible with a single-threaded concurrency model. The ASGI specification has a function to deal with these situations named `sync_to_async`.

In chapter 7, we saw that we could run synchronous APIs in thread pool executors and get back awaitables we could use with asyncio. The `sync_to_async` function essentially does that with a few noteworthy caveats.

The first caveat is that `sync_to_async` has a notion of thread sensitivity. In many contexts, synchronous APIs with shared state weren't designed to be called from multiple threads, and doing so could cause race conditions. To deal with this, `sync_to_async` defaults to a "thread sensitive" mode (specifically, this function has a `thread_sensitive` flag that defaults to `True`). This makes any sync code we pass in run in

Django's main thread. This means that any blocking we do here will block the entire Django application (well, at least one WSGI/ASGI worker if we're running multiple), making us lose some benefits of an async stack by doing this.

If we're in a situation where thread sensitivity isn't an issue (in other words, when there is no shared state, or the shared state does not rely on being in a specific thread), we can change `thread_sensitive` to `False`. This will make things run in a new thread per each call, giving us something that won't block Django's main thread and preserving more benefits of an asynchronous stack.

To see this in action, let's make a new view to test out the variations of `sync_to_async`. We'll create a function that uses `time.sleep` to put a thread to sleep, and we'll pass that in to `sync_to_async`. We'll add a query parameter to our endpoint, so we can easily switch between thread sensitivity modes to see the impact. First, add the following definition to `async_views/async_api/views.py`:

Listing 9.14 The `sync_to_async` view

```python
from functools import partial
from django.http import HttpResponse
from asgiref.sync import sync_to_async


def sleep(seconds: int):
    import time
    time.sleep(seconds)


async def sync_to_async_view(request):
    sleep_time: int = int(request.GET['sleep_time'])
    num_calls: int = int(request.GET['num_calls'])
    thread_sensitive: bool = request.GET['thread_sensitive'] == 'True'
    function = sync_to_async(partial(sleep, sleep_time),
     thread_sensitive=thread_sensitive)
    await asyncio.gather(*[function() for _ in range(num_calls)])
    return HttpResponse('')
```

Next, add the following to `async_views/async_api/urls.py` to the `urlpatterns` list to wire up the view:

```python
path('sync_to_async', views.sync_to_async_view)
```

Now, you'll be able to hit the endpoint. To test this out, let's sleep for 5 seconds five times in thread-insensitive mode with the following URL:

```
http://127.0.0.1:8000/requests/sync_to_async?sleep_time=5&num_calls=
    5&thread_sensitive=False
```

You'll notice that this only takes 5 seconds to complete since we're running multiple threads. You'll also notice if you hit this URL more than once that each request still takes only 5 seconds, indicating the requests aren't blocking each other. Now, let's change the `thread_sensitive url` parameter to `True`, and you'll see quite different behavior. First, the view will take 25 seconds to return since it is making five 5-second calls sequentially. Second, if you hit the URL multiple times, each will block until the other completed, since we're blocking Django's main thread. The `sync_to_async` function offers us several options to use existing code with async views, but you need to be aware of the thread-sensitivity of what you're running, as well as the limitations that this can place on async performance benefits.

9.4.2   *Using async code in synchronous views*

The next logical question is, "What if I have a synchronous view, but I want to use an asyncio library?" The ASGI specification also has a special function named `async_to_sync`. This function accepts a coroutine and runs it in an event loop, returning the results in a synchronous fashion. If there is no event loop (as is the case in a WSGI application), a new one will be created for us on each request; otherwise, this will run in the current event loop (as is the case when we run as an ASGI application). To try this out, let's create a new version of our `requests` endpoint as a synchronous view, while still using our async request function.

Listing 9.15   Calling async code in a synchronous view

```
from asgiref.sync import async_to_sync


def requests_view_sync(request):
    url: str = request.GET['url']
    request_num: int = int(request.GET['request_num'])
    context = async_to_sync(partial(make_requests, url, request_num))()
    return render(request, 'async_api/requests.html', context)
```

Next, add the following to the `urlpatterns` list in `urls.py`:

```
path('async_to_sync', views.requests_view_sync)
```

Then, you'll be able to hit the following url and see the same results as we saw with our first async view:

```
http://localhost:8000/requests/async_to_sync?url=http://example.com&request_
    num=10
```

Even in a synchronous WSGI world, `sync_to_async` lets us get some of the performance benefits of an asynchronous stack without being fully asynchronous.

Summary

- We've learned how to create basic RESTful APIs that hook up to a database with aiohttp and asyncpg.
- We've learned how to create ASGI compliant web applications with Starlette.
- We've learned how to use WebSockets with Starlette to build web applications with up-to-date information without HTTP polling.
- We've learned how to use asynchronous views with Django, and also learned how to use async code in synchronous views and vice versa.

Microservices

This chapter covers

- The basics of microservices
- The backend-for-frontend pattern
- Using asyncio to handle microservice communication
- Using asyncio to handle failures and retries

Many web applications are structured as monoliths. A *monolith* generally refers to a medium-to-large-sized application containing multiple modules that are independently deployed and managed as one unit. While there is nothing inherently wrong with this model (monoliths are perfectly fine, and even preferable, for most web applications, as they are generally simpler), it does have its drawbacks.

As an example, if you make a small change to a monolithic application, you need to deploy the entire application, even parts that may be unaffected by your change. For instance, a monolithic e-commerce application may have order management and product listing endpoints in one application, meaning a tweak to a product endpoint would require a redeploy of order management code. A microservice architecture can help with such pain points. We could create separate services for orders and products, then a change in one service wouldn't affect the other.

In this chapter, we'll learn a bit more about microservices and the motivations behind them. We'll learn a pattern called *backend-for-frontend* and apply this to an e-commerce microservice architecture. We'll then implement this API with aiohttp and asyncpg, learning how to employ concurrency to help us improve the performance of our application. We'll also learn how to properly deal with failure and retries with the circuit breaker pattern to build a more robust application.

10.1 Why microservices?

First, let's define what microservices are. This is a rather tricky question, as there is no standardized definition, and you'll probably get different answers depending on who you ask. Generally, *microservices* follow a few guiding principles:

- They are loosely coupled and independently deployable.
- They have their own independent stack, including a data model.
- They communicate with one another over a protocol such as REST or gRPC.
- They follow the "single responsibility" principle; that is, a microservice should "do one thing and do it well."

Let's apply these principles to a concrete example of an e-commerce storefront. An application like this has users that provide shipping and payment information to our hypothetical organization who then buy our products. In a monolithic architecture, we'd have one application with one database to manage user data, account data (such as their orders and shipping information), and our available products. In a microservice architecture, we would have multiple services, each with their own database for separate concerns. We might have a product API with its own database, which only handles data around products. We might have a user API with its own database, which handles user account information, and so on.

Why would we choose this architectural style over monoliths? Monoliths are perfectly fine for most applications; they are simpler to manage. Make a code change, and run all the test suites to make sure your seemingly small change does not affect other areas of the system. Once you've run tests, you deploy the application as one unit. Is your application not performing well under load? In this case you can scale horizontally or vertically, either deploying more instances of your application or deploying to more powerful machines to handle the additional users. While managing a monolith is operationally simpler, this simplicity has drawbacks that may matter a lot, depending on which tradeoffs you want to make.

10.1.1 Complexity of code

As the application grows and acquires new features its complexity grows. Data models may become more coupled, causing unforeseen and hard-to-understand dependencies. Technical debt gets larger and larger, making development slower and more complicated. While this is true of any growing system, a large codebase with multiple concerns can exacerbate this.

10.1.2 Scalability

In a monolithic architecture, if you need to scale you need to add more instances of your *entire* application, which can lead to technology cost inefficiencies. In the context of an e-commerce application, you will typically get much fewer orders than people just browsing products. In a monolithic architecture, to scale up to handle more people viewing your products, you'll need to scale up your order capabilities as well. In a microservice architecture, you can just scale the product service and leave the order service untouched if it has no issues.

10.1.3 Team and stack independence

As a development team grows, new challenges emerge. Imagine you have five teams working on the same monolithic codebase with each team committing code several times per day. Merge conflicts will become an increasing issue that everyone needs to handle, as will coordinating deploys across teams. With independent, loosely coupled microservices, this becomes less of an issue. If a team owns a service, they can work on it and deploy it mostly independently. This also allows for teams to use different tech stacks if desired, one service can be in Java and one in Python.

10.1.4 How can asyncio help?

Microservices generally need to communicate with one another over a protocol such as REST or gRPC. Since we may be talking to multiple microservices at the same time, this opens up the possibility to run requests concurrently, creating an efficiency that we otherwise wouldn't have in a synchronous application.

In addition to the resource efficiency benefits we get from an async stack, we also get the error-handling benefits of the asyncio APIs, such as `wait` and `gather`, which allow us to aggregate exceptions from a group of coroutines or tasks. If a particular group of requests takes too long or a portion of that group has an exception, we can handle them gracefully. Now that we understand the basic motivations behind microservices, let's learn one common microservice architecture pattern and see how to implement it.

10.2 *Introducing the backend-for-frontend pattern*

When we're building UIs in a microservice architecture, we'll typically need to get data from multiple services to create a particular UI view. For example, if we're building a user order history UI, we'll probably have to get the user's order history from an order service and merge that with product data from a product service. Depending on requirements, we may need data from other services as well.

This poses a few challenges for our frontend clients. The first is a user experience issue. With standalone services, our UI clients will have to make one call to each service over the internet. This poses issues with latency and time to load the UI. We can't assume all our users will have a good internet connection or fast computer; some may be on a mobile phone in a poor reception area, some may be on older computers, and some may be in developing countries without access to high-speed internet at all. If we make five slow requests to five services, there is the potential to cause more issues than making one slow request.

In addition to network latency challenges, we also have challenges related to good software design principles. Imagine we have both web-based UIs as well as iOS and Android mobile UIs. If we directly call each service and merge the resulting responses, we need to replicate the logic to do so across three different clients, which is redundant and puts us at risk of having inconsistent logic across clients.

While there are many microservice design patterns, one that can help us address the above issues is the *backend-for-frontend pattern*. In this design pattern, instead of our UIs directly communicating with our services, we create a new service that makes these calls and aggregates the responses. This addresses our issues, and instead of making multiple requests we can just make one, cutting down on our round trips across the internet. We can also embed any logic related to failovers or retries inside of this service, saving our clients the work of having to repeat the same logic and introducing one place for us to update the logic when we need to change it. This also enables multiple backend-for-frontend services for different types of clients. The services we need to communicate with may need to vary depending on if we're a mobile client versus a web-based UI. This is illustrated in figure 10.1. Now that we understand the backend-for-frontend design pattern and the problems it addresses, let's apply it to build a backend-for-frontend service for an e-commerce storefront.

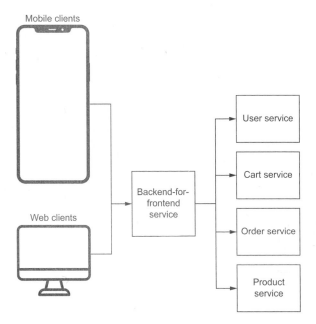

Figure 10.1 The backend-for-frontend pattern

10.3 *Implementing the product listing API*

Let's implement the backend-for-frontend pattern for an *all products* page of our e-commerce storefront's desktop experience. This page displays all products available on our site, along with basic information about our user's cart and favorited items in a menu bar. To increase sales, the page has a low inventory warning when only a few items are left available. This page also has a navigation bar up on top with information about our user's favorite products as well as what data is in their cart. Figure 10.2 illustrates our UI.

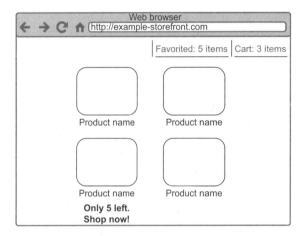

Figure 10.2   A mockup of the products listing page

Given a microservice architecture with several independent services, we'll need to request the appropriate data from each service and stitch them together to form a cohesive response. Let's first start by defining the base services and data models we'll need.

10.3.1 *User favorite service*

This service keeps track of a mapping from a user to the product IDs they have put in their favorites list. Next, we'll need to implement these services to support our backend-for-frontend product, inventory, user cart, and user favorites.

> **User cart service**
>
> This contains a mapping from user ID to product IDs they have put in the cart; the data model is the same as the user favorite service.

> **Inventory service**
>
> This contains a mapping from a product ID to the available inventory for that product.

> **Product service**
>
> This contains product information, such as descriptions and SKUs. This is similar to the service we implemented in chapter 9 around our products database.

10.3.2 *Implementing the base services*

Let's start by implementing an aiohttp application for our inventory service, as we'll make this our simplest service. For this service we won't create a separate data model; instead, we'll just return a random number from 0 to 100 to simulate available inventory. We'll also add a random delay to simulate our service being intermittently slow, and we'll use this to demonstrate how to handle timeouts in our product list service. We'll host this service on port 8001 for development purposes, so it does not interfere with our product service from chapter 9, which runs on port 8000.

Listing 10.1   The inventory service

```python
import asyncio
import random
from aiohttp import web
from aiohttp.web_response import Response

routes = web.RouteTableDef()


@routes.get('/products/{id}/inventory')
async def get_inventory(request: Request) -> Response:
    delay: int = random.randint(0, 5)
    await asyncio.sleep(delay)
    inventory: int = random.randint(0, 100)
    return web.json_response({'inventory': inventory})


app = web.Application()
app.add_routes(routes)
web.run_app(app, port=8001)
```

Next, let's implement the user cart and user favorite service. The data model for these two is identical, so the services will be almost the same, with the difference being table names. Let's start with the two data models, "user cart" and "user favorite." We'll also insert a few records in these tables, so we have some data to start with. First, we'll start with the user cart table.

Listing 10.2   User cart table

```sql
CREATE TABLE user_cart(
    user_id    INT NOT NULL,
    product_id INT NOT NULL
);
```

```
INSERT INTO user_cart VALUES (1, 1);
INSERT INTO user_cart VALUES (1, 2);
INSERT INTO user_cart VALUES (1, 3);
INSERT INTO user_cart VALUES (2, 1);
INSERT INTO user_cart VALUES (2, 2);
INSERT INTO user_cart VALUES (2, 5);
```

Next, we'll create the user favorite table and insert a few values; this will look very similar to the previous table.

Listing 10.3   User favorite table

```
CREATE TABLE user_favorite
(
    user_id    INT NOT NULL,
    product_id INT NOT NULL
);

INSERT INTO user_favorite VALUES (1, 1);
INSERT INTO user_favorite VALUES (1, 2);
INSERT INTO user_favorite VALUES (1, 3);
INSERT INTO user_favorite VALUES (3, 1);
INSERT INTO user_favorite VALUES (3, 2);
INSERT INTO user_favorite VALUES (3, 3);
```

To simulate multiple databases, we'll want to create these tables each in their own Postgres database. Recall from chapter 5 that we can run arbitrary SQL with the psql command-line utility, meaning that we can create two databases for user favorites and user cart with the following two commands:

```
sudo -u postgres psql -c "CREATE DATABASE cart;"
sudo -u postgres psql -c "CREATE DATABASE favorites;"
```

Since we'll now need to set up and tear down connections to multiple different databases, let's create some reusable code across our services to create asyncpg connection pools. We'll reuse this in our aiohttp on_startup and on_cleanup hooks.

Listing 10.4   Creating and tearing down database pools

```
import asyncpg
from aiohttp.web_app import Application
from asyncpg.pool import Pool

DB_KEY = 'database'


async def create_database_pool(app: Application,
                               host: str,
                               port: int,
                               user: str,
                               database: str,
                               password: str):
```

```
        pool: Pool = await asyncpg.create_pool(host=host,
                                                port=port,
                                                user=user,
                                                password=password,
                                                database=database,
                                                min_size=6,
                                                max_size=6)
        app[DB_KEY] = pool


async def destroy_database_pool(app: Application):
    pool: Pool = app[DB_KEY]
    await pool.close()
```

The preceding listing should look similar to code we wrote in chapter 5 to set up database connections. In create_database_pool, we create a connection pool and then put it in our Application instance. In destroy_database_pool, we grab the connection pool from the application instance and close it.

Next, let's create the services. In REST terms, both favorites and cart are a subentity of a particular user. This means that each endpoint's root will be users and will accept a user ID as an input. For example, /users/3/favorites will fetch the favorite products for user id 3. First, we'll create the user favorite service:

Listing 10.5 The user favorite service

```
import functools
from aiohttp import web
from aiohttp.web_request import Request
from aiohttp.web_response import Response
from chapter_10.listing_10_4 import DB_KEY, create_database_pool, \
    destroy_database_pool


routes = web.RouteTableDef()


@routes.get('/users/{id}/favorites')
async def favorites(request: Request) -> Response:
    try:
        str_id = request.match_info['id']
        user_id = int(str_id)
        db = request.app[DB_KEY]
        favorite_query = 'SELECT product_id from user_favorite where user_id = $1'
        result = await db.fetch(favorite_query, user_id)
        if result is not None:
            return web.json_response([dict(record) for record in result])
        else:
            raise web.HTTPNotFound()
    except ValueError:
        raise web.HTTPBadRequest()
```

```
app = web.Application()
app.on_startup.append(functools.partial(create_database_pool,
                                         host='127.0.0.1',
                                         port=5432,
                                         user='postgres',
                                         password='password',
                                         database='favorites'))
app.on_cleanup.append(destroy_database_pool)

app.add_routes(routes)
web.run_app(app, port=8002)
```

Next, we'll create the user cart service. This code will look mostly similar to our previous service with the main difference being we'll interact with the user_cart table.

Listing 10.6   The user cart service

```
import functools
from aiohttp import web
from aiohttp.web_request import Request
from aiohttp.web_response import Response
from chapter_10.listing_10_4 import DB_KEY, create_database_pool, \
    destroy_database_pool

routes = web.RouteTableDef()


@routes.get('/users/{id}/cart')
async def time(request: Request) -> Response:
    try:
        str_id = request.match_info['id']
        user_id = int(str_id)
        db = request.app[DB_KEY]
        favorite_query = 'SELECT product_id from user_cart where user_id = $1'
        result = await db.fetch(favorite_query, user_id)
        if result is not None:
            return web.json_response([dict(record) for record in result])
        else:
            raise web.HTTPNotFound()
    except ValueError:
        raise web.HTTPBadRequest()


app = web.Application()
app.on_startup.append(functools.partial(create_database_pool,
                                         host='127.0.0.1',
                                         port=5432,
                                         user='postgres',
                                         password='password',
                                         database='cart'))
app.on_cleanup.append(destroy_database_pool)

app.add_routes(routes)
web.run_app(app, port=8003)
```

Finally, we'll implement the product service. This will be similar to the API we built in chapter 9 with the difference being that we'll fetch all products from our database instead of just one. With the following listing, we've created four services to power our theoretical e-commerce storefront!

Listing 10.7 The product service

```
import functools
from aiohttp import web
from aiohttp.web_request import Request
from aiohttp.web_response import Response
from chapter_10.listing_10_4 import DB_KEY, create_database_pool, 
    destroy_database_pool

routes = web.RouteTableDef()


@routes.get('/products')
async def products(request: Request) -> Response:
    db = request.app[DB_KEY]
    product_query = 'SELECT product_id, product_name FROM product'
    result = await db.fetch(product_query)
    return web.json_response([dict(record) for record in result])


app = web.Application()
app.on_startup.append(functools.partial(create_database_pool,
                                        host='127.0.0.1',
                                        port=5432,
                                        user='postgres',
                                        password='password',
                                        database='products'))
app.on_cleanup.append(destroy_database_pool)

app.add_routes(routes)
web.run_app(app, port=8000)
```

10.3.3 *Implementing the backend-for-frontend service*

Next, let's build the backend-for-frontend service. We'll first start with a few requirements for our API based on the needs of our UI. Product load times are crucial for our application, as the longer our users must wait, the less likely they are to continue browsing our site and the less likely they are to buy our products. This makes our requirements center around delivering the minimum viable data to the user as quickly as possible:

- The API should never wait for the product service more than 1 second. If it takes longer than 1 second, we should respond with a timeout error (HTTP code 504), so the UI does not hang indefinitely.
- The user cart and favorites data is optional. If we can get it in within 1 second, that's great! If not, we should just return what product data we have.

■ The inventory data for products is optional as well. If we can't get it, just return the product data.

With these requirements, we've given ourselves a few ways to short-circuit around slow services or services that have crashed or have other network issues. This makes our service, and therefore the user interfaces that consume it, more resilient. While it may not always have all the data to provide a complete user experience, it has enough to create a usable experience. Even if the result is a catastrophic failure of the product service, we won't leave the user hanging indefinitely with a busy spinner or some other poor user experience.

Next, let's define what we want our response to look like. All we need for the navigation bar is the number of items in our cart and in our favorites list, so we'll have our response just represent these as scalar values. Since our cart or favorite service could time out or could have an error, we'll allow this value to be null. For our product data, we'll just want our normal product data augmented with the inventory value, so we'll add this data in a products array. This means we'll have a response similar to the following:

```
{
 "cart_items": 1,
 "favorite_items": null,
 "products": [{"product_id": 4, "inventory": 4},
              {"product_id": 3, "inventory": 65}]
}
```

In this case, the user has one item in their cart. They may have favorite items, but the result is null because there was an issue reaching the favorite service. Finally, we have two products to display with 4 and 65 items in stock respectively.

So how should we begin implementing this functionality? We'll need to communicate with our REST services over HTTP, so aiohttp's web client functionality is a natural choice for this, as we're already using the framework's web server. Next, what requests do we make, and how do we group them and manage timeouts? First, we should think about the most requests we can run concurrently. The more we can run concurrently, the faster we can theoretically return a response to our clients. In our case, we can't ask for inventory before we have product IDs, so we can't run that concurrently, but our products, cart, and favorite services are not dependent on one another. This means we can run them concurrently with an asyncio API such as wait. Using wait with a timeout will give us a done set where we can check which requests finished with error and which are still running after the timeout, giving us a chance to handle any failures. Then, once we have product IDs and potentially user favorite and cart data, we can begin to stitch together our final response and send that back to the client.

We'll create an endpoint /products/all to do this that will return this data. Normally, we'd want to accept the currently logged-in user's ID somewhere in the URL, the request headers, or a cookie, so we can use that when making requests to our downstream services. In this example, for simplicity's sake, we'll just hardcode this ID to the user for whom we've already inserted data into our database.

Listing 10.8 The product backend-for-frontend

```
import asyncio
from asyncio import Task
import aiohttp
from aiohttp import web, ClientSession
from aiohttp.web_request import Request
from aiohttp.web_response import Response
import logging
from typing import Dict, Set, Awaitable, Optional, List

routes = web.RouteTableDef()

PRODUCT_BASE = 'http://127.0.0.1:8000'
INVENTORY_BASE = 'http://127.0.0.1:8001'
FAVORITE_BASE = 'http://127.0.0.1:8002'
CART_BASE = 'http://127.0.0.1:8003'


@routes.get('/products/all')
async def all_products(request: Request) -> Response:
    async with aiohttp.ClientSession() as session:
        products = asyncio.create_task(session.get(f'{PRODUCT_BASE}/products'))
        favorites =
            asyncio.create_task(session.get(f'{FAVORITE_BASE}/users/3/favorites'))
        cart = asyncio.create_task(session.get(f'{CART_BASE}/users/3/cart'))

        requests = [products, favorites, cart]
        done, pending = await asyncio.wait(requests, timeout=1.0)

        if products in pending:
            [request.cancel() for request in requests]
            return web.json_response({'error': 'Could not reach products service.'},
                status=504)
        elif products in done and products.exception() is not None:
            [request.cancel() for request in requests]
            logging.exception('Server error reaching product service.',
             exc_info=products.exception())
            return web.json_response({'error': 'Server error reaching products
             service.'}, status=500)
        else:
            product_response = await products.result().json()
            product_results: List[Dict] = await get_products_with_inventory(session,
             product_response)

            cart_item_count: Optional[int] = await get_response_item_count(cart,
                                                                           done,
                                                                           pending,
                                                                           'Error getting
                user cart.')
            favorite_item_count: Optional[int] = await get_response_item_count(favorites,
                                                                               done,
                                                                               pending,
                                                                               'Error
                getting user favorites.')
```

Create tasks to query the three services we have and run them concurrently.

If the products request times out, return an error, as we can't proceed.

Extract data from the product response, and use it to get inventory data.

```
                return web.json_response({'cart_items': cart_item_count,
                                          'favorite_items': favorite_item_count,
                                          'products': product_results})
```

> **Given a product response, make requests for inventory.**

```
async def get_products_with_inventory(session: ClientSession,
            product_response) -> List[Dict]:
    def get_inventory(session: ClientSession, product_id: str) -> Task:
        url = f"{INVENTORY_BASE}/products/{product_id}/inventory"
        return asyncio.create_task(session.get(url))

    def create_product_record(product_id: int, inventory: Optional[int]) -> Dict:
        return {'product_id': product_id, 'inventory': inventory}

    inventory_tasks_to_product_id = {
        get_inventory(session, product['product_id']): product['product_id'] for product
            in product_response
    }

    inventory_done, inventory_pending = await \
            asyncio.wait(inventory_tasks_to_product_id.keys(), timeout=1.0)

    product_results = []

    for done_task in inventory_done:
        if done_task.exception() is None:
            product_id = inventory_tasks_to_product_id[done_task]
            inventory = await done_task.result().json()
            product_results.append(create_product_record(product_id,
                inventory['inventory']))
        else:
            product_id = inventory_tasks_to_product_id[done_task]
            product_results.append(create_product_record(product_id, None))
            logging.exception(f'Error getting inventory for id {product_id}',
                            exc_info=inventory_tasks_to_product_id[done_task]
                .exception())

    for pending_task in inventory_pending:
        pending_task.cancel()
        product_id = inventory_tasks_to_product_id[pending_task]
        product_results.append(create_product_record(product_id, None))

    return product_results
```

> **Convenience method to get the number of items in a JSON array response**

```
async def get_response_item_count(task: Task,
                                  done: Set[Awaitable],
                                  pending: Set[Awaitable],
                                  error_msg: str) -> Optional[int]:
    if task in done and task.exception() is None:
        return len(await task.result().json())
    elif task in pending:
        task.cancel()
    else:
        logging.exception(error_msg, exc_info=task.exception())
```

```
                return None
```

```
app = web.Application()
app.add_routes(routes)
web.run_app(app, port=9000)
```

In the preceding listing, we first define a route handler named all_products. In all_products, we send requests to our products, cart, and favorite services concurrently, giving these requests 1 second to complete with wait. Once either all of them finish, or we have waited for 1 second, we begin to process the results.

Since the product response is critical, we check its status first. If it is still pending or has an exception, we cancel any pending requests and return an error to the client. If there was an exception, we respond with a HTTP 500 error, indicating a server issue. If there was a timeout, we respond with a 504 error, indicating we couldn't reach the service. This specificity gives our clients a hint as to whether they should try again and also gives us more information useful for any monitoring and altering we may have (we can have alerts specifically to watch 504 response rates, for example).

If we have a successful response from the product service, we can now start to process it and ask for inventory numbers. We do this work in a helper function called get_products_with_inventory. In this helper function, we pull product IDs from the response body and use these to construct requests to the inventory service. Since our inventory service only accepts one product ID at a time (ideally, you would be able to batch these into a single request, but we'll pretend the team that manages the inventory service has issues with this approach), we'll create a list of tasks to request inventory per each product. We'll again pass these into the wait coroutine, giving them all 1 second to complete.

Since inventory numbers are optional, once our timeout is up, we begin processing everything in both the done and pending sets of inventory requests. If we have a successful response from the inventory service, we create a dictionary with the product information alongside the inventory number. If there was either an exception or the request is still in the pending set, we create a record with the inventory as None, indicating we couldn't retrieve it. Using None will give us a null value when we turn our response into JSON.

Finally, we check the cart and favorite responses. All we need to do for both these requests is count the number of items returned. Since this logic is nearly identical for both services, we create a helper method to count items named get_response_item_count. In get_response_item_count, if we have a successful result from either the cart or favorite service, it will be a JSON array, so we count and return the number of items in that array. If there was an exception or the request took longer than 1 second, we set the result to None, so we get a null value in our JSON response.

This implementation provides us with a reasonably robust way to deal with failures and timeouts of our non-critical services, ensuring that we give a sensible response quickly even in the result of downstream issues. No single request to a downstream service will take longer than 1 second, creating an approximate upper bound for how slow our service can be. However, while we've created something fairly robust, there are still a few ways we can make this even more resilient to issues.

10.3.4 *Retrying failed requests*

One issue with our first implementation is that it pessimistically assumes that if we get an exception from a service, we assume we can't get results and we move on. While this can make sense, it is the case that an issue with a service could be transient. For example, there may be a networking hiccup that disappears rather quickly, there may be a temporary issue with any load balancers we're using, or there could be any other host of temporary issues.

In these cases, it can make sense to retry a few times with a short delay in between retries. This gives the error a chance to clear up and can give our users more data than they would otherwise have if we were pessimistic about our failures. This of course comes with the tradeoff of having our users wait longer, potentially just to see the same failure they would have otherwise.

To implement this functionality, the `wait_for` coroutine function is a perfect candidate. It will raise any exception we get, and it lets us specify a timeout. If we surpass that timeout, it raises a `TimeoutException` and cancels the task we started. Let's try and create a reusable retry coroutine that does this for us. We'll create a `retry` coroutine function that takes in coroutine as well as a number of times to retry. If the coroutine we pass in fails or times out, we'll retry up to the number of times we specified.

Listing 10.9   A retry coroutine

```
import asyncio
import logging
from typing import Callable, Awaitable


class TooManyRetries(Exception):
    pass


async def retry(coro: Callable[[], Awaitable],
                max_retries: int,
                timeout: float,
                retry_interval: float):                           Wait for a response
    for retry_num in range(0, max_retries):                       for the specified
        try:                                                      timeout.
            return await asyncio.wait_for(coro(), timeout=timeout)   ◁┘
        except Exception as e:
            logging.exception(f'Exception while waiting (tried {retry_num}
    times), retrying.', exc_info=e)        ◁┐   If we get an exception,
            await asyncio.sleep(retry_interval)   log it and sleep for the
    raise TooManyRetries()      ◁─────────┐       retry interval.

            If we've failed too many times,
          raise an exception to indicate that.
```

In the preceding listing, we first create a custom exception class that we'll raise when we are still failing after the maximum amount of retries. This will let any callers catch this exception and handle this specific issue as they see fit. The `retry` coroutine takes in a few arguments. The first argument is a callable that returns an awaitable; this is the coroutine that we'll retry. The second argument is the number of times we'd like to retry, and the final arguments are the timeout and the interval to wait to retry after a failure. We create a loop that wraps the coroutine in `wait_for`, and if this completes successfully, we return the results and exit the function. If there was an error, timeout or otherwise, we catch the exception, log it, and sleep for the specified interval time, retrying again after we've slept. If our loop finishes without an error-free call of our coroutine, we raise a `TooManyRetries` exception.

We can test this out by creating a couple of coroutines that exhibit the failure behavior we'd like to handle. First, one which always throws an exception and second, one which always times out.

Listing 10.10   Testing the retry coroutine

```
import asyncio
from chapter_10.listing_10_9 import retry, TooManyRetries


async def main():
    async def always_fail():
        raise Exception("I've failed!")

    async def always_timeout():
        await asyncio.sleep(1)

    try:
        await retry(always_fail,
                    max_retries=3,
                    timeout=.1,
                    retry_interval=.1)
    except TooManyRetries:
        print('Retried too many times!')

    try:
        await retry(always_timeout,
                    max_retries=3,
                    timeout=.1,
                    retry_interval=.1)
    except TooManyRetries:
        print('Retried too many times!')


asyncio.run(main())
```

For both retries, we define a timeout and retry interval of 100 milliseconds and a max retry amount of three. This means we give the coroutine 100 milliseconds to complete, and if it doesn't complete within that time, or it fails, we wait 100 milliseconds before trying again. Running this listing, you should see each coroutine try to run three times and finally print `Retried too many times!`, leading to output similar to the following (tracebacks omitted for brevity):

```
ERROR:root:Exception while waiting (tried 1 times), retrying.
Exception: I've failed!
ERROR:root:Exception while waiting (tried 2 times), retrying.
Exception: I've failed!
ERROR:root:Exception while waiting (tried 3 times), retrying.
Exception: I've failed!
Retried too many times!
ERROR:root:Exception while waiting (tried 1 times), retrying.
ERROR:root:Exception while waiting (tried 2 times), retrying.
ERROR:root:Exception while waiting (tried 3 times), retrying.
Retried too many times!
```

Using this, we can add some simple retry logic to our product backend-for-frontend. For example, let's say we wanted to retry our initial requests to the products, cart, and favorite services a few times before considering their error unrecoverable. We can do this by wrapping each request in the retry coroutine like so:

```
product_request = functools.partial(session.get, f'{PRODUCT_BASE}/products')
favorite_request = functools.partial(session.get,
    f'{FAVORITE_BASE}/users/5/favorites')
cart_request = functools.partial(session.get, f'{CART_BASE}/users/5/cart')

products = asyncio.create_task(retry(product_request,
                                     max_retries=3,
                                     timeout=.1,
                                     retry_interval=.1))

favorites = asyncio.create_task(retry(favorite_request,
                                      max_retries=3,
                                      timeout=.1,
                                      retry_interval=.1))

cart = asyncio.create_task(retry(cart_request,
                                 max_retries=3,
                                 timeout=.1,
                                 retry_interval=.1))

requests = [products, favorites, cart]
done, pending = await asyncio.wait(requests, timeout=1.0)
```

In this example, we try each service a maximum of three times. This lets us recover from issues with our services that may be transient. While this is an improvement, there is another potential issue that can hurt our service. For example, what happens if our product service always times out?

10.3.5 *The circuit breaker pattern*

One issue we still have in our implementation occurs when a service is consistently slow enough such that it always times out. This can happen when a downstream service is under load, there is some other network issue happening, or a multitude of other application or network errors.

You may be tempted to ask, "Well, our application handles the timeout gracefully; the user won't wait for more than 1 second before seeing an error or getting partial data, so what is the problem?" And you're not wrong to ask. However, while we've designed our system to be robust and resilient, consider the user experience. For example, if the cart service is experiencing an issue such that it always takes 1 second to time out, this means that all users will be stuck waiting for 1 second for results from the service.

In this instance, since this issue with the cart service could last for some time, anyone who hits our backend-for-frontend will be stuck waiting for 1 second when we *know* that this issue is highly likely to happen. Is there a way we can short-circuit a call that is likely to fail, so we don't cause unneeded delays to our users?

There is an aptly named pattern to handle this called the *circuit breaker pattern*. Popularized by Michael Nygard's book *Release It* (The Pragmatic Bookshelf, 2017), this pattern lets us "flip a circuit breaker," and when we have a specified number of errors in each time period, we can use this to bypass the slow service until the issues with it clear up, ensuring our response to our users remains as fast as possible.

Much like an electrical circuit breaker, a basic circuit breaker pattern has two states associated with it that are the same as a normal circuit breaker on your electrical panel: an open state and a closed state. The closed state is a happy path; we make a request to a service and it returns normally. The open state happens when the circuit is tripped. In this state, we don't bother to call the service, as we know it has a problem; instead, we instantly return an error. The circuit breaker pattern stops us from sending electricity to the bad service. In addition to these two states there is a "half-open" state. This happens when we're in the open state after a certain time interval. In this state we issue a single request to check if the issue with the service is fixed. If it is, we close the circuit breaker, and if not, we keep it open. For the sake of keeping our example simple, we'll skip the half-open state and just focus on the closed and open states, as shown in figure 10.3.

Let's implement a simple circuit breaker to understand how this works. We'll allow the users of the circuit breaker to specify a time window and a maximum number of failures. If more than the maximum number of errors happens within the time window, we'll open the circuit breaker and fail any other calls. We'll do this with a class that takes the coroutine we wish to run and keeps track if we are in the open or closed state.

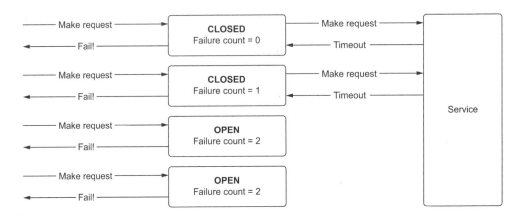

Figure 10.3   A circuit breaker that opens after two failures. Once opened, all requests will fail instantly.

Listing 10.11   A simple circuit breaker

```
import asyncio
from datetime import datetime, timedelta


class CircuitOpenException(Exception):
    pass


class CircuitBreaker:

    def __init__(self,
                 callback,
                 timeout: float,
                 time_window: float,
                 max_failures: int,
                 reset_interval: float):
        self.callback = callback
        self.timeout = timeout
        self.time_window = time_window
        self.max_failures = max_failures
        self.reset_interval = reset_interval
        self.last_request_time = None
        self.last_failure_time = None
        self.current_failures = 0

    async def request(self, *args, **kwargs):
        if self.current_failures >= self.max_failures:
            if datetime.now() > self.last_request_time +
    timedelta(seconds=self.reset_interval):
                self._reset('Circuit is going from open to closed, resetting!')
                return await self._do_request(*args, **kwargs)
```

Make the request, failing fast if we've exceeded the failure count.

```
            else:
                print('Circuit is open, failing fast!')
                raise CircuitOpenException()
        else:
            if self.last_failure_time and datetime.now() >
    self.last_failure_time + timedelta(seconds=self.time_window):
                self._reset('Interval since first failure elapsed, resetting!')
            print('Circuit is closed, requesting!')
            return await self._do_request(*args, **kwargs)

    def _reset(self, msg: str):          ◁────┐  Reset our
        print(msg)                              │  counters and last
        self.last_failure_time = None           │  failure time.
        self.current_failures = 0

                                                   Make the request, keeping
                                                   track of how many failures
    async def _do_request(self, *args, **kwargs):  ◁───  we've had and when they
        try:                                           last happened.
            print('Making request!')
            self.last_request_time = datetime.now()
            return await asyncio.wait_for(self.callback(*args, **kwargs),
    timeout=self.timeout)
        except Exception as e:
            self.current_failures = self.current_failures + 1
            if self.last_failure_time is None:
                self.last_failure_time = datetime.now()
            raise
```

Our circuit breaker class takes five constructor parameters. The first two are the callback we wish to run with the circuit breaker and a timeout which represents how long we'll allow the callback to run before failing with a timeout. The next three are related to handling failures and resets. The max_failure parameter is the maximum number of failures we'll tolerate within time_window seconds before opening the circuit. The reset_interval parameter is how many seconds we wait to reset the breaker from the open to closed state after max_failure failures have occurred.

We then define a coroutine method request, which calls our callback and keeps track of how many failures we've had, returning the result of the callback if there were no errors. When we have a failure, we keep track of this in a counter failure_count. If the failure count exceeds the max_failure threshold we set within the specified time interval, any further calls to request will raise a CircuitOpenException. If the reset interval has elapsed, we reset the failure_count to zero and begin making requests again (if our breaker was closed, which it may not be).

Now, let's see our breaker in action with a simple example application. We'll create a slow_callback coroutine that sleeps for just 2 seconds. We'll then use that in our breaker, setting a short timeout that will let us easily trip the breaker.

Listing 10.12   The breaker in action

```
import asyncio
from chapter_10.listing_10_11 import CircuitBreaker
```

```
async def main():
    async def slow_callback():
        await asyncio.sleep(2)

    cb = CircuitBreaker(slow_callback,
                        timeout=1.0,
                        time_window=5,
                        max_failures=2,
                        reset_interval=5)

    for _ in range(4):
        try:
            await cb.request()
        except Exception as e:
            pass

    print('Sleeping for 5 seconds so breaker closes...')
    await asyncio.sleep(5)

    for _ in range(4):
        try:
            await cb.request()
        except Exception as e:
            pass


asyncio.run(main())
```

In the preceding listing, we create a breaker with a 1-second timeout that tolerates two failures within a 5-second interval and resets after 5 seconds once the breaker is open. We then try to make four requests rapidly to the breaker. The first two should take 1 second before failing with a timeout, then every subsequent call will fail instantly as the breaker is open. We then sleep for 5 seconds; this lets the breaker's reset_interval elapse, so it should move back to the closed state and start to make calls to our callback again. Running this, you should see output as follows:

```
Circuit is closed, requesting!
Circuit is closed, requesting!
Circuit is open, failing fast!
Circuit is open, failing fast!
Sleeping for 5 seconds so breaker closes...
Circuit is going from open to closed, requesting!
Circuit is closed, requesting!
Circuit is open, failing fast!
Circuit is open, failing fast!
```

Now that we have a simple implementation, we can combine this with our retry logic and use it in our backend-for-frontend. Since we've purposefully made our inventory service slow to simulate a real-life legacy service, this is a natural place to add our circuit breaker. We'll set a timeout of 500 milliseconds and tolerate five failures within 1 second, after which we'll set a reset interval of 30 seconds. We'll need to rewrite our get_inventory function into a coroutine to do this like so:

```
async def get_inventory(session: ClientSession, product_id: str):
    url = f"{INVENTORY_BASE}/products/{product_id}/inventory"
    return await session.get(url)


inventory_circuit = CircuitBreaker(get_inventory, timeout=.5, time_window=5.0,
    max_failures=3, reset_interval=30)
```

Then, in our all_products coroutine we'll need to change how we create our inventory service requests. We'll create a task with a call to our inventory circuit breaker instead of the get_inventory coroutine:

```
inventory_tasks_to_pid = {
  asyncio.create_task(inventory_circuit.request(session,
    product['product_id'])): product['product_id']
  for product in product_response
}

inventory_done, inventory_pending = await
    asyncio.wait(inventory_tasks_to_pid.keys(), timeout=1.0)
```

Once we've made these changes, you should see call time decrease to the products' backend-for-frontend after a few calls. Since we're simulating an inventory service that is slow under load, we'll eventually trip the circuit breaker with a few timeouts and then any subsequent call won't make any more requests to the inventory service until the breaker resets. Our backend-for-frontend service is now more robust in the face of a slow and failure-prone inventory service. We could also apply this to all our other calls if desired to increase the stability of these as well.

In this example, we've implemented a very simple circuit breaker to demonstrate how it works and how to build it with asyncio. There are several existing implementations of this pattern with many other features to tune to your specific needs. If you're considering this pattern, take some time to do research on the circuit breaker libraries available before implementing it yourself.

Summary

- Microservices have several benefits over monoliths, including, but not limited to, independent scalability and deployability.
- The backend-for-frontend pattern is a microservice pattern that aggregates the calls from several downstream services. We've learned how to apply a microservice architecture to an e-commerce use case, creating multiple independent services with aiohttp.

- We've used asyncio utility functions such as `wait` to ensure that our backend-for-frontend service remains resilient and responsive to failures of downstream services.
- We've created a utility to manage retries of HTTP requests with asyncio and aiohttp.
- We've implemented a basic circuit breaker pattern to ensure a service failure does not negatively impact other services.

Synchronization

When we write applications using multiple threads and multiple processes, we need to worry about race conditions when using non-atomic operations. Something as simple as incrementing an integer concurrently can cause subtle, hard-to-reproduce bugs. When we are using asyncio, however, we're always using a single thread (unless we're interoperating with multithreading and multiprocessing), so doesn't that mean we don't need to worry about race conditions? It turns out it is not quite so simple.

While certain concurrency bugs that would occur in multithreaded or multiprocessing applications are eliminated by asyncio's single-threaded nature, they are not completely eliminated. While you likely won't need to use synchronization often with asyncio, there are still cases where we need these constructs. asyncio's *synchronization primitives* can help us prevent bugs unique to a single-threaded concurrency model.

Synchronization primitives are not limited to preventing concurrency bugs and have other uses as well. As an example, we may be working with an API that lets us make only a few requests concurrently as per a contract we have with a vendor, or there may be an API we're concerned about overloading with requests. We may also have a workflow with several workers that need to be notified when new data is available.

In this chapter, we'll look at a few examples where we can introduce race conditions in our asyncio code and learn how to solve them with locks and other concurrency primitives. We'll also learn how to use semaphores to limit concurrency and control access to a shared resource, such as a database connection pool. Finally, we'll look at events and conditions that we can use to notify tasks when something occurs and gain access to shared resources when that happens.

11.1 *Understanding single-threaded concurrency bugs*

In earlier chapters on multiprocessing and multithreading, recall that when we were working with data that is shared among different processes and threads, we had to worry about race conditions. This is because a thread or process could read data while it is being modified by a different thread or process, leading to an inconsistent state and therefore corruption of data.

This corruption was in part due to some operations being non-atomic, meaning that while they appear like one operation, they comprise multiple separate operations under the hood. The example we gave in chapter 6 dealt with incrementing an integer variable; first, we read the current value, then we increment it, then we reassign it back to the variable. This gives other threads and processes ample opportunities to get data in an inconsistent state.

In a single-threaded concurrency model, we avoid race conditions caused by non-atomic operations. In asyncio's single-threaded model, we only have one thread executing one line of Python code at any given time. This means that even if an operation is non-atomic, we'll always run it to completion without other coroutines reading inconsistent state information.

To prove this to ourselves, let's try and re-create the race condition we looked at in chapter 7 with multiple threads trying to implement a shared counter. Instead of having multiple threads modify the variable, we'll have multiple tasks. We'll repeat this 1,000 times and assert that we get the correct value back.

Listing 11.1 Attempting to create a race condition

```
import asyncio

counter: int = 0


async def increment():
    global counter
    await asyncio.sleep(0.01)
    counter = counter + 1
```

```
async def main():
    global counter
    for _ in range(1000):
        tasks = [asyncio.create_task(increment()) for _ in range(100)]
        await asyncio.gather(*tasks)
        print(f'Counter is {counter}')
        assert counter == 100
        counter = 0


asyncio.run(main())
```

In the preceding listing, we create an increment coroutine function that adds one to a global counter, adding a 1-millisecond delay to simulate a slow operation. In our main coroutine, we create 100 tasks to increment the counter and then run them all concurrently with gather. We then assert that our counter is the expected value, which, since we ran 100 increment tasks, should always be 100. Running this, you should see that the value we get is always 100 even though incrementing an integer is non-atomic. If we ran multiple threads instead of coroutines, we should see our assertion fail at some point in execution.

Does this mean that with a single-threaded concurrency model we've found a way to completely avoid race conditions? Unfortunately, it's not quite the case. While we avoid race conditions where a single non-atomic operation can cause a bug, we still have the problem where multiple operations executed in the wrong order can cause issues. To see this in action, let's make incrementing an integer in the eyes of asyncio non-atomic.

To do this, we'll replicate what happens under the hood when we increment a global counter. We read the global value, increment it, then write it back. The basic idea is if other code modifies state while our coroutine is suspended on an await, once the await finishes we may be in an inconsistent state.

Listing 11.2 A single-threaded race condition

```
import asyncio

counter: int = 0


async def increment():
    global counter
    temp_counter = counter
    temp_counter = temp_counter + 1
    await asyncio.sleep(0.01)
    counter = temp_counter


async def main():
    global counter
    for _ in range(1000):
        tasks = [asyncio.create_task(increment()) for _ in range(100)]
        await asyncio.gather(*tasks)
```

```
    print(f'Counter is {counter}')
    assert counter == 100
    counter = 0


asyncio.run(main())
```

Instead of our increment coroutine directly incrementing the counter, we first read it into a temporary variable and then increment the temporary counter by one. We then `await asyncio.sleep` to simulate a slow operation, suspending our coroutine, and only then do we reassign it back to the global counter variable. Running this, you should see this code fail with an assertion error instantly, and our counter only ever gets set to 1! Each coroutine reads the counter value first, which is 0, stores it to a temp value, then goes to sleep. Since we're single-threaded, each read to a temporary variable runs sequentially, meaning each coroutine stores the value of counter as 0 and increments this to 1. Then, once the sleep is finished, every coroutine sets the value of the counter to 1, meaning despite running 100 coroutines to increment our counter, our counter is only ever 1. Note that if you remove the `await` expression, things will operate in the correct order because there is no opportunity to modify the application state while we're paused at an `await` point.

This is admittedly a simplistic and somewhat unrealistic example. To better see when this may occur, let's create a slightly more complex race condition. Imagine we're implementing a server that sends messages to connected users. In this server, we keep a dictionary of usernames to sockets we can use to send messages to these users. When a user disconnects, a callback runs that will remove the user from the dictionary and close their socket. Since we close the socket on disconnect, attempting to send any other messages will fail with an exception. What happens if a user disconnects while we're in the process of sending messages? Let's assume the desired behavior is for all users to receive a message if they were connected when we started to send messages.

To test this out, let's implement a mock socket. This mock socket will have a `send` coroutine and a `close` method. Our `send` coroutine will simulate a message send over a slow network. This coroutine will also check a flag to see if we've closed the socket, and if we have it will throw an exception.

We'll then create a dictionary with a few connected users and create mock sockets for each of them. We'll send messages to each user and manually trigger a disconnect for a single user while we're sending messages to see what happens.

> **Listing 11.3   A race condition with dictionaries**

```
import asyncio


class MockSocket:
    def __init__(self):
        self.socket_closed = False
```

```
async def send(self, msg: str):                    ◄──────┐   Simulate a slow
    if self.socket_closed:                                 │   send of a message
        raise Exception('Socket is closed!')               │   to a client.
    print(f'Sending: {msg}')
    await asyncio.sleep(1)
    print(f'Sent: {msg}')

def close(self):
    self.socket_closed = True


user_names_to_sockets = {'John': MockSocket(),
                         'Terry': MockSocket(),
                         'Graham': MockSocket(),
                         'Eric': MockSocket()}
                                                       Disconnect a user and
                                                       remove them from
                                                       application memory.
async def user_disconnect(username: str):          ◄───┘
    print(f'{username} disconnected!')
    socket = user_names_to_sockets.pop(username)
    socket.close()

                                              Send messages to all
                                              users concurrently.
async def message_all_users():             ◄──┘
    print('Creating message tasks')
    messages = [socket.send(f'Hello {user}')
                for user, socket in
                user_names_to_sockets.items()]
    await asyncio.gather(*messages)


async def main():
    await asyncio.gather(message_all_users(), user_disconnect('Eric'))


asyncio.run(main())
```

If you run this code, you will see the application crash with the following output:

```
Creating message tasks
Eric disconnected!
Sending: Hello John
Sending: Hello Terry
Sending: Hello Graham
Traceback (most recent call last):
  File 'chapter_11/listing_11_3.py', line 45, in <module>
    asyncio.run(main())
  File "asyncio/runners.py", line 44, in run
    return loop.run_until_complete(main)
  File "python3.9/asyncio/base_events.py", line 642, in run_until_complete
    return future.result()
  File 'chapter_11/listing_11_3.py', line 42, in main
    await asyncio.gather(message_all_users(), user_disconnect('Eric'))
  File 'chapter_11/listing_11_3.py', line 37, in message_all_users
    await asyncio.gather(*messages)
```

```
File 'chapter_11/listing_11_3.py', line 11, in send
  raise Exception('Socket is closed!')
Exception: Socket is closed!
```

In this example, we first create the message tasks, then we `await`, suspending our `message_all_users` coroutine. This gives `user_disconnect('Eric')` a chance to run, which will close Eric's socket and remove it from the `user_names_to_sockets` dictionary. Once this is finished, `message_all_users` resumes; and we start to send out messages. Since Eric's socket was closed, we see an exception, and he won't get the message we intended to send. Note that we also modified the `user_names_to_sockets` dictionary. If we somehow needed to use this dictionary and relied on Eric still being in there, we could potentially have an exception or another bug.

These are the types of bugs you tend to see in a single-threaded concurrency model. You hit a suspension point with `await`, and another coroutine runs and modifies some shared state, changing it for the first coroutine once it resumes in an undesired way. The key difference between multithreaded concurrency bugs and single-threaded concurrency bugs is that in a multithreaded application, race conditions are possible anywhere you modify a mutable state. In a single-threaded concurrency model, you need to modify the mutable state during an `await` point. Now that we understand the types of concurrency bugs in a single-threaded model, let's see how to avoid them by using asyncio locks.

11.2 Locks

asyncio locks operate similarly to the locks in the multiprocessing and multithreading modules. We acquire a lock, do work inside of a critical section, and when we're done, we release the lock, letting other interested parties acquire it. The main difference is that asyncio locks are awaitable objects that suspend coroutine execution when they are blocked. This means that when a coroutine is blocked waiting to acquire a lock, other code can run. In addition, asyncio locks are also asynchronous context managers, and the preferred way to use them is with `async with` syntax.

To get familiar with how locks work, let's look at a simple example with one lock shared between two coroutines. We'll acquire the lock, which will prevent other coroutines from running code in the critical section until someone releases it.

Listing 11.4 Using an asyncio lock

```
import asyncio
from asyncio import Lock
from util import delay


async def a(lock: Lock):
    print('Coroutine a waiting to acquire the lock')
    async with lock:
        print('Coroutine a is in the critical section')
        await delay(2)
    print('Coroutine a released the lock')
```

```
async def b(lock: Lock):
    print('Coroutine b waiting to acquire the lock')
    async with lock:
        print('Coroutine b is in the critical section')
        await delay(2)
    print('Coroutine b released the lock')


async def main():
    lock = Lock()
    await asyncio.gather(a(lock), b(lock))


asyncio.run(main())
```

When we run the preceding listing, we will see that coroutine a acquires the lock first, leaving coroutine b waiting until a releases the lock. Once a releases the lock, b can do its work in the critical section, giving us the following output:

```
Coroutine a waiting to acquire the lock
Coroutine a is in the critical section
sleeping for 2 second(s)
Coroutine b waiting to acquire the lock
finished sleeping for 2 second(s)
Coroutine a released the lock
Coroutine b is in the critical section
sleeping for 2 second(s)
finished sleeping for 2 second(s)
Coroutine b released the lock
```

Here we used async with syntax. If we had wanted, we could use the acquire and release methods on the lock like so:

```
await lock.acquire()
try:
    print('In critical section')
finally:
    lock.release()
```

That said, it is best practice to use async with syntax where possible.

One important thing to note is that we created the lock inside of the main coroutine. Since the lock is shared globally amongst the coroutines we create, we may be tempted to make it a global variable to avoid passing it in each time like so:

```
lock = Lock()

# coroutine definitions

async def main():
    await asyncio.gather(a(), b())
```

If we do this, we'll quickly see a crash with an error reporting multiple event loops:

```
Task <Task pending name='Task-3' coro=<b()> got Future <Future pending>
    attached to a different loop
```

Why is this happening when all we've done is move our lock definition? This is a confusing quirk of the asyncio library and is not unique to just locks. Most objects in asyncio provide an optional loop parameter that lets you specify the specific event loop to run in. When this parameter is not provided, asyncio tries to get the currently running event loop, but if there is none, it creates a new one. In the above case, creating a Lock creates a new event loop, since when our script first runs we haven't yet created one. Then, asyncio.run(main()) creates a second event loop, and when we attempt to use our lock we intermingle these two separate event loops, which causes a crash.

This behavior is tricky enough that in Python 3.10, event loop parameters are going to be removed, and this confusing behavior will go away, but until then you'll need to think through these cases when using global asyncio variables carefully.

Now that we know the basics, let's see how to use a lock to solve the bug we had in listing 11.3, where we attempted to send a message to a user whose socket we closed too early. The idea to solve this is to use a lock in two places: first, when a user disconnects, second, when we send out messages to users. This way, if a disconnect happens while we're sending out messages, we'll wait until they all finish before finally closing any sockets.

Listing 11.5 Using locks to avoid a race condition

```python
import asyncio
from asyncio import Lock


class MockSocket:
    def __init__(self):
        self.socket_closed = False

    async def send(self, msg: str):
        if self.socket_closed:
            raise Exception('Socket is closed!')
        print(f'Sending: {msg}')
        await asyncio.sleep(1)
        print(f'Sent: {msg}')

    def close(self):
        self.socket_closed = True


user_names_to_sockets = {'John': MockSocket(),
                         'Terry': MockSocket(),
                         'Graham': MockSocket(),
                         'Eric': MockSocket()}
```

```
async def user_disconnect(username: str, user_lock: Lock):
    print(f'{username} disconnected!')
    async with user_lock:
        print(f'Removing {username} from dictionary')
        socket = user_names_to_sockets.pop(username)
        socket.close()
```

Acquire the lock before removing a user and closing the socket.

```
async def message_all_users(user_lock: Lock):
    print('Creating message tasks')
    async with user_lock:
        messages = [socket.send(f'Hello {user}')
                    for user, socket in
                    user_names_to_sockets.items()]
        await asyncio.gather(*messages)
```

Acquire the lock before sending.

```
async def main():
    user_lock = Lock()
    await asyncio.gather(message_all_users(user_lock),
                         user_disconnect('Eric', user_lock))


asyncio.run(main())
```

When we run the following listing, we won't see any more crashes, and we'll get the following output:

```
Creating message tasks
Eric disconnected!
Sending: Hello John
Sending: Hello Terry
Sending: Hello Graham
Sending: Hello Eric
Sent: Hello John
Sent: Hello Terry
Sent: Hello Graham
Sent: Hello Eric
Removing Eric from dictionary
```

We first acquire the lock and create the message tasks. While this is happening, Eric disconnects, and the code in disconnect tries to acquire the lock. Since message_all_users still holds the lock, we need to wait for it to finish before running the code in disconnect. This lets all the messages finish sending out before closing out the socket, preventing our bug.

You likely won't often need to use locks in asyncio code because many concurrency issues are avoided by its single-threaded nature. Even when race conditions occur, sometimes you can refactor your code such that state isn't modified while a coroutine is suspended (by using immutable objects, for example). When you can't refactor in this way, locks can force modifications to happen in a desired synchronized order. Now that we understand the concepts around avoiding concurrency bugs with locks, let's look at how to use synchronization to implement new functionality in our asyncio applications.

11.3 *Limiting concurrency with semaphores*

Resources that our applications need to use are often finite. We may have a limited number of connections we can use concurrently with a database; we may have a limited number of CPUs that we don't want to overload; or we may be working with an API that only allows a few concurrent requests, based on our current subscription pricing. We could also be using our own internal API and may be concerned with overwhelming it with load, effectively launching a distributed denial of service attack against ourselves.

Semaphores are a construct that can help us out in these situations. A semaphore acts much like a lock in that we can acquire it and we can release it, with the major difference being that we can acquire it multiple times up to a limit we specify. Internally, a semaphore keeps track of this limit; each time we acquire the semaphore we decrement the limit, and each time we release the semaphore we increment it. If the count reaches zero, any further attempts to acquire the semaphore will block until someone else calls release and increments the count. To draw parallels to what we just learned with locks, you can think of a lock as a special case of a semaphore with a limit of one.

To see semaphores in action, let's build a simple example where we only want two tasks running at the same time, but we have four tasks to run in total. To do this, we'll create a semaphore with a limit of two and acquire it in our coroutine.

Listing 11.6   Using semaphores

```
import asyncio
from asyncio import Semaphore


async def operation(semaphore: Semaphore):
    print('Waiting to acquire semaphore...')
    async with semaphore:
        print('Semaphore acquired!')
        await asyncio.sleep(2)
    print('Semaphore released!')


async def main():
    semaphore = Semaphore(2)
    await asyncio.gather(*[operation(semaphore) for _ in range(4)])


asyncio.run(main())
```

In our main coroutine, we create a semaphore with a limit of two, indicating we can acquire it twice before additional acquisition attempts start to block. We then create four concurrent calls to operation—this coroutine acquires the semaphore with an async with block and simulates some blocking work with sleep. When we run this, we'll see the following output:

```
Waiting to acquire semaphore...
Semaphore acquired!
Waiting to acquire semaphore...
Semaphore acquired!
Waiting to acquire semaphore...
Waiting to acquire semaphore...
Semaphore released!
Semaphore released!
Semaphore acquired!
Semaphore acquired!
Semaphore released!
Semaphore released!
```

Since our semaphore only allows two acquisitions before it blocks, our first two tasks successfully acquire the lock while our other two tasks wait for the first two tasks to release the semaphore. Once the work in the first two tasks finishes and we release the semaphore, our other two tasks can acquire the semaphore and start doing their work.

Let's take this pattern and apply it to a real-world use case. Let's imagine you're working for a scrappy, cash-strapped startup, and you've just partnered with a third-party REST API vendor. Their contracts are particularly expensive for unlimited queries, but they offer a plan that allows for only 10 concurrent requests that is more budget-friendly. If you make more than 10 requests concurrently, their API will return a status code of 429 (too many requests). You could send a set of requests and retry if you get a 429, but this is inefficient and places extra load on your vendor's servers, which probably won't make their site reliability engineers happy. A better approach is to create a semaphore with a limit of 10 and then acquire that whenever you make an API request. Using a semaphore when making a request will ensure that you only ever have 10 requests in flight at any given time.

Let's see how to do this with the aiohttp library. We'll make 1,000 requests to an example API but limit the total concurrent requests to 10 with a semaphore. Note that aiohttp has connection limits we can tweak as well, and by default it only allows 100 connections at a time. It is possible achieve the same as below by tweaking this limit.

Listing 11.7 Limiting API requests with semaphores

```python
import asyncio
from asyncio import Semaphore
from aiohttp import ClientSession


async def get_url(url: str,
                  session: ClientSession,
                  semaphore: Semaphore):
    print('Waiting to acquire semaphore...')
    async with semaphore:
        print('Acquired semaphore, requesting...')
        response = await session.get(url)
```

```
        print('Finished requesting')
        return response.status


async def main():
    semaphore = Semaphore(10)
    async with ClientSession() as session:
        tasks = [get_url('https://www.example .com', session, semaphore)
                 for _ in range(1000)]
        await asyncio.gather(*tasks)


asyncio.run(main())
```

While output will be nondeterministic depending on external latency factors, you should see output similar to the following:

```
Acquired semaphore, requesting...
Acquired semaphore, requesting...
Acquired semaphore, requesting...
Acquired semaphore, requesting...
Acquired semaphore, requesting...
Finished requesting
Finished requesting
Acquired semaphore, requesting...
Acquired semaphore, requesting...
```

Each time a request finishes, the semaphore is released, meaning a task that is blocked waiting for the semaphore can begin. This means that we only ever have at most 10 requests running at a given time, and when one finishes, we can start a new one.

This solves the issue of having too many requests running concurrently, but the code above is *bursty*, meaning that it has the potential to burst 10 requests at the same moment, creating a potential spike in traffic. This may not be desirable if we're concerned about spikes of load on the API we're calling. If you need to only burst up to a certain number of requests per some unit of time, you'll need to use this with an implementation of a traffic-shaping algorithm, such as the "leaky bucket" or "token bucket."

11.3.1 *Bounded semaphores*

One aspect of semaphores is that it is valid to call release more times than we call acquire. If we always use semaphores with an async with block, this isn't possible, since each acquire is automatically paired with a release. However, if we're in a situation where we need finer-grained control over our releasing and acquisition mechanisms (for example, perhaps we have some branching code where one branch lets us release earlier than another), we can run into issues. As an example, let's see what happens when we have a normal coroutine that acquires and releases a semaphore with an async with block, and while that coroutine is executing another coroutine calls release.

Listing 11.8   Releasing more than we acquire

```python
import asyncio
from asyncio import Semaphore

async def acquire(semaphore: Semaphore):
    print('Waiting to acquire')
    async with semaphore:
        print('Acquired')
        await asyncio.sleep(5)
    print('Releasing')

async def release(semaphore: Semaphore):
    print('Releasing as a one off!')
    semaphore.release()
    print('Released as a one off!')

async def main():
    semaphore = Semaphore(2)

    print("Acquiring twice, releasing three times...")
    await asyncio.gather(acquire(semaphore),
                         acquire(semaphore),
                         release(semaphore))

    print("Acquiring three times...")
    await asyncio.gather(acquire(semaphore),
                         acquire(semaphore),
                         acquire(semaphore))


asyncio.run(main())
```

In the preceding listing, we create a semaphore with two permits. We then run two calls to acquire and one call to release, meaning we'll call release three times. Our first call to gather seems to run okay, giving us the following output:

```
Acquiring twice, releasing three times...
Waiting to acquire
Acquired
Waiting to acquire
Acquired
Releasing as a one off!
Released as a one off!
Releasing
Releasing
```

However, our second call where we acquire the semaphore three times runs into issues, and we acquire the lock three times at once! We've inadvertently increased the number of permits our semaphore has available:

```
Acquiring three times...
Waiting to acquire
```

```
Acquired
Waiting to acquire
Acquired
Waiting to acquire
Acquired
Releasing
Releasing
Releasing
```

To deal with these types of situations, asyncio provides a `BoundedSemaphore`. This semaphore behaves exactly as the semaphore we've been using, with the key difference being that release will throw a `ValueError: BoundedSemaphore released too many times` exception if we call `release` such that it would change the available permits. Let's look at a very simple example in the following listing.

Listing 11.9 Bounded semaphores

```
import asyncio
from asyncio import BoundedSemaphore


async def main():
    semaphore = BoundedSemaphore(1)

    await semaphore.acquire()
    semaphore.release()
    semaphore.release()


asyncio.run(main())
```

When we run the preceding listing, our second call to release will throw a `ValueError` indicating we've released the semaphore too many times. You'll see similar results if you change the code in listing 11.8 to use a `BoundedSemaphore` instead of a `Semaphore`. If you're manually calling `acquire` and `release` such that dynamically increasing the number of permits your semaphore has available would be an error, it is wise to use a `BoundedSemaphore`, so you'll see an exception to warn you of the mistake.

We've now seen how to use semaphores to limit concurrency, which can be useful in situations where we need to constrain concurrency within our applications. asyncio synchronization primitives not only allow us to limit concurrency but also allow us to notify tasks when something happens. Next, let's see how to do this with the `Event` synchronization primitive.

11.4 *Notifying tasks with events*

Sometimes, we may need to wait for some external event to happen before we can proceed. We might need to wait for a buffer to fill up before we can begin to process it, we might need to wait for a device to connect to our application, or we may need to wait for some initialization to happen. We may also have multiple tasks waiting to process data that may not yet be available. Event objects provide a mechanism to help us out in situations where we want to idle while waiting for something specific to happen.

Internally, the Event class keeps track of a flag that indicates whether the event has happened yet. We can control this flag is with two methods, set and clear. The set method sets this internal flag to True and notifies anyone waiting that the event happened. The clear method sets this internal flag to False, and anyone who is waiting for the event will now block.

With these two methods, we can manage internal state, but how do we block until an event happens? The Event class has one coroutine method named wait. When we await this coroutine, it will block until someone calls set on the event object. Once this occurs, any additional calls to wait will not block and will return instantly. If we call clear once we have called set, then calls to wait will start blocking again until we call set again.

Let's create a dummy example to see events in action. We'll pretend we have two tasks that are dependent on something happening. We'll have these tasks wait and idle until we trigger the event.

Listing 11.10   Event basics

```
import asyncio
import functools
from asyncio import Event


def trigger_event(event: Event):
    event.set()


async def do_work_on_event(event: Event):        Wait until the
    print('Waiting for event...')                event occurs.
    await event.wait()              ◁────────────
    print('Performing work!')
    await asyncio.sleep(1)          ◁──── Once the event occurs,
    print('Finished work!')              wait will no longer block,
    event.clear()           ◁──────      and we can do work.

                          Reset the event, so future
async def main():         calls to wait will block.
    event = asyncio.Event()                                Trigger the event
    asyncio.get_running_loop().call_later(5.0,             5 seconds in the
      functools.partial(trigger_event, event))  ◁────      future.
    await asyncio.gather(do_work_on_event(event), do_work_on_event(event))


asyncio.run(main())
```

In the preceding listing, we create a coroutine method do_work_on_event, this coroutine takes in an event and first calls its wait coroutine. This will block until someone calls the event's set method to indicate the event has happened. We also create a simple method trigger_event, which sets a given event. In our main coroutine, we create an event object and use `call_later` to trigger the event 5 seconds in the future. We then call `do_work_on_event` twice with `gather`, which will create two concurrent tasks for us. We'll see the two `do_work_on_event` tasks idle for 5 seconds until we trigger the event, after which we'll see them do their work, giving us the following output:

```
Waiting for event...
Waiting for event...
Triggering event!
Performing work!
Performing work!
Finished work!
Finished work!
```

This shows us the basics; waiting on an event will block one or more coroutines until we trigger an event, after which they can proceed to do work. Next, let's look at a more real-world example. Imagine we're building an API to accept file uploads from clients. Due to network latency and buffering, a file upload may take some time to complete. With this constraint, we want our API to have a coroutine to block until the file is fully uploaded. Callers of this coroutine can then wait for all the data to come in and do anything they want with it.

We can use an event to accomplish this. We'll have a coroutine that listens for data from an upload and stores it in an internal buffer. Once we've reached the end of the file, we'll trigger an event indicating the upload is finished. We'll then have a coroutine method to grab the file contents, which will wait for the event to be set. Once the event is set, we can then return the fully formed uploaded data. Let's create this API in a class called `FileUpload:`.

> **Listing 11.11 A file upload API**

```python
import asyncio
from asyncio import StreamReader, StreamWriter


class FileUpload:
    def __init__(self,
                 reader: StreamReader,
                 writer: StreamWriter):
        self._reader = reader
        self._writer = writer
        self._finished_event = asyncio.Event()
        self._buffer = b''
        self._upload_task = None

    def listen_for_uploads(self):
        self._upload_task = asyncio.create_task(self._accept_upload())    ⟵┐
                                                                           Create a task to listen
    async def _accept_upload(self):                                        for the upload and
        while data := await self._reader.read(1024):                       append it to a buffer.
            self._buffer = self._buffer + data
        self._finished_event.set()
```

```
        self._writer.close()
        await self._writer.wait_closed()

    async def get_contents(self):          ◄──┐  Block until the finished
        await self._finished_event.wait()      │  event is set, then return
        return self._buffer                    │  the contents of the buffer.
```

Now let's create a file upload server to test out this API. Let's say that on every successful upload we want to dump contents to standard out. When a client connects, we'll create a `FileUpload` object and call `listen_for_uploads`. Then, we'll create a separate task that awaits the results of `get_contents`.

Listing 11.12 Using the API in a file upload server

```
import asyncio
from asyncio import StreamReader, StreamWriter
from chapter_11.listing_11_11 import FileUpload


class FileServer:

    def __init__(self, host: str, port: int):
        self.host = host
        self.port = port
        self.upload_event = asyncio.Event()

    async def start_server(self):
        server = await asyncio.start_server(self._client_connected,
                                            self.host,
                                            self.port)
        await server.serve_forever()

    async def dump_contents_on_complete(self, upload: FileUpload):
        file_contents = await upload.get_contents()
        print(file_contents)

    def _client_connected(self, reader: StreamReader, writer: StreamWriter):
        upload = FileUpload(reader, writer)
        upload.listen_for_uploads()
        asyncio.create_task(self.dump_contents_on_complete(upload))


async def main():
    server = FileServer('127.0.0.1', 9000)
    await server.start_server()


asyncio.run(main())
```

In the preceding listing, we create a `FileServer` class. Each time a client connects to our server we create an instance of the `FileUpload` class that we created in the previous listing, which starts listening for an upload from a connected client. We also concurrently create a task for the `dump_contents_on_complete` coroutine. This calls the get_contents coroutine (which will only return once the upload is complete) on the file upload and prints the file to standard out.

We can test this server out by using netcat. Pick a file on your filesystem, and run the following command, replacing file with the file of your choice:

```
cat file | nc localhost 9000
```

You should then see any file you upload printed to standard out once all the contents have fully uploaded.

One drawback to be aware of with events is that they may fire more frequently than your coroutines can respond to them. Suppose we're using a single event to wake up multiple tasks in a type of producer–consumer workflow. If our all our worker tasks are busy for a long time, the event could run while we're doing work, and we'll never see it. Let's create a dummy example to demonstrate this. We'll create two worker tasks each of which does 5 seconds of work. We'll also create a task that fires an event every second, outpacing the rate that our consumers can handle.

Listing 11.13   A worker falling behind an event

```
import asyncio
from asyncio import Event
from contextlib import suppress


async def trigger_event_periodically(event: Event):
    while True:
        print('Triggering event!')
        event.set()
        await asyncio.sleep(1)


async def do_work_on_event(event: Event):
    while True:
        print('Waiting for event...')
        await event.wait()
        event.clear()
        print('Performing work!')
        await asyncio.sleep(5)
        print('Finished work!')


async def main():
    event = asyncio.Event()
    trigger = asyncio.wait_for(trigger_event_periodically(event), 5.0)

    with suppress(asyncio.TimeoutError):
        await asyncio.gather(do_work_on_event(event),
    do_work_on_event(event), trigger)


asyncio.run(main())
```

When we run the preceding listing, we'll see our event fires and our two workers start their work concurrently. In the meantime, we keep triggering our event. Since our workers are busy, they won't see that our event fired a second time until they finish their work and call `event.wait()` a second time. If you care about responding every time an event occurs, you'll need to use a queueing mechanism, which we'll learn about in the next chapter.

Events are useful for when we want to alert when a specific event happens, but what happens if we need a combination of waiting for an event alongside exclusive access to a shared resource, such as a database connection? Conditions can help us solve these types of workflows.

11.5 *Conditions*

Events are good for simple notifications when something happens, but what about more complex use cases? Imagine needing to gain access to a shared resource that requires a lock on an event, waiting for a more complex set of facts to be true before proceeding or waking up only a certain number of tasks instead of all of them. Conditions can be useful in these types of situations. They are by far the most complex synchronization primitives we've encountered so far, and as such, you likely won't need to use them all that often.

A *condition* combines aspects of a lock and an event into one synchronization primitive, effectively wrapping the behavior of both. We first acquire the condition's lock, giving our coroutine exclusive access to any shared resource, allowing us to safely change any state we need. Then, we wait for a specific event to happen with the `wait` or `wait_for` coroutine. These coroutines release the lock and block until the event happens, and once it does it reacquires the lock giving us exclusive access.

Since this is a bit confusing, let's create a dummy example to understand how to use conditions. We'll create two worker tasks that each attempt to acquire the condition lock and then wait for an event notification. Then, after a few seconds, we'll trigger the condition, which will wake up the two worker tasks and allow them to do work.

Listing 11.14   Condition basics

```python
import asyncio
from asyncio import Condition


async def do_work(condition: Condition):
    while True:
        print('Waiting for condition lock...')
        async with condition:                      ←──  Wait to acquire the condition lock; once acquired, release the lock.
            print('Acquired lock, releasing and waiting for condition...')
            await condition.wait()                 ←──  Wait for the event to fire; once it does, reacquire the condition lock.
            print('Condition event fired, re-acquiring lock and doing work...')
            await asyncio.sleep(1)
        print('Work finished, lock released.')     ←──  Once we exit the async with block, release the condition lock.
```

```
async def fire_event(condition: Condition):
    while True:
        await asyncio.sleep(5)
        print('About to notify, acquiring condition lock...')
        async with condition:
            print('Lock acquired, notifying all workers.')
            condition.notify_all()                              ◁─────  Notify all tasks
            print('Notification finished, releasing lock.')             that the event
                                                                        has happened.

async def main():
    condition = Condition()

    asyncio.create_task(fire_event(condition))
    await asyncio.gather(do_work(condition), do_work(condition))


asyncio.run(main())
```

In the preceding listing, we create two coroutine methods: do_work and fire_event. The do_work method acquires the condition, which is analogous to acquiring a lock, and then calls the condition's wait coroutine method. The wait coroutine method will block until someone calls the condition's notify_all method.

The fire_event coroutine method sleeps for a little bit and then acquires the condition and calls the notify_all method, which will wake up any tasks that are currently waiting on the condition. Then, in our main coroutine we create one fire_event task and two do_work tasks and run them concurrently. When running this you'll see the following repeated if the application runs:

```
Worker 1: waiting for condition lock...
Worker 1: acquired lock, releasing and waiting for condition...
Worker 2: waiting for condition lock...
Worker 2: acquired lock, releasing and waiting for condition...
fire_event: about to notify, acquiring condition lock...
fire_event: Lock acquired, notifying all workers.
fire_event: Notification finished, releasing lock.
Worker 1: condition event fired, re-acquiring lock and doing work...
Worker 1: Work finished, lock released.
Worker 1: waiting for condition lock...
Worker 2: condition event fired, re-acquiring lock and doing work...
Worker 2: Work finished, lock released.
Worker 2: waiting for condition lock...
Worker 1: acquired lock, releasing and waiting for condition...
Worker 2: acquired lock, releasing and waiting for condition...
```

You'll notice that the two workers start right away and block waiting for the fire_event coroutine to call notify_all. Once fire_event calls notify_all, the worker tasks wake up and then proceed to do their work.

Conditions have an additional coroutine method called wait_for. Instead of blocking until someone notifies the condition, wait_for accepts a predicate (a no-argument function that returns a `Boolean`) and will block until that predicate returns `True`. This proves useful when there is a shared resource with some coroutines dependent on certain states becoming true.

As an example, let's pretend we're creating a class to wrap a database connection and run queries. We first have an underlying connection that can't run multiple queries at the same time, and the database connection may not be initialized before someone tries to run a query. The combination of a shared resource and an event we need to block gives us the right conditions to use a `Condition`. Let's simulate this with a mock database connection class. This class will run queries but will only do so once we've properly initialized a connection. We'll then use this mock connection class to try to run two queries concurrently before we've finished initializing the connection.

Listing 11.15 Using conditions to wait for specific states

```python
import asyncio
from enum import Enum


class ConnectionState(Enum):
    WAIT_INIT = 0
    INITIALIZING = 1
    INITIALIZED = 2


class Connection:

    def __init__(self):
        self._state = ConnectionState.WAIT_INIT
        self._condition = asyncio.Condition()

    async def initialize(self):
        await self._change_state(ConnectionState.INITIALIZING)
        print('initialize: Initializing connection...')
        await asyncio.sleep(3)  # simulate connection startup time
        print('initialize: Finished initializing connection')
        await self._change_state(ConnectionState.INITIALIZED)

    async def execute(self, query: str):
        async with self._condition:
            print('execute: Waiting for connection to initialize')
            await self._condition.wait_for(self._is_initialized)
            print(f'execute: Running {query}!!!')
            await asyncio.sleep(3)  # simulate a long query

    async def _change_state(self, state: ConnectionState):
        async with self._condition:
            print(f'change_state: State changing from {self._state} to {state}')
            self._state = state
            self._condition.notify_all()

    def _is_initialized(self):
        if self._state is not ConnectionState.INITIALIZED:
```

```
            print(f'_is_initialized: Connection not finished initializing,
      state is {self._state}')
            return False
        print(f'_is_initialized: Connection is initialized!')
        return True

async def main():
    connection = Connection()
    query_one = asyncio.create_task(connection.execute('select * from table'))
    query_two = asyncio.create_task(connection.execute('select * from
     other_table'))
    asyncio.create_task(connection.initialize())
    await query_one
    await query_two


asyncio.run(main())
```

In the preceding listing, we create a connection class that contains a condition object and keeps track of an internal state that we initialize to WAIT_INIT, indicating we're waiting for initialization to happen. We also create a few methods on the Connection class. The first is initialize, which simulates creating a database connection. This method calls the _change_state method to set the state to INITIALIZING when first called and then once the connection is initialized, it sets the state to INITIALIZED. Inside the _change_state method, we set the internal state and then call the conditions notify_all method. This will wake up any tasks that are waiting for the condition.

In our execute method, we acquire the condition object in an async with block and then we call wait_for with a predicate that checks to see if the state is INITIALIZED. This will block until our database connection is fully initialized, preventing us from accidently issuing a query before the connection exists. Then, in our main coroutine, we create a connection class and create two tasks to run queries, followed by one task to initialize the connection. Running this code, you'll see the following output, indicating that our queries properly wait for the initialization task to finish before running the queries:

```
execute: Waiting for connection to initialize
_is_initialized: Connection not finished initializing, state is
    ConnectionState.WAIT_INIT
execute: Waiting for connection to initialize
_is_initialized: Connection not finished initializing, state is
    ConnectionState.WAIT_INIT
change_state: State changing from ConnectionState.WAIT_INIT to
    ConnectionState.INITIALIZING
initialize: Initializing connection...
_is_initialized: Connection not finished initializing, state is
    ConnectionState.INITIALIZING
_is_initialized: Connection not finished initializing, state is
    ConnectionState.INITIALIZING
initialize: Finished initializing connection
change_state: State changing from ConnectionState.INITIALIZING to
    ConnectionState.INITIALIZED
```

```
_is_initialized: Connection is initialized!
execute: Running select * from table!!!
_is_initialized: Connection is initialized!
execute: Running select * from other_table!!!
```

Conditions are useful in scenarios in which we need access to a shared resource and there are states that we need to be notified about before doing work. This is a somewhat complicated use case, and as such, you won't likely come across or need conditions in asyncio code.

Summary

- We've learned about single-threaded concurrency bugs and how they differ from concurrency bugs in multithreading and multiprocessing.
- We know how to use asyncio locks to prevent concurrency bugs and synchronize coroutines. This happens less often due to asyncio's single-threaded nature, they can sometimes be needed when shared state could change during an `await`.
- We've learned how to use semaphores to control access to finite resources and limit concurrency, which can be useful in traffic-shaping.
- We know how to use events to trigger actions when something happens, such as initialization or waking up worker tasks.
- We know how to use conditions to wait for an action and, because of an action, gain access to a shared resource.

Asynchronous queues

12

This chapter covers

- Asynchronous queues
- Using queues for producer–consumer workflows
- Using queues with web applications
- Asynchronous priority queues
- Asynchronous LIFO queues

When designing applications to process events or other types of data, we often need a mechanism to store these events and distribute them to a set of workers. These workers can then do whatever we need to do based on these events concurrently, yielding time savings as opposed to processing events sequentially. asyncio provides an asynchronous queue implementation that lets us do this. We can add pieces of data into a queue and have several workers running concurrently, pulling data from the queue and processing it as it becomes available.

These are commonly referred to as *producer–consumer workflows*. Something produces data or events that we need to handle; processing these work items could take a long time. Queues can also help us transmit long-running tasks while keeping a responsive user interface. We put an item on the queue for later processing and inform the user that we've started this work in the background. Asynchronous queues also have an added benefit of providing a mechanism to limit concurrency, as each queue generally permits a finite amount of worker tasks. This can be used in cases in which we need to limit concurrency in a similar way to what we saw with semaphores in chapter 11.

In this chapter, we'll learn how to use asyncio queues to handle producer–consumer workflows. We'll master the basics first by building an example grocery store queue with cashiers as our consumers. We'll then apply this to an order management web API, demonstrating how to respond quickly to users while letting the queue process work in the background. We'll also learn how to process tasks in priority order, which is useful when one task is more important to process first, despite being put in the queue later. Finally, we'll look at LIFO (last in, first out) queues and understand the drawbacks of asynchronous queues.

12.1 *Asynchronous queue basics*

Queues are a type of FIFO data structure. In other words, the first element in a queue is the first element to leave the queue when we ask for the next element. They're not much different from the queue you're a part of when checking out in a grocery store. You join the line at the end and wait for the cashier to check out anyone in front of you. Once they've checked someone out, you move up in the queue while someone who joins after you waits behind you. Then, when you're first in the queue you check out and leave the queue entirely.

The checkout queue as we have described it is a synchronous workflow. One cashier checks out one customer at a time. What if we reimagined the queue to better take advantage of concurrency and perform more like a supermarket checkout? Instead of one cashier, there would be multiple cashiers and a single queue. Whenever a cashier is available, they can flag down the next person to the checkout counter. This means there are multiple cashiers directing customers from the queue concurrently in addition to multiple cashiers concurrently checking out customers.

This is the core of what asynchronous queues let us do. We add multiple work items waiting to be processed into the queue. We then have multiple workers pull items from the queue when they are available to perform a task.

Let's explore this by building our supermarket example. We'll think of our worker tasks as cashiers, and our "work items" will be customers to check out. We'll implement customers with individual lists of products that the cashier needs to scan. Some items take longer than others to scan; for instance, bananas must be weighed and have their SKU code entered. Alcoholic beverages require a manager to check the customer's ID.

For our supermarket checkout scenario, we'll implement a few data classes to represent products with integers used to represent the time (in seconds) they take for a cashier to check out. We'll also build a customer class that has a random set of products they'd like to buy. Then, we'll put these customers in an asyncio queue to represent our checkout line. We'll also create several worker tasks to represent our

cashiers. These tasks will pull customers from the queue, looping through all their
products and sleeping for the time needed to check out their items to simulate the
checkout process.

Listing 12.1   A supermarket checkout queue

```
import asyncio
from asyncio import Queue
from random import randrange
from typing import List


class Product:
    def __init__(self, name: str, checkout_time: float):
        self.name = name
        self.checkout_time = checkout_time


class Customer:
    def __init__(self, customer_id: int, products: List[Product]):
        self.customer_id = customer_id
        self.products = products


async def checkout_customer(queue: Queue, cashier_number: int):
    while not queue.empty():                                          ◄─┐ Keep checking
        customer: Customer = queue.get_nowait()                          out customers if
        print(f'Cashier {cashier_number} '                               there are any in
            f'checking out customer '                                    the queue.
            f'{customer.customer_id}')
        for product in customer.products:         ◄── Check out each customer's product.
            print(f"Cashier {cashier_number} "
                f"checking out customer "
                f"{customer.customer_id}'s {product.name}")
            await asyncio.sleep(product.checkout_time)
            print(f'Cashier {cashier_number} '
                f'finished checking out customer '
                f'{customer.customer_id}')
            queue.task_done()


async def main():
    customer_queue = Queue()

    all_products = [Product('beer', 2),
                    Product('bananas', .5),
                    Product('sausage', .2),
                    Product('diapers', .2)]          ◄─┐ Create 10 customers
                                                         with random products.
    for i in range(10):
        products = [all_products[randrange(len(all_products))]
                    for _ in range(randrange(10))]
        customer_queue.put_nowait(Customer(i, products))
```

```
cashiers = [asyncio.create_task(checkout_customer(customer_queue, i))
           for i in range(3)]

await asyncio.gather(customer_queue.join(), *cashiers)

asyncio.run(main())
```

Create three "cashiers" or worker tasks to check out customers.

In the preceding listing, we create two data classes: one for a product and one for a supermarket customer. A product consists of a product name and the amount of time (in seconds) it takes for a cashier to enter that item in the register. A customer has a number of products they are bringing to the cashier to buy. We also define a checkout_customer coroutine function, which does the work of checking out a customer. While our queue has customers in it, it pulls a customer from the front of the queue with queue.get_nowait() and simulates the time to scan a product with asyncio.sleep. Once a customer is checked out, we call queue.task_done. This signals to the queue that our worker has finished its current work item. Internally within the Queue class, when we get an item from the queue a counter is incremented by one to track the number of unfinished tasks remain. When we call task_done, we tell the queue that we've finished, and it decrements this count by one (why we need to do this will make sense shortly, when we talk about join).

In our main coroutine function, we create a list of available products and generate 10 customers, each with random products. We also create three worker tasks for the checkout_customer coroutine that are stored in a list called cashiers, which is analogous to three human cashiers working at our imaginary supermarket. Finally, we wait for the cashier checkout_customer tasks to finish alongside the customer_queue.join() coroutine using gather. We use gather so that any exceptions from our cashier tasks will rise up to our main coroutine function. The join coroutine blocks until the queue is empty and all customers have been checked out. The queue is considered empty when the internal counter of pending work items reaches zero. Therefore, it is important to call task_done in your workers. If you don't do this, the join coroutine may receive an incorrect view of the queue and may never terminate.

While the customer's items are randomly generated, you should see output similar to the following, showing that each worker task (cashier) is concurrently checking out customers from the queue:

```
Cashier 0 checking out customer 0
Cashier 0 checking out customer 0's sausage
Cashier 1 checking out customer 1
Cashier 1 checking out customer 1's beer
Cashier 2 checking out customer 2
Cashier 2 checking out customer 2's bananas
Cashier 0 checking out customer 0's bananas
Cashier 2 checking out customer 2's sausage
Cashier 0 checking out customer 0's sausage
Cashier 2 checking out customer 2's bananas
Cashier 0 finished checking out customer 0
Cashier 0 checking out customer 3
```

Our three cashiers start checking out customers from the queue concurrently. Once they've finished checking out one customer, they pull another from the queue until the queue is empty.

You may notice that our methods for putting items into the queue and retrieving them are oddly named: `get_nowait` and `put_nowait`. Why is there a `nowait` at the end of each of these methods? There are two ways of getting and retrieving an item from a queue: one that is a coroutine and blocks, and one that is nonblocking and is a regular method. The `get_nowait` and `put_nowait` variants instantly perform the non-blocking method calls and return. Why would we need a blocking queue insertion or retrieval?

The answer lies in how we want to handle the upper and lower bounds of our queue. This describes happens when there are too many items in the queue (the upper bound) and what happens when there are no items in the queue (the lower bound).

Going back to our supermarket queue example, let's address two things that aren't quite real-world about it, using the coroutine versions of `get` and `put`.

- It is unlikely we'll just have one line of 10 customers who all show up at the same time, and once the line is empty the cashiers stop working altogether.
- Our customer queue probably shouldn't be unbounded; say, the latest desirable gaming console just came out, and you're the only store in town to carry it. Naturally, mass hysteria has ensued, and your store is flooded with customers. We probably couldn't fit 5,000 customers in the store, so we need a way to turn them away or make them wait outside.

For the first issue, let's say we wanted to refactor our application so that we randomly generate some customers every few seconds to simulate a realistic supermarket queue. In our current implementation of `checkout_customer`, we loop while the queue is not empty and grab a customer with `get_nowait`. Since our queue could be empty, we can't loop on `not queue.empty`, since our cashiers will be available even if no one is in line, so we'll need a `while True` in our worker coroutine. So what happens in this case when we call `get_nowait` and the queue is empty? This is easy to test out in a few lines of code; we just create an empty queue and call the method in question:

```
import asyncio
from asyncio import Queue


async def main():
    customer_queue = Queue()
    customer_queue.get_nowait()

asyncio.run(main())
```

Our method will throw an `asyncio.queues.QueueEmpty` exception. While we could wrap this in a `try catch` and ignore this exception, this wouldn't quite work, as whenever the queue is empty, we've made our worker task CPU-bound, spinning and catching exceptions. In this case, we can use the `get` coroutine method. This will block (in a non-CPU-bound fashion) until an item is in the queue to process and won't throw an exception. This is the equivalent of the worker tasks idling, standing by for some customer to come into the queue giving them work to do at the checkout counter.

To address our second issue of thousands of customers trying to get in line concurrently, we need to think about the bounds of our queue. By default, queues are unbounded, and they can grow to store an infinite amount of work items. In theory this is acceptable, but in the real world, systems have memory constraints, so placing an upper bound on our queue to prevent running out of memory is a good idea. In this case, we need to think through what we want our behavior to be when our queue is full. Let's see what happens when we create a queue that can only hold one item and try to add a second with put_nowait:

```python
import asyncio
from asyncio import Queue


async def main():
    queue = Queue(maxsize=1)

    queue.put_nowait(1)
    queue.put_nowait(2)

asyncio.run(main())
```

In this case, much like get_nowait, put_nowait throws an exception of the type asyncio.queues.QueueFull. Like get, there is also a coroutine method called put. This method will block until there is room in the queue. With this in mind, let's refactor our customer example to use the coroutine variants of get and put.

Listing 12.2 Using coroutine queue methods

```python
import asyncio
from asyncio import Queue
from random import randrange


class Product:
    def __init__(self, name: str, checkout_time: float):
        self.name = name
        self.checkout_time = checkout_time


class Customer:
    def __init__(self, customer_id, products):
        self.customer_id = customer_id
        self.products = products


async def checkout_customer(queue: Queue, cashier_number: int):
    while True:
```

```
        customer: Customer = await queue.get()
        print(f'Cashier {cashier_number} '
              f'checking out customer '
              f'{customer.customer_id}')
        for product in customer.products:
            print(f"Cashier {cashier_number} "
                  f"checking out customer "
                  f"{customer.customer_id}'s {product.name}")
            await asyncio.sleep(product.checkout_time)
        print(f'Cashier {cashier_number} '
              f'finished checking out customer '
              f'{customer.customer_id}')
        queue.task_done()


def generate_customer(customer_id: int) -> Customer:
    all_products = [Product('beer', 2),
                    Product('bananas', .5),
                    Product('sausage', .2),
                    Product('diapers', .2)]
    products = [all_products[randrange(len(all_products))]
                for _ in range(randrange(10))]
    return Customer(customer_id, products)


async def customer_generator(queue: Queue):
    customer_count = 0

    while True:
        customers = [generate_customer(i)
                     for i in range(customer_count,
                     customer_count + randrange(5))]
        for customer in customers:
            print('Waiting to put customer in line...')
            await queue.put(customer)
            print('Customer put in line!')
        customer_count = customer_count + len(customers)
        await asyncio.sleep(1)


async def main():
    customer_queue = Queue(5)

    customer_producer = asyncio.create_task(customer_generator(customer_queue))

    cashiers = [asyncio.create_task(checkout_customer(customer_queue, i))
                for i in range(3)]

    await asyncio.gather(customer_producer, *cashiers)


asyncio.run(main())
```

Annotations:
- **Generate a random customer.** (pointing to `def generate_customer`)
- **Generate several random customers every second.** (pointing to `async def customer_generator`)

In the preceding listing, we create a generate_customer coroutine that creates a customer with a random list of products. Alongside this we create a customer_generator coroutine function that generates between one and five random customers every second and adds them to the queue with put. Because we use the coroutine put, if our queue is full, customer_generator will block until the queue has free spaces. Specifically, this means that if there are five customers in the queue and the *producer* tries to add a sixth, the queue will block, allowing that customer into the queue until there is a space freed up by a cashier checking someone out. We can think of customer_generator as our *producer*, as it produces customers for our cashiers to check out.

We also refactor checkout_customer to run forever, since our cashiers remain on call when the queue is empty. We then refactor checkout_customer to use the queue get coroutine, and the coroutine will block if the queue has no customers in it. Then, in our main coroutine we create a queue that allows five customers in line at a time and create three checkout_customer tasks running concurrently. We can think of the cashiers as our *consumers*; they consume customers to check out from the queue.

This code randomly generates customers, but at some point, the queue should fill up such that the cashiers aren't processing customers as fast as the producer is creating them. Thus, we'll see output similar to the following where the producer waits to add a customer into the line until a customer has finished checking out:

```
Waiting to put customer in line...
Cashier 1 checking out customer 7's sausage
Cashier 1 checking out customer 7's diapers
Cashier 1 checking out customer 7's diapers
Cashier 2 finished checking out customer 5
Cashier 2 checking out customer 9
Cashier 2 checking out customer 9's bananas
Customer put in line!
```

We now understand the basics of how asynchronous queues work, but since we're usually not building supermarket simulations in our day jobs, let's look at a few real-world scenarios to see how we would apply this in applications we really might build.

12.1.1 Queues in web applications

Queues can be useful in web applications when we have a potentially time-consuming operation that we can run in the background. If we ran this operation in the main coroutine of the web request, we would block the response to the user until the operation finished, potentially leaving the end user with a slow, unresponsive page.

Imagine we're part of an e-commerce organization, and we're operating with a slow order management system. Processing an order can take several seconds, but we don't want to keep the user waiting for a response that their order has been placed. Furthermore, the order management system does not handle load well, so we'd like to limit how many requests we make to it concurrently. In this circumstance a queue can solve both problems. As we saw before, a queue can have a maximum number of elements we allow before adding more either blocks or throws an exception. This means if we have a queue with an upper limit, we'll at most have however many consumer tasks we create that are running concurrently. This provides a natural limit to concurrency.

A queue also solves the issue of the user waiting too long for a response. Putting an element on the queue happens instantly, meaning we can notify the user that their order has been placed right away, providing a fast user experience. In the real world, of course, this opens up the potential for the background task to fail without the user being notified, so you'll need some form of data persistence and logic to combat this.

To try this out, let's create a simple web application with aiohttp that employs a queue to run background tasks. We'll simulate interacting with a slow order management system by using `asyncio.sleep`. In a real world microservice architecture you'd likely be communicating over REST with aiohttp or a similar library, but we'll use `sleep` for simplicity.

We'll create an aiohttp startup hook to create our queue as well as a set of worker tasks that will interact with the slow service. We'll also create a `HTTP POST` endpoint/order that will place an order on the queue (here, we'll just generate a random number for our worker task to `sleep` to simulate the slow service). Once the order is put on the queue, we'll return a `HTTP 200` and a message indicating the order has been placed.

We'll also add some graceful shutdown logic in an aiohttp shutdown hook, since if our application shuts down, we might still have some orders being processed. In the shutdown hook, we'll wait until any workers that are busy have finished.

Listing 12.3   Queues with a web application

```python
import asyncio
from asyncio import Queue, Task
from typing import List
from random import randrange
from aiohttp import web
from aiohttp.web_app import Application
from aiohttp.web_request import Request
from aiohttp.web_response import Response

routes = web.RouteTableDef()

QUEUE_KEY = 'order_queue'
TASKS_KEY = 'order_tasks'


async def process_order_worker(worker_id: int, queue: Queue):      ◁┐  Grab an order from the
    while True:                                                       │  queue, and process it.
        print(f'Worker {worker_id}: Waiting for an order...')
        order = await queue.get()
        print(f'Worker {worker_id}: Processing order {order}')
        await asyncio.sleep(order)
        print(f'Worker {worker_id}: Processed order {order}')
        queue.task_done()


@routes.post('/order')
async def place_order(request: Request) -> Response:
```

```
        order_queue = app[QUEUE_KEY]
        await order_queue.put(randrange(5))              Put the order on the
        return Response(body='Order placed!')            queue, and respond to
                                                         the user immediately.

async def create_order_queue(app: Application):          Create a queue with a
    print('Creating order queue and tasks.')             maximum of 10 elements,
    queue: Queue = asyncio.Queue(10)                     and create 5 worker tasks.
    app[QUEUE_KEY] = queue
    app[TASKS_KEY] = [asyncio.create_task(process_order_worker(i, queue))
                      for i in range(5)]


async def destroy_queue(app: Application):               Wait for any busy
    order_tasks: List[Task] = app[TASKS_KEY]             tasks to finish.
    queue: Queue = app[QUEUE_KEY]
    print('Waiting for pending queue workers to finish....')
    try:
        await asyncio.wait_for(queue.join(), timeout=10)
    finally:
        print('Finished all pending items, canceling worker tasks...')
        [task.cancel() for task in order_tasks]


app = web.Application()
app.on_startup.append(create_order_queue)
app.on_shutdown.append(destroy_queue)

app.add_routes(routes)
web.run_app(app)
```

In the preceding listing, we first create a process_order_worker coroutine. This pulls an item from the queue, in this case an integer, and sleeps for that amount of time to simulate working with a slow order management system. This coroutine loops forever, continually pulling items from the queue and processing them.

We then create the coroutines to set up and tear down the queue, create_order_queue and destroy_order_queue, respectively. Creating the queue is straightforward, as we create an asyncio queue with a maximum of 10 elements and we create five worker tasks, storing them in our Application instance.

Destroying the queue is a bit more involved. We first wait for the queue to finish processing all its elements with Queue.join. Since our application is shutting down, it won't be serving any more HTTP requests, so no other orders can go into our queue. This means that anything already in the queue will be processed by a worker, and anything a worker is currently processing will finish as well. We also wrap join in a wait_for with a timeout of 10 seconds as well. This is a good idea because we don't want a runaway task taking a long time preventing our application from shutting down.

Finally, we define our application route. We create a POST endpoint at /order. This endpoint creates a random delay and adds it to the queue. Once we've added the order to the queue, we respond to the user with a HTTP 200 status code and a short message. Note that we used the coroutine variant of put, which means that if our queue is full the request will block until the message is on the queue, which could take time. You may want to use the put_nowait variant and then respond with a HTTP 500 error or other error code asking the caller to try again later. Here, we've made a tradeoff of a request potentially taking some time so that our order always goes on the queue. Your application may require "fail fast" behavior, so responding with an error when the queue is full may the correct behavior for your use case.

Using this queue, our order endpoint will respond nearly instantly when our order was placed so long as the queue isn't full. This provides the end user with a quick and smooth ordering experience—one that hopefully keeps them coming back to buy more.

One thing to keep in mind when using asyncio queues in web applications is the failure modes of queues. What if one of our API instances crashed for some reason, such as running out of memory, or if we needed to restart the server for a redeploy of our application? In this case, we would lose any unprocessed orders that are in the queue, as they are only stored in memory. Sometimes, losing an item in a queue isn't a big deal, but in the case of a customer order, it probably is.

asyncio queues provide no out-of-the-box concept of task persistence or queue durability. If we want tasks in our queue to be robust against these types of failures, we need to introduce somewhere a method to save our tasks, such as a database. More correctly, however, is using a separate queue outside of asyncio that supports task persistence. Celery and RabbitMQ are two examples of task queues that can persist to disk.

Of course, using a separate architectural queue comes with added complexity. In the case of durable queues with persistent tasks, it also comes with a performance challenge of needing to persist to disk. To determine the best architecture for your application, you'll need to carefully weigh the tradeoffs of an in-memory-only asyncio queue versus a separate architectural component.

12.1.2 A web crawler queue

Consumer tasks can also be producers if our consumer generates more work to put in the queue. Take for instance a web crawler that visits all links on a particular page. You can imagine one worker downloading and scanning a page for links. Once the worker has found links it can add them to a queue. This lets other available workers pull links onto the queue and visit them concurrently, adding any links they encounter back to the queue.

Let's build a crawler that does this. We'll create an unbounded queue (you may want to bound it if you're concerned about memory overruns) that will hold URLs to download. Then, our workers will pull URLs off the queue and use aiohttp to download them. Once we've downloaded them, we'll use a popular HTML parser, Beautiful Soup, to extract links to put back into the queue.

At least with this application, we don't want to scan the entire internet, so we'll only scan a set number of pages away from the root page. We'll call this our "maximum depth"; if our maximum depth is set to three, it means we'll only follow links three pages away from the root.

To get started, let's install Beautiful Soup version 4.9.3 with the following command:

```
pip install -Iv beautifulsoup4==4.9.3
```

We'll assume some knowledge of Beautiful Soup. You can read more in the documentation at https://www.crummy.com/software/BeautifulSoup/bs4/doc.

Our plan will be to create a worker coroutine that will pull a page from the queue and download it with aiohttp. Once we've done this, we'll use Beautiful Soup to get all the links of the form `<a href="url">` from the page, adding them back to the queue.

Listing 12.4 A queue-based crawler

```python
import asyncio
import aiohttp
import logging
from asyncio import Queue
from aiohttp import ClientSession
from bs4 import BeautifulSoup


class WorkItem:
    def __init__(self, item_depth: int, url: str):
        self.item_depth = item_depth
        self.url = url


async def worker(worker_id: int, queue: Queue, session: ClientSession,
        max_depth: int):
    print(f'Worker {worker_id}')
    while True:
        work_item: WorkItem = await queue.get()
        print(f'Worker {worker_id}: Processing {work_item.url}')
        await process_page(work_item, queue, session, max_depth)
        print(f'Worker {worker_id}: Finished {work_item.url}')
        queue.task_done()


async def process_page(work_item: WorkItem, queue: Queue, session:
        ClientSession, max_depth: int):
    try:
        response = await asyncio.wait_for(session.get(work_item.url), timeout=3)
        if work_item.item_depth == max_depth:
            print(f'Max depth reached, '
                  f'for {work_item.url}')
        else:
            body = await response.text()
            soup = BeautifulSoup(body, 'html.parser')
            links = soup.find_all('a', href=True)
            for link in links:
                queue.put_nowait(WorkItem(work_item.item_depth + 1,
                                          link['href']))
```

Grab a URL from the queue to process and then begin to download it.

Download the URL contents, and parse all links from the page, putting them back on the queue.

```
    except Exception as e:
        logging.exception(f'Error processing url {work_item.url}')
```

```
async def main():                    ◁──────────┐  Create a queue and
    start_url = 'http://example.com'             │  100 worker tasks
    url_queue = Queue()                          │  to process URLs.
    url_queue.put_nowait(WorkItem(0, start_url))
    async with aiohttp.ClientSession() as session:
        workers = [asyncio.create_task(worker(i, url_queue, session, 3))
                   for i in range(100)]
        await url_queue.join()
        [w.cancel() for w in workers]
```

```
asyncio.run(main())
```

In the preceding listing, we first define a WorkItem class. This is a simple data class to hold a URL and the depth of that URL. We then define our worker, which pulls a WorkItem from the queue and calls process_page. The process_page coroutine function downloads the contents of the URL if it can do so (a timeout or exception could occur, which we just log and ignore). It then uses Beautiful Soup to get all the links and adds them back to the queue for other workers to process.

In our main coroutine, we create the queue and bootstrap it with our first Work-Item. In this example we hardcode example.com, and since it is our root page, its depth is 0. We then create an aiohttp session and create 100 workers, meaning we can download 100 URLs concurrently, and we set its max depth to 3. We then wait for the queue to empty and all workers to finish with Queue.join. Once the queue is finished processing, we cancel all our worker tasks. When you run this code, you should see 100 worker tasks fire up and start looking for links from each URL it downloads, giving you output like the following:

```
Found 1 links from http://example.com
Worker 0: Finished http://example.com
Worker 0: Processing https://www.iana.org/domains/example
Found 68 links from https://www.iana.org/domains/example
Worker 0: Finished https://www.iana.org/domains/example
Worker 0: Processing /
Worker 2: Processing /domains
Worker 3: Processing /numbers
Worker 4: Processing /protocols
Worker 5: Processing /about
Worker 6: Processing /go/rfc2606
Worker 7: Processing /go/rfc6761
Worker 8: Processing http://www.icann.org/topics/idn/
Worker 9: Processing http://www.icann.org/
```

The workers will continue to download pages and process links, adding them to the queue until we reach the maximum depth we've specified.

We've now seen the basics of asynchronous queues by building a fake supermarket checkout line as well as by building an order management API and a web crawler. So far, our workers have given equal weight to each element in the queue, and they just pull whoever is at the front of the line out to work on. What if we wanted some tasks to happen sooner even if they're toward the back of the queue? Let's take a look at priority queues to see how to do this.

12.2 Priority queues

Our previous examples of queues processed items in FIFO, or first-in, first-out, ordering. Whoever was first in line gets processed first. This works well in many cases, both in software engineering and in life.

In certain applications, however, having all tasks be considered equal is not always desirable. Imagine we're building a data processing pipeline where each task is a long-running query that can take several minutes. Let's say two tasks come in at roughly the same time. The first task is a low priority data query, but the second is a mission-critical data update that should be processed as soon as possible. With simple queues, the first task will be processed, leaving the second, more important task waiting for the first one to finish. Imagine the first task takes hours, or if all our workers are busy, our second task could be waiting for a long time.

We can use a priority queue to solve this problem and make our workers work on our most important tasks first. Internally, priority queues are backed by *heaps* (using the `heapq` module) instead of Python lists like simple queues. To create an asyncio priority queue, we create an instance of `asyncio.PriorityQueue`.

We won't get too much into data structure specifics here, but a heap is a binary tree with the property that every parent node has a value less than all its children (see figure 12.1). This is unlike binary search trees typically used in sorting and searching problems where the only property is that a node's left-hand child is smaller than its parent and the node's right-hand child is larger. The property of heaps we take advantage of is that the topmost node is always the smallest element in the tree. If we always make the smallest node our highest priority one, then the high priority node will always be the first in the queue.

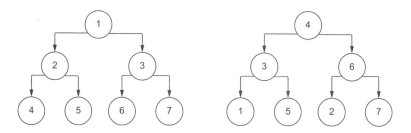

Figure 12.1 On the left, a binary tree that satisfies the heap property; on the right, a binary search tree that does not satisfy the heap property

It is unlikely the work items we put in our queue will be plain integers, so we'll need some way to construct a work item with a sensible priority rule. One way to do this is with a tuple, where the first element is an integer representing the priority and the second is any task data. The default queue implementation looks to the first value of the tuple to decide priority with the lowest numbers having the highest priority. Let's look at an example with tuples as work items to see the basics of how a priority queue works.

Listing 12.5 Priority queues with tuples

```
import asyncio
from asyncio import Queue, PriorityQueue
from typing import Tuple


async def worker(queue: Queue):
    while not queue.empty():
        work_item: Tuple[int, str] = await queue.get()
        print(f'Processing work item {work_item}')
        queue.task_done()


async def main():
    priority_queue = PriorityQueue()

    work_items = [(3, 'Lowest priority'),
                  (2, 'Medium priority'),
                  (1, 'High priority')]

    worker_task = asyncio.create_task(worker(priority_queue))

    for work in work_items:
        priority_queue.put_nowait(work)

    await asyncio.gather(priority_queue.join(), worker_task)


asyncio.run(main())
```

In the preceding listing, we create three work items: one with high priority, one with medium priority, and one with low priority. We then add them in the priority queue in reverse priority order, meaning we insert the lowest priority item first and the highest last. In a normal queue, this would mean we'd process the lowest priority item first, but if we run this code, we'll see the following output:

```
Processing work item (1, 'High priority')
Processing work item (2, 'Medium priority')
Processing work item (3, 'Lowest priority')
```

This indicates that we processed the work items in the order of their priority, not how they were inserted into the queue. Tuples work for simple cases, but if we have a lot of data in our work items, a tuple could get messy and confusing. Is there a way for us to create a class of some sort that will work the way we want with heaps? We can, in fact, and the tersest way to do this is by using a data class (we could also implement the proper *dunder* methods __lt__, __le__, __gt__, and __ge__ if data classes aren't an option).

Listing 12.6 Priority queues with data classes

```python
import asyncio
from asyncio import Queue, PriorityQueue
from dataclasses import dataclass, field


@dataclass(order=True)
class WorkItem:
    priority: int
    data: str = field(compare=False)


async def worker(queue: Queue):
    while not queue.empty():
        work_item: WorkItem = await queue.get()
        print(f'Processing work item {work_item}')
        queue.task_done()


async def main():
    priority_queue = PriorityQueue()

    work_items = [WorkItem(3, 'Lowest priority'),
                  WorkItem(2, 'Medium priority'),
                  WorkItem(1, 'High priority')]

    worker_task = asyncio.create_task(worker(priority_queue))

    for work in work_items:
        priority_queue.put_nowait(work)

    await asyncio.gather(priority_queue.join(), worker_task)


asyncio.run(main())
```

In the preceding listing, we create a dataclass with ordered set to True. We then add a priority integer and a string data field, excluding this from the comparison. This means that when we add these work items to the queue, they'll only be sorted by the priority field. Running the code above, we can see that this is processed in the proper order:

```
Processing work item WorkItem(priority=1, data='High priority')
Processing work item WorkItem(priority=2, data='Medium priority')
Processing work item WorkItem(priority=3, data='Lowest priority')
```

Now that we know the basics of priority queues, let's translate this back into the earlier example of our order management API. Imagine we have some "power user" customers who spend a lot of money on our e-commerce site. We want to ensure that their orders always get processed first to ensure the best experience for them. Let's adapt our earlier example to use a priority queue for these users.

Listing 12.7　A priority queue in a web application

```python
import asyncio
from asyncio import Queue, Task
from dataclasses import field, dataclass
from enum import IntEnum
from typing import List
from random import randrange
from aiohttp import web
from aiohttp.web_app import Application
from aiohttp.web_request import Request
from aiohttp.web_response import Response

routes = web.RouteTableDef()

QUEUE_KEY = 'order_queue'
TASKS_KEY = 'order_tasks'


class UserType(IntEnum):
    POWER_USER = 1
    NORMAL_USER = 2


@dataclass(order=True)          ◁──┐ An order class to represent
class Order:                         our work item with a priority
    user_type: UserType              based on user type.
    order_delay: int = field(compare=False)


async def process_order_worker(worker_id: int, queue: Queue):
    while True:
        print(f'Worker {worker_id}: Waiting for an order...')
        order = await queue.get()
        print(f'Worker {worker_id}: Processing order {order}')
        await asyncio.sleep(order.order_delay)
        print(f'Worker {worker_id}: Processed order {order}')
        queue.task_done()


@routes.post('/order')
async def place_order(request: Request) -> Response:
    body = await request.json()
    user_type = UserType.POWER_USER if body['power_user'] == 'True' else
     UserType.NORMAL_USER
    order_queue = app[QUEUE_KEY]
    await order_queue.put(Order(user_type, randrange(5)))    ◁──┐ Parse the
    return Response(body='Order placed!')                        request into
                                                                 an order.

async def create_order_queue(app: Application):
    print('Creating order queue and tasks.')
```

```
queue: Queue = asyncio.PriorityQueue(10)
app[QUEUE_KEY] = queue
app[TASKS_KEY] = [asyncio.create_task(process_order_worker(i, queue))
                    for i in range(5)]


async def destroy_queue(app: Application):
    order_tasks: List[Task] = app[TASKS_KEY]
    queue: Queue = app[QUEUE_KEY]
    print('Waiting for pending queue workers to finish....')
    try:
        await asyncio.wait_for(queue.join(), timeout=10)
    finally:
        print('Finished all pending items, canceling worker tasks...')
        [task.cancel() for task in order_tasks]


app = web.Application()
app.on_startup.append(create_order_queue)
app.on_shutdown.append(destroy_queue)

app.add_routes(routes)
web.run_app(app)
```

The preceding listing looks very similar to our initial API to interact with a slow order management system with the difference being that we use a priority queue and create an Order class to represent an incoming order. When we get an incoming order, we now expect it to have a payload with a "power user" flag set to True for VIP users and False for other users. We can hit this endpoint with cURL like so

```
curl -X POST -d '{"power_user":"False"}' localhost:8080/order
```

passing in the desired power user value. If a user is a power user, their orders will always be processed by any available workers ahead of regular users.

One interesting corner case that can come up with priority queues is what happens when you add two work items with the same priority right after one another. Do they get processed by workers in the order they were inserted? Let's make a simple example to test this out.

Listing 12.8 A work item priority tie

```
import asyncio
from asyncio import Queue, PriorityQueue
from dataclasses import dataclass, field


@dataclass(order=True)
class WorkItem:
    priority: int
    data: str = field(compare=False)
```

```
async def worker(queue: Queue):
    while not queue.empty():
        work_item: WorkItem = await queue.get()
        print(f'Processing work item {work_item}')
        queue.task_done()


async def main():
    priority_queue = PriorityQueue()

    work_items = [WorkItem(3, 'Lowest priority'),
                  WorkItem(3, 'Lowest priority second'),
                  WorkItem(3, 'Lowest priority third'),
                  WorkItem(2, 'Medium priority'),
                  WorkItem(1, 'High priority')]

    worker_task = asyncio.create_task(worker(priority_queue))

    for work in work_items:
        priority_queue.put_nowait(work)

    await asyncio.gather(priority_queue.join(), worker_task)


asyncio.run(main())
```

In the preceding listing, we put three low-priority tasks in the queue first. We might expect these to be processed in order of insertion, but we don't exactly get that behavior when we run this:

```
Processing work item WorkItem(priority=1, data='High priority')
Processing work item WorkItem(priority=2, data='Medium priority')
Processing work item WorkItem(priority=3, data='Lowest priority third')
Processing work item WorkItem(priority=3, data='Lowest priority second')
Processing work item WorkItem(priority=3, data='Lowest priority')
```

It turns out that we process the low-priority items in the reverse order we inserted them. This is happening because the underlying heapsort algorithm is not a stable sort algorithm, as equal items are not guaranteed to be in the same order of insertion. Order when there are ties in priority may not be an issue, but if you care about it, you'll need to add a tie-breaker key that gives you the ordering you want. One simple way to do this and preserve insertion order is to add an item count to the work item, though there are many ways you could do this.

Listing 12.9   Breaking ties in a priority queue

```
import asyncio
from asyncio import Queue, PriorityQueue
from dataclasses import dataclass, field
```

```
@dataclass(order=True)
class WorkItem:
    priority: int
    order: int
    data: str = field(compare=False)


async def worker(queue: Queue):
    while not queue.empty():
        work_item: WorkItem = await queue.get()
        print(f'Processing work item {work_item}')
        queue.task_done()


async def main():
    priority_queue = PriorityQueue()

    work_items = [WorkItem(3, 1, 'Lowest priority'),
                  WorkItem(3, 2, 'Lowest priority second'),
                  WorkItem(3, 3, 'Lowest priority third'),
                  WorkItem(2, 4, 'Medium priority'),
                  WorkItem(1, 5, 'High priority')]

    worker_task = asyncio.create_task(worker(priority_queue))

    for work in work_items:
        priority_queue.put_nowait(work)

    await asyncio.gather(priority_queue.join(), worker_task)


asyncio.run(main())
```

In the previous listing, we add an order field to our WorkItem class. Then, when we insert work items, we add an integer representing the order we insert it into the queue. When there is a tie in priority, this will be the field that we order on. In our case, this gives us the desired ordering of insertion for the low priority items:

```
Processing work item WorkItem(priority=1, order=5, data='High priority')
Processing work item WorkItem(priority=2, order=4, data='Medium priority')
Processing work item WorkItem(priority=3, order=1, data='Lowest priority')
Processing work item WorkItem(priority=3, order=2, data='Lowest priority second')
Processing work item WorkItem(priority=3, order=3, data='Lowest priority third')
```

We've now seen how to process work items in a FIFO queue order and in a priority queue order. What if we want to process the most recently added work items first? Next, let's see how to do this with a LIFO queue.

12.3 *LIFO queues*

LIFO queues are more commonly referred to *stacks* in the computer science world. We can imagine these like a stack of poker chips: As you place bets, you take chips from the top of your stack (or "pop" them), and as you hopefully win hands, you put chips back on the top of the stack (or "push" them). These are useful for when we want our workers to process the most recently added items first.

We won't build much more than a simple example to demonstrate the order that workers process elements. As for when to use a LIFO queue, it depends on the order your application needs to process items in the queue. Do you need to process the most recently inserted item in the queue first? In this case, you'll want to use a LIFO queue.

Listing 12.10   A LIFO queue

```python
import asyncio
from asyncio import Queue, LifoQueue
from dataclasses import dataclass, field


@dataclass(order=True)
class WorkItem:
    priority: int
    order: int
    data: str = field(compare=False)


async def worker(queue: Queue):
    while not queue.empty():
        work_item: WorkItem = await queue.get()       ◁─┐  Get an item from the
        print(f'Processing work item {work_item}')        │  queue, or "pop" it,
        queue.task_done()                                 │  from the stack.


async def main():
    lifo_queue = LifoQueue()

    work_items = [WorkItem(3, 1, 'Lowest priority first'),
                  WorkItem(3, 2, 'Lowest priority second'),
                  WorkItem(3, 3, 'Lowest priority third'),
                  WorkItem(2, 4, 'Medium priority'),
                  WorkItem(1, 5, 'High priority')]

    worker_task = asyncio.create_task(worker(lifo_queue))

    for work in work_items:
        lifo_queue.put_nowait(work)          ◁─┤  Put an item into the queue,
                                                 or "push" it, onto the stack.

    await asyncio.gather(lifo_queue.join(), worker_task)


asyncio.run(main())
```

In the preceding listing, we create a LIFO queue and a set of work items. We then insert them one after another into the queue, pulling them out and processing them. Running this, you'll see the following output:

```
Processing work item WorkItem(priority=1, order=5, data='High priority')
Processing work item WorkItem(priority=2, order=4, data='Medium priority')
Processing work item WorkItem(priority=3, order=3, data='Lowest priority third')
Processing work item WorkItem(priority=3, order=2, data='Lowest priority second')
Processing work item WorkItem(priority=3, order=1, data='Lowest priority first')
```

Notice that we process items in the queue in the reverse order that we inserted them into the queue. As this is a stack, this makes sense, since we're processing the most recently added work item to our queue first.

We've now seen all the flavors of queue that the asyncio queue library has to offer. Are there any pitfalls to using these queues? Can we just use them whenever we need a queue in our application? We'll address this in chapter 13.

Summary

- asyncio queues are task queues that are useful in workflows in which we have coroutines that produce data and coroutines responsible for processing that data.
- Queues decouple data generation from data processing, as we can have a producer put items into a queue that multiple workers can then process independently and concurrently.
- We can use priority queues to give certain tasks priority over one another. This is useful for instances in which certain work is of higher importance than others and should always be handled first.
- asyncio queues are not distributed, not persistent, and not durable. If you need any of these qualities, you'll need to look towards a separate architectural component, such as Celery or RabbitMQ.

Managing subprocesses

13

This chapter covers

- Running multiple subprocesses asynchronously
- Handling standard output from subprocesses
- Communicating with subprocesses using standard input
- Avoiding deadlocks and other pitfalls with subprocesses

Many applications will never need to leave the world of Python. We'll call code from other Python libraries and modules or use multiprocessing or multithreading to run Python code concurrently. However, not everything we'll want to interact with is written in Python. We may have an already built application that is written in C++, Go, Rust, or some other language that provides better runtime characteristics or is simply already there for us to use without reimplementing. We may also want to use OS provided command-line utilities, such as GREP for searching through large files, cURL for making HTTP requests, or any of the numbers of applications we have at our disposal.

In standard Python, we can use the subprocess module to run different applications in separate processes. Like most other Python modules, the standard subprocess

312

API is blocking, making it incompatible with asyncio without multithreading or multiprocessing. asyncio provides a module modeled on the subprocess module to create and manage subprocesses asynchronously with coroutines.

In this chapter, we'll learn the basics of creating and managing subprocesses with asyncio by running an application written in a different language. We'll also learn how to handle input and output, reading standard output, and sending input from our application to our subprocesses.

13.1 Creating a subprocess

Suppose you'd like to extend the functionality of an existing Python web API. Another team within your organization has already built the functionality you'd like in a command-line application for a batch processing mechanism they have, but there is a major problem in that the application is written in Rust. Given the application already exists, you don't want to reinvent the wheel by reimplementing it in Python. Is there a way we can still use this application's functionality within our existing Python API?

Since this application has a command-line interface, we can use subprocesses to reuse this application. We'll call the application via its command-line interface and run it in a separate subprocess. We can then read the results of the application and use it within our existing API as needed, saving us the trouble of having to reimplement the application.

So how do we create a subprocess and execute it? asyncio provides two coroutine functions out of the box to create subprocesses: `asyncio.create_subprocess_shell` and `asyncio.create_subprocess_exec`. Each of these coroutine functions returns an instance of a `Process`, which has methods to let us wait for the process to finish and terminate the process as well as a few others. Why are there two coroutines to accomplish seemingly the same task? When would we want to use one over the other? The `create_subprocess_shell` coroutine function creates a subprocess within a shell installed on the system it runs on such as `zsh` or `bash`. Generally speaking, you'll want to use `create_subprocess_exec` unless you need to use functionality from the shell. Using the shell can have pitfalls, such as different machines having different shells or the same shell configured differently. This can make it hard to guarantee your application will behave the same on different machines.

To learn the basics of how to create a subprocess, let's write an asyncio application to run a simple command-line program. We'll start with the `ls` program, which lists the contents of the current directory to test things out, although we wouldn't likely do this in the real world. If you're running on a Windows machine, replace `ls -l` with `cmd /c dir`.

Listing 13.1 Running a simple command in a subprocess

```
import asyncio
from asyncio.subprocess import Process


async def main():
    process: Process = await asyncio.create_subprocess_exec('ls', '-l')
```

```
print(f'Process pid is: {process.pid}')
status_code = await process.wait()
print(f'Status code: {status_code}')
```

```
asyncio.run(main())
```

In the preceding listing, we create a Process instance to run the ls command with create_subprocess_exec. We can also specify other arguments to pass to the program by adding them after. Here we pass in -l, which adds some extra information around who created the files in the directory. Once we've created the process, we print out the process ID and then call the wait coroutine. This coroutine will wait until the process finishes, and once it does it will return the subprocesses status code; in this case it should be zero. By default, standard output from our subprocess will be piped to standard output of our own application, so when you run this you should see something like the following, differing based in what you have in your directory:

```
Process pid is: 54438
total 8
drwxr-xr-x    4 matthewfowler  staff  128 Dec 23 15:20 .
drwxr-xr-x   25 matthewfowler  staff  800 Dec 23 14:52 ..
-rw-r--r--    1 matthewfowler  staff    0 Dec 23 14:52 __init__.py
-rw-r--r--    1 matthewfowler  staff  293 Dec 23 15:20 basics.py
Status code: 0
```

Note that the wait coroutine will block until the application terminates, and there are no guarantees as to how long a process will take to terminate, let alone if it will terminate at all. If you're concerned about a runaway process, you'll need to introduce a timeout with asyncio.wait_for. There is a caveat to this, however. Recall that wait_for will terminate the coroutine that it is running if it times out. You may assume that this will terminate the process, but it does not. It only terminates the task that is waiting for the process to finish, and not the underlying process.

We'll need a better way to shut down the process when it times out. Luckily, Process has two methods that can help us out in this situation: terminate and kill. The terminate method will send the SIGTERM signal to the subprocess, and kill will send the SIGKILL signal. Note that both these methods are not coroutines and are also non-blocking. They just send the signal. If you want to try and get the return code once you've terminated the subprocess or you want to wait for any cleanup, you'll need to call wait again.

Let's test out terminating a long-running application with the sleep command line application (for Windows users, replace 'sleep', '3' with the more complicated 'cmd', 'start', '/wait', 'timeout', '3'). We'll create a subprocess that sleeps for a few seconds and try to terminate it before it has a chance to finish.

Listing 13.2   Terminating a subprocess

```python
import asyncio
from asyncio.subprocess import Process


async def main():
    process: Process = await asyncio.create_subprocess_exec('sleep', '3')
    print(f'Process pid is: {process.pid}')
    try:
        status_code = await asyncio.wait_for(process.wait(), timeout=1.0)
        print(status_code)
    except asyncio.TimeoutError:
        print('Timed out waiting to finish, terminating...')
        process.terminate()
        status_code = await process.wait()
        print(status_code)


asyncio.run(main())
```

In the preceding listing, we create a subprocess that will take 3 seconds to complete but wrap it in a `wait_for` with a 1-second timeout. After 1 second, `wait_for` will throw a `TimeoutError`, and in the except block we terminate the process and wait for it to finish, printing out its status code. This should give us output similar to the following:

```
Process pid is: 54709
Timed out waiting to finish, terminating...
-15
```

One thing to watch out for when writing your own code is the `wait` inside of the except block still has a chance of taking a long time, and you may want to wrap this in a `wait_for` if this is a concern.

13.1.1   Controlling standard output

In the previous examples, the standard output of our subprocess went directly to our application's standard output. What if we don't want this behavior? Perhaps we want to do additional processing on the output, or maybe the output is inconsequential, and we can safely ignore it. The `create_subprocess_exec` coroutine has a `stdout` parameter that let us specify where we want standard output to go. This parameter takes in an `enum` that lets us specify if we want to redirect the subprocess's output to our own standard output, pipe it to a `StreamReader`, or ignore it entirely by redirecting it to `/dev/null`.

Let's say we're planning to run multiple subprocesses concurrently and echo their output. We'd like to know which subprocess generated the output to avoid confusion. To make this output easier to read, we'll add some extra data about which subprocess generated the output before writing it to our application's standard output. We'll prepend the command that generated the output before printing it out.

To do this, the first thing we'll need to do is set the stdout parameter to asyncio
.subprocess.PIPE. This tells the subprocess to create a new StreamReader instance
we can use to read output from the process. We can then access this stream reader
with the Proccess.stdout field. Let's try this with our ls -la command.

Listing 13.3   Using the standard output stream reader

```
import asyncio
from asyncio import StreamReader
from asyncio.subprocess import Process


async def write_output(prefix: str, stdout: StreamReader):
    while line := await stdout.readline():
        print(f'[{prefix}]: {line.rstrip().decode()}')


async def main():
    program = ['ls', '-la']
    process: Process = await asyncio.create_subprocess_exec(*program,
                                                  stdout=asyncio
                                                  .subprocess.PIPE)
    print(f'Process pid is: {process.pid}')
    stdout_task = asyncio.create_task(write_output(' '.join(program),
     process.stdout))

    return_code, _ = await asyncio.gather(process.wait(), stdout_task)
    print(f'Process returned: {return_code}')


asyncio.run(main())
```

In the preceding listing, we first create a coroutine write_output to prepend a prefix to
output from a stream reader line by line. Then, in our main coroutine, we create a subprocess specifying we want to pipe stdout. We also create a task to run write_output,
passing in the process's standard output stream reader, and run this concurrently with
wait. When running this, you'll see the output prepended with the command:

```
Process pid is: 56925
[ls -la]: total 32
[ls -la]: drwxr-xr-x    7 matthewfowler   staff   224 Dec 23 09:07 .
[ls -la]: drwxr-xr-x   25 matthewfowler   staff   800 Dec 23 14:52 ..
[ls -la]: -rw-r--r--    1 matthewfowler   staff     0 Dec 23 14:52 __init__.py
Process returned: 0
```

One crucial aspect of using pipes, and dealing with subprocesses input and output in
general, is that they are susceptible to deadlocks. The wait coroutine is especially susceptible to this if our subprocess generates a lot of output, and we don't properly consume it. To demonstrate this, let's look at a simple example by generating a Python
application that writes a lot of data to standard output and flushes it all at once.

Listing 13.4 Generating a lot of output

```
import sys

[sys.stdout.buffer.write(b'Hello there!!\n') for _ in range(1000000)]

sys.stdout.flush()
```

The preceding listing writes Hello there!! to the standard output buffer 1,000,000 times and flushes it all at once. Let's see what happens if we use a pipe with this application but don't consume the data.

Listing 13.5 A deadlock with pipes

```
import asyncio
from asyncio.subprocess import Process


async def main():
    program = ['python3', 'listing_13_4.py']
    process: Process = await asyncio.create_subprocess_exec(*program,
                                                    stdout=asyncio
                                                    .subprocess.PIPE)
    print(f'Process pid is: {process.pid}')

    return_code = await process.wait()
    print(f'Process returned: {return_code}')


asyncio.run(main())
```

If you run the preceding listing, you'll see the process pid printed out and then nothing more. The application will hang forever, and you'll need to forcefully terminate it. If this does not happen on your system, simply increase the number of times we output data in the output application, and you'll eventually run into the problem.

Our application seems simple enough, so why are we running into this deadlock? The issue lies in how the stream reader's buffer works. When the stream reader's buffer fills up, any more calls to write into it block until more space in the buffer becomes available. While our stream reader buffer is blocked because its buffer is full, our process is still trying to finish writing its large output to the stream reader. This makes our process dependent on the stream reader becoming unblocked, but the stream reader will never become unblocked because we never free up any space in the buffer. This is a circular dependency and therefore a deadlock.

Previously, we avoided this issue entirely by reading from the standard output stream reader concurrently as we were waiting for the process to finish. This meant that even if the buffer filled, we would drain it such that the process wouldn't block indefinitely waiting to write additional data. When dealing with pipes, you'll need to be careful about consuming stream data, so you don't run into deadlocks.

You can also address this issue by avoiding use of the `wait` coroutine. In addition, the `Process` class has another coroutine method called `communicate` that avoids deadlocks entirely. This coroutine blocks until the subprocess completes and concurrently consumes standard output and standard error, returning the output complete once the application finishes. Let's adapt our previous example to use `communicate` to fix the issue.

Listing 13.6 Using `communicate`

```python
import asyncio
from asyncio.subprocess import Process


async def main():
    program = ['python3', 'listing_13_4.py']
    process: Process = await asyncio.create_subprocess_exec(*program,
                                                            stdout=asyncio
                                                            .subprocess.PIPE)

    print(f'Process pid is: {process.pid}')

    stdout, stderr = await process.communicate()
    print(stdout)
    print(stderr)
    print(f'Process returned: {process.returncode}')


asyncio.run(main())
```

When you run the preceding listing, you'll see all the application's output printed to the console all at once (and `None` printed once, since we didn't write anything to standard output). Internally, `communicate` creates a few tasks that constantly read output from standard output and standard error into an internal buffer, thus, avoiding any deadlock issues. While we avoid potential deadlocks, we have a serious drawback in that we can't interactively process output from standard output. If you're in a situation in which you need to react to output from an application (perhaps you need to terminate when you encounter a certain message or spawn another task), you'll need to use `wait`, but be careful to read output from your stream reader appropriately to avoid deadlocks.

An additional drawback is that communicate buffers *all* the data from standard output and standard input in memory. If you're working with a subprocess that could produce a large amount of data, you run the risk of running out of memory. We'll see how to address these shortcomings in the next section.

13.1.2 *Running subprocesses concurrently*

Now that we know the basics of creating, terminating, and reading output from subprocesses, it is added with our existing knowledge to run multiple applications concurrently. Let's imagine we need to encrypt multiple pieces of text that we have in memory, and for security purposes we'd like to use the Twofish cipher algorithm. This algorithm isn't supported by the hashlib module, so we'll need an alternative. We can use the gpg (short for GNU Privacy Guard, which is a free software replacement of PGP [pretty good privacy]) command-line application. You can download gpg at https://gnupg.org/download/.

First, let's define the command we'll want to use for our encryption. We can use gpg by defining a passcode and setting an algorithm with command line parameters. Then, it is a matter of echoing text to the application. For example, to encrypt the text "encrypt this!", we can run the following:

```
echo 'encrypt this!' | gpg -c --batch --passphrase 3ncryptm3 --cipher-algo TWOFISH
```

This should produce encrypted output to standard output similar to the following:

```
?
Q+??/??*??C??H`??`)R??u??7þ_{f{R;n?FE .?b5??(?i??????o\k?b<????`%
```

This will work on our command line, but it won't work if we're using create_subprocess_exec, since we won't have the | pipe operator available (create_subprocess_shell will work if you truly need a pipe). So how can we pass in the text we want to encrypt? In addition to allowing us to pipe standard output and standard error, communicate and wait let us pipe in standard input as well. The communicate coroutine also lets us specify input bytes when we start the application. If we've piped standard input when we created our process, these bytes will get sent to the application. This will work nicely for us; we'll simply pass the string we want to encrypt with the communicate coroutine.

Let's try this out by generating random pieces of text and encrypting them concurrently. We'll create a list of 100 random text strings with 1,000 characters each and run gpg on each of them concurrently.

Listing 13.7 Encrypting text concurrently

```python
import asyncio
import random
import string
import time
from asyncio.subprocess import Process


async def encrypt(text: str) -> bytes:
    program = ['gpg', '-c', '--batch', '--passphrase', '3ncryptm3',
        '--cipher-algo', 'TWOFISH']

    process: Process = await asyncio.create_subprocess_exec(*program,
                                                stdout=asyncio
                                                .subprocess.PIPE,
                                                stdin=asyncio
                                                .subprocess.PIPE)
```

```
        stdout, stderr = await process.communicate(text.encode())
        return stdout


async def main():
    text_list = [''.join(random.choice(string.ascii_letters) for _ in
     range(1000)) for _ in range(100)]

    s = time.time()
    tasks = [asyncio.create_task(encrypt(text)) for text in text_list]
    encrypted_text = await asyncio.gather(*tasks)
    e = time.time()

    print(f'Total time: {e - s}')
    print(encrypted_text)


asyncio.run(main())
```

In the preceding listing, we define a coroutine called encrypt that creates a gpg process and sends in the text we want to encrypt with communicate. For simplicity, we just return the standard output result and don't do any error handling; in a real-world application you'd likely want to be more robust here. Then, in our main coroutine we create a list of random text and create an encrypt task for each piece of text. We then run them all concurrently with gather and print out the total runtime and encrypted bits of text. You can compare the concurrent runtime with the synchronous runtime by putting await in front of asyncio.create_task and removing the gather, and you should see a reasonable speedup.

In this listing, we only had 100 pieces of text. What if we had thousands or more? Our current code takes 100 pieces of text and tries to encrypt them all concurrently; this means that we create 100 processes at the same time. This poses a challenge because our machines are resource constrained, and one process could eat up a lot of memory. In addition, spinning up hundreds or thousands of processes creates non-trivial context-switching overhead.

In our case we have another wrinkle caused by gpg, since it relies on shared state to encrypt data. If you take the code in listing 13.7 and increase the number of pieces of text into the thousands, you'll likely start to see the following printed to standard error:

```
gpg: waiting for lock on `/Users/matthewfowler/.gnupg/random_seed'...
```

So not only have we created a lot of processes and all the overhead associated with that, but we've also created processes that are actually blocked on shared state that gpg needs. So how can we limit the number of processes running to circumvent this issue? This is a perfect example of when a semaphore comes in handy. Since our work is CPU-bound, adding a semaphore to limit the number of processes to the number of CPU cores we have available makes sense. Let's try this out by using a semaphore that is limited to the number of CPU cores on our system and encrypting 1,000 pieces of text to see if this can improve our performance.

Listing 13.8 Subprocesses with a semaphore

```python
import asyncio
import random
import string
import time
import os
from asyncio import Semaphore
from asyncio.subprocess import Process


async def encrypt(sem: Semaphore, text: str) -> bytes:
    program = ['gpg', '-c', '--batch', '--passphrase', '3ncryptm3',
      '--cipher-algo', 'TWOFISH']

    async with sem:
        process: Process = await asyncio.create_subprocess_exec(*program,
                                                stdout=asyncio
                                                .subprocess.PIPE,
                                                stdin=asyncio
                                                .subprocess.PIPE)
        stdout, stderr = await process.communicate(text.encode())
        return stdout


async def main():
    text_list = [''.join(random.choice(string.ascii_letters) for _ in
      range(1000)) for _ in range(1000)]
    semaphore = Semaphore(os.cpu_count())
    s = time.time()
    tasks = [asyncio.create_task(encrypt(semaphore, text)) for text in text_list]
    encrypted_text = await asyncio.gather(*tasks)
    e = time.time()

    print(f'Total time: {e - s}')


asyncio.run(main())
```

Comparing this with the runtime of 1,000 pieces of text with an unbounded set of subprocesses you should see some performance improvement, alongside a reduction in memory usage. You might think this is similar to what we saw in chapter 6 with a `ProcessPoolExecutor`'s concept of maximum workers, and you'd be correct. Internally, a `ProcessPoolExecutor` uses a semaphore to manage how many processes run concurrently.

We've now seen the basics around creating, terminating, and running multiple subprocesses concurrently. Next, we'll take a look at how to communicate with subprocesses in a more interactive manner.

13.2 *Communicating with subprocesses*

Up to this point, we've been using one-way, noninteractive communication with processes. But what if we're working with an application that may require user input? For example, we may be asked for a passphrase, username, or any other number of inputs.

In the case in which we know we only have one piece of input to deal with, using `communicate` is ideal. We saw this previously using gpg to send in text to encrypt, but let's try it when the subprocess explicitly asks for input. We'll first create a simple Python program to ask for a username and echo it to standard output.

Listing 13.9   Echoing user input

```python
username = input('Please enter a username: ')
print(f'Your username is {username}')
```

Now, we can use `communicate` to input the username.

Listing 13.10   Using `communicate` with standard input

```python
import asyncio
from asyncio.subprocess import Process


async def main():
    program = ['python3', 'listing_13_9.py']
    process: Process = await asyncio.create_subprocess_exec(*program,
                                                            stdout=asyncio
                                                            .subprocess.PIPE,
                                                            stdin=asyncio
                                                            .subprocess.PIPE)

    stdout, stderr = await process.communicate(b'Zoot')
    print(stdout)
    print(stderr)


asyncio.run(main())
```

When we run this code, we'll see `b'Please enter a username: Your username is Zoot\n'` printed to the console, as our application terminates right after our first user input. This won't work if we have a more interactive application. For example, take this application, which repeatedly asks for user input and echoes it until the user types `quit`.

Listing 13.11   An echo application

```python
user_input = ''

while user_input != 'quit':
    user_input = input('Enter text to echo: ')
    print(user_input)
```

Since `communicate` waits until the process terminates, we'll need to use `wait` and process standard output and standard input concurrently. The `Process` class exposes `StreamWriter` in a `stdin` field we can use when we've set standard input to `PIPE`. We can use this concurrently with the standard output `StreamReader` to handle these types of applications. Let's see how to do this with the following listing, where we'll create an application to write a few pieces of text to our subprocess.

Listing 13.12 Using the echo application with subprocesses

```python
import asyncio
from asyncio import StreamWriter, StreamReader
from asyncio.subprocess import Process


async def consume_and_send(text_list, stdout: StreamReader, stdin:
        StreamWriter):
    for text in text_list:
        line = await stdout.read(2048)
        print(line)
        stdin.write(text.encode())
        await stdin.drain()


async def main():
    program = ['python3', 'listing_13_11.py']
    process: Process = await asyncio.create_subprocess_exec(*program,
                                                stdout=asyncio
                                                .subprocess.PIPE,
                                                stdin=asyncio
                                                .subprocess.PIPE)

    text_input = ['one\n', 'two\n', 'three\n', 'four\n', 'quit\n']

    await asyncio.gather(consume_and_send(text_input, process.stdout,
     process.stdin), process.wait())


asyncio.run(main())
```

In the preceding listing, we define a `consume_and_send` coroutine that reads standard output until we receive the expected message for a user to specify input. Once we've received this message, we dump the data to our own application's standard output and write the strings in `'text_list'` to standard input. We repeat this until we've sent all data into our subprocess. When we run this, we should see all of our output was sent to our subprocess and properly echoed:

```
b'Enter text to echo: '
b'one\nEnter text to echo: '
b'two\nEnter text to echo: '
b'three\nEnter text to echo: '
b'four\nEnter text to echo: '
```

The application we're currently running has the luxury of producing deterministic output and stopping at deterministic points to ask for input. This makes managing standard output and standard input relatively straightforward. What if the application we're running in a subprocess only asks for input sometimes or could write a lot of data before asking for input? Let's adapt our sample echo program to be a bit more complicated. We'll have it echo user input between 1 and 10 times randomly, and we'll sleep for a half second between each echo.

> **Listing 13.13   A more complex echo application**

```
from random import randrange
import time

user_input = ''

while user_input != 'quit':
    user_input = input('Enter text to echo: ')
    for i in range(randrange(10)):
        time.sleep(.5)
        print(user_input)
```

If we run this application as a subprocess with a similar approach to listing 13.12, it will work because we're still deterministic in that we eventually ask for input with a known piece of text. However, the drawback of using this approach is that our code to read from standard output and write to standard input is strongly coupled. This combined with increasing complexity of our input/output logic can make the code hard to follow and maintain.

We can address this by decoupling reading standard output from writing data to standard input, thus, separating the concerns of reading standard output and writing to standard input. We'll create one coroutine to read standard output and one coroutine to write text to standard input. Our coroutine that reads standard output will set an event once it has received the input prompt we expect. Our coroutine that writes to standard input will wait for that event to be set, then once it is, it will write the specified text. We'll then take these two coroutines and run them concurrently with gather.

> **Listing 13.14   Decoupling output reading from input writing**

```
import asyncio
from asyncio import StreamWriter, StreamReader, Event
from asyncio.subprocess import Process


async def output_consumer(input_ready_event: Event, stdout: StreamReader):
    while (data := await stdout.read(1024)) != b'':
        print(data)
        if data.decode().endswith("Enter text to echo: "):
            input_ready_event.set()
```

```
async def input_writer(text_data, input_ready_event: Event, stdin:
    StreamWriter):
    for text in text_data:
        await input_ready_event.wait()
        stdin.write(text.encode())
        await stdin.drain()
        input_ready_event.clear()


async def main():
    program = ['python3', 'interactive_echo_random.py']
    process: Process = await asyncio.create_subprocess_exec(*program,
                                                stdout=asyncio
                                                .subprocess.PIPE,
                                                stdin=asyncio
                                                .subprocess.PIPE)

    input_ready_event = asyncio.Event()

    text_input = ['one\n', 'two\n', 'three\n', 'four\n', 'quit\n']

    await asyncio.gather(output_consumer(input_ready_event, process.stdout),
                         input_writer(text_input, input_ready_event,
                         process.stdin),
                         process.wait())


asyncio.run(main())
```

In the preceding listing, we first define an output_consumer coroutine function. This function takes in an input_ready event as well as a StreamReader that will reference standard output and reads from standard output until we encounter the text Enter text to echo:. Once we see this text, we know that the standard input of our subprocess is ready to accept input, so we set the input_ready event.

Our input_writer coroutine function iterates over our input list and waits on our event for standard input to become ready. Once standard input is ready, we write out our input and clear the event so that on the next iteration of our for loop we'll block until standard input becomes ready again. With this implementation we now have two coroutine functions, each with one clear responsibility: one to write to standard input and one to read to standard output, increasing the readability and maintainability of our code.

Summary

- We can use asyncio's subprocess module to launch subprocesses asynchronously with create_subprocess_shell and create_subprocess_exec. Whenever possible, prefer create_subprocess_exec, as it ensures consistent behavior across machines.
- By default, output from subprocesses will go to our own application's standard output. If we need to read and interact with standard input and standard output, we'll need to configure them to pipe to StreamReader and StreamWriter instances.

- When we pipe standard output or standard error, we need to be careful to consume output. If we don't, we could deadlock our application.
- When we have a large amount of subprocesses to run concurrently, semaphores can make sense to avoid abusing system resources and creating unneeded contention.
- We can use the `communicate` coroutine method to send input to standard input on a subprocess.

Advanced asyncio

14

This chapter covers

- Designing APIs for both coroutines and functions
- Coroutine context locals
- Yielding to the event loop
- Using different event loop implementations
- The relationship between coroutines and generators
- Creating your own event loop with custom awaitables

We've learned the vast majority of what asyncio has to offer. Using the modules of asyncio covered in previous chapters, you should be able to complete almost any task you need. That said, there are still a few lesser-known techniques that you may need to use, especially if you're designing your own asyncio APIs.

In this chapter, we'll learn a smorgasbord of more advanced techniques available in asyncio. We'll learn how to design APIs that can handle both coroutines and regular Python functions, how to force iterations of the event loop, and how to pass state between tasks without ever passing arguments. We'll also dig into more details on how exactly asyncio uses generators to fully understand what is happening under the hood. We'll do this by implementing our own custom awaitables and using them to build our own simple implementation of an event loop that can run multiple coroutines concurrently.

You're not likely to need a lot of what is covered in this chapter in your day-to-day development tasks unless you're building new APIs or frameworks that rely on the internals of asynchronous programming. These techniques are primarily for these applications and for the curious who'd like a deeper understanding of the internals of asynchronous Python.

14.1   *APIs with coroutines and functions*

If we're building an API on our own, we may not want to assume that our users are using our library in their own asynchronous application. They may not have migrated yet, or they may not get any benefits from an async stack and will never migrate. How can we design an API that accepts both coroutines and plain old Python functions to accommodate these types of users?

asyncio provides a couple of convenience functions to help us do this: `asyncio.iscoroutine` and `asyncio.iscoroutinefunction`. These functions let us test if a callable object is a coroutine or not, letting us apply different logic based on this. These functions are the basis of how Django can handle both synchronous and asynchronous views seamlessly, as we saw in chapter 9.

To see this, let's build a sample task runner class that accepts both functions and coroutines. This class will let users add functions to an internal list that we'll then run concurrently (if they are coroutines) or serially (if they are normal functions) when the user calls a start method on our task runner.

Listing 14.1   A task runner class

```
import asyncio


class TaskRunner:

    def __init__(self):
        self.loop = asyncio.new_event_loop()
        self.tasks = []

    def add_task(self, func):
        self.tasks.append(func)

    async def _run_all(self):
        awaitable_tasks = []

        for task in self.tasks:
            if asyncio.iscoroutinefunction(task):
                awaitable_tasks.append(asyncio.create_task(task()))
            elif asyncio.iscoroutine(task):
                awaitable_tasks.append(asyncio.create_task(task))
```

```
        else:
            self.loop.call_soon(task)

    await asyncio.gather(*awaitable_tasks)

def run(self):
    self.loop.run_until_complete(self._run_all())


if __name__ == "__main__":

    def regular_function():
        print('Hello from a regular function!')


    async def coroutine_function():
        print('Running coroutine, sleeping!')
        await asyncio.sleep(1)
        print('Finished sleeping!')


    runner = TaskRunner()
    runner.add_task(coroutine_function)
    runner.add_task(coroutine_function())
    runner.add_task(regular_function)

    runner.run()
```

In the preceding listing, our task runner creates a new event loop and an empty task list. We then define an add method which just adds a function (or coroutine) to the pending task list. Then, once a user calls run(), we kick off the _run_all method in the event loop. Our _run_all method iterates through our task list and checks to see if the function in question is a coroutine. If it is a coroutine, we create a task; otherwise, we use the event loops call_soon method to schedule our plain function to run on the next iteration of the event loop. Then once we've created all the tasks we need to, we call gather on them and wait for them all to finish.

We then define two functions: a normal Python function aptly named regular_ function and a coroutine named coroutine_function. We create an instance of TaskRunner and add three tasks, calling coroutine_function twice to demonstrate the two different ways we can reference a coroutine in our API. This gives us the following output:

```
Running coroutine, sleeping!
Running coroutine, sleeping!
Hello from a regular function!
Finished sleeping!
Finished sleeping!
```

This demonstrates that we've successfully run both coroutines and normal Python functions. We've now built an API which can handle both coroutines as well as normal

Python functions, increasing the ways available for our end users to consume our API. Next, we'll look at context variables, which let us store a state that is local to a task without having to explicitly pass it around as a function argument.

14.2   *Context variables*

Imagine we're using a REST API built with thread-per-request web server. When a request to the web server comes in, we may have common data about the user making the request we need to keep track of, such as a user ID, access token, or other information. We may be tempted to store this data globally across all threads in the web servers, but this has drawbacks. Chief among the drawbacks is that we need to handle the mapping from a thread to its data as well as any locking to prevent race conditions. We can resolve this by using a concept called *thread locals*. Thread locals are global state that are specific to one thread. This data we set in a thread local will be seen by the thread that set it and only by that thread, avoiding any thread to data mapping as well as race conditions. While we won't go into to details of thread locals, you can read more about them in the documentation for the threading module available at https://docs.python.org/3/library/threading.html#thread-local-data.

Of course, in asyncio applications we usually have only one thread, so anything we store as a thread local is available anywhere in our application. In PEP-567 (https://www.python.org/dev/peps/pep-0567) the concept of *context variables* was introduced to handle the concept of a thread local within a single-threaded concurrency model. Context variables are similar to thread locals with the difference being that they are local to a particular task instead of to a thread. This means that if a task creates a context variable, any inner coroutine or task within that initial task will have access to that variable. No other tasks outside of that chain will be able to see or modify the variable. This lets us keep track of a state specific to one task without ever having to pass it as an explicit argument.

To see an example of this, we'll create a simple server that listens for data from connected clients. We'll create a context variable to keep track of a connected user's address, and when a user sends a message, we'll print out their address along with the message they sent.

Listing 14.2   A server with a context variables

```python
import asyncio
from asyncio import StreamReader, StreamWriter
from contextvars import ContextVar


class Server:
    user_address = ContextVar('user_address')    ◁─── Create a context
                                                       variable with the name
    def __init__(self, host: str, port: int):          'user_address'.
        self.host = host
        self.port = port
```

```
async def start_server(self):
    server = await asyncio.start_server(self._client_connected,
                                        self.host, self.port)
    await server.serve_forever()

def _client_connected(self, reader: StreamReader, writer: StreamWriter):
    self.user_address.set(writer.get_extra_info('peername'))    ◁─────────┐
    asyncio.create_task(self.listen_for_messages(reader))

async def listen_for_messages(self, reader: StreamReader):
    while data := await reader.readline():
        print(f'Got message {data} from {self.user_address.get()}')  ◁─┐
```

Display the user's message alongside their address from the context variable.

```
async def main():
    server = Server('127.0.0.1', 9000)
    await server.start_server()


asyncio.run(main())
```

When a client connects, store the client's address in the context variable.

In the preceding listing, we first create an instance of a `ContextVar` to hold our user's address information. Context variables require us to provide a string name, so here we give it a descriptive name of `user_address`, primarily for debugging purposes. Then in our `_client_connected` callback, we set the data of the context variable to the client's address. This will allow any tasks spawned from this parent task to have access to the information we set; in this instance, this will be tasks that listen for messages from the clients.

In our `listen_for_messages` coroutine method we listen for data from our clients, and when we get it, we print it out alongside the address that we stored in our context variable. When you run this application and connect with multiple clients and send some messages, you should see output like the following:

```
Got message b'Hello!\r\n' from ('127.0.0.1', 50036)
Got message b'Okay!\r\n' from ('127.0.0.1', 50038)
```

Note that the port number of the address is different, indicating we got the message from two separate clients on localhost. Even though we created only one context variable, we're still able to access unique data specific to each individual client. This gives us a clean way to pass data among tasks without having to explicitly pass data into tasks or other method calls within that task.

14.3 *Forcing an event loop iteration*

How the event loop operates internally is mostly outside of our control. It decides when and how to execute coroutines and tasks. That said, there is a way to trigger an event loop iteration if we need to do so. This can come in handy for long-running tasks to avoid blocking the event loop (though you should also consider threads in this case) or ensuring that a task starts instantly.

Recall that if we're creating several tasks, none of them will start to run until we hit an `await`, which will trigger the event loop to schedule and start to run them. What if we wanted each task to start running right away?

asyncio provides an optimized idiom to suspend the current coroutine and force an iteration of the event loop by passing in zero to `asyncio.sleep`. Let's see how to use this to start running tasks as soon as we create them. We'll create two functions: one that does not use `sleep` and one which does to compare the order in which things run.

Listing 14.3   Forcing an event loop iteration

```
import asyncio
from util import delay


async def create_tasks_no_sleep():
    task1 = asyncio.create_task(delay(1))
    task2 = asyncio.create_task(delay(2))
    print('Gathering tasks:')
    await asyncio.gather(task1, task2)


async def create_tasks_sleep():
    task1 = asyncio.create_task(delay(1))
    await asyncio.sleep(0)
    task2 = asyncio.create_task(delay(2))
    await asyncio.sleep(0)
    print('Gathering tasks:')
    await asyncio.gather(task1, task2)


async def main():
    print('--- Testing without asyncio.sleep(0) ---')
    await create_tasks_no_sleep()
    print('--- Testing with asyncio.sleep(0) ---')
    await create_tasks_sleep()


asyncio.run(main())
```

When we run the preceding listing, we'll see the following output:

```
--- Testing without asyncio.sleep(0) ---
Gathering tasks:
sleeping for 1 second(s)
sleeping for 2 second(s)
finished sleeping for 1 second(s)
finished sleeping for 2 second(s)
--- Testing with asyncio.sleep(0) ---
sleeping for 1 second(s)
sleeping for 2 second(s)
Gathering tasks:
finished sleeping for 1 second(s)
finished sleeping for 2 second(s)
```

We first create two tasks and then `gather` them without using `asyncio.sleep(0)`, and this runs as we would normally expect with our two `delay` coroutines not running until our `gather` statement. Next, we insert an `asyncio.sleep(0)` after we create each task. In the output, you'll notice that the messages from the `delay` coroutine print immediately before we call `gather` on the tasks. Using the `sleep` forces an event loop iteration, which causes the code in our tasks to execute immediately.

We've been almost exclusively using the asyncio implementation of an event loop. However, other implementations exist that we can swap in if we have a need. Next, let's look at how to use different event loops.

14.4 *Using different event loop implementations*

asyncio provides a default implementation of an event loop that we have been using up until this point, but it is entirely possible to use a different implementation that may have different characteristics. There are a few ways to use a different implementation. One is to subclass the `AbstractEventLoop` class and implement its methods, create an instance of this, then set it as the event loop with the `asyncio.set_event_loop` function. If we're building our own custom implementation this makes sense, but there are off-the-shelf event loops we can use. Let's look at one such implementation called *uvloop*.

So, what is uvloop, and why would you want to use it? uvloop is an implementation of an event loop that heavily relies on the `libuv` library (https://libuv.org), which is the backbone of the `node.js` runtime. Since `libuv` is implemented in C, it has better performance than pure interpreted Python code. As a result, uvloop can be faster than the default asyncio event loop. It tends to perform particularly well when writing socket and stream-based applications. You can read more about benchmarks on the project's github site at https://github.com/magicstack/uvloop. Note that at the time of writing, uvloop is only available on *Nix platforms.

To get started, let's first install the latest version of uvloop with the following command:

```
pip -Iv uvloop==0.16.0
```

Once we've installed `libuv`, we're ready to use it. We'll make a simple echo server and will use the uvloop implementation of the event loop.

Listing 14.4   Using uvloop as an event loop

```
import asyncio
from asyncio import StreamReader, StreamWriter
import uvloop


async def connected(reader: StreamReader, writer: StreamWriter):
    line = await reader.readline()
    writer.write(line)
    await writer.drain()
```

```
        writer.close()
        await writer.wait_closed()


async def main():
    server = await asyncio.start_server(connected, port=9000)
    await server.serve_forever()


uvloop.install()          ⊲─────┐  Install the uvloop
asyncio.run(main())              │  event loop.
```

In the preceding listing, we call `uvloop.install()`, which will switch out the event loop for us. We can do this manually with the following code instead of calling install if we'd like:

```
loop = uvloop.new_event_loop()
asyncio.set_event_loop(loop)
```

The important part is to call this *before* calling `asyncio.run(main())`. Internally, `asyncio.run` calls `get_event_loop` that will create an event loop if one does not exist. If we do this before properly installing uvloop, we'll get a typical asyncio event loop, and installation after the fact will have no effect.

You may want to complete an exercise to benchmark if an event loop such as uvloop helps performance characteristics of your application. The uvloop project on Github has code that will run benchmarking both in terms of throughput and requests per second.

We've now seen how to use an existing event loop implementation instead of the default event loop implementation. Next, we'll see how to create our own event loop completely outside of the confines of asyncio. This will let us gain a deeper understanding of how the asyncio event loop, as well as coroutines, tasks, and futures, work under the hood.

14.5 *Creating a custom event loop*

One potentially non-obvious aspect of asyncio is that it is conceptually distinct from async/await syntax and coroutines. The coroutine class definition isn't even in the asyncio library module!

Coroutines and async/await syntax are concepts that are independent of the ability to execute them. Python comes with a default event loop implementation, asyncio, which is what we have been using to run them until now, but we could use any event loop implementation, even our own. In the previous section, we saw how we could swap out the asyncio event loop with different implementations with potentially better (or at least, different) runtime performance. Now, let's see how to build our own simple event loop implementation that can handle non-blocking sockets.

14.5.1 Coroutines and generators

Before `async` and `await` syntax were introduced in Python 3.5, the relationship between coroutines and generators was obvious. Let's build a simple coroutine which sleeps for 1 second with the old syntax using decorators and generators to understand this.

Listing 14.5 Generator-based coroutines

```
import asyncio


@asyncio.coroutine
def coroutine():
    print('Sleeping!')
    yield from asyncio.sleep(1)
    print('Finished!')


asyncio.run(coroutine())
```

Instead of the async keyword, we apply the `@asyncio.coroutine` decorator to specify the function is a coroutine function and instead of the `await` keyword we use the `yield from` syntax we're familiar with in generators. Currently, the `async` and `await` keywords are just syntactic sugar around this construct.

14.5.2 Generator-based coroutines are deprecated

Note that generator based coroutines are currently scheduled to be removed entirely in Python version 3.10. You may run into them in legacy codebases, but you should not write new async code in this style anymore.

So why do generators make sense at all for a single-threaded concurrency model? Recall that a coroutine needs to suspend execution when it runs into a blocking operation to allow other coroutines to run. Generators suspend execution when they hit a yield point, effectively pausing them midstream. This means if we have two generators, we can interleave their execution. We let the first generator run until it hits a yield point (or, in coroutine language, an `await` point), then we let the second generator run until it hits its yield point, and we repeat this until both generators are exhausted. To see this in action, let's build a very simple example that interleaves two generators, using some background methods we'll need to use to build our event loop.

Listing 14.6 Interleaving generator execution

```
from typing import Generator


def generator(start: int, end: int):
    for i in range(start, end):
        yield i
```

```
one_to_five = generator(1, 5)
five_to_ten = generator(5, 10)
```

Run one
step of the
generator.

```
def run_generator_step(gen: Generator[int, None, None]):
    try:
        return gen.send(None)
    except StopIteration as si:
        return si.value
```

Interleave
execution of both
generators.

```
while True:
    one_to_five_result = run_generator_step(one_to_five)
    five_to_ten_result = run_generator_step(five_to_ten)
    print(one_to_five_result)
    print(five_to_ten_result)

    if one_to_five_result is None and five_to_ten_result is None:
        break
```

In the preceding listing, we create a simple generator that counts from a start integer to an end integer, yielding values along the way. We then create two instances of that generator: one that counts from one to four and one that counts from five to nine.

We also create a convenience method, run_generator_step, to handle running one step of the generator. The generator class has a send method, which advances the generator to the next yield statement, running all code up to that point. After we call send, we can consider the generator paused until we call send again, letting us run code in other generators. The send method takes in a parameter for any values we want to send as arguments to the generator. Here we don't have any, so we just pass in None. Once a generator reaches its end, it raises a StopIteration exception. This exception contains any return value from the generator, and here we return it. Finally, we create a loop and run each generator step by step. This has the effect of interleaving the two generators at the same time, giving us the following output:

```
1
5
2
6
3
7
4
8
None
9
None
None
```

Imagine instead of yielding numbers, we yielded to some slow operation. Once the slow operation was complete, we could resume the generator, picking up where we left off, while other generators that aren't paused can run other code. This is the core of how the event loop works. We keep track of generators that have paused their execution on a slow operation. Then, any other generators can run while that other generator is paused. Once the slow operation is finished, we can wake up the previous generator by calling `send` on it again, advancing to its next yield point.

As mentioned, `async` and `await` are just syntactical sugar around generators. We can demonstrate this by creating a coroutine instance and calling `send` on it. Let's make an example with two coroutines that just print simple messages and a third coroutine, which calls the other two with `await` statements. We'll then use the generator's send method to see how to call our coroutines.

Listing 14.7 Using coroutines with send

```
async def say_hello():
    print('Hello!')


async def say_goodbye():
    print('Goodbye!')


async def meet_and_greet():
    await say_hello()
    await say_goodbye()


coro = meet_and_greet()

coro.send(None)
```

When we run the code in the preceding listing, we'll see the following output:

```
Hello!
Goodbye!
Traceback (most recent call last):
  File "chapter_14/listing_14_7.py", line 16, in <module>
    coro.send(None)
StopIteration
```

Calling send on our coroutine runs all our coroutines in `meet_and_greet`. Since there is nothing that we actually "pause" on waiting for a result, as all code is run right away, even in our `await` statements.

So how do we get a coroutine to pause and wake up on a slow operation? To do this, let's define how to make a custom awaitable, so we can use `await` syntax instead of generator-style syntax.

14.5.3 *Custom awaitables*

How do we define awaitables, and how do they work under the hood? We can define an awaitable by implementing the __await__ method on a class, but how do we implement this method? What should it even return?

The only requirement of the __await__ method is that it returns an iterator, and by itself this requirement isn't very helpful. Can we make the concept of an iterator make sense in the context of an event loop? To understand how this works, we'll implement our own version of an asyncio Future we'll call CustomFuture, which we'll then use in our own event loop implementation.

Recall that a Future is a wrapper around a value that may be there at some point in the future, having two states: complete and incomplete. Imagine we're in an infinite event loop, and we want to check if a future is done with an iterator. If the operation is finished, we can just return the result and the iterator is done. If it isn't done, we need some way of saying "I'm not finished; check me again later," and in this case, the iterator can just yield itself!

This is how we'll implement our __await__ method for our CustomFuture class. If the result is not there yet, our iterator just returns the CustomFuture itself; if the result is there, we return the result, and the iterator is complete. If it isn't done, we just yield self. If the result isn't there, the next time we attempt to advance the iterator we run the code inside of the __await__ again. In this implementation, we'll also implement a method to add a callback to our future that runs when the value is set. We'll need this later when implementing our event loop.

Listing 14.8   A custom future implementation

```
class CustomFuture:

    def __init__(self):
        self._result = None
        self._is_finished = False
        self._done_callback = None

    def result(self):
        return self._result

    def is_finished(self):
        return self._is_finished

    def set_result(self, result):
        self._result = result
        self._is_finished = True
        if self._done_callback:
            self._done_callback(result)

    def add_done_callback(self, fn):
        self._done_callback = fn

    def __await__(self):
        if not self._is_finished:
            yield self
        return self.result()
```

In the preceding listing, we define our CustomFuture class with __await__ defined alongside methods to set the result, get the result, and add a callback. Our __await__ method checks to see if the future is finished. If it is, we just return the result, and the iterator is done. If it is not finished, we return `self`, meaning our iterator will continue to infinitely return itself until the value is set. In terms of generators, this means we can keep calling __await__ forever until someone sets the value for us.

Let's look at a small example of this to get a sense for how the flow might look in an event loop. We'll create a custom future and set the value of it after a few iterations, calling __await__ at each iteration.

Listing 14.9 The custom future in a loop

```
from listing_14_8 import CustomFuture

future = CustomFuture()

i = 0

while True:
    try:
        print('Checking future...')
        gen = future.__await__()
        gen.send(None)
        print('Future is not done...')
        if i == 1:
            print('Setting future value...')
            future.set_result('Finished!')
        i = i + 1
    except StopIteration as si:
        print(f'Value is: {si.value}')
        break
```

In the preceding listing, we create a custom future and a loop that calls the `await` method and then attempts to advance the iterator. If the future is done, a `StopIteration` exception gets thrown with the result of the future. Otherwise, our iterator will just return the future, and we move on to the next iteration of the loop. In our example, we set the value after a couple of iterations, giving us the following output:

```
Checking future...
Future is not done...
Checking future...
Future is not done...
Setting future value...
Checking future...
Value is: Finished!
```

This example is just to reinforce the way to think about awaitables, we wouldn't write code like this in real life, as we'd normally want something else to set the result of our future. Next, let's extend this to do something more useful with sockets and the selector module.

14.5.4 *Using sockets with futures*

In chapter 3, we learned a bit about the selector module, which lets us register call-backs to be run when a socket event, such as a new connection or data being ready to read, occurs. Now we'll expand on this knowledge by using our custom future class to interact with selectors, setting results on futures when socket events occur.

Recall that selectors let us register callbacks to run when an event, such as a read or write, occurs on a socket. This concept nicely fits in with the future we've built. We can register the set_result method as a callback when a read happens on a socket. When we want to asynchronously wait for a result from a socket, we create a new future, register that future's set_result method with the selector module for that socket, and return the future. We can then await it, and we'll get the result when the selector calls the callback for us.

To see this in action, let's build an application that listens for a connection from a non-blocking socket. Once we get a connection, we'll just return it and let the application terminate.

Listing 14.10 Sockets with custom futures

```
import functools
import selectors
import socket
from listing_14_8 import CustomFuture
from selectors import BaseSelector


def accept_connection(future: CustomFuture, connection: socket):
    print(f'We got a connection from {connection}!')
    future.set_result(connection)


async def sock_accept(sel: BaseSelector, sock) -> socket:
    print('Registering socket to listen for connections')
    future = CustomFuture()
    sel.register(sock, selectors.EVENT_READ,
      functools.partial(accept_connection, future))
    print('Pausing to listen for connections...')
    connection: socket = await future
    return connection


async def main(sel: BaseSelector):
    sock = socket.socket()
    sock.setsockopt(socket.SOL_SOCKET, socket.SO_REUSEADDR, 1)

    sock.bind(('127.0.0.1', 8000))
    sock.listen()
    sock.setblocking(False)

    print('Waiting for socket connection!')
    connection = await sock_accept(sel, sock)
    print(f'Got a connection {connection}!')
```

Set the connection socket on the future when a client connects.

Register the accept_connection function with the selector and pause to wait for a client connection.

Wait for the client to connect.

```
selector = selectors.DefaultSelector()

coro = main(selector)

while True:
    try:
        state = coro.send(None)

        events = selector.select()

        for key, mask in events:
            print('Processing selector events...')
            callback = key.data
            callback(key.fileobj)
    except StopIteration as si:
        print('Application finished!')
        break
```

Loop forever, calling send on the main coroutine. Each time a selector event occurs, run the registered callback.

In the preceding listing, we first define an accept_connection function. This function takes in a CustomFuture as well as a client socket. We print a message that we have a socket and then set that socket as the result of the future. We then define sock_accept; this function takes a server socket as well as a selector and registers accept_connection (bound to a CustomFuture) as a callback on read events from the server socket. We then await the future, pausing until we have a connection, and then return it.

We then define a main coroutine function. In this function, we create a server socket and then await the sock_accept coroutine until we receive a connection, logging a message and terminating once we do so. With this we can build a *minimally viable event loop*. We create an instance of our main coroutine function, passing in a selector and then loop forever. In our loop, we first call send to advance our main coroutine to its first await statement, then we call selector.select, which will block until a client connects. Then we call any registered callbacks; in our case, this will always be accept_connection. Once someone connects, we'll call send a second time, which will advance all coroutines again and will let our application finish. If you run the following code and connect over Telnet, you should see output similar to the following:

```
Waiting for socket connection!
Registering socket to listen for connections
Pausing to listen for connections...
Processing selector events...
We got a connection from <socket.socket fd=4, family=AddressFamily.AF_INET,
    type=SocketKind.SOCK_STREAM, proto=0, laddr=('127.0.0.1', 8000)>!
Got a connection <socket.socket fd=4, family=AddressFamily.AF_INET,
    type=SocketKind.SOCK_STREAM, proto=0, laddr=('127.0.0.1', 8000)>!
Application finished!
```

We've now built a basic asynchronous application using only the async and await keywords without any asyncio! Our while loop at the end is a simplistic event loop and demonstrates the key concept of how the asyncio event loop works. Of course, we can't do too much concurrently without the ability to create tasks.

14.5.5 A task implementation

Tasks are a combination of a future and a coroutine. A task's future is complete when the coroutine it wraps finishes. With inheritance, we can wrap a coroutine in a future by subclassing our CustomFuture class and writing a constructor that takes a coroutine, but we still need a way to *run* that coroutine. We can do this by building a method we'll call step that will call the coroutine's send method and keep track of the result, effectively running one step of our coroutine per call.

One thing we'll need to keep in mind as we implement this method is that send may also return other futures. To handle this, we'll need to use the add_done_callback method of any futures that send returns. We'll register a callback that will call send on the task's coroutine with the resulting value when the future is finished.

> **Listing 14.11   A task implementation**

```
from chapter_14.listing_14_8 import CustomFuture


class CustomTask(CustomFuture):

    def __init__(self, coro, loop):
        super(CustomTask, self).__init__()
        self._coro = coro
        self._loop = loop
        self._current_result = None          Register the
        self._task_state = None              task with the
        loop.register_task(self)             event loop.

    def step(self):          Run one step of
        try:                 the coroutines.
            if self._task_state is None:                             If the coroutine
                self._task_state = self._coro.send(None)             yields a future,
            if isinstance(self._task_state, CustomFuture):           add a done
                self._task_state.add_done_callback(self._future_done)  callback.
        except StopIteration as si:
            self.set_result(si.value)
                                      Once the future is
    def _future_done(self, result):  done, send the result
        self._current_result = result  to the coroutine.
        try:
            self._task_state = self._coro.send(self._current_result)
        except StopIteration as si:
            self.set_result(si.value)
```

In the preceding listing, we subclass CustomFuture and create a constructor that accepts a coroutine and an event loop, registering the task with the loop by calling loop.register_task. Then, in our step method, we call send on the coroutine, and if the coroutine yields a `CustomFuture`, we add a `done` callback. In this case, our `done` callback will take the result of the future and send it to the coroutine we wrap, advancing it when the future is complete.

14.5.6 *Implementing an event loop*

We now know how to run coroutines and have created implementations of both futures and tasks, giving us all the building blocks we need to build an event loop. What does our event API need to look like to build an asynchronous socket application? We'll need a few methods with different purposes:

- We'll need a method to accept a main entry coroutine, much like `asyncio.run`.
- We'll need methods to accept connections, receive data, and close a socket. These methods will register and deregister sockets with a selector.
- We'll need a method to register a `CustomTask`; this is just an implementation of the method we used in the `CustomTask` constructor previously.

First, let's talk about our main entry point; we'll call this method `run`. This is the powerhouse of our event loop. This method will take a main entrypoint coroutine and call `send` on it, keeping track of the result of the generator in an infinite loop. If the main coroutine produces a future, we'll add a `done` callback to keep track of the result of the future once it is complete. Once we do this, we'll run the `step` method of any registered tasks and then call the selector waiting for any socket events to fire. Once they run, we'll run the associated callbacks and trigger another iteration of the loop. If at any point our main coroutine throws a `StopIteration` exception, we know our application is finished, and we can exit returning the value inside the exception.

Next, we'll need coroutine methods to accept socket connections and receive data from a client socket. Our strategy here will be to create a `CustomFuture` instance that a callback will set the result of, registering this callback with the selector to fire on read events. We'll then await this future.

Finally, we'll need a method to register tasks with the event loop. This method will simply take a task and add it to a list. Then, on each iteration of the event loop we'll call `step` on any tasks we've registered with the event loop, advancing them if they are ready. Implementing all of this will yield a minimum viable event loop.

Listing 14.12 An event loop implementation

```
import functools
import selectors
from typing import List
from chapter_14.listing_14_11 import CustomTask
from chapter_14.listing_14_8 import CustomFuture


class EventLoop:
    _tasks_to_run: List[CustomTask] = []
```

```
    def __init__(self):
        self.selector = selectors.DefaultSelector()
        self.current_result = None

    def _register_socket_to_read(self, sock, callback):
        future = CustomFuture()
        try:
            self.selector.get_key(sock)
        except KeyError:
            sock.setblocking(False)
            self.selector.register(sock, selectors.EVENT_READ,
 functools.partial(callback, future))
        else:
            self.selector.modify(sock, selectors.EVENT_READ,
 functools.partial(callback, future))
        return future

    def _set_current_result(self, result):
        self.current_result = result

    async def sock_recv(self, sock):
        print('Registering socket to listen for data...')
        return await self._register_socket_to_read(sock, self.recieved_data)

    async def sock_accept(self, sock):
        print('Registering socket to accept connections...')
        return await self._register_socket_to_read(sock,
 self.accept_connection)

    def sock_close(self, sock):
        self.selector.unregister(sock)
        sock.close()

    def register_task(self, task):
        self._tasks_to_run.append(task)

    def recieved_data(self, future, sock):
        data = sock.recv(1024)
        future.set_result(data)

    def accept_connection(self, future, sock):
        result = sock.accept()
        future.set_result(result)

    def run(self, coro):
        self.current_result = coro.send(None)

        while True:
            try:
                if isinstance(self.current_result, CustomFuture):
                    self.current_result.add_done_callback(
 self._set_current_result)
                    if self.current_result.result() is not None:
                        self.current_result =
 coro.send(self.current_result.result())
```

Register a socket with the selector for read events.

Register a socket to receive data from a client.

Register a socket to accept connections from a client.

Register a task with the event loop.

Run a main coroutine until it finishes, executing any pending tasks at each iteration.

```
            else:
                self.current_result = coro.send(self.current_result)
        except StopIteration as si:
            return si.value

    for task in self._tasks_to_run:
        task.step()

    self._tasks_to_run = [task for task in self._tasks_to_run if not
task.is_finished()]

        events = self.selector.select()
        print('Selector has an event, processing...')
        for key, mask in events:
            callback = key.data
            callback(key.fileobj)
```

We first define a _register_socket_to_read convenience method. This method takes in a socket and a callback and registers them with the selector if the socket isn't already registered. If the socket is registered, we replace the callback. The first argument to our callback needs to be a future, and in this method we create a new one and partially apply it to the callback. Finally, we return the future bound to the callback, meaning callers of our method can now await it and suspend execution until the callback is complete.

We then define coroutine methods to receive socket data and accept new client connections, sock_recv, and sock_accept, respectively. These methods call the _register_socket_to_read convenience method we just defined, passing in callbacks that handle data and new connections when they are available (these methods just set this data on a future).

Finally, we build our run method. This method accepts our main entry point coroutine and calls send on it, advancing it to its first suspension point and storing the result from send. We then kick off an infinite loop, first checking to see if the current result from the main coroutine is a CustomFuture; if it is, we register a callback to store the result, which we can then send back to the main coroutine if needed. If the result is not a CustomFuture, we just send it to the coroutine. Once we've controlled the flow of our main coroutine, we run any tasks that are registered with our event loop by calling step on them. Once we've run our tasks, we remove any that are finished from our task list.

Finally, we call selector.select, blocking until there are any events fired on the sockets we've registered. Once we have a socket event, or set of events, we loop through them, calling the callback we registered for that socket back in _register_socket_to_read. In our implementation, any socket event will trigger an iteration of the event loop. We've now implemented our EventLoop class, and we're ready to create our first asynchronous application without asyncio!

14.5.7 *Implementing a server with a custom event loop*

Now that we have an event loop, we'll build a very simple server application to log messages we receive from connected clients. We'll create a server socket and write a coroutine function to listen for connections in an infinite loop. Once we have a connection, we'll create a task to read data from that client until they disconnect. This will look very similar to what we built in chapter 3, with the main difference being that here we use our own event loop instead of asyncio's.

Listing 14.13   Implementing a server

```python
import socket

from chapter_14.listing_14_11 import CustomTask
from chapter_14.listing_14_12 import EventLoop


async def read_from_client(conn, loop: EventLoop):          # Read data from
    print(f'Reading data from client {conn}')               # the client, and
    try:                                                     # log it.
        while data := await loop.sock_recv(conn):
            print(f'Got {data} from client!')
    finally:
        loop.sock_close(conn)
                                                  # Listen for client connections,
                                                  # creating a task to read data
                                                  # when a client connects.
async def listen_for_connections(sock, loop: EventLoop):
    while True:
        print('Waiting for connection...')
        conn, addr = await loop.sock_accept(sock)
        CustomTask(read_from_client(conn, loop), loop)
        print(f'I got a new connection from {sock}!')


async def main(loop: EventLoop):
    server_socket = socket.socket()
    server_socket.setsockopt(socket.SOL_SOCKET, socket.SO_REUSEADDR, 1)

    server_socket.bind(('127.0.0.1', 8000))
    server_socket.listen()
    server_socket.setblocking(False)

    await listen_for_connections(server_socket, loop)


event_loop = EventLoop()              # Create an event loop instance,
event_loop.run(main(event_loop))      # and run the main coroutines.
```

In the preceding listing, we first define a coroutine function to read data from a client in a loop, printing the results as we get them. We also define a coroutine function to listen for client connections from a server socket in an infinite loop, creating a CustomTask to concurrently listen for data from that client. In our main coroutine, we create a server socket and call our `listen_for_connections` coroutine function. Then, we create an instance of our event loop implementation, passing in the `main` coroutine to the `run` method.

Running this code, you should be able to connect with multiple clients concurrently over Telnet and send messages to the server. For example, two clients connecting and sending a few test messages may look something like the following:

```
Waiting for connection...
Registering socket to accept connections...
Selector has an event, processing...
I got a new connection from <socket.socket fd=4, family=AddressFamily.AF_INET,
    type=SocketKind.SOCK_STREAM, proto=0, laddr=('127.0.0.1', 8000)>!
Waiting for connection...
Registering socket to accept connections...
Reading data from client <socket.socket fd=7, family=AddressFamily.AF_INET,
    type=SocketKind.SOCK_STREAM, proto=0, laddr=('127.0.0.1', 8000),
    raddr=('127.0.0.1', 58641)>
Registering socket to listen for data...
Selector has an event, processing...
Got b'test from client one!\r\n' from client!
Registering socket to listen for data...
Selector has an event, processing...
I got a new connection from <socket.socket fd=4, family=AddressFamily.AF_INET,
    type=SocketKind.SOCK_STREAM, proto=0, laddr=('127.0.0.1', 8000)>!
Waiting for connection...
Registering socket to accept connections...
Reading data from client <socket.socket fd=8, family=AddressFamily.AF_INET,
    type=SocketKind.SOCK_STREAM, proto=0, laddr=('127.0.0.1', 8000),
    raddr=('127.0.0.1', 58645)>
Registering socket to listen for data...
Selector has an event, processing...
Got b'test from client two!\r\n' from client!
Registering socket to listen for data...
```

In the above output, one client connects, triggering the selector to resume `listen_for_connections` from its suspension point on `loop.sock_accept`. This also registers the client connection with the selector when we create a task for `read_from_client`. The first client sends the message `"test from client one!"`, which again triggers the selector to fire any callbacks. In this case we advance the `read_from_client` task, outputting our client's message to the console. Then, a second client connects, and the same process happens again.

While this isn't a production-worthy event loop by any stretch of the imagination (we don't really handle exceptions properly, and we only allow socket events to trigger event loop iteration, among other shortcomings), this should give you an idea as to how the inner workings of the event loop and asynchronous programming in Python work. An exercise would be to take the concepts here and build a production-ready event loop. Perhaps you can create the next-generation asynchronous Python framework.

Summary

- We can check if a callable argument is a coroutine to create APIs that handle both coroutines and regular functions.
- Use context locals when you have state that you need to pass between coroutines, but you want this state independent from your parameters.
- asyncio's `sleep` coroutine can be used to force an iteration of the event loop. This is useful when we need to trigger the event loop to do something but don't have a natural `await` point.
- asyncio is merely Python's standard implementation of an event loop. Other implementations exist, such as uvloop, and we can change them as we wish and still use `async` and `await` syntax. We can also create our own event loop if we'd like to design something with different characteristics to better suit our needs.

index